T. W. Allies

The Formation Of Christendom Vol. 7

Peter's Rock in Mohammed's Flood: Gregory to Leo III

T. W. Allies

The Formation Of Christendom Vol. 7
Peter's Rock in Mohammed's Flood: Gregory to Leo III

ISBN/EAN: 9783742835796

Manufactured in Europe, USA, Canada, Australia, Japa

Cover: Foto ©Lupo / pixelio.de

Manufactured and distributed by brebook publishing software (www.brebook.com)

T. W. Allies

The Formation Of Christendom Vol. 7

PETER'S ROCK
IN
MOHAMMED'S FLOOD

FROM ST. GREGORY THE GREAT TO ST. LEO III.

BEING THE SEVENTH VOLUME OF THE FORMATION
OF CHRISTENDOM

BY
THOMAS W. ALLIES, K.C.S.G.

LONDON: BURNS & OATES, Ld.
NEW YORK: CATHOLIC PUBLICATION SOCIETY CO.
1890

PROLOGUE TO THE SEVEN VOLUMES OF THE FORMATION OF CHRISTENDOM.

This work being from the beginning one in idea, I place here together the titles of the fifty-six chapters composing it. For each of these was intended to be complete in itself, so far as its special subject reached; but each was likewise to form a distinct link in a chain. The Church of God comes before the thoughtful mind as the vast mass of a kingdom. Its greatest deeds are but parts of something immeasurably greater. The most striking evidence of its doctrines and of its works is cumulative. Those who do not wish to let it so come before them often confine their interest in very narrow bounds of time and space. Thus I have known one, who thought himself a bishop, accept Wycliffe as the answer of a child to his question, Who first preached the Gospel in England? And not only this. They also seize upon a particular incident, or person, and so invest with extraordinary importance facts which they suppose, and which so conceived are convenient for their purpose, but in historical truth are anything but undisputed. In this tone of mind, or shortness of vision, that which is gigantic becomes puny, that which is unending becomes transient. The sequel and coherence of nations, the mighty roll of the ages spoken of by St. Augustine, are lost sight of. Again, in English-speaking countries alone more than two hundred sects call themselves Christian. Their enjoyment of perfect civil freedom and equality veils to them the horror of doctrinal anarchy, in virtue of which alone they exist. By this anarchy the very conception of unity as the corollary of truth is lost to the popular mind. But through the eight centuries of which I have treated, the loss of unity was the one conclusive test of falsehood, and the Christian Faith stood out to its possessors with the fixed solidity of a mountain range whose summit pierced the heaven.

It has been my purpose to exhibit the profound unity of the Christian Faith together with the infinite variety of its effects on individual character, on human society, on the action of nations towards each other, on universal as well as national legislation. Like the figure of the great Mother of God bearing her Divine Son in her arms, and so including the Incarnation and all its works, the Faith stands before us in history, "veste deaurata, circumdata varietate". And as the personal unity appears in the symbol of the Divine Love to man expressed in her Maternity, so it appears also in the figure of the Church through the ages in which that Divine Love executes His work. A divided creed means a marred gospel and an incredulous world.

I offer this work as a single stone, though costing the labour of thirty years, if perchance it may be accepted in the structure of that Cathedral of human thought and action wherein our Crucified God is the central figure, around which all has grown.

Be it allowed me to quote here words of the present Sovereign Pontiff addressed on the 18th August, 1883, to the Cardinals de Luca, Pitra, and Hergenröther :—

"It is the voice of all history that God with the most careful providence directs the various and never-ending movements of human affairs. Even against man's intention he makes them serve the advancement of His Church. History says further that the Roman Pontificate has ever escaped victorious from its contests and the violence employed against it, while its assaulters have failed in the hope which they cherished, and have wrought their own destruction. Not less openly does history attest the divine provision made concerning the city of Rome from its very beginning. This was to give for ever a home and seat to the successors of St. Peter, from which as a centre, being free from all control of a superior, they might guide the whole Christian commonwealth. And no one has ventured to resist this counsel of the divine Providence without sooner or later perceiving the vanity of his efforts.

"It cannot be expedient, nor is it wise counsel, to fight with a power for whose perpetuity God has pledged Himself, while history attests the performance of the pledge. Since Catholics throughout the whole world pay it religious veneration, it is their interest to defend it with all their power. Nay even the rulers of secular governments must acknowledge this, and lay it to heart, especially in times so dangerous, when the very foundations on which human society rests appear well nigh to shake and totter."

CONTENTS.

VOLUME I.

*INAUGURAL LECTURE ON THE PHILOSOPHY OF HISTORY, 1854.—
THE CHRISTIAN FAITH AND THE INDIVIDUAL.*

Chapter I.
The Consummation of the Old World.

Chapter II.
The New Creation of Individual Man.

Chapter III.
Heathen and Christian Man compared.

Chapter IV.
Effect of the Christian People on the World.

Chapter V.
New Creation of the Primary Relation between Man and Woman.

Chapter VI.
The Creation of the Virginal Life.

VOLUME II.

THE CHRISTIAN FAITH AND SOCIETY.

Chapter VII.
The gods of the Nations when Christ appeared.

Chapter VIII.
The First and the Second Man.

Chapter IX.
The Second Man verified in history.

Chapter X.
The First Age of the Martyr Church.

Chapter XI.
The Second Age of the Martyr Church.

Chapter XII.
The Third Age of the Martyr Church.

Chapter XIII.
The Christian Church and the Greek Philosophy, I.

Chapter XIV.
The Christian Church and the Greek Philosophy, II.

VOLUME III.

THE CHRISTIAN FAITH AND PHILOSOPHY.

Chapter XV.
The Foundation of the Roman Church, the Type and Form of every particular Church; its contrast with Philosophy, and its development of the Judaic embryo.

Chapter XVI.

Neostoicism and the Christian Church.

Chapter XVII.

The First Resurrection of Cultured Heathenism in the Neopythagorean School.

Chapter XVIII.

Standing-ground of Philosophy from the accession of Nerva to that of Severus.

Chapter XIX.

The Gospel of Philosophic Heathenism.

Chapter XX.

The Neoplatonic Philosophy and Epoch.

Chapter XXI.

The respective power of the Greek Philosophy and the Christian Church to construct a Society.

Chapter XXII.

The Church reconstructing the Natural Order by the Supernatural.

VOLUME IV.

CHURCH AND STATE IN THE FORMATION OF CHRISTENDOM.

Chapter XXIII.

Prologue.—The Kingdom as prophesied and as fulfilled.

Chapter XXIV.

Relation between the Civil and the Spiritual Powers from Adam to Christ.

Chapter XXV.

Relation between the Spiritual and the Civil Powers after Christ.

Chapter XXVI.

Transmission of Spiritual Authority from the Person of our Lord to Peter and the Apostles, as set forth in the New Testament.

Chapter XXVII.

Transmission of Spiritual Authority as witnessed in the history of the Church from A.D. 29 to A.D. 325.

Chapter XXVIII.

The One Episcopate resting upon the One Sacrifice.

Chapter XXIX.

Independence of the Antenicene Church shown in her organic growth.

Chapter XXX.

Independence of the Antenicene Church shown in her mode of positive teaching and in her mode of resisting error.

Chapter XXXI.

The Church's battle for independence over against the Roman Empire.

VOLUME V.

THE THRONE OF THE FISHERMAN BUILT BY THE CARPENTER'S SON, THE ROOT, THE BOND, AND THE CROWN OF CHRISTENDOM.

Chapter XXXII.

The witness of Eighteen Centuries to the See of Peter.

Chapter XXXIII.

From St. Peter to St. Sylvester, No. 1.

Chapter XXXIV.

From St. Peter to St. Sylvester, No. 2.

CHAPTER XXXV.

Constantine and the Church.

CHAPTER XXXVI.

Constantine and his Sons: Julian, Valentinian, Valens.

CHAPTER XXXVII.

From Constantine at Nicæa to Theodosius at Constantinople.

CHAPTER XXXVIII.

Church and State under the Theodosian House.

CHAPTER XXXIX.

Church and State and the Primacy from 380 to 440.

CHAPTER XL.

The flowering of Patristic Literature, No. 1.

CHAPTER XLI.

The flowering of Patristic Literature, No. 2.

CHAPTER XLII.

St. Leo the Great.

VOLUME VI.

THE HOLY SEE AND THE WANDERING OF THE NATIONS: LEO I. TO GREGORY I.

CHAPTER XLIII.

The Holy See and the Wandering of the Nations.

CHAPTER XLIV.

Cæsar fell down.

CHAPTER XLV.

Peter stood up.

Justinian.

CHAPTER XLVI.

CHAPTER XLVII.

St. Gregory the Great.

VOLUME VII.

PETER'S ROCK IN MOHAMMED'S FLOOD.

CHAPTER XLVIII.

The Pope and the Byzantine.

CHAPTER XLIX.

Pope Martin: his Council, and his Martyrdom.

CHAPTER L.

Heraclius betrays the Faith, and cuts his empire in two.

CHAPTER LI.

Christendom and Islam.

CHAPTER LII.

Old Rome and New Rome.

CHAPTER LIII.

An Emperor-Priest and four great Popes.

CHAPTER LIV.

Rome's Three Hundred Years, 455-756, from Genseric to Aistulf, between the Goth, the Lombard, and the Byzantine.

CHAPTER LV.

From Servitude to Sovereignty.

CHAPTER LVI.

The Making of Christendom.

PETER'S ROCK IN MOHAMMED'S FLOOD.

BEING THE SEVENTH VOLUME OF THE FORMATION OF CHRISTENDOM.

THIS volume is strictly in continuance of the two which it follows—"The Throne of the Fisherman built by the Carpenter's Son," and "The Holy See and the Wandering of the Nations". It is bulk alone which prevents my offering the three in one cover as historic proof, from original documents, of the first eight centuries that the Holy See by the institution of Christ is the Root, the Bond, and the Crown of Christendom. The works chiefly used in it are before and above all the letters of the Popes in their office of governing the Christian Commonwealth, which are contained in the great collection of Mansi, thirty-one volumes folio. The full titles of other works chiefly referred to are Cardinal Hergenröther, to whose work, *Photius, Patriarch von Constantinopel, sein Leben, seine Schriften, und das griechische Schisma*, and to his *Handbuch der allgemeinen Kirchengeschichte*, I owe great obligations— they are each in three volumes; Alfred von Reumont,

Geschichte der Stadt Rom, in three volumes; Gregorovius, *Geschichte der Stadt Rom*, in eight volumes; Kurth, *Les origines de la Civilisation moderne*, in two volumes; Jungmann, *Dissertationes*, in seven volumes; the German edition of Rohrbacher's History, vol. x. by Rump, vol. xi. by Kellner; Hefele, *Concilien-Geschichte*, in seven volumes; Muratori, *Annali d'Italia;* Brunengo, *Le Origini della Sovranità Temporale dei Papi*, and *I primi Papi-Re e l'ultimo Re dei Longo-bardi;* F. von Hoensbroech, *Enstehung und Entwicklung des Kirchenstaates;* Niehues, *Kaiserthum und Papstthum*, Döllinger, *Muhammed's Religion, nach ihrer inneren Entwicklung und ihrem Einflusse auf das Leben der Völker.* Regensburg, 1838.

CONTENTS.

FORMATION OF CHRISTENDOM.—CHAP. XLVIII.

CHAPTER I.

PETER'S ROCK IN MOHAMMED'S FLOOD.

I.—THE POPE AND THE BYZANTINE.

	PAGE
Connection with the preceding time and specification of the period here treated,	1
The essential condition for reading aright the history of the Church,	2
The constant enemy during St. Gregory's pontificate,	5
The rivalry of the Byzantine patriarch,	6
War between the Eastern and Persian empires,	7
The Emperor Phocas and St. Theodore of Siceon,	7
Slaughter of emperors—Mauritius by Phocas, Phocas by Heraclius,	8
Frightful cruelty of Justinian II., deposed, restored, and finally executed,	10
Losses of the Eastern empire during 18 years, A.D. 604-622,	11
Capture of Mar Sabas, and martyrdom of 44 monks,	12
John the Almsgiver, last great patriarch of Alexandria,	13
The twelve years' inactivity of Heraclius,	15
The awakening of Heraclius,	16
Who conquers Persia in five campaigns,	17
The end of king Chosroes,	20
Heraclius brings back the true Cross to Jerusalem in triumph,	21

	PAGE
The successes of Heraclius viewed as a whole, . . .	21
The triumph of Heraclius and the pretension of Mohammed exactly contemporaneous, ...	22
Mohammed estimated by Döllinger, ...	23
The Persian empire has nine sovereigns in four years, and collapses finally in 651, ...	24
The emperor Phocas repeats to Pope Boniface III. the declarations of Marcian and Justinian to his predecessors, ...	25
The Popes in succession from St. Gregory, ...	26
How the imperial confirmation of their election was used, .	27
The extreme of disloyalty shown by the emperors to the Popes, ...	27
Pope Boniface IV. consecrates the Pantheon for a Church, .	28
Succession of Pope Honorius in 625; his building and ornamenting churches and burial in St. Peter's, . .	30
His deception by the patriarch Sergius and subsequent condemnation, ...	31
The Ecthesis of the patriarch Sergius and the emperor Heraclius, ...	33
The Ecthesis confirmed by Sergius in a council at Constantinople, ...	33
And by the patriarchs of Antioch and Alexandria, . .	35
Death of Honorius and election of Severinus in 638, . .	36
The Lateran palace plundered by the exarch Isaac, . .	37
The chartular Mauritius concerned in this, ...	38
Papal commissioners at Constantinople ask the confirmation of the election of Severinus from Heraclius, . . .	38
Finally Severinus sits two months out of twenty-two since his election, ...	39
The forty years' oppression of the Popes by the Monothelites,	40
Coincidence with this of the Mohammedan conquests over the empire, ...	41
Pope John IV. condemns the Monothelite heresy and defends the orthodoxy of Honorius, ...	42
In doing so sets forth the true doctrine of the Incarnation,	43
Struggle of Pope John IV. against Byzantium, and violent revolutions there, ...	44

	PAGE
The actions and epitaph of Isaac, the model exarch,	45
Pope Theodorus receives in St. Peter's Pyrrhus after his renouncement of heresy,	46
Admonishes and afterwards condemns the Monothelite patriarch Paul,	48
Who compels the eastern bishops to subscribe a fresh doctrinal decree,	49

FORMATION OF CHRISTENDOM.—CHAP. XLIX.

VOLUME VII.

PETER'S ROCK IN MOHAMMED'S FLOOD.

II.—POPE MARTIN, HIS COUNCIL, AND HIS MARTYRDOM.

Pope Theodorus succeeded by Pope Martin,	51
Notice by Anastasius of events in his time,	52
The exarch Olympius attempts to assassinate him,	53
His first act to convoke a Council at the Lateran in 649,	55
After which he directs an encyclical to all bishops and peoples,	56
Informs the emperor Constans II. that his Typus is condemned,	56
Four Popes, immediate succcessors of Honorius, condemn the Monothelite heresy,	56
The Popes during forty years persecuted on account of this heresy,	57
The Typus as read and considered at the Lateran Council,	58
The Ecthesis of Sergius and the Typus of Paul II. compared,	60
Five theological acts of Byzantine despotism,	61
The Typus the most complete and, as it were, model act,	64
The march of doctrinal usurpation from Constantine to Constans II.,	64
The secular power of Byzantium declines as its spiritual usurpation advances,	65
Pope Martin begins his pontificate by summoning the Council,	65

	PAGE
Speech of the Pope on opening the Council,	66
Memorial to the Council of Stephen, bishop of Dor in Palestine,	68
The appeal of the patriarch Sophronius to the Apostolic See at the Mohammedan inroad,	69
Presented to Pope Martin afresh in the name of eastern bishops and peoples,	70
Result and creed of the Lateran Council in 649,	71
Letter to the Pope from the province of Africa, read at the Council,	72
Letter of Pope Martin after the Council to the African bishops,	73
To the bishop of Thessalonica and to his clergy and people,	74
How these letters exhibit the actual working of the Primacy,	75
The chief contents of the Pope's encyclical letter,	76
Contrast between the Roman See and the eastern patriarchates,	77
The exarch Olympius succeeded by the exarch Kalliopas,	79
The kidnapping of the Pope described by himself,	79
The Lateran basilica violated and the Pope taken away,	81
The Pope carried a prisoner to Constantinople,	82
Calumnies spread against the faith of the Pope,	83
Commemoration by an eyewitness of Pope Martin's sufferings,	85
The Pope arraigned for high treason before the senate of Constantinople,	86
He is condemned, and exposed to mockery,	87
He is dragged through the city with the sword borne before him,	89
And taken to the guard-house in fetters,	90
The emperor hears from the dying patriarch his plaint over the Pope,	92
St. Martin questioned about the ex-patriarch Pyrrhus,	93
Is confined in the guard-house during eighty-five days,	95
His leave-taking of those in the prison,	95
The Pope banished to Cherson in great misery, with which the commemoration of the eye-witness ends,	96
Letters of Pope St. Martin from the Crimea,	97
The record of Pope St. Martin's death,	99

St. Martin repeats the Passion of Christ, and Constans II.
the tyranny of Trajan, ... 100

FORMATION OF CHRISTENDOM.—CHAP. L.

VOLUME VII.

PETER'S ROCK IN MOHAMMED'S FLOOD.

III.—HERACLIUS BETRAYS THE FAITH, AND CUTS HIS EMPIRE IN TWO.

Heraclius in 629 bringing back the Cross to Jerusalem, . 101
The nature of the revolution which followed, . . . 102
Heraclius lends the imperial authority to a compromise of doctrine contrived by Sergius, ... 103
The action of Cyrus made patriarch of Alexandria, . . 105
Which Sergius suggests to Pope Honorius as the restoration of unity in Egypt, ... 106
Sophronius remonstrates with Cyrus and Sergius, . . 106
Synodical letter of Sophronius as patriarch of Jerusalem, . 107
He sets forth the orthodox and condemns the Monophysite doctrine, ... 108
Sergius repudiates his letter, and draws up the Ecthesis against it, ... 109
The Byzantine despotism, both religious and civil, . . 110
Religious despotism, beginning with the last days of Constantine, ... 111
Progressive diminution of the Church's original independence, ... 112
The long Eastern tampering with heresy, ... 113
Alexandria and Antioch fall under the ecumenical patriarch, 115
Civil despotism exhausting the provinces for Byzantium, . 116
The heretical spirit destroys the empire, ... 117
Monothelite heresy the pioneer of Mohammedan conquest, . 118
Abu Bekr elected the first chalif, ... 119

	PAGE
The chalifate of Omar,	120
Fall of Syria, and surrender of Jerusalem,	121
Terms of capitulation granted by Omar,	123
The loss of Mesopotamia, and the doom of Egypt,	124
Amrou besieges Alexandria,	125
Egypt, and Northern Africa as far as Tripolis, lost,	127
Deaths of Heraclius and Omar, and Omar's conquests,	128
The character of Omar's rule,	129
Effect of his chalifate on the Eastern empire,	131
The new Empire ruled from Medina,	133
Its disparity with all preceding it,	134
The blow dealt by it to the Christian Church,	135
Fall of the Antiochine patriarchate,	137
St. Jerome's view of his own times,	138
How he describes the Northern wandering of the nations,	139
The causes which he assigns for its being allowed,	141
The two centuries of declension in the Eastern patriarchates,	142
History of Antioch from the time of St. Chrysostom,	143
History of the Alexandrian See from Dioscorus to the welcome of the Mohammedans by the Coptic Christians,	144
The subjection of the three Eastern patriarchs to the See of the royal residence coeval with the Mohammedan inroad,	146
The act of Constantine reaches full development in Heraclius,	147
The Nestorian and Monothelite heresies, following on the Arian, dissolve the Eastern empire,	148
The Northern and the Southern wandering of the nations,	149
The chalifate of Osman,	152
The chalifate of Ali,	153
Disposition of things at Constantinople on the death of Heraclius,	155
Pope John IV. calls on the successor of Heraclius to withdraw the Ecthesis,	155
Constans II., succeeding in 642, persecutes Pope Martin,	156
St. Maximus the Confessor,	157
His work in opposing the Monothelite heresy,	158
He is counsellor of Pope Martin in calling the Lateran Synod,	159
Testimonies of Maximus to the Apostolic See,	160

	PAGE
First trial of Maximus before the Senate at Byzantium,	162
Further attempts to make him accept the Typus,	163
Maximus rejects the Imperial offers of honour,	168
The final condemnation and death of Maximus and his companions,	169

FORMATION OF CHRISTENDOM.—CHAP. LI.

VOLUME VII.

PETER'S ROCK IN MOHAMMED'S FLOOD.

IV.—CHRISTENDOM AND ISLAM.

The sword and the word,	171
The personal conduct of Mohammed,	172
Change in his life after the death of Chadidja,	173
Proclaims force as the instrument of spreading his religion,	174
A marauding excursion ordered by him on one of the holy months,	175
Produces verses of the Koran to justify his act,	176
His first battle with the Meccans at Bedr,	177
Is defeated in the second battle at Ohod,	179
Defends Medina in a siege, and loses reputation,	180
Puts to death the men of a Jewish clan, and enslaves their wives,	181
Attempts a pilgrimage to Mecca, and is obliged to retire,	182
His polygamy after Chadidja's death,	183
Rebukes by aid of the Koran a revolt of his wives,	184
Takes the wife of his adopted son, and justifies it as the command of God by the Koran,	185
Forbids, by the Koran, his wives to marry after his death,	186
Obtains possession of Mecca in the eighth year of the Hegira, 630,	186
Issues a new law of nations and war, proclaims his religion to be universal, and dies,	187

	PAGE
Four principles of Mohammed's life from the Hegira to his death:	189
1. Employment of force to propagate Islam,	190
The relation of Mohammed to Arius,	190
2. His imposture in using the Angel Gabriel's name,	191
3. His privilege as to the number and choice of his wives,	192
4. His disregard of human life,	193
Mohammed's personal character as founder of a religion,	194
Contrast between his character and that of Christ,	195
How Mohammed's life has infected the life of his followers,	196
Degradation of women in all Mohammed's countries arising from it,	197
The position of Mohammed at the time of his death,	199
Certain virtues of Mohammed amid his vices,	200
The invention of Gabriel destroys the basis of Mohammed's title,	201
Which rested upon a claim utterly falsified,	202
Mohammed at his death simply a successful robber,	203
The Arabians before him, as described by themselves,	204
The first chalif made by election, not by inheritance,	205
The first twelve years of the Christian faith compared with the first twelve years of the Mohammedan,	206
Mohammed in his system holds the place of Christ in ours,	208
The radical antagonism of that system with the Christian faith,	209
St. John Damascene's record of Mohammed,	211
His reproach that Mohammed had no witness to the truth,	213
The Koran: its character and formation,	214
How its edition was brought about,	216
The meaning of the first chalif's election	217
Christendom and Islam contemporaneous in their origin,	218
Absolute despotism the proper offspring of Mohammed,	219
Illustrated in the three Mohammedan kingdoms,	220
The Cæsarean attack on the Church followed by Mohammedan despotism,	224
The locust people,	225

FORMATION OF CHRISTENDOM.—CHAP. LII.

VOLUME VII.

PETER'S ROCK IN MOHAMMED'S FLOOD.

V.—OLD ROME AND NEW ROME.

	PAGE
Depression of Rome in the middle of the Seventh Century,	226
Damascus made the Saracenic Capital,	227
Constans II. leaves Constantinople and visits Rome,	228
Eugenius made Pope by Constans in St. Martin's life-time,	229
Election of Pope Vitalian,	229
The visit of Constans II. to Rome described by Anastasius,	230
Pope Vitalian received him as legitimate Roman emperor,	232
The acts of Constance at Rome represent the Byzantine spirit,	233
Constans assassinated in his bath at Syracuse,	234
Pope Vitalian's action on the young English church,	235
Pontificates of Adeodatus, Donus, and Agatho,	237
The Saracens during seven years attempt in vain to take Constantinople,	237
Constantine IV., the Bearded, solicits union with the West by writing to the Pope,	238
Pope Agatho orders councils through the West and holds one at Rome,	239
The Sixth Council opened under the presidency of the Papal Legates,	240
Its condemnation of the Monothelites,	241
Definition of the Faith by the Council,	245
What Pope Agatho claims in his letter to the emperor,	246
The Council in its answer assents to this claim,	247
The emperor in his answer addresses the Pope as the Living Peter,	249
The confirmation of the Council as to its faith and as to its condemnations by Pope St. Leo II.,	250
In confirming, he modifies the terms used by the Council,	251
The Popes and the patriarchs between Honorius and the Sixth Council,	253

	PAGE
The firmness of ten successive Popes saves the Church from heresy,	256
The ground of that firmness belief in the succession from St. Peter,	259
The danger of the empire traced by St. Maximus and by Theophanes to the misconduct of its rulers,	260
The emperor Constantine the Bearded at the Sixth Council,	261
Justinian II. succeeds, and summons the Greek Council in Trullo,	262
Spirit of its 102 Canons,	263
Position of the emperor as marked in the subscription to the Canons,	264
Position given in the 36th Canon to the patriarch of Constantinople,	265
The Byzantine idea of Church and empire thus involved,	266
Short pontificates and Greek parentage of several Popes at this time,	268
The exarch unable to prevent the election of Sergius, exacts a great fine,	269
Anglo-Saxon kings pilgrims to Rome,	271
Justinian II. orders his protospathair Zacharias to deport Pope Sergius to Constantinople,	272
The attempt frustrated by the rising of the emperor's Italian forces,	273
Treatment by Justinian II. of his patriarch, followed by his deposition,	274
Leontius and Apsimar successive emperors, and Justinian II. restored,	275
Theophylact, exarch of the emperor Apsimar, repulsed from Rome by Italian soldiers,	276
Massacre at Ravenna by order of the restored Justinian II.,	277
Pope Constantine summoned by him to Constantinople,	278
The Pope makes a triumphal entry,	279
Is received by Justinian II. at Nicomedia with the highest honour,	279
The end of Justinian II. and of the race of Heraclius,	280
Philippicus Bardanes: his reign of eighteen months,	281
Artemius, first secretary, is made emperor, and named Anastasius,	282

TABLE OF CONTENTS.

	PAGE
The patriarch, John VI., asks pardon of Pope Constantine,	282
And describes his pre-eminence as that of the head in the human body,	283
The visit of five Popes, John I., Agapetus, Vigilius, Martin I., and Constantine, to Constantinople,	284
Deposition of the emperors Anastasius II. and Theodosius III. and succession of Leo III., the Isaurian,	288
Pope Constantine followed by St. Gregory II.,	290
The time from St. Gregory I. to St. Gregory II.,	290
The twenty-four Popes between the two Gregories,	292
Roman fortitude and Byzantine fluctuation,	295

FORMATION OF CHRISTENDOM.—CHAP. LIII.

VOLUME VII.

PETER'S ROCK IN MOHAMMED'S FLOOD.

VI.—AN EMPEROR PRIEST AND FOUR GREAT POPES.

Pretension of a new emperor to abrogate the Sixth Council,	297
Accession, and success of Leo III., the Isaurian,	298
Muratori's account of the Iconoclast contest,	299
The character and actions of Pope Gregory II.,	301
His letter to the emperor Leo III.,	302
There are both holy and unholy things made with hands,	303
The bearing of God Incarnate on the making of images,	305
Images and pictures of Christ and of the Martyrs made,	306
The act of Leo III. compared with that of Ozias, the Jewish king,	308
Effects on the mind of portraying divine actions,	309
The words of Constantine the Bearded asking the Pope for a Council,	310
The separate bounds of Church and State, and their joint action invaluable,	311
The Pope declines the request of Leo III. for an ecumenical Council,	312

xxviii   TABLE OF CONTENTS.

	PAGE
The impiety of the emperor in breaking up the image of Christ,	312
The Pope replies to his threat that he will destroy the image of St. Peter,	313
Whom all the kings of the West look upon as a God upon earth,	314
Gregory's second letter to Leo, who claims to be priest as well as emperor,	315
Dogma belongs not to emperors but to bishops,	317
Church discipline and State punishment contrasted,	318
The Pope and the patriarch commissioned by God to receive the emperor to penitence and to pardon his sin,	319
These letters a picture of the time in which they were written,	321
Especially in the relation existing between the Two Powers,	322
And in the unjealous unity of the Papal and Episcopal power,	324
The answer of Leo III. to the Pope is to attempt his life five times,	325
Leo III. deposes the patriarch Germanus, and substitutes Anastasius,	326
Persecution of bishops and monks by Leo III. and Anastasius,	326
St. John of Damascus censures Iconoclasm as the invasion of a robber,	327
St. Gregory II. rejects Leo's attack on the faith, but maintains allegiance,	328
King Liutprand advances upon Rome and retires at the Pope's intervention,	329
Gregory II. calls on the Doge of Venice to support the emperor,	330
Character of St. Gregory II. as estimated by Baronius,	332
St. Gregory III., Anastasius on his pontificate,	333
Leo III. sends a great fleet against Ravenna and Rome,	335
And failing, confiscates the patrimonies of St. Peter in his realm,	336
And severs the Illyrian provinces from the Pope, bestowing their spiritual jurisdiction on his own patriarch,	336

	PAGE
The structure of Byzantine pride begun in 381, completed in 733,	337
Liutprand takes Spoleto and appears before Rome,	338
St. Gregory III. turns for aid to Charles Martell,	339
Death of Leo III., Charles Martell, and Pope Gregory III., in 741,	343
How Anastasius records the works of St. Gregory III.,	343
Election and immediate consecration of Pope Zacharias, 1st December, 741,	344
His character by Anastasius, before and after his consecration,	345
He succeeds in prevailing over king Liutprand at Terni,	346
And again at Pavia in 743, inducing him to give back the exarchate to the empire,	347
Again Zacharias in person prevails on king Rachis at Perugia to retire,	348
Rachis further resigns his kingdom and receives the Benedictine cowl from the Pope's hands,	349
The three pacific victories of Pope Zacharias,	349
Aistulf become king, takes Ravenna in 751, and names himself king of Italy,	350
Pipin invites Pope Zacharias to sanction his reigning in France,	351
Zacharias assents, and Pipin is elected king at Soissons, 752,	351
Death of Zacharias and election of Pope Stephen II. in 752,	352
Aistulf attacks the duchy of Rome, and imposes a poll tax on Rome,	353
Pope Stephen II. appeals to Kopronymus to defend Rome,	353
The Byzantine sovereignty supported by the Popes until Kopronymus sent no defence to Pope Stephen II.,	354
Stephen receiving no aid journeys to Pavia,	355
Unable to persuade Aistulf, he crosses the Alps,	356
At meeting with Pipin, Jan. 6, 754, Stephen ceases to recognise the Byzantine sovereignty,	357
Pipin engages by treaty to restore to the Pope the Lombard captures,	359
Stephen II. crowns the king, his wife, and his sons, at the Abbey of St. Denys, in July, 754,	360

Pipin advances on Pavia—Aistulf yields—Pope Stephen
 returns in triumph to Rome, ... 360
Aistulf begins a fresh siege of Rome in 756, . . . 361
Pope Stephen writes to king Pipin in the name of St. Peter, 362
Pipin takes Pavia, and bestows the enfranchised cities in
 full sovereignty upon St. Peter, and the Pope returns
 head of the Roman State, ... 363
The State of the Church thus created, ... 365

FORMATION OF CHRISTENDOM.—CHAP. LIV.

VOLUME VII.

PETER'S ROCK IN MOHAMMED'S FLOOD.

VII.—ROME'S THREE HUNDRED YEARS, 455-756, FROM GENSERIC
 TO AISTULF, BETWEEN THE GOTH, THE LOMBARD, AND THE
 BYZANTINE.

The three hundred years of suffering and glory date from
 the acknowledged primacy of St. Leo I., . . . 369
And end with Leo the Isaurian and his son Kopronymus, . 370
The Arian domination in Italy a cause of suffering, . . 372
Theodorich's political clemency ends in blood, . . . 373
Odoacer and Theodorich emissaries of the eastern emperor, . 374
The emperor ever considered himself the overlord of Italy, . 375
1. The first usurpation of confirming the Papal election, . 376
At the election of Pope Symmachus that right was not
 exercised by emperor or king, ... 377
Theodorich's interference with the election of Pope Felix IV., 378
Pope Boniface II. attempts to nominate his successor, . 379
Athalarich imposes a fee for confirming the Pope's election, 380
Justinian, becoming lord of Rome by right of conquest, seizes
 on the nomination of Popes, ... 381
The election of Pope Gregory III., in 731, the last confirmed
 at Ravenna, ... 382
Mode of Papal election and confirmation, ... 383

		PAGE
Form of letter announcing the election to the exarch,		384
Confirmation of the Popes from 526 to 731,		385

2. Exarchal government the second arm of Byzantine oppression, ... 386
Deeds of the exarchs, Isaac, Olympius, Theodore Kalliopa, John Platina, ... 387
Zacharias, the guardsman, fails to seize Pope Sergius, . 388
Effect of the Lombard invasion on the position of the Popes, 389
The Pope in the middle of the long struggle between Lombard and Byzantine, ... 390
3. The Byzantine oppression of doctrine the third weapon, 391
The full mind of Justinian as depicted in his legislation, . 392
Justinian theologising, ... 393
The unbending constancy of the Popes from Gelasius to Gregory II., ... 394
What this constancy effects in a free Pope, ... 395
Contrasts presented at this time by the East and West, . 396

  1. The emperor Leo III. and Pope Gregory II. on the Two Powers, ... 397
  2. Leo III. sends a fleet against Italy—Gregory III. appeals to Charles Martell, ... 398
  3. Leo III. bestows ten provinces taken from the Pope on his patriarch—Stephen II. crowns Pipin at St. Denys, ... 399
  4. Stephen II., refused help by Kopronymus, is made sovereign of the exarchate, and Rome restored to him by Pipin. 400
  5. Kopronymus names his ecumenical patriarch to the Council which he has called at Constantinople, . 403
The end of the ecumenical patriarch Constantine, . 405
His deposition, ... 407
He is beaten—degraded in Sancta Sophia—exposed in the circus, ... 408
His head struck off—fastened up in the amphitheatre—his body dissected, ... 408
  6. Condition to which despotism had reduced the Eastern episcopate, ... 409
In the West the bishops followed the stedfastness of the Popes, ... 410

	PAGE
In Constantine Kopronymus the thraldom of Italy ceases,	411
The fifty-eight bishops of Constantinople from Metrophanes to Methodius,	412
The twenty-one heretics included among these fifty-eight bishops,	413
The seventy Popes who sat in the same period,	414
During three centuries the Primacy works in fetters,	416
The guarantee of truth offered by this conduct of the Primacy,	419

FORMATION OF CHRISTENDOM.—CHAP. LV.

VOLUME VII.

PETER'S ROCK IN MOHAMMED'S FLOOD.

VIII.—FROM SERVITUDE TO SOVEREIGNTY.

The Lateran Palace first landed possession of the Roman See,	420
Rapid increase of estates left to it,	421
After Constantine no emperor or king makes Rome his seat,	422
Odoacer and Theodorich took Ravenna in preference,	423
The twenty-three patrimonies in St. Gregory's time,	424
The political influence which thus accrued to the Popes,	425
The independence following as its crown,	426
Muratori on the Pope's position before the donation of Pipin,	426
Adolf Menzel on the right to make the donation,	428
The return of Pope Stephen II. as king to Rome and the death of Aistulf in 756,	429
Letter of thanksgiving from Stephen II. to king Pipin in 757,	430
Close of the line of subject Popes in Stephen II.,	432
Pontificate of Paul I. defended by Pipin from Desiderius,	433
Seizure of the Papal chair by the duke Toto for his brother, a layman,	434
The intruded Constantine deposed, and succession of Stephen III.,	435

TABLE OF CONTENTS.

	PAGE
Death of king Pipin; Charles and Carloman kings of the Franks, 768,	436
A Council held at Rome to prevent future intrusions,	436
Desiderius obtains Charles for his daughter,	437
Who sends her back repudiated after a year,	438
Desiderius at Rome effects the ruin of Christophorus and Sergius,	439
Charles by the death of Carloman becomes king of the whole Frank empire, Dec. 4, 771,	440
Accession and character of Pope Adrian I.,	441
How he replies to the embassy of Desiderius,	442
Desiderius, while his ambassadors profess his fidelity, seizes on fresh cities,	443
Advances with his army towards Rome,	443
Adrian arms Rome against Desiderius, and stops him by an interdict at Viterbo,	445
Charles, after fully proving the perfidy of Desiderius, marches into Italy against him,	446
Charles invests Pavia, October, 773,	448
Charles at Rome on the Easter of 774,	449
How Charles entered St. Peter's and was received by Adrian,	450
Lauds sung to Charles, as patricius, on Easter Monday, in St. Peter's,	452
Pope Adrian holds conferences with Charles,	453
Renewal and confirmation of the pact of Quiersy by Charles,	454
The donation laid by Charles upon the altar in the Confession,	455
Capture of Verona and Pavia, and conquest of the Lombard kingdom by Charles,	457
Length of time required to execute the gift of Charles to the State of the Church,	459
The Pope appears as a sovereign from the compact with Pipin at Quiersy,	460
The Pope's own language that of a monarch,	461
The visit of Charles to Rome in 774 inaugurates his reign,	463
The loyalty of Charles in repeating his father's act,	465
Contemporary acknowledgement by the Popes of the acts of Pipin and Charlemagne,	465

xxxiv   TABLE OF CONTENTS.

	PAGE
Two great benefits to Italy—the overthrow of Lombard domination,	466
And the substitution of Papal for Byzantine rule,	467

FORMATION OF CHRISTENDOM.—CHAP. LVI.

VOLUME VII.

PETER'S ROCK IN MOHAMMED'S FLOOD.

IX.—THE MAKING OF CHRISTENDOM.

The northern and the southern wandering of the nations in relation to the Church,	469
The range and nature of these two wanderings,	470
Extension of the Saracen conquests in the seventh century,	471
The danger of the Christian Church in 715,	473
The Iconoclast attack, its motive and its result,	474
Nova Roma in its first century, A.D. 330-430,	476
Nova Roma in its second century, A.D. 430-519,	477
Nova Roma in Justinian's time, A.D. 519-604,	479
Nova Roma under Heraclius and his race, A.D. 610-711,	480
Nova Roma in the century of Leo the Isaurian, A.D. 715-785,	481
The other eastern patriarchates in these times,	482
The Rock of St. Peter from the First to the Second Nicene Council, 330-785,	483
The descent of the Greek empire during this period,	484
What the East wanted the West possessed,	486
The Papacy fountain head of political sense,	491
Rise of the family of Arnulf and of Pipin,	493
The battle of Saracen and Christian by Tours,	494
The farthest advance of the Saracen to the West,	496
Visits of Charles to Rome during Adrian's pontificate,	497
Leo III. succeeds Pope Adrian I., A.D. 795,	498
Jurisdiction exercised in Rome by its patricius as protector,	499
Attack made during a procession on the person of the Pope,	500

	PAGE
Consultation between the Pope and Charles at Paderborn,	501
Charles comes from Aix-le-Chapelle to Rome,	501
The Pope is not judged but acquitted on his personal word,	502
Crowns Charles Emperor of the Romans on Christmas Day, 800,	503
The course of events from A.D. 476 to the renovation of the western empire,	504
The Pope alone made the emperor to be protector of the Church,	505
The making and the charge acknowledged by Charles and all his subjects,	506
Effect in recognising the proper nature of civil government,	507
Christian legislation established in the person of Charlemagne,	509
The action of Charlemagne in the Champs de Mai,	511
Institution of the Missi Dominici—specimen of their action in Istria,	512
The Christian hierarchy Charles' model in his civil government,	513
Effect of that government in civilising the West,	515
Constantine and Charlemagne,	516
Bearing of Charlemagne's empire on the Byzantine,	516
Charlemagne and the chalifate,	518

PETER'S ROCK IN MOHAMMED'S FLOOD.

CHAPTER I.

THE POPE AND THE BYZANTINE.

I HAVE hitherto conducted the history of the Throne of the Fisherman built by the Carpenter's Son in unbroken succession from St. Peter to St. Gregory the Great. It is a period of 575 years from the Day of Pentecost A.D. 29 to St. Gregory's death in A.D. 604. This period is very nearly bisected by the conversion of Constantine. The first half contains the action of the Primacy over against a hostile heathen empire. The second half contains its action upon an empire which, at least in principle, acknowledged union with the Catholic Church as a duty, a privilege, and a necessity. The testimony rendered by Councils and by Fathers to the Roman Primacy may be said to be complete in the time of St. Gregory. Subsequent Councils can only add a closer precision to the testimony of the Council of Chalcedon. Subsequent acts of the Eastern empire can scarcely go beyond the submission of its episcopate, its emperor, and its nobles to Pope Hormisdas. The point of that submission consists in the solemn acceptance of the line of Roman bishops as inheriting the charge given by our Lord to St. Peter. Subsequent legislation can but apply in detail the acceptance by Justinian of the Pope's right to examine everything which belongs to the doctrine or concerns the conduct of the Church throughout the world. And force is even added to this acceptance, because it was made when the Pope, John II., to whom it was made, was not in fact his temporal subject.

I propose to treat in this volume of a period embracing two hundred years. It runs from the time of St. Gregory the Great to the founding of the holy Roman empire, in the person of Charlemagne, by Pope St. Leo III.

But, before entering on this treatment, it seems to me called for to make one remark on all which I have hitherto written or am hereafter to write, and to draw out distinctly a principle which affects every line of my narrative. This is the necessity of considering the Church as the one kingdom of Christ in all ages : one and the same polity from the Day of Pentecost to the Day of Judgment. This idea has always been before me as the rule of faith in writing the six preceding volumes. It has been the major premiss of my whole argument. To a Catholic the unity of the Church is as necessary as the unity of God ; and, equally, to say that the Church is fallible is to deny the existence of any such thing as the kingdom of God upon earth. The sooner that anything which is fallible is swept away the better. The one duty which we owe to fallibility is to label it. The thing called public opinion[1] is fallible, and,

---
[1] Der Zeit-geist.

accordingly, every generation sweeps it away and substitutes a fresh fallibility, destined to disappear after a similar ascendency, which waxes and wanes in varying durations of time. Division is the strongest proof of fallibility in that which is divided, as unity is of truth in that which remains one mass. For this cause those who substitute national churches in a particular country under the political head of that country, whether king, president, or parliament, for the one divine polity in all countries, are divided from my argument by an impassable gulf. They no more believe in the Church which is "the house of God, the pillar and basis of the truth," than he who sets up three gods believes in one Infinite Creator and Rewarder of His creatures. The decrees of a General Council in matters of faith are not recognised by them as part of the divine deposit; for to them they are not acts of the Sovereign Lord in His plenary council. The lessons of history fail to convey any definite impressions to minds in which this idea is wanting. Rather the lessons of history affect them as the heathen was affected who heard the description of our Lord's sufferings undergone for his redemption only to exclaim, "Was it not a long time ago?" There are facts, but no connection. A strong instance of this is that the want of written records in the first three centuries is not made up to them by the acts of the Church in the fourth, fifth, and sixth centuries, because to them the Church is not a polity instinct with one life and following from the beginning identical rules of government. On the contrary, they argue from the silence of perished documents in the three earliest centuries against the recorded practice of the three centuries following. Thus to them the acts of the Church in the Council of Ephesus in 431,[1] the next ecumenical council to the Nicene, throw no light upon the acts of the Church in the Nicene, of which no full record exists. Nor, again, do the acts of the Council of Chalcedon illustrate to them the antecedent constitution of the Church. And the supplication of the Eastern emperor, Marcian, to Pope St. Leo to confirm those acts tells them nothing as to the relation of the Council to the Pope in the time of the Nicene Council. Less even than infidels, who reject the Christian revelation altogether, but have a regard for historical sequence, do the nurslings of a national church, especially if it was in origin a queen's love-child, and then dandled on the knees of successive kings, understand the majesty of the Apostolic See, as set forth in the words of our Lord, or as unfolded in the course of ages. If the political constitution under which they live be a system of compromise, they are tempted to make the constitution of the Church a similar system, in which a change of ministry alters or even reverses the policy of a kingdom. "The holy Catholic Church, the communion of saints," is not an entity to such minds. Therefore they fail to appreciate the proof of the one polity at the head of which St. Peter's successor stands.

[1] It is ever to be borne in mind that at the time of the Council of Ephesus the Council of Constantinople in 381 ranked only as a local council of Eastern bishops, partially confirmed by Pope Damasus.

For some that polity ceased to exist in the fifth century; for others in the ninth; for others in the sixteenth; for all such it is non-existent in the nineteenth. It is for them as the human soul for the infidel surgeon: he cannot find it under his knife. Or as God for the infidel astronomer: he cannot see God in the order of the universe, though he will receive what physicists tell him, that the universe is absolutely one.

But I write for those to whom history is intelligible, because it is an order of events unrolling itself as a drama at once human and divine; to whom the human soul makes itself known by its acts; to whom "the heavens declare the glory of God, and the firmament shows his handiwork—day unto day utters speech, and night unto night showeth knowledge." To whom likewise there is one "Jesus Christ yesterday and to-day, and the same for ever": yesterday at Pentecost with St. Peter and the apostles and our Blessed Lady; to-day with Leo XIII. at Rome and nineteen hundred years of doctors, martyrs, and saints; "the same for ever" at the Day of Judgment.

And now I turn another leaf in the book of human actions, which our Lord holds on His knees and unfolds in His history of His one Church.

During the whole pontificate of St. Gregory he was defending himself against the deceit and despotism of the man whom he acknowledged as his lawful sovereign, the Byzantine emperor. The despotism usually veiled itself in deceit, while the deceit rested upon the despotism rooted in the heart of the eastern that he was lord of the world.[1] Worse than the Lombards, who pursued to the very gates of Rome the people nourished by Gregory on the Church's patrimonium, who spoiled, maimed, and tortured those whom they could catch, were the intrigues of the imperial lieutenants, the exarchs of Ravenna, plotting with the Lombards, enemies of the emperor, against his subjects, the Pope and his Romans. With this state of things the seventh century begins, and so it continues to the end. We have to consider the great events which took place in this century, and especially to point out their connection with this fact of the Byzantine temporal despotism as it was turned upon the spiritual power.

Again, during his whole pontificate, St. Gregory was resisting the attempts of the bishops of Constantinople to extend their power. In his own time it would seem to have been an effect of Justinian's legislation that the Roman See accepted them as patriarchs, which Pope Gelasius denied them to be. Not only so but in every step of their advancement they were backed by the emperors to go on yet further by pushing their See under the title of Ecumenical to a position over the eastern empire parallel to that of the Pope over the West, while it was subordinate at the same time to the emperor himself. The four-and-twenty immediate successors of St. Gregory, from Pope Sabinian, elected in 604, to Pope Constantine, who died in 715, were exposed to the full force of this attempt. The bearing of it upon

---

[1] Orbis dominus : ὁ Δεσπότης τῆς οἰκουμένης.

the rise of the Mohammedan empire will appear more and more as we proceed in the history of this terrible century.

The first event on which we must dwell for a time on account of its great effect upon the history of the century, is the long continued hostility between the eastern and the Persian empires. In the year 602 the general Phocas had deposed the emperor Mauritius.[1] From his reign most Byzantine historians date the ever increasing calamities of the empire. The popular feeling that a bad ruler is a judgment from God was expressed in the story that a pious monk once asked, O God, why hast Thou set this man over us as emperor? when he received for answer, Because I could find none worse. Phocas reigned about seven years, and his end was as follows. The patriarch Thomas had, by his entreaties, drawn to Constantinople Theodore of Siceon, who enjoyed a great reputation for holiness. The mind of patriarch Thomas had been greatly moved by auguries of misfortune which as it were filled the air. He urged the saint to pray and then to give him his advice. The saint at last yielded to his entreaties and said, "It was my mind not to disturb you. It is not for your good to know these things. But since you will have it so, learn that the incident which troubles you betokens many great misfortunes. Many will leave our religion. Incursions of barbarians will follow, and great bloodshedding. Devastation and insurrection through the whole world. Churches will be deserted. The fall of

[1] Photius, i. 193.

the divine service and of the empire is approaching: and the adversary is nigh at hand."

Whilst St. Theodore was at Constantinople the emperor Phocas suffered from gout in hands and feet. He sent for the saint, who laid his hands upon him and prayed for him. The emperor felt relief, and commended himself and his realm to Theodore's prayers. The saint replied that if he wished such a prayer to be heard he must cease from oppression and shedding of blood. Phocas had great need of such warning, but profited little by it. Narses was the ablest and bravest general whom he had to send against the Persians, but he broke his word, and had him burnt alive. This frightful execution moved the patrician Germanus to try after the place of emperor which Phocas had once offered to him. He planned a conspiracy with Constantina, widow of the emperor Mauritius. She had taken asylum with her daughters in Sancta Sophia. This was in 606. At the sight of her the people flocked together and took up arms. Phocas sent orders to bring out Constantina with her daughters. The patriarch Cyriakus refused: only when he had compelled Phocas to swear that no harm should be done to them, he gave them up. Phocas kept his word, and only confined them in a monastery. Germanus was forced to become a priest. In the next year, 607, Germanus and Constantine with other persons of high rank made a new conspiracy. It was discovered. Germanus with his daughter, the widow of prince Theodosius, eldest son of the preceding emperor Mauritius, was beheaded. The same lot befel Constantina and her daughters at Chalcedon, on the spot where, five years before, the emperor Mauritius had witnessed the execution of five sons, one after another, uttering at each stroke only the words: "Just art Thou, O Lord, and just is Thy judgment": and then offering his own head to the sword. Phocas put to death the other conspirators with fearful tortures. Such executions were followed by fresh conspiracies, and these by similar punishments. At last, Crispus, the very stepson of Phocas, rose against him, and invited Heraclius, governor of Africa, to depose the emperor. Heraclius despatched a fleet under the command of his son, bearing the same name. Only as it drew near Constantinople did Phocas hear of it. He prepared for defence, but Crispus secretly traversed all his efforts, pretending to be on his side. After a bloody engagement the fleet appeared before the walls of the capital on Sunday the 4th October, 610. The next morning a senator, whose wife Phocas had dishonoured, appeared with a troop of soldiers at the palace. Phocas was seized, stripped of the purple, his hands bound behind his back, and carried through the city and the fleet before the young Heraclius, who was still on board his vessel. "Wretch," said Heraclius, "hast thou governed the empire so?" "And wilt thou," answered Phocas, "govern it better?" Heraclius trampled on him, cut off his hands and feet, and then his head, in sight of the vast throng which lined the shore. His head and limbs were carried on spears through the city, the trunk dragged through the streets, and all at last burnt.

Heraclius, accompanied by Crispus, disembarked. He

invited Crispus to put on the imperial robe, since he was not come to invest himself with it, but only to avenge Mauritius and his children. Crispus refused, and then Heraclius had nothing to oppose to the request of the patriarch Sergius, who had just succeeded Thomas, that he should be crowned by him. Crispus was given the government of Cappadocia: but becoming a few years later unfaithful to Heraclius, as he had been to his stepfather Phocas, was compelled to receive the torture, and pass the rest of his days in banishment.

It may here be said that the dynasty thus begun occupied the throne for five generations. Justinian II., great-great-grandson of Heraclius, was more cruel if possible, than Phocas: he was deposed by an adventurer in 695, and his nose cut off to incapacitate him for any future recovery of the throne. His successor lasted three years: and another for seven; after which Justinian, who wore a golden nose for the one which he had lost, recovered the throne; practised during five years atrocious cruelties, was deposed by a third adventurer, Philippicus Bardanes in 711: put to death, and his head carried to Rome to assure all men that they were delivered from a tyrant, and a special oppressor of the Church.

Such in personal conduct was the manner of men who sat on the eastern throne of the great Constantine during the seventh century: whom four-and-twenty Popes found themselves bound to acknowledge as "Christian kings and Roman princes". What they were in this capacity, which was the first and greatest of all their duties, as recognised by the imperial laws, will be seen as the narrative proceeds. Under these men the Popes, utterly deprived of temporal power, in the midst of a province an outlying domain of a distant despot, had to maintain the unity of the Christian faith, and the independence of the Holy See as its guardian. In the midst of these things the chalifs of Mohammed broke upon the eastern empire, and severed from it its fairest provinces. It is requisite to follow closely the series of events, and the connection of times.

Upon his accession to the throne in 603 Phocas had sent an embassy to the Persian emperor Chosroes, expressing his desire to maintain peace with him. But Chosroes under pretext of avenging his benefactor, the late emperor Mauritius, began a war which lasted more than four and twenty years, inflicted fearful sufferings on both empires, and had the most important consequences by leaving them in a state of great weakness to meet the assault of a new enemy, the Mohammedan chalifate.

During the first eighteen years of this war, that is, from 604 to 622, the Greek empire suffered a series of defeats and disasters. Through the whole East, from the ruins of Babylon to the Bosphorus, cities were burnt and destroyed, the country ravaged and left without cultivation, the inhabitants slain or carried away into slavery. The Persians tore from the empire province after province—Armenia, Mesopotamia, Cappadocia. In 610 they came up to the walls of Chalcedon. The accession of Heraclius produced no pause in their destructive course. In 611 they took Edessa, Apamea, and Antioch. In 615 they plundered Palestine, and took Jerusalem. The Church of Gethsemane, on the Mount of Olives, and Constantine's Basilica of the Holy Sepulchre were destroyed or burnt. Among the inhabitants carried away was the patriarch Zacharias. The Persians seized in plunder all that was valuable, and the priceless relic of the Holy Cross was taken away by the fire-worshipper Chosroes. The Sponge and the Lance were saved by the patrician Nicetas, who purchased them at a high price from a Persian soldier, and then brought them to Constantinople, where they were exposed for veneration of the faithful.

It is to be noted that in 610 the Jews at Antioch had an insurrection, and massacred a great number of the most considerable inhabitants. They seized the patriarch Anastasius II., whom we have seen St. Gregory treat with such regard; they frightfully maimed him, dragged him by the feet through his city, and finished by casting him upon a funeral pile. When Jerusalem was captured in 615, the Jews of Palestine bought of the Persians as many Christians as they could get, for the pleasure of strangling them. It is recorded that they murdered seventy thousand in this manner.

Eight days before the taking of Jerusalem the fortress monastery of Mar Sabas, 2000 feet above the Dead Sea, then, as now, of the greatest renown, was assaulted by the Arabs. All but fourty-four of the oldest monks had fled, but these remained, and, after its capture, suffered first grievous tortures, and at last martyrdom.

When the monks who had fled returned, they found the bodies of their brethren unburied; the abbot Modestus gave them holy burial. He afterwards superintended the diocese of Jerusalem during the absence of the captive patriarch. What Monte Cassino is to Italy, and Mount Athos to Greece, Mar Sabas was then and is now to Palestine.

At this time St. John the Almsgiver—the last great patriarch of Alexandria—gave every help to the fugitives from the Persian seizure of the Holy Land. It is a sign of the secular power wielded by the Egyptian patriarch that he ordered the confiscation of the goods of those who used in his city false weights and measures. After he had lovingly received and supported the fugitives from Syria and Palestine, he had, in the next year, 616, to fly himself in order to escape the sword of the Persians. He was on his way with the patrician Nicetas to Constantinople, when, at Rhodes, he had a vision, in consequence of which he said to his companion: "You invite me to the king of this world, but the Lord of heaven comes before you". He told Nicetas the vision, and left him to go to Amathus in Cyprus, his birthplace. There he made his will in these words: "I thank Thee, O Lord, that Thou hast heard my prayer, and that only one-third of one gold piece remains to me, though at my consecration I found 8000 pounds' weight of gold in the bishop's house at Alexandria, not reckoning those countless sums which I have received from the friends of Christ. Therefore, I order that this small remnant be given to Thy servants." Ten years he sat in the See of Alexandria. George was his successor. But from this time nothing more is known of this Church's history. Alexandria fell first under the Persians, and then under Amrou, the Mohammedan. The Arabian domination supported Christian errors only, and from that time the Church of St. Athanasius has never lifted its head again, and the land of the Desert Fathers is become the chief seat of the religion which puts an impostor in the place of the Redeemer.

In the year 616, the Persians broke into Egypt, took and plundered Alexandria, and carried their ravages to the borders of Æthiopia. Another Persian army besieged Chalcedon. Still Heraclius remained inactive. He only sent an embassy to Chosroes. In 619 he sent another, beseeching mercy in the name of the senate. Chosroes replied : " I will spare the Romans when they renounce their Crucified One and worship the sun ". He remembered not that he had to thank the Romans for his crown, that in his time of trouble he had found help only from the God of the Christians. Heraclius lost courage at this answer. Since the loss of Egypt Constantinople was suffering from famine, as well as a grievous pestilence. The emperor resolved to quit his capital, and take refuge with his father in Africa. He embarked his chief treasures, and directed the fleet to Carthage. Most of it was wrecked in a storm. A panic fell on his people, and they besought him with tears and cries not to forsake them. The patriarch Sergius went to the palace, led Heraclius to Sancta Sophia, and compelled him before the altar to swear aloud not to desert his capital. Heraclius submitted against his will.

In 619 he was very nearly taken captive by the Khan of the Avars, who had asked him for an interview, ostensibly to settle terms of peace, in reality to secure his person and riches, and to fall upon Constantinople. The emperor came in great pomp, was surprised, and scarcely escaped in disguise. The Avars obtained an immense booty, and, according to the patriarch Nicephorus, carried away captive beyond the Danube 270,000 men, women, and children.

At length, in the twelfth year of his reign, Heraclius awoke from his torpor, and his awakening was one of the most marvellous events recorded in history. His treasury was empty and his credit not good enough to borrow; but he resolved to attack the Persians in their own country. To secure Constantinople he made peace with the Avars, and to hold them in check he ceded provinces to other races, Slaves, Croatians, and Servians. He made churches and monasteries supply a forced loan. He took even the candlesticks and holy vessels of Sancta Sophia and coined them. When all was ready for his departure, he declared his eldest son, Heraclius Constantinus, ten years old, regent of the kingdom under tutorship of Sergius the patriarch and Bonosus, patrician. Then he celebrated the Easter festival, 4th April, 622. The next day he went to Sancta Sophia, threw himself before the altar and cried: "Lord, deliver us not for the punishment of our transgressions to our enemies, but look upon us in Thy mercy and grant us victory, that the wicked cease to exalt themselves and to mock Thine inheritance". Then he turned to the patriarch Sergius with the words: "My city and my son I leave to God's protection, the Blessed Virgin's, and thine". Upon this he took into his hands an image of our Saviour, which was said not to have been made by hands, marched to the Bosphorus and crossed over to Asia.

A train of defeats by the Persians had demoralised the Greek soldiers. Heraclius reinforced his army with allied troops, amongst them a number of Turks. He spent some months at first in restoring courage to his forces. "See," he said, "my children, how the enemies of God trample on our land, lay waste our cities, burn our sanctuaries, desecrate our altars, pollute our churches with the vilest abominations." When he had thus enheartened them he reviewed them together, and swore to fight with them and on equal terms unto death, to share all their dangers, to be inseparable from them as a father with his children. And moreover, he kept his word.

Heraclius was ever at the head of his soldiers: he united valour with caution: he entered Armenia and defeated the Persians in several battles. Then he made a show of taking up his winter-quarters in Pontus, but suddenly burst into Persia, and utterly discomfited a large force. He took the enemy's camp, together with immense treasure. His troops were astounded at their own victories, and he wintered them in Armenia. The next campaign was no less glorious. He kept Easter

Day in 623, which fell on the 27th March, with his family at Nicomedia. By the 20th April he was in Persia. He had written to Chosroes, and offered him peace. The Persian king not only rejected his offer, but put the bearers of it to death. Heraclius used all these circumstances to give courage and confidence to his troops. He penetrated to the heart of Persia : he burnt the cities and villages which he passed on his way, and marched on Ganzac, now Tauris, where Chosroes was encamped with forty thousand men. At the first onset, Chosroes took flight. His troops were mown down, captured, or scattered. Ganzac was the capital of Atropatene. The Persian kings kept there a treasure, said to be that of Crœsus and to have been brought thither by Cyrus. The most renowned fire-temple of the chief god of the Persians was in this city. Here Zoroaster, the founder of that worship, had been born and lived. There was also here a colossal statue of Chosroes. He was seated in the middle of the palace under a great baldachin representing heaven. Round him were the sun, moon and stars, and angels bearing sceptres. The statue, by means of machinery, caused rain to fall, and thunder to sound. In fact, Chosroes assumed here divine worship. The emperor ordered the statue to be overthrown and broken to pieces. Heraclius burnt palace and temple, with part of the city. Then he marched into Albania for the winter, and, out of pity, set free fifty thousand Persian prisoners, to whom he likewise gave maintenance. This humanity so won their hearts that they burst into tears, and prayed that he might restore freedom to Persia, and put to flight Chosroes, whom they called the Waster of the human race—so hateful had he made himself by oppression and cruelty.

In the campaign of 624, Chosroes brought up three armies against the emperor. Heraclius defeated them in three great battles. He made so sudden a night attack upon what remained that their general, Sarbar, wakened by the clash of arms, had scarcely time to spring from his bed on horseback, and ride away at full speed, while the conqueror took possession of his golden shield, and even his clothes. In his fourth campaign, that of 625, Heraclius was also victorious. Chosroes avenged the defeat of his troops by falling on the churches of Persia, which he stripped of all their ornaments: and to punish the emperor, he compelled the Christians of his realm to become Nestorians. Fifteen years before, he had, to please his physician, compelled the inhabitants of Edessa to become Eutycheans. Chosroes rallied all his forces for the campaign of 626. He raised three great armies, composed indifferently of freemen and slaves, of natives and foreigners. Sarbar led one of these armies to Chalcedon to besiege Constantinople, on the Asiatic side, while the Khan of the Avars, breaking truce, appeared on the European side, to demand the surrender of the city and all its wealth. Its inhabitants, however, defended themselves with such valour as to repulse both Avars and Persians. The fall of the Avar power begins at this moment. It was henceforth occupied by intestine struggles. Sais led the second army of Chosroes, which was defeated by Theodore, brother of the emperor Heraclius. Heraclius himself broke the third army under the command of Rhazates, at Nineveh, on the 12th December, 627. The battle began in early morning, and ended only in the evening. The Persians lost, besides the commanding general, his three lieutenants, almost all their officers, and nearly the half of their soldiers. The Romans had only fifty killed, but many thousands wounded. These the emperor tended with so much care that only ten died.

Nineveh, at that time, was only a village on the ruins of the old capital. Heraclius marched thence upon Ctesiphon, the capital of Persia, built upon the remains of old Babylon, at a little distance. On his road he passed palaces, seats, and chaces wherein the Persian nobles pursued their hunting. Heraclius suffered his soldiers to sack and burn them all. Chosroes fled from city to city. Heraclius made him new peace-proposals at the beginning of 628. Chosroes refused them all, and became perfectly hated by the Persians. He thought not of the justice of God, which was pursuing him. Thirty-eight years before he had murdered his father Hermisdas to obtain his throne. What he had done to his father was to happen to him from his eldest son. He had been struck by a violent dysentery : and wished to make Medarses, his son by his favourite wife Syra, a Christian, his successor in the throne. His eldest son, Siroes, irritated by this preference, gained the nobles and the army, was proclaimed king, and sent an embassy to Heraclius. Chosroes was captured in his flight, and brought to Ctesiphon, on the 24th February, 628. He was put in chains and imprisoned in the strong tower, Tenebres, which he had built to keep his treasures. The next day Siroes was crowned : the first act of his government was to condemn his father to die of starvation. " Let him eat," he said, " the gold for which he has desolated the world, and condemned so many to die of hunger." The Satraps and all his enemies were made to mock the fallen ruler, and spit in his face. Siroes ordered Medarses and all his brethren to be strangled before his father's eyes : and, as the old king was still living on the fifth day, had him shot to death with arrows. So ended Chosroes, king of Persia, murdered by his son as he murdered his father.

These victories the emperor Heraclius reported at Constantinople, and also sent a letter, in which Siroes announced his coronation, and proclaimed his wish for peace. This letter was read from the ambo of Sancta Sophia on the Feast of Pentecost, 15th May, 628.

Siroes, in fact, established a stable peace with the emperor. He restored him all Christian prisoners in Persia, among them, Zacharias, patriarch of Jerusalem. He delivered to him also the true Cross, which Sarbar had taken away fourteen years before at the capture of Jerusalem. This was at first carried to Constantinople : but in the following year, 629, the emperor took ship to bring it back to Jerusalem, and give thanks to God for his victories. Here he replaced the Cross on its old spot.

It had remained in its case, as it was taken away. The patriarch, with his clergy, recognised the seal as intact, opened with its key the shrine, worshipped the Cross, and showed it to the people. The Church celebrates, by the Feast of the Exaltation of the Holy Cross, this event on the same day, the 14th September, on which she had before celebrated the apparition of the Cross to Constantine. Heraclius, in the same year, came to Edessa, and restored to the Catholics the church which Chosroes had given to the Nestorians. And he paid back, in the shape of a yearly income to Sancta Sophia and its clergy, the sums which he had borrowed for the costs of the war.

Let us dwell for a moment on these acts of Heraclius, from 622 to 629.

No Roman emperor, in the course of many hundred years, during the whole time in which Rome and Persia stood as rivals over against each other, obtained such a triumph over the king of kings, as did Heraclius. He surpassed by far Trajan at the culmination of the empire. Heraclius, commending his city and his son to the protection of God, of our Blessed Lady, and of the bishop of his city, God's representative, went forth on what seemed a desperate expedition, borrowing from churches and monasteries the means to equip it. For seven years victory crowned his course. Trajan stopped at the Mesopotamian provinces. Julian perished in them. Mark Antony won no honour of Rome's eastern rival: Crassus and his host never returned. Galerius was stuffed and served as a footstool for the great king to mount on horseback. Into the heart of that eastern realm Heraclius threw himself fearlessly. He made his own army out of divers peoples, and shared their dangers. Host after host he overthrew, as only the son of Philip, the conqueror without his match, had done before him. In the end, on the very spot where a Roman emperor, the special despiser of the Nazarene, and fostering in his heart the destruction of the Church as the crowning work of his reign, to be achieved upon his return as conqueror, perished by a Persian lance, Heraclius, after driving to despair the great king, the persecutor of the Cross, its possessor by conquest, saw him dethroned, famished, and at last shot to death by his son. He received from that son, the successor of the murdered father, abundant satisfaction for the wrongs which the Roman empire had suffered from its great rival of so many hundred years.

But, moreover, during these very seven years in which Heraclius won a perpetual victory in the name of the Cross—the wood of which he brought back as a conqueror to Jerusalem, giving thanks and worship, and replaced it with the seal which guarded it unbroken in its old sanctuary—an Arabian trafficker who had gained his living by carrying goods from city to city, and lived virtuously with one wife much his elder, upon her death, when he was more than fifty years of age, was assuming the name of a prophet and the position of a conqueror. The year in which Heraclius started is the same in which this pretension was set up. His claim to be a prophet is exactly coincident with the years in which he was

taking to himself wife after wife, in which, entering
suddenly the tent of his adopted son, he was seduced
by a casual glance on that wife's beauty to desire her,
to obtain her, and to forge a permission from the Most
High to take as many wives as he pleased, and the wives
of others—a forgery as yet unique in all the history of
imposture; for many bad men have taken the wives of
others, but no one except Mohammed has pretended to
have a divine sanction for an act which treads under foot
all human justice, and pulls down for the lust of one
man the very foundation of domestic life.

It is of this man that one who has analysed his
religion and described its course opens his work with
these words [1] :—

"Since the beginning of the world has no other man
—mere man—ever exerted so boundless an influence
on the human race in the relations of religion, morality,
and polity as Mohammed, the Arab. A man, by no
means one of those rare spirits whom Providence at
times evokes and endues with genius to open a path for
a new world—a man rather whose mind was enclosed
in narrow limits, poor in ideas for the construction of a
new religion: a man such as this has for twelve hundred
years cast his net of artless yet impenetrable links of
doctrine round a hundred million souls—roots of teaching which have sunk into the marrow of men's minds,
have taken up into themselves and mastered the whole
of life, and impressed a uniform stamp on the thoughts
and deeds of races as well as individuals."

[1] Döllinger, *Muhanmed's Religion*, p. 1.

The seven years of Heraclius form part of the ten years of this Mohammed, in which the trader turns prophet and the reformer of religion endeavours to put a divine sanction on polygamy, in conjunction with a boundless concubinage of which captives were the prey.

As eighteen years of continual defeat by the Persians, from 604 to 622, had reduced the Eastern empire to a state of demoralised weakness, so the seven succeeding years, from 622 to 629, in which Heraclius wrought a full revenge on the Persian king, inflicted no passing collapse upon the empire resuscitated by the Sassanides in the third century. King Siroes did not long enjoy the fruit of his parricide. He reigned six months and then he died—some say of the plague, some of remorse. After his death the throne of Persia seemed to become a seat of murder. His young son, Ardeschir, or Artaxerxes, was killed after reigning seven months by his uncle, the general Sarbar. Sarbar kept the throne two months and was killed. Devanschir took his place. He was followed by Borane, a daughter of Chosroes. She was replaced by a certain Tschaschindeh, who was followed by Borane's sister, Azermidokt. A certain Kesra, or Chosroes, succeeded, and he gave way to a Ferokzad. Finally, Jezdedjerd, a grandson of the last Chosroes, was crowned in the year 632. Thus in the short space of four years about nine persons succeeded to the throne by murder. Jezdedjerd III. began his reign in the year Mohammed died. He is called by Theophanes, Hormisdas. He had the honour to be the last king of Persia and to end his days by the sword of the Arab in 651. His son, Peroxes, became a captain in the life-guards of the emperor of China at Singapore, and left no posterity.

After this glimpse at the action of the Byzantine and Persian empires on each other during the thirty years which follow immediately on the death of St. Gregory, we turn to consider the conduct of the temporal liege-lord of the Pope towards him whom he recognised as successor of St. Peter.

The emperor Phocas, following in this his predecessor Justinian, had expressly enjoined on the patriarch of Constantinople to recognise the Primacy of Rome.[1] What the chroniclers remark is important, that Boniface III., the next to succeed St. Gregory, received a decree from Phocas, in which he solemnly declared that the See of the Roman Church was to be considered the head of Christendom. It may be remarked here that Phocas did not say a word more than his predecessor, Marcian, said to St. Leo a hundred and fifty years before. Phocas may be named a tyrant, but Marcian has left an unspotted reputation as a Christian king and Roman prince, who received the empire with the hand of Pulcheria, heiress of the great Theodosius, and the only descendant worthy of his greatness, whose name stands also on the diptychs of the Catholic Church as a virgin saint.[2]

Upon the history of the City of Rome during the first

---

[1] Gregorovius, ii. 112-3, first edition (afterwards a little altered), p. 102.
[2] As such she has merited and received the scoffs of Gibbon in full Voltairian foulness.

half of the seventh century the greatest obscurity rests.[1] It was indeed the most frightful and destructive century for the former queen-city of the world. The Book of the Popes by Anastasius[2] trickles in a slender thread amid war, famine, and pestilence, and inundations of the Tiber; but it is all we have to look at.

With the death of the great Pontiff, who guarded and fed his city while the calamities which he saw all round the sphere of his vision over the whole Church led him to look for the end of the world, the See of Peter remained half a year unfilled until his successor, Sabinianus of Volterra, formerly Papal Nuncio at the Byzantine court, received the confirmation of his election from the exarch or the emperor. The confirmation of each pope's election was, as a rule, obtained either from the exarch or direct from the emperor. It was a business both costly and protracted. It also made the spiritual head of Rome dependent for his recognition on the imperial court. I find that in the period of 111 years, running from the death of St. Gregory in 604 to the death of Pope Constantine in 715, twenty-four popes succeeded. Of these the first, Sabinian, in 604, had to wait six months. Phocas confirmed the election of Boniface III., the next pope, after a year. He died in November, 607, and Boniface IV. following took his seat in August, 608. When he died, Pope Deusdedit waited five months. At his death Boniface V. succeeded after a year, in 619.

---

[1] Gregorovius, ii. 112, 3rd edit.
[2] See the article on this writer's adventurous life by Card. Hergenröther in the *Kirchen-lexicon*, i. 788.

Pope Honorius followed Boniface in five days and sat during thirteen years, but at his death the confirmation of his successor, Pope Severinus, was delayed by Greek intrigue, and for a purpose hereafter to be mentioned, during nineteen months and sixteen days, so that he only sat from the 28th May to the 1st August, 640. St. Martin in 649 did not wait for the imperial confirmation; he was first banished and then martyred by the emperor Constans II., who put in by threats his successor, Eugenius, during his lifetime. St. Leo II. waited eighteen months in 682, after the death of Pope Agatho, and the next Pope, Benedict II., a year in 684.

This privation of its original freedom, according to which the Pope's consecration followed at once upon his complete and legitimate election by clergy and people, the Roman Church owed to the Arian Herule Odoacer, during his occupation of Italy. It was eagerly grasped, after Theodorich and Theodatus had exercised it, by Justinian, when he became, by conquest, lord of Rome. I have already recorded the infamous violence exerted by Belisarius as soon as he had entered Rome, at the bidding of the Empress Theodora, upon St. Silverius. Now we have the eastern emperors, through the seventh century, exerting, sometimes directly, sometimes by delegation to their exarch, this stolen privilege. It was taken by Odoacer ostensibly for the preservation of order in the election, and the prevention of violence. I suppose it is the furthest reach of disloyalty to exercise a power which has been entrusted for protection to the injury of the party protected. This disloyalty was perpetually shown by the eastern emperors to the Popes, whose Primacy over the Church they acknowledged, until they finally lost the opportunity by the new-creation of the Western empire, and the acquisition of temporal sovereignty by the Popes.

At the accession of Honorius I., in 625, it is stated to have been the custom, upon the death of a Pope, that the Archpriest, the Archdeacon, and the first of the Notaries signified his death to the exarch. The Acts of the new election, subscribed by clergy and laity, were deposited in the archives of the Lateran. A copy of them was sent to the emperor. The report sent to the exarch was the more important. This Viceroy of Italy was humbly besought for his consent: nay, even the Archbishop and Judges of Ravenna were asked to obtain it from him. The clergy and people of Rome had to look to the exarch, the emperor's delegate, even more than to the emperor, since he stood in more immediate relation to Rome, and determined the decision of the Byzantine court. The Romans, suffering from the delay of their bishop's consecration, would entreat the emperor to lessen the time of disturbance by allowing the exarch to confirm their choice.[1]

In the short pontificates of the Popes, who sat from St. Gregory to Honorius, we may note one remarkable fact. Full six centuries after its erection by Agrippa, as the vestibule of his baths in the centre of the Campus Martius, stood what was called the Pantheon, with its

[1] Gregorovius ii. 113, referring to Pagi, upon Baronius, year 625, sec. 17.

superb portico of granite pillars and white marble
capitals, untouched in their beauty—the fairest relic of
ancient Rome. It had withstood all the inundations of
the Tiber: all the devastations of the Gothic war: all
the injuries of time. Every winter the floods forced
themselves up over its floor: day and night the dome,
through its aperture, received the waters of heaven.
The images of Augustus[1] and Agrippa probably stood still
in their niches : the beams of gilded brass supported its
roof, covered with the gilt tiles of bronze, which neither
Vandal, nor Goth, nor Byzantine robber had yet carried
away. Pliny had given it the name of Pantheon: Dio
Cassius had seen in it the statues of Mars and Venus,
and of the deified Cæsars. A tablet of the Fratres
Arvales has been found, dating from the year 59, in
Nero's time, and showing that worship to the pagan
gods was then offered in it.

Pope Boniface IV. beheld this wonder of ancient art,
and longed to make a church of that beautiful dome
which hung like the vault of heaven over the broadest
expanse ever covered by a roof. He asked it of the
emperor Phocas, and received it as a gift. He assembled
the clergy of Rome, and a procession, singing hymns,
entered that noble doorway, and the Pope sprinkled
with holy water the marble-encrusted walls, from which
every vestige of heathendom was cleared away. The
" Gloria in Excelsis " resounded for the first time in
that dome from which Michael Angelo took his most
beautiful creation. The temple of all the demons was

---

[1] See Gregorovius, ii. 105.

purified: and Pope Boniface IV. preserved it for all succeeding ages, under its dedication to the Ever-virgin Mother of God, and all martyrs. So it was saved from becoming, in mediæval times, the hold of some noble robber. And from it the devotion to All Saints, on the 1st November, and for All Souls, on the 2nd, was propagated amongst the nations of the West. What was originally a Roman festival passed beyond the Alps and the dome of Agrippa, the partner of Augustus and the husband of Julia, and through her progenitor of Cæsars, became the shrine from which the glorious office of all the saints in the Church triumphant, and that of intercession for all souls in the Church suffering, went forth to the Christian world.

From 604 to 625, five Pontiffs had ascended the Roman chair, and all had to wait, after their election, for the good pleasure of the Byzantine emperor, that they should take their seat. In 625, there succeeded a man of great distinction. He was a Campanian of high birth, and he strove to follow the example of his master, St. Gregory. Honorius I. sat for 13 years, and with Vitalian, A.D. 657-672, and Sergius, 687-701, alone reached that length of pontificate, while twenty-one other Popes share between them, including vacancies and delays interposed by the Byzantine, the remaining 69 years. We have no documents existing to account for such a number of short pontificates. Honorius busied himself much in the conversion of the southern Saxon kingdoms in England, where St. Bede[1] attests

[1] Hist., iii. 7.

that the Bishop Birinus came by his instance. Anastasius gives a long account of the gifts which he bestowed on the churches of Rome; among them, that he covered the confession of St. Peter with pure silver, weighing 187 pounds : and the whole church with brazen tiles which, with the consent of the emperor Heraclius, he took from the temple of Roma : that he built the church of St. Agnes, and made her a silver shrine, weighing 252 pounds; also, the church of the Four-crowned. Of his character, the Abbot Jonas, near his time, writes : he was " a venerable prelate, sagacious, strong in counsel, clear in doctrine, powerful by his gentleness and humility ". He also clothed with silver plates, weighing 975 pounds, the middle or royal door of St. Peter's, on which there was an inscription, calling him "Honorius, the good bishop, the leader of the people. Your own prelate, blessed Peter, made your doors of silver; O doorkeeper of heaven, maintain for this in tranquillity all the times of your flock." And there, in the great Basilica, he was buried in all honour.

But, in his person, one of the State-made patriarchs of Constantine's city is able to make the solitary boast that he once deceived one Roman Pontiff. Sergius, who sat in that See, from 610 to 638, and who seems to have obtained as great a mastery over the mind of the emperor Heraclius as his predecessor, Acacius, had over the emperor Zeno, constructed a doctrinal exposition called the Ecthesis, which he induced the emperor to father and promulgate. He was desirous, above all things, to obtain the Pope's approval of the doctrine which he afterwards set forth in this document. He wrote to the Pope letters, the purpose of which the successor of St. Peter, instead of seeing through, appears to have misconceived. After the death of Honorius, the Monothelite emperors and patriarchs claimed to have received the support of that Pope. His not having detected, and actively condemned the deceit of Sergius, brought upon the memory of Honorius the heavy rebuke that Pope St. Leo. II. assented so far to the sentence of the Sixth General Council in 682, as to have written to the Spanish bishops :—" Those who had been traitors to the purity of the Apostolic tradition were punished with eternal condemnation : they are Theodore of Pharan, Cyrus of Alexandria, Sergius, Pyrrhus, Paulus, Petrus of Constantinople, together with Honorius, who, instead of extinguishing, when it began to arise, the flame of heretical doctrine, fostered it by his neglect".[1]

Much light would appear to be thrown upon the belief of Pope Honorius by the history of the forty years succeeding his death.

He sat within a few days of thirteen years. He was buried, says Anastasius, on the 12th October, 638, in St. Peter's, and the See remained vacant one year seven months and seventeen days. Why did it so remain vacant ?

The era and the question are both most important to note. The following narrative [2] will explain why the

---

[1] See Hefele, iii. 267.
[2] See Rohrbacher-Rump, x. 247.

Papal See was kept vacant nineteen months after the election of a successor to Pope Honorius.

In the year 638, Sergius, patriarch of Constantinople, composed in the name of the emperor Heraclius an edict which he called Ecthesis or exposition, as if it were merely an exposition of the Catholic faith respecting the dispute about the One or the Two Operations in our Lord. He then brought about that the emperor subscribed and published it. Perhaps Sergius wished to take advantage of the vacancy in the Papal See to make the Monothelite error a law of the State, and to compel the future Pope to subscribe it, for which he wished to get the imperial subscription making it a law.

The Ecthesis begins with a confession of faith in the Holy Trinity which is quite orthodox. It then enlarges upon the Incarnation, and draws out the distinction of the Two Natures and the Unity of the Person. It proceeds :—" We acknowledge one Son and Lord Jesus Christ, who is at once capable and incapable of suffering, visible and invisible. We teach that the miracles and the sufferings belong to one and the same ; we ascribe all divine and human Operation to one and the same Word become flesh ; we offer . . . to Him one adoration, and allow no man to hold and teach either One or Two Operations in the Divine Incarnation of the Lord ; but rather, according to the tradition of the holy General Councils, that one and the same only-begotten Son, our Lord Jesus Christ, works both the divine and the human actions, and that the whole Operation belonging at once to God and to man proceeds from one and the same Incarnate God, the Word, indivisibly and unconfusedly, and is to be referred to one and the same. Since the expression, One Operation, if used by some fathers, still sounds strange and disturbs the ears of some who conceive that it is used for the doing away of the Two Natures personally united in Christ our God, and in like manner the expression Two Operations offends many, as not used by any one of the chief doctors of the Church, and because there follow from it two Wills opposed to each other, as if God the Word willed to fulfil His saving passion, while His Manhood resisted that will of His, and so two are introduced willing contrary things, an impious thing opposed to Christian doctrine. For even the impious Nestorius, though he divided the divine taking of the manhood from the Lord, and introduced two Sons, did not venture to speak of two Wills. Rather he taught identity of will in the two persons invented by him. How then can they who confess the right faith, and glorify one Son, our Lord Jesus Christ, the true God, receive two Wills and those opposed to each other in Him? Following, therefore, the holy Fathers in all things and in this, we confess One Will of our Lord Jesus Christ, the true God, so that at no time did His Flesh, animated by the mind, make a natural movement of itself separately and by its own impulse, which was contrary to the bidding of God the Word personally united with it; but when and such and as much as God the Word Himself willed . . . and we exhort all Christians to be so minded, and so to hold, adding nothing and taking away nothing. I, Heraclius, the faithful emperor in Jesus Christ our Lord, have subscribed."

Sergius did not fail to have the Ecthesis confirmed by a council at Constantinople. He died himself in December, 638, but before this he had it read, probably, to his Resident Council, and asked for the judgment of its members. The bishops answered, like good courtiers; "The exposition of our great and most wise Emperor agrees in truth with the teaching of the Apostles. This is the doctrine of the Fathers, this the support of the Church. This the confessions of the Five Councils teach; by this the unity of the Christian people is assured, the weakness of the simple strengthened. This works the salvation of mankind. This we also believe; this we confirm; with this we agree." Sergius gave his solemn confirmation, and added, "If any one henceforth, disregarding the prohibition of the Emperor and the Council, dares to teach that there is One Operation or that there are Two in Christ he shall, if he be bishop, priest, deacon, or clerk, be deposed; but if monk or layman, be excluded from Communion in the Body and Blood of our Lord until he return to his duty". Thereupon the Ecthesis was attached publicly to the narthex of Sancta Sophia.

The Ecthesis had been specially drawn up against the teaching of the champion of orthodoxy in the East, Sophronius, patriarch of Jerusalem, who had appealed to Pope Honorius, and expressed full trust in his defence of the truth. But before its appearance Sophronius was already dead, and his see had come into the hands of the Monothelite Sergius, Bishop of Joppa. Macedonius had, contrary to the canons, been imposed on the see of Antioch, and consecrated by Sergius of Constantinople. It is true he had never entered his city, which was already captured by the Arabs. He had remained in Constantinople.

Cyrus, patriarch of Alexandria, in an epistle read afterwards at the Roman Council of Pope St. Martin, expressed to his spiritual brother and fellow-ministrant, Sergius of Constantinople, his intense delight at the Ecthesis which his great sovereign had drawn up in behalf of the faith, which was ready to be sent to the exarch Isaac at Ravenna, and was to be accepted by his brother Severinus, elected at Rome. I have read it, he said, not once or twice but many times. I admire an exposition brilliant as the sun's light, announcing with unswerving accuracy the true faith ; and I sung praises to God who had bestowed on us so wise a governor, guiding to harbour the holy churches. He has saved us once, twice, and thrice from tyrannous power, from Persian boastfulness, from Saracen domination.[1]

In the meantime Sergius had died, and Heraclius had put his friend Pyrrhus, who shared his Monothelite heresy, in his place at Constantinople. We learn from the letter just quoted that the death of Pope Honorius and the choice of Severinus to succeed him had already been made known at Constantinople before the Ecthesis

[1] I have shortened this from the original in Mansi, x. 1003, as read at St. Martin's Council.

was sent to Rome,¹ which was, therefore, never presented for acceptance to Honorius.

I will now take another narrative² of what was happening at Rome. Honorius died on 12th October, 638, and was buried in peace and great renown at St. Peter's. The Romans chose their countryman Severinus, son of Labienus, for his successor. The confirmation was delayed during nineteen months and sixteen days, as it seems, because the elected refused to subscribe the Ecthesis of the patriarch Sergius, being a formulary favouring Monothelism.

Before Severinus was yet consecrated the imperial officers practised a robbery upon the treasury of the Church, in which the violence exercised reminds of the dealing of Turkish pashas, with whom in general Byzantine ministers may be compared. The treasures of the Roman Church were kept in the vestiary of the episcopal palace.³ There were the costly presents which various Christian emperors, patricians, and consuls had left to the blessed Apostle Peter for the redemption of their souls, to be given, as occasion might be, in alms to the poor or for ransoming of captives. There was a report that Honorius had stored up vast sums, and his magnificent buildings caused full credence to be given to this report. Isaac, the exarch in Ravenna, found himself in want of money. The imperial troops riotously demanded to be paid. Isaac had long cast his eyes on

---

¹ Noted by Hefele, iii. 159.
² Gregorovius, ii. 128. 3rd Ed. From Anastasius, Mansi, x. 675.
³ From the *Liber Pontificalis*.

the Church's treasury, and now devised a plan to get possession of it. The Book of the Popes gives a detailed description of this incident, and it is not only an exception to the scantiness of historical accounts about Rome, but casts a passing light on the circumstances of the city.

The chartular Mauritius was then at Rome, perhaps as Magister Militum and commander of the Roman army. This consisted of troops in Byzantine pay, but no doubt was already organised as a city militia. Mauritius led by deceit against the Church of God, and taking counsel with certain ill-minded persons, stirred up this Roman force. What good, he said, is it that such a mass of money has been laid up by Pope Honorius in his Lateran Palace while your wages are not paid, which our lord the emperor has sent, and the holy man has put them in his treasury? Kindled by these words, all the armed men in the city of Rome, young and old, flocked to the Lateran Palace. They could not force an entrance, because those who attended on Severinus, the Pope elect, resisted. Mauritius, seeing this, encamped his army there for three days. Then he summoned the judges, that is, the high officers of the city, who were in his counsel. They broke in and set the imperial seal upon the treasure. Then Mauritius wrote an account of what he had done to the exarch Isaac at Ravenna, saying that he had put his seal on the treasury and they could take without harm anything which they liked. When Isaac learnt this he came to Rome; he banished all the chief persons of the church who resided in the several cities, so that none of the clergy could resist him, and, after some days, he entered the Lateran Palace; he stayed there eight days, and plundered everything. Part he sent to the emperor in the imperial city, part he gave to the troops, part he kept for himself. Anastasius concludes with the words: After this the most holy Severinus was consecrated, and Isaac returned to Ravenna. The meaning of which seems to be that Isaac had come to Rome under pretence of confirming the election of Severinus, which he made the elected Pope pay for by the plunder of his treasury.[1]

In the meantime Roman Commissioners were urging upon the emperor Heraclius at Constantinople to issue the imperial consent to the consecration of the Pope. After many negotiations, the chief of the clergy there showed them a doctrinal writing, the Ecthesis, and said, "We will only support you in your matter if you promise us to persuade the Pope to subscribe this act and to recognise without reserve the doctrines therein contained". The Commissioners, who perceived the drift of the act, and that on account of this the first See of Christendom had so long remained unfilled, answered calmly and prudently: "In this affair we can do nothing. A message has been entrusted to us, but no order given us to make a confession of faith. We will give you the assurance that we will inform the Elect of everything that you have said; that we will show him this paper and beseech him, if he approve of

---

[1] From the contemporaneous letter of St. Maximus to the Abbot Thalassius. Mansi, x. 677. Rohrbacher-Rump, x. 249.

its contents, to subscribe it. Be so good, therefore, as to put no hindrance to our mission for this matter, to do us no violence, and not to detain us without end. None can do violence to another, especially in a matter of faith ; for in such a case even the weakest becomes very strong, even the quietest feels himself a hero ; and since he strengthens his soul with the word of God, the most violent attacks serve only to confirm not to weaken him. And how much more does this apply to the Church and clergy of Rome, who, from the beginning to the present, as eldest of all the churches under the sun, presides over all! Having received this privilege according to the canons, as well from councils and apostles as from their supreme Head, in this matter of succession in the Pontificate, it is subject to no writings whatsoever, to no issue of synodical documents ; but in all these matters all are subject to it according to sacerdotal law." This is what with a most sacred and becoming confidence, fearing nothing, those intrepid ministers[1] of the immovable Rock said to the clergy of Constantinople ; who thereupon ceased from their pretension, and promised to obtain for them the imperial confirmation.

Pope Severinus, after suffering the double humiliation of having the treasury of the Church sacked by the emperor's viceroy, and his own election unconfirmed for nearly twenty months, ascended the throne of Peter on the 28th May, 640, and sat two months and six days. " He loved the clergy, and was most liberal to them all,"

[1] Stabiles illi et firmæ revera et immobilis Petræ ministri.

says of him the Book of the Popes; "holy, benignant above all men, a lover of the poor, large-handed, most gentle." In this short Pontificate he found time to reject the imperial decree, called the Ecthesis.

Had Pope Severinus at this moment failed in his duty, the whole Church would have been involved in the Monothelite heresy. Not only Pope Severinus, but his successors during forty years, were the sole stay of the Church against a heresy—the last root of the condemned Eutychean heresy—which overthrew the true doctrine of the Incarnation, making our Lord Jesus Christ not God and Man in one Person, but a Person compounded out of God and Man, and therefore not Man at all. The whole temporal power of the Byzantine sovereign, at that time despotic lord of Rome, and backed by subservient patriarchs, Sergius, Pyrrhus, Paulus, and Peter, was exerted to compel the Popes who sat during these forty years to accept the false doctrine presented to them in an imperial decree.[1] The successive Popes in this time, Severinus, John IV., Theodore I., St. Martin I., St. Eugenius I., St. Vitalian, Deusdedit, Donus I., rejected and condemned the decision urged upon them by the imperial and patriarchal pressure, all of them at the risk of every sort of persecution—one, St. Martin, at the cost of a singularly painful and glorious martyrdom. The next Pope, St. Agatho, condemned the heresy in a General Council allowed at Constantinople itself by an orthodox emperor over which his legatees presided. The Pope succeeding him,

---

[1] See Hefele, iii. 154, 160.

St. Leo II. ratified the condemnation by the Council of four successive Byzantine patriarchs, Sergius, Pyrrhus, Paulus and Peter, as heretics, and censured the negligence of Honorius in not extinguishing at once so dangerous a flame. In truth it had held the life of the Church in suspense during more than forty years. Had one of the ten successors of Honorius failed, all would have been lost, so near to the precipice was the Byzantine despotism and the State patriarchate, subservient to it, and supplying it obediently with theological knowledge sufficient to formulate heresy, allowed by the Divine Providence in that fearful century to drive the Church. And precisely during these years the new Arabian conqueror—the chalif of Mohammed —cut in two the empire which was attempting this parricide. When Heraclius went forth committing his city and his son to God, to the holy Mother of God, and to his bishop, he triumphed for the only time in the long Roman history over Rome's eastern rival, and brought back the Cross from Persia to Constantinople, and then carried it in dutiful homage to be replaced in its old shrine where our Lord suffered at Jerusalem. When at the bidding of that very bishop Sergius he tampered with the Christian faith, and oppressed the successor of St. Peter, he lost Jerusalem, Alexandria, and Antioch, with the great provinces which belonged to them. Out of the four patriarchates of his empire, three became subject to the Mohammedan chalif. The subjection came suddenly, but has lasted with a short interval from that time to this. The conquest, as yet unbroken, of Mohammed over Christian peoples dates from the perfidy of Heraclius and of his grandson Constans II, and the heresy propagated by four Byzantine patriarchs.

Returning to the history of this time we find that the successor of Pope Severinus, John IV., was consecrated 24th December, 640, and held a council at Rome immediately after his accession, and condemned under anathema the Monothelite heresy. Heraclius died February 11th, 641. Upon his death Pope John IV. sent a letter to his successors, Constantinus-Heraclius, and Heracleonas, setting forth the same faith. He also informed the new Patriarch, Pyrrhus, that he had condemned the Ecthesis: and St. Maximus informs us that Heraclius I., to turn away the Western displeasure at the Ecthesis from his own person, at the beginning of the year 641 wrote to Pope John IV. that " the Ecthesis is not mine, nor did I command it to be drawn up, but the patriarch Sergius prepared it five years ago, and besought me on my return from the East to publish it with my subscription ". The purpose of John IV. in writing to the new emperors was to set forth the doctrine of the two Operations and Wills in Christ, and in doing this to defend the orthodoxy of his predecessor Honorius. It is to be observed that after the death of Honorius, when the eastern patriarchs began to assert that Honorius in his answers to Sergius, which up to that time had been private, favoured the heresy which Sergius had imposed upon the eastern bishops, and was trying to put upon the Pope, his successors denied with much care that

Honorius had any such meaning. Thus in this document of Pope John IV. directed to the sons of Heraclius, which bears the title,[1] Defence of Pope Honorius, he says :—

"My predecessor, teaching concerning the mystery of Christ's Incarnation, said that there were not in Him, as there are in us, opposing wills of the spirit and the flesh. Certain men, twisting this to their own meaning, threw out the suspicion that he had taught that there was one Will of the Godhead and the Manhood, which is utterly contrary to the truth. I could wish them to reply to my question, in regard to which nature do they assert that there is one Will of Christ our God? If it be only in regard to the Divine Nature, what is their reply concerning His Human Nature? For he is likewise Perfect Man, lest they be condemned with Manichæus. If they speak in regard to the Manhood of Christ that this Will is Perfect God, let them see whether they do not fall under the condemnation of Photinus and Ebion. But if they assert that in the Two Natures there is only one Will, they will confuse not only the Natural Wills but the Natures themselves, so that neither the one nor the other, that is, the Divine and the Human, can be understood. For as we do not, like the impious Nestorius, suffer Two Natures to make up one Christ, so we do anything but deny, yet neither do we confuse, the difference of Natures, inasmuch as we confess the Two Natures united in the one Person of Christ our God with an agreement which language is not able to express. For in that they assert One Will of Christ's Godhead and

---

[1] Gallandi, *Bibliotheca veterum Patrum*, Tom. xiii. 33.

Manhood and at the same time one Operation, what else do they assert than that one Nature of Christ our God operates according to the division of Eutyches and Severus. As a last argument, the orthodox Fathers, who have flourished in the whole world, are proved to teach in full accordance at once Two Natures and Two Wills and Operations."

In these words, which John IV. writes as Pope to the immediate successors of Heraclius within three years after the death of Honorius, he would seem not only to have set forth in plain language the immense importance of the doctrine itself, but to be an unimpeachable witness of the meaning of Honorius, one of whose priests he had been, and as such well acquainted with his doctrine.

The pontificate of John IV., for the confirmation of which he had to wait four months, lasted only twenty-one months, and was disquieted throughout by the conflict with the Byzantine court and patriarch respecting the Ecthesis.[1] There was war between the exarch and the Lombard king, Rotharis, but it did not touch Rome. All misfortunes which threatened it came from Byzantium. The struggle against the eastern heresy embittered the feeling of Constantinople to Rome. At the same time, the Byzantine court was disturbed by intestine revolutions. Heraclius ended his reign of 31 years in February, 641. His eldest son, Heraclius Constantinus, succeeded, but, after seven months, was poisoned by his stepmother, Martina, and the Mono-

---

[1] Gregorovius, ii. 130.

thelite patriarch Pyrrhus was charged with concurrence.
In a few months, Martina's own son, Heracleonas, was
deposed by an insurrection. His nose was cut off, and
the tongue of the empress Martina cut out, and both
were banished. The grandson of Heraclius, Constans
II., became emperor in 642, a boy of twelve years, and
reigned 26 years, until 668. The reign of this emperor
is much to be noted, because it is contemporaneous with
the second, third, and fourth chalifs: Constans II.
stands in history over against Omar, Osman, and Ali.

On the death of John IV., Theodorus, a Greek of
Jerusalem, was made Pope : it is supposed by the influence of the exarch Isaac. He was the first of many
Greeks, who, in this period, were made Popes : of all
of whom, without exception, it is recorded that their
integrity, as Popes, was in no way affected by any
national feeling : they sacrificed nothing to Byzantine
policy.

At the beginning of this pontificate, Mauritius, the
officer called chartular, whose proceeding in the robbery
of the Lateran treasury has been recorded above, raised
a rebellion in Rome. He found people, nobility, and
army embittered by the Byzantine domination, and
used this feeling for his own purposes. He spread a
report that Isaac was striving to be king, made party
with those same turbulent Romans who had joined in
the attack upon the Lateran, and induced the garrisons
in all the castles of the Roman territory to refuse obedience to the exarch. When Isaac heard this, that all
the army of Italy had taken the oath to Mauritius, he

sent Donus as commander with an army to Rome. Thereupon the Roman army gave up Mauritius, and joined Donus. Mauritius took asylum at St. Mary of the Crib.[1] He was taken out and sent with an iron collar about his neck, as well as the others implicated in the insurrection, to the exarch at Ravenna : but, before he arrived there, was beheaded, and his head carried to Ravenna and impaled. Isaac kept the other conspirators in prison, collared in the same way, but they escaped execution by the death of Isaac himself. Isaac was buried in the beautiful church of St. Vitale, in Ravenna, and his epitaph is preserved in Greek, and being a picture not only of the man, but of his time, is worth transcribing. It runs thus :—

"Here lies one, a brilliant commander, who for six years, preserved Rome and the West without injury for our serene lords, Isaac, the fellow-worker with emperors, the great ornament of all Armenia, where he was of illustrious race. Upon his death in great renown, his wife Susannah mourns over her loss like a chaste dove, the loss of a husband who gained glory by his labours both in the East and in the West, for he commanded the army of both."

Isaac may be considered as the ideal exarch, and by contemplating his deeds, we may attain to a knowledge of the race of exarchs, viceroys of Italy, and images, in common clay, of their masters in marble, towards whom, for 200 years, St. Gregory and his successors had to exercise the virtue of loyalty.

[1] Sta. Maria Maggiore.

Upon the accession of Constans II., in 642, the patriarch Pyrrhus, under suspicion of complicity with the empress Martina in the poisoning of the emperor Heraclius Constantinus, fled to Africa. His place was taken by Paulus, a still more zealous Monothelite. Pyrrhus, coming to the West, which was unanimous in rejecting that heresy, represented himself to have been convinced by the eloquence of the Abbot Maximus, in an African Council in 645, and came to Rome to lay the confession of his faith at the feet of the Apostle Peter. Pope Theodorus received the repentant patriarch with great ceremony in the Vatican Basilica before the assembled clergy and people, to whom he solemnly condemned his own errors. But, when he went to Ravenna, Pyrrhus fell back again. Pope Theodorus thereupon condemned him in a Roman Council.[1]

In 646, the African bishops, in four councils, had condemned the Monothelite doctrine with the Ecthesis. Pope Theodorus, in accordance with the wish of these African Councils, admonished the new patriarch, Paulus II., at Constantinople, to return to the faith of the Church. Paulus sent a long answer,[2] in which he expressed the Monothelite doctrine. Pope Theodorus condemned him after his nuncios at Constantinople had in vain endeavoured to draw from him an orthodox confession. At the same time Pope Theodorus

---

[1] Photius, i. 202-3.
[2] See the whole as read in the Lateran Council of Pope Martin, in Mansi, x. 1019-1025.

named Stephen, Bishop of Dor, Apostolic Vicar for Palestine, with the charge to resist the heresy which Sergius, Bishop of Joppa, was spreading, and to depose the bishops intruded by him. The patriarchal chair at Jerusalem was, in fact, vacant, and the patriarchate laid waste by this usurper. Hence the Pope took charge of it. So afterwards John of Philadelphia was appointed Apostolic Vicar.

Paulus did not give way. He moved the emperor Constans II. in 648 to issue a new doctrinal decree, drawn up by himself, called the Typus, which was to take the place of the Ecthesis, and prepare in another way the spread of Monothelite error. It was to forbid under the severest secular punishments any dispute respecting One or Two Operations in our Lord or One or Two Wills. In itself it seemed intended to quiet the westerns, but in the actual state of things only for the prejudice of Catholics. Maximus the Confessor shewed that in it truth and error were alike intended to be suppressed. The eastern bishops were again compelled to subscribe. Those who refused were persecuted, even the papal legates. Their altar in the Placidia palace was destroyed, and they were forbidden to celebrate, and severe ill-treatment added.

While the Greek emperor, led by his patriarch Paulus, was issuing his edict concerning the Christian faith, Muawia, as general of the third chalif, Osman, with a fleet of 1700 ships, great and small, being already in possession of Syria, had made a descent on Cyprus, occupied the city of Constantia, subjected and laid waste the whole island.[1]

Pope Theodorus is recorded in the book of the Popes as "a lover of the poor, large-handed, kind to all, and very merciful".

---

[1] Gregorovius, ii. 138.

CHAPTER II.

POPE MARTIN, HIS COUNCIL, AND HIS MARTYRDOM.

Martinus prærogativa martyrii ter maximus nuncupandus.
Baronius, Tom. viii., Preface.

IN the mean time Pope Theodorus, having during the seven years of his pontificate maintained the faith against the aggression of the Byzantine emperor and patriarch with the same resolution as his predecessors, Popes Severinus and John IV., died on the 13th May, 649, and was buried at St. Peter's. His death occurred just after the Typus had been issued, and perhaps before he had seen it. On the 5th of the following July, Martin was chosen to succeed him.[1] Martin was then a Roman priest, had been a nuncio at Constantinople, a man distinguished by his virtue and knowledge, as well as by his personal beauty. By the fifteenth letter of this Pope we learn that the Roman clergy would not wait for the imperial consent to his consecration, and so in due time the Greeks pretended that he had taken possession of the episcopate irregularly. This pontiff, one of the most remarkable and vigorous that ever sat on the throne of St. Peter, although aware of the

---

[1] Hefele, iii. 189; Muratori, *Annali d'Italia*, anno 649.

penalty imposed by the emperor Constans, in his Typus, shrunk not the least, but was rather kindled with greater zeal to summon immediately a council of the Bishops of Italy, which met on the 5th October in this year at the Sacristy of the Lateran Basilica.

Anastasius,[1] the librarian, gives the following narrative of events which now took place concerning Pope Martin :—

"In his time Paulus, bishop of Constantinople, inflated with the spirit of pride against the holy Church of God, presumed in his audacity to go against the definitions of the Fathers. Moreover he took pains to veil his own error for the seduction of others, so that he induced the emperor also to set forth the Typus for the destruction of Catholic belief. In this he deprived of their strength all the voices of the holy Fathers by the expressions of the worst heretics, laying down that one should confess neither One nor Two Wills or Operations in Christ our Lord.

"In defending his own perversion he did a deed which no former heretic had ventured to do. He pulled down the altar belonging to our Holy See[2] in the chapel of the Placidia palace, prohibiting our nuncios from offering therein to God the adorable and immaculate Victim, or receiving the sacraments of communion. These nuncios by command of the apostolic authority had enjoined him to desist from his heretical intention. They also

---
[1] Mansi, x., 785-8.
[2] These facts are taken from the words of Pope Martin himself, in the Lateran Council.

bore witness in suffering diverse persecutions with other orthodox men, and venerable priests, some of whom he imprisoned, some he banished, some he scourged. Well nigh the whole world being thus disturbed, many of the orthodox brought up complaints from various places to our Apostolic See, intreating that the web of all this malice and destruction might be rent by the Apostolic authority, so that the disease of their Ecthesis might not break up the whole body of the Catholic Church. Then most blessed Martin, the bishop, sent and assembled 105 bishops in the city of Rome, and called a Synod according to the institution of the orthodox Fathers in the church of the Saviour at the Lateran episcopal palace. Bishops and priests sitting, deacons and the whole clergy standing, they condemned Cyrus of Alexandria, Sergius, Pyrrhus, and Paulus, patriarchs of Constantinople, who presumed to mix up their innovations with the immaculate faith. That is, in their haste to exclude this, they dressed up a confusion of heretical dogmas against God's Catholic church, for which they were smitten with anathema. This council now forms part of the Church's archives. And the Pope causing copies to be made, sent them throughout the East and West, placing them in the hands of the orthodox faithful. At that very time the emperor sent into Italy his chamberlain and exarch Olympius, to be viceroy of the whole land. His commands were:—' You are to carry out what Paulus, patriarch of this heaven defended city, has suggested to us. And if you find the province itself agreeing in the Typus set forth by us then lay hold of all the bishops, landed proprietors, dwellers, and strangers, and let them subscribe it. But, if, as Plato, the patrician, and Euphranius have suggested to us, you can carry with you the armed force there, we command you to lay hold of Martin, who was nuncio here, in the imperial city. And afterwards let all the churches read afresh the orthodox Typus, because it has been made by us, and let all the bishops in Italy set their names to it. But if you find the armed force opposed, keep it secret till you have got possession of the province, and are able to have on your side the army of the Roman city, and of Ravenna, that you may be able to execute our commands as soon as possible.' The said Olympius, coming to Rome, found the holy Church of Rome united with all the bishops of Italy, whether priests or clergy, and wishing to execute the commands received he tried, by help of the army, to make a schism in the Church. This took a long time, and Almighty God did not permit him to accomplish what he was trying to do. Seeing then that he was overcome by the holy Catholic and Apostolic Church of God, he thought it necessary to veil his bad intention, and to accomplish what he had not been able to do with the armed hand in heretical fashion at mass in the Church of God's Holy Mother, the Ever-virgin Mary, at the Crib. For while the holy Pope was giving him communion he had instructed one of his guards to murder him. But, Almighty God, who is wont to protect His orthodox servants, and to deliver them from all evil, Himself blinded the eyes of the swordsman of the exarch Olympius, and he was not allowed to see the Pontiff at the moment of giving communion, or the kiss of peace, that he might shed his blood and subject to heresy the Catholic Church of God. The soldier attested this afterwards on his oath to several. So Olympius, seeing that the hand of God protected the holy Pope Martin, thought it necessary to agree with him, and to disclose the commands which he had received. Then having made peace with the Church, he collected his army and went to Sicily against the Saracens who were there. And through the sin a great destruction fell on the Roman army, and then the exarch died of disease."

In the Council of the Lateran, held by Pope Martin in 649, the Pope carefully examined the whole history and documents concerning the attempt of the patriarch Sergius, and the emperor Heraclius, and the succeeding patriarchs at Alexandria, Constantinople, and Antioch, to alter the faith of the Church. The imperial documents, the Ecthesis of Heraclius, composed by Sergius, the Typus of Constans II. composed by the sitting patriarch, Paulus, both of them one after the other imposed by violence on the eastern episcopate, letters from many bishops, documents, in fact, of every kind, were subjected to careful reading. The Council drew up twenty canons which it imposed under anathema. The Pope at the head of the Bishops, subscribed in these words: "I, Martin, by the grace of God, Bishop of the holy Catholic and Apostolic Church of the City of Rome, ordain and subscribe this definition, confirmatory of the orthodox faith, and condemning Sergius, formerly Bishop of Constantinople, Cyrus, Bishop of Alexandria, Theodorus, Bishop, Pyrrhus, and Paulus, also, Bishop of Constantinople, together with their heretical writings ". Then follow the signatures of the Bishops of Italy, the Archbishop of Aquileia and Grado first, the Archbishop of Milan adding his assent afterwards.

Pope Martin also wrote to the emperor Constans II., sending him the acts of the Council, together with a Greek translation. Thus, with the utmost force, and with the presentiment of hard trials, he strove to prevent the further spread of Monothelite error. He also declared himself against the heretical patriarchs, Peter of Alexandria and Macedonius of Antioch, deposed Paul, Archbishop of Thessalonica, and provided for sending Catholic bishops and clergy to the East.

In these events, we have this very striking fact, that within eleven years after the death of Pope Honorius in 638, we find four Popes his immediate successors, Severinus, John IV., Theodorus, and Martin, opposing two emperors, Heraclius, and his grandson, Constans II., censuring three patriarchs of Constantinople, Sergius, Pyrrhus, and Paulus, besides other eastern patriarchs, and the last of them solemnly condemning "the impious Ecthesis and still more impious Typus," and all manner of heretical expositions, whether made by patriarchs, or imposed by emperors. There can be no doubt that all these four Popes had been clergy of Honorius himself, and as little doubt that they were maintaining the doctrine which he held. There is no appearance that any one at Rome was the least inclined to the Monothelite heresy, and the insidious manner in which it was propagated by those who held it is conspicuous on every occasion. Nor must it be forgotten that the publication of this judgment of Pope Martin fulfils all the conditions of a judgment *ex cathedra*.

But the events which now took place are of so great an importance for all subsequent time that it seems necessary to enlarge upon the epitome of them just given, and to draw out the full range of their bearing, not only on the doctrine of the Church, but on its government at the time.

We are witnessing a deliberate attempt by successive patriarchs of Constantinople to alter the faith of the Church as it had been laid down at the Council of Chalcedon. And not this only, but to make the mouth of their emperor the instrument for disseminating their heresy, and to use the whole material power of that emperor as despotic lord of Rome to overthrow the defence of the faith by the Roman See, the superior authority of which, at the same time, neither emperor nor patriarch denied. This attempt continues during forty years from the death of Pope Honorius in 638, and in the whole of that time, it was the constancy of the Roman See, the purely spiritual power of the successor of St. Peter, in the midst of the greatest danger and a helpless temporal position, which preserved the life of the Church, and foiled the Byzantine oppressor, together with the underplay of the Byzantine patriarch.

I take from the Acts of the Lateran Council of 649 the following :—

"Pope Martin said, 'Let the copy of the Typus lately composed against the orthodox faith, by persuasion of Paul, Bishop of Constantinople, be brought before our consideration'.

"Theophylact, first of the notaries of the Apostolic See, said, 'I bear in my hands the copy of the Typus ordered by your Beatitude'.

"Pope Martin said, 'Let it be read in the presence of the holy Council, that we may accurately examine its meaning'.

"Theodorus, regionary notary of the Apostolic See, read it thus, translated from the Greek into Latin." It must be remembered that the following are words of the emperor, spoken in that character.

"Since we are accustomed to do everything and to consider everything which concerns our Christian polity, and especially whatever touches the purity of our faith, through which we look for all our prosperity, we recognise how greatly our orthodox people has been disturbed. Some of them maintain One Will in the dispensation of our great God and Saviour, Jesus Christ, and His One Operation in divine and human things. Others maintain Two Wills and Two Operations in the same dispensation of the Incarnate Word. The one support themselves by saying that our Lord Jesus Christ, because of the One Person, wills and operates both divine and human things in the two natures, without confusion, and without separation. The others say, because in one and the same Person two natures are bound together without division, their distinction from each other remains, and according to the quality of the natures one and the same Christ operates both what is divine and what is human. Hence our Christian polity has been led into much variance and strife; the parties do not agree, and thus it is injured in many ways. Led therefore by Almighty God, we thought it fit to quench the flame of dissension thus enkindled, and not allow it further to feed upon human souls. We therefore proclaim to our subjects, who continue in orthodoxy, and the immaculate Christian faith, and belong to the Catholic and Apostolic Church, that it is no longer open to them to introduce any question, strife, or contention with each other concerning One Will or One Operation, or Two Operations or Two Wills. This we command, not as taking anything away from the pious belief of the holy approved Fathers concerning the dispensation of our Incarnate God the Word, but intending to put a stop to further contest on account of the said questions, and in these to follow and be satisfied with the sacred Scriptures and the traditions of the five holy Ecumenical Councils, and the simple unquestioned usages and expressions of the holy approved Fathers. Their dogmas, canons, and laws are those of the holy Catholic and Apostolic Church. Add to them nothing of your own: take from them nothing: interpret them not according to your own view, but keep the form which existed everywhere before the contention upon these questions arose. None then laid down One Will or One Operation, or Two Wills or Two Operations, under any contention. . . . Now to ensure perfect unity and concord, and to leave no opportunity to those who would contend for ever, we have ordered the documents (*i.e.*, the Ecthesis) attached to the narthex of the great church in our imperial city, which contain the questions above mentioned, to be removed. Now those who transgress these commands will first be subject to the judgment of Almighty God, and then to the severe imperial indignation for contempt. If it be a bishop or clerk, he shall be deposed from his particular rank; if a monk, he shall be banished; if noble or military, he shall be deposed. If they be private persons, when of rank, their property shall be confiscated; when of low degree, they shall be scourged and banished for ever. So that all shall be restrained by the fear of God, and seeing the punishments respectively threatened, shall maintain unshaken and undisturbed, the peace of God's holy Churches."

As[1] one Bishop of Constantinople, Sergius, composed the Ecthesis, so another, his second successor, Paul, composed the Typus, but as Sergius did not give to his work the fitting form of an imperial decree, but the theological form of a creed, Paul showed himself more skilful, and dressed his Typus in imperial clothing. Constans himself says that he meant to restore the peace of the Church by this new decree. There is no reason to doubt this, since, in tearing down the Ecthesis from the wall of Sancta Sophia, he plainly purposed to

[1] Hefele, iii, 188. Translated to "cruelty".

quiet the minds of the Westerns and those who held with them. It is further clear that while the Ecthesis forbade contention concerning One or Two Operations, it inconsistently proclaimed One Will, that is Monothelism. But the Typus consistently rejected not only One Operation, but One Will. It wished in this to be impartial. This apparent impartiality is likewise the chief distinction between the Typus and the Ecthesis, for they are like each other in the main thought, which is, that the development of doctrine should remain at the point to which it had come in the five general councils, and that further questions should not be entered into. However, that impartiality is but a false *via media*, for it puts the true doctrine of the Two Wills upon the same footing with the heresy, and forbids both one and the other. Another distinction between the Ecthesis and the Typus lies in this, that the Ecthesis only required obedience in general. Constans, on the contrary, threatened every transgressor of his Typus with the severest civil punishments, and these he executed with the utmost cruelty.

The Typus is the fifth specimen of doctrinal despotism proceeding from the Byzantine emperors since the time of St. Leo. In all these the effort was the same. So far as the relation between the emperor and the Pope is concerned, the principle at issue is whether the Byzantine emperor, with the Byzantine patriarch as his chief agent, should dictate the creed and direct the government of the Church, or the Pope and the bishops.

The first attempt proceeds from Basiliscus, who, by

insurrection got possession of the imperial throne for about twenty months, and in that short time issued the Encyclikon, in which Timotheus Ailouros, patriarch of Alexandria, helped him as to the composition, and 500 Greek bishops were found to accept and praise it. Basiliscus with his wife and children, was presently starved to death by the emperor Zeno.

The second attempt was by Zeno, when he had recovered the throne, and fallen into the hands of his patriarch Acacius. He then issued the Henoticon, which Acacius had drawn up, which was imposed by force on the bishops, and which Fravita, Euphemius, Macedonius, and Timotheus, successive patriarchs of Constantinople, submitted to subscribe, the first under Zeno, the following three under Anastasius. The wisdom and firmness of successive Popes frustrated this attempt, and Hormisdas finally obtained a full reparation, and the acknowledgment of his own charge over the whole Church, by the gift of Christ to St. Peter, which the bishops of the Apostolic See inherited.

Yet, notwithstanding this most solemn confession on the part of the bishop of Constantinople, of the emperor, and of the nobles of the East, some thirty years later, Justinian, having become direct lord of Rome, and having summoned Pope Vigilius as his temporal subject, to go to Constantinople, makes a third attempt, and issues to the Fifth General Council his own "Confession of Faith," which a recreant court-archbishop, Theodore Askidas, supplies him with, and which the patriarch of Constantinople, Eutychius, then, by the emperor's nomination, presiding over the Council, as well as the eastern bishops in the Council, receive. The whole attitude and conduct of Justinian at the Fifth Council show how deeply this most distinguished of the eastern emperors was imbued with the doctrinal despotism of his throne. And from that time, the contention of his successors is still more pronounced, and their temporal power over the Pope, as their subject, is unsparingly exercised, not to deny his spiritual supremacy in itself, but to make its exercise subject to their imperial power, and in this the patriarchs of Constantinople, assuming by and with the consent of the emperors, the title of Ecumenical Patriarch, serve their sovereign as the chief instrument for reducing the Church to servitude. It is to be observed that Justinian conferred this title upon them in his laws. From that time they one and all clung to it.

The fourth attempt is made by Heraclius at the end of his long reign, when he had fallen under the influence of Sergius, as his predecessor, Zeno, had fallen under the influence of Acacius. Not only did Sergius hold the great see of the capital during twenty-eight years from 610 to 638, but things recorded of him seem to indicate that he was a man of extraordinary resolution. He had preserved Heraclius from deserting his capital, and flying back for refuge to his father at Carthage, after a long series of defeats from the Persians. He had acted as guardian of his son, and administrator of the empire during the marvellous six years when Heraclius, shaking off twelve years of apathy, and going forth in the name of God, and in publicly uttered commendation of his kingdom to the Blessed Mother of God, had triumphed over the Great King. Servius finally supplied him with the exposition, which was to present in seeming concord the wrangling episcopacy of his eastern empire, and overcome the Roman Pontiff in his maintenance of the faith.

The fifth attempt was made by Constans II., grandson of Heraclius, for whom Paul II., patriarch of Constantinople, invested his heresy in fitting language, and presented it in the Typus as an imperial decree which all were to accept under punishment to property, freedom, or life. And Pope Martin I. had to fight the old battle of the Church as a subject to a sovereign who was at once without mercy and without scruple.

The Typus is the perfect specimen of the theologising emperor, who begins by attributing to himself the charge over the whole Church, and puts himself precisely in the place of the Pope and the bishops in formulating the true Christian doctrine, wherein he claims the initiative, and the ultimate decision.

It need only be added that in all this succession of attempts to deprive the Church of God of her liberty, and the Pope of that guardianship of the faith which alone is adequate to its maintenance, the successors of Constantine departed essentially from the position which the first of Christian emperors took at the first General Council. He did not sit in that Council. He placed himself with the sword of empire at the entrance to guard the approach. He made the decrees of the

Council laws of the Roman empire; but he acknowledged that the power to make them rested in the bishops alone.

Nor would it be unhistorical to note that in proportion as the emperors, whose seat was Byzantium, encroached upon the liberty of the Church, and sought domination over the successor of St. Peter, in whose prerogatives that liberty was seated, their temporal empire declined. The despotism which flung itself with insolence and violence against the Church became odious to its own subjects. We shall see an instance of this which almost passes belief when the patriarchate of St. Athanasius embraces the Moslem conqueror, to escape the Byzantine sovereign, and terms the defenders of the Christian faith Melchites, that is, Royalists, because, while they rejected the Eutychean heresy, they were likewise loyal to the eastern emperor.

Let us see how Pope Martin meets this attempt. No sooner is he invested with "the great mantle,"[1] than he summons a Council to meet in the basilica of Constantine, then called the Church of the Saviour, now St. John Lateran, adjoining the papal palace, the Mother Church of Rome. He called this council in order to judge the doctrine which two emperors, using two Byzantine patriarchs, and at the same time used by them, seek to impose upon the Church, instead of the doctrine of St. Leo the Great, accepted and set forth at the Council of Chalcedon. It held from the 5th to the 31st October, 649, five sittings. It was attended by

[1] *Inferno*, xix. 69. Sappi ch'io fui vestito del gran manto

105 bishops, chiefly from Italy (excluding the Lombard dominion), Sicily and Sardinia, with some African, and a few foreign. The acts have come to us complete, both in Greek and Latin, the former being the proper language of the two documents, the Ecthesis and Typus. I give the following epitome of the Pope's speech to the Council:—

"Christ has commanded pastors to be watchful: this concerns us also, and especially must we watch over the purity of the faith, since certain bishops, who do not deserve this name, have lately sought to spoil our confession of belief by new invented expressions. Every one knows them, since they have come forward openly to injure the Church: such are Cyrus of Alexandria, Sergius of Constantinople, and his followers, Pyrrhus and Paulus. Cyrus eighteen years ago taught in Alexandria One Operation in Christ, and published from the pulpit nine heads of doctrine. Sergius approved this, issued somewhat later the Ecthesis under the name of the emperor Heraclius, and taught One Will and One Operation, which leads to One Nature of Christ. The Fathers distinctly taught that Operation answers to Nature, and whoever has like Operation must likewise be of like Nature. Since then the Fathers teach Two Natures in Christ, it follows that Two Wills and Operations are united without mixture and without division in one and the same Incarnate Word. That both are naturally one thing is not possible. Pope Leo also taught Two Wills, and so holy Scripture indicates. So Christ wrought what belonged to the Godhead corporeally, since He manifested it through His flesh animated by a reasonable soul; but what belonged to the Manhood, He wrought by the Godhead, since He took upon Him freely for our sake human weaknesses, that is, sufferings, but without sin. Cyrus, in issuing his nine heads of doctrine, Sergius, in issuing the Ecthesis, contradicted the doctrine of Leo, and of the Council of Chalcedon. But Pyrrhus and Paulus spread the error more widely; in particular, Pyrrhus by threats and flatteries seduced many bishops to subscribe his impiety. When he had afterwards come to shame, he came hither, and presented to our Holy See a writing in which he anathematised his former error. But he returned as a dog to his vomit, and was therefore rightly deposed. But Paulus went even beyond his predecessor; he confirmed the Ecthesis, and contradicted the true doctrine.

"Therefore he also was deposed by the Holy See. Specially imitating Sergius, to cover his error he counselled the emperor to issue the Typus, which annuls the Catholic doctrine, denies to Christ properly all will and all operation, and therewith likewise each nature, for nature is shown by its operation. He has done what hitherto no heretic has dared; he has destroyed the altar of our Holy See in the Placidia Palace, and forbidden our Nuncios to celebrate thereon. He has persecuted those nuncios because they exhorted him to give up his error, as well as other orthodox men, imprisoning some, banishing others, beating others. As these men (that is, Sergius and the rest) have disturbed well-nigh the whole world, complaints both written and oral have come to us from various sides urging us to put down the falsehood by apostolic authority. Our predecessors have both by writing and by their nuncios tried to correct them, but without success. We have, therefore, thought it needful to convoke you, to consider together with you them and the new teaching." [1]

Pope Theodorus had named Stephen, Bishop of Dor, in Palestine, to be Apostolic Vicar in that province. He was the prelate whom the patriarch of Jerusalem, Sophronius, had sent to Rome in the time of Honorius to solicit support for the faith of that Pope, and to set before him the dangerous state of affairs. He was introduced in the Lateran Council at its second sitting, and read to it the following memorial :—[2]

"To the holy Apostolic Council held by the grace of God and the regular authority of most blessed Pope Martin presiding, in the great city of the elder Rome, for the confirmation and defence of the definitions received from our fathers and councils, I, Stephen, Bishop, and sitting in the first see of the council under the throne of Jerusalem, make the following report :—Jerusalem was in peace and tranquillity when the tempest broke upon it. For first of all Theodorus, Bishop of Pharan, then Cyrus, Bishop of Alexandria, then Sergius, Bishop of Constantinople, and Pyrrhus and Paulus, who succeeded him, set up afresh the doctrine of the heretics Apolli-

---

[1] As the Pope's speech occupies six columns in Mansi, I have taken from Hefele, iii. 190-1, the above, which, he says, contains its chief import.

[2] See Mansi, x. 891-901. I have selected parts and omitted redundancies.

naris and Severus. By these men the whole Catholic Church has been thrown into confusion. I speak to your supreme see, which is set over all sees, for the healing of every wound, for this it has been accustomed to do with power from of old and from the beginning by apostolical authority. Since Peter, the great head of the Apostles, was manifestly invested not only with the keys of heaven to open to those who believe and to close to those who disbelieve the gospel, but he first had the charge to feed the sheep of the whole Catholic Church—to convert and confirm his spiritual brethren of the same order, as he received this dignity over all, given to him providentially by God Himself for our sakes incarnate.

"Knowing which things, Sophronius, of blessed memory, formerly patriarch of Christ's holy city, took me and placed me on the holy spot of Calvary, and there indissolubly bound me with these words :—Thou shalt answer to God Himself who on this spot chose to be crucified for us, when He comes at His glorious epiphany to judge the living and the dead, if thou delayest and disregardest His endangered faith, for I myself am bodily prevented from doing this by the Saracen invasion which has come upon us for our sins.[1] Go, then, swiftly from end to end of the earth, until thou reach the Apostolic See in which the foundations of our

---

[1] Ταχέως οὖν ἀπὸ περάτων εἰς πέρατα δίελθε, μέχρις ἂν εἰς τὸν ἀποστολικὸν ἀπαντήσειας θρόνον, ἔνθα τῶν εὐσεβῶν δογμάτων εἰσὶν αἱ κρηπίδες. Μὴ ἅπαξ, μὴ δὶς, ἀλλὰ πολλάκις γνωρίζων τοῖς ἐκεῖσε πανιέροις ἀνδράσιν πάντα διακριβείας τὰ ἐνταῦθα κεκινημένα, καὶ μὴ ἐνδόσης ἐντόνως παρακαλῶν καὶ δεόμενος, ἕως ἂν ἐξ ἀποστολικῆς θεοσοφίας εἰς νεῖκος τὴν κρίσιν ἀγάγωσι, καὶ τῶν ἐπεισάκτων δογμάτων τελείαν ποιήσονται κανονικῶς τὴν κατάργησιν.

The Pope thus solemnly addressed was Honorius. Mansi, x. 895, c.

holy doctrines rest. Not once, not twice, but again and again make known to the holy men there what is being here mooted, until with apostolic prudence they bring forth judgment to victory, and effect, according to the canons, a complete annulment of these innovating doctrines. Shuddering at the adjuration put on me in this most holy spot, remembering also the episcopal dignity granted to me by God, further bearing in mind the entreaties from almost all the bishops of the East and their Christian people, agreeing with Sophronius, who is now among the saints, as first of the Episcopal Council of Jerusalem, I gave no sleep to my eyes nor slumber to my eyelids in fulfilling this command. This now is the third time that I take refuge at your apostolical feet, beseeching you, as all beseech you, to help the faith of Christians in its danger. The enemy pursue me from place to place to have me imprisoned and delivered to them in fetters, but the Lord has saved me from my persecutors. Nor has God failed to the prayers of His supplicants, but has raised up your predecessors, the apostolic prelates, to no slight exertions in correcting these men, though they would not be softened, and now he has raised up the most blessed Pope Martin. . . . I beseech you, therefore, not to despise the earnest entreaties of the orthodox bishops and peoples throughout the East, and of my now sainted lord Sophronius, brought to your blessedness now by me the least of all."

In further sittings of this Council abundant testimony from the Greek and Latin fathers was presented to show how contrary to them was the teaching which the emperors and the patriarchs of Byzantium were seeking by crude force to impose on bishops and people. In the end the Council passed twenty canons fully setting forth the true doctrine, and condemning the heresy as contrary to what had been taught up to that time: especially "the most impious Ecthesis which was made by Heraclius, formerly emperor, under persuasion of Sergius, against the orthodox faith"; and with it "the atrocious Typus lately drawn up by the most serene prince, the Emperor Constans, against the Catholic Church, by persuasion of Paulus".

In[1] rank this council stands near to the General Councils; its twenty canons being issued by Pope Martin under anathema upon matters of faith are as binding on the Church now as when they were first published. The creed of this Council is a simple repetition and exhibition of the creed of the Council of Chalcedon, until we come to the addition which at once transfixes the heresy and sets forth the faith. After the words "we believe one and the same only-begotten Son, God, the Word, our Lord Jesus Christ," the addition runs, "and we believe as Two Natures of the same, united without confusion, so likewise Two Natural Wills, the divine and the human, and Two Natural Operations, the divine and the human, for the perfect and unfailing assurance that He is truly perfect God and perfect Man in very deed, one and the same our Lord and God, Jesus Christ, willing and working divinely and humanly our salvation, as the prophets of old and our Lord Jesus

[1] Hefele, iii. 190.

Christ Himself taught us, and the creed of the holy fathers handed down, and in general all the holy universal Councils and the whole band of approved doctors in the Catholic Church. This, in agreement with them all according to their inspired teaching, we one and all confess and define."

Among the documents read at the Lateran Council was one from the whole African episcopate addressed to Pope Theodorus three years before, in 646, in the following titles: "To our most blessed Lord, seated in the apostolic headship, the Father of Fathers, Theodorus, most holy Pope and Chief Shepherd of all Prelates, Columbus Bishop of the first See of the Byzacene Council, and Reparatus Bishop of the first See of the Mauritanian Council, and with us all the bishops of the three Councils of Africa." It is to be noted that the Archbishop of Carthage is not mentioned, for Fortunatus was elected somewhat later to take the place of a Monothelite. "No one can question that a great and neverfailing spring of grace wells forth from your Apostolic See, enriching all Christians. Thence in abundance rivulets come forth, irrigating the whole Christian world, whence, O Father of Fathers, in honour of most holy Peter, your Apostolic See has been appointed, by divine decree in a peculiar and unique manner, to search into and to treat the sacred doctrines of the Church, receiving which as truly handed down it is the most necessary function of the high priest of that supreme and apostolic See to certify." Then the African bishops, by quoting, made their own that famous answer given by Pope Innocent I. to the African bishops in the time of St. Augustine, 230 years before. "This obedience," they proceed, "we humbly render to your apostolic supremacy, and beseech the Pope to do away with the hateful novelty which has sprung up in the Church of Constantinople."

This letter has a double interest, being one of the last recorded acts of the ancient African episcopate, which was already in conflict with the Mohammedan assault, and about fifty years later was entirely swept away. It would be difficult to find stronger words than it uses to describe the Papal authority and the special gift which it recognises as belonging to the See of Peter by divine ordinance.[1]

Several of the letters written by Pope Martin after the Lateran Synod testify his zeal to overthrow the Monothelite heresy. Among these is his answer to the just-quoted letter,[2] which he addresses to the Church of Carthage, and all the bishops, clergy, and laity subject to it. He praises them for the synodical letters drawn up by the Church's glorious orator, Augustine, through the Holy Ghost, to his Apostolic See, alluding to that great confession of his[3] Primacy which we have in the letters of the Saint, and which, he says, their words repeat, and so he presents to them the acts of the Lateran Council.

[1] ὅθεν εἰς τὴν τοῦ παναγίου Πέτρου τιμὴν, ὦ πάτερ πατρῶν, αὐτὸς ὁ ὑμέτερος ἀποστολικὸς θρόνος ἰδιοτρόπως ἤτοι μονογενῶς κατὰ θεῖον κεκλήρωται θέσπισμα τὰ ἱερὰ τῆς ἐκκλησίας δόγματα διερευνᾶσθαι καὶ ἀναψηλαφᾷν. Mansi, x. 920.

[2] Mansi, x. 797-804.

[3] Ep. 186. Quoted in "Formation of Christendom," vol. v., p. 335.

Particularly remarkable is the Pope's letter[1] to the bishops under the Sees of Jerusalem and Antioch, that is, the patriarchates which had fallen under Mohammedan domination. He announces to them that, after due examination, he had condemned "the Exposition of the Emperor Heraclius, and the formula of the present serene emperor," and he deplores the havoc which heretics had made in the East, irregularly setting up a false bishop at Antioch, the heretic Macedonius, and another, Peter, at Alexandria. The Pope adds that in his anxiety to build up the Church of God, which they were laying waste, he had, according to the power given him by the Lord in the person of blessed Peter, ordered his brother John, Bishop of Philadelphia, to supply his place in all ecclesiastical matters through the East, and to create in all cities episcopally subject to the Sees of Antioch and Jerusalem bishops, priests, and deacons, and he begs them as sons of obedience " to help our Vicar set by Apostolic authority ".

The Bishop of Thessalonica, in the course of 200 years since St. Leo and the succeeding Popes had made him their Vicar for the great province of Eastern Illyricum, had become a prelate of very high rank. Paul was actually bishop, but he favoured the new heresy, and the Pope, after warning him in vain,[2] wrote deposing him, unless he received without the least omission everything which had been synodically ratified and defined at the Council. At the same time he wrote to the people of

[1] See Mansi, x. 827-832.
[2] Mansi, x. 834-843, and 843-850.

Thessalonica, enjoining them to have no society, agreement, or connection with such a man.

Thus, in the case of any diocese, whether that of a simple bishop, or a primate, or a patriarch, the Pope does not hesitate to tell their several diocesans that they are set free from all duty of obedience to one condemned by him. No act can show the superior authority of the universal Primate more strongly than this. St. Gregory the Great had said that all bishops were equal when performing their respective work in their own diocese; but if that work is not duly performed, he knows of no bishop who is not subject to the Apostolic See. The power of the Primacy is essentially for edification of the whole Church, and so is exerted whenever the Church and the faith of the Church are anywhere in danger. The acts of St. Martin I. at a crisis of singular danger follow exactly the rule of St. Gregory. If an emperor supports heresy, he condemns his act, though he may be a lawful sovereign; if a patriarch is false to the faith, he sets a vicar of his own to appoint fresh bishops in the patriarchate. If his own vicar sins against the power which appointed him, he dissolves the primary bond according to which the people of that diocese is bound to their own bishop.

But the supreme authority of the Roman See is indicated most plainly in the encyclical letter issued by the Pope. It is addressed[1] "Martin, Servant of the Servants of God, by grace Bishop of God's holy Catholic and Apostolic Church of the Romans, together with the

[1] Mansi, x. 1169.

Synod of Bishops here canonically assembled with us for the confirmation of the true dogmas of the Catholic Church, to those who have inherited the like precious faith as we of our Lord and Saviour Jesus Christ, through the laver of regeneration, who sojourn in holiness and justice in every part of His dominion, our brethren the bishops, priests, deacons, heads of monasteries, monks, ascetics, and to the whole sacred plenitude of the Catholic Church ".

I give the main contents of this letter thus addressed to the whole world to announce the decision of the Council by Pope Martin. It expresses in every line, supported by constant quotations of Scripture, the solicitude of the Pope for the maintenance of the doctrine concerning the Person of the Lord which had been held from the beginning. " Our predecessors, the Pontiffs of Catholic memory, have not ceased to admonish the innovators to recede from this their heresy. Bishops from various provinces, and, what is more, general synods, have not only by their own writings called upon them to amend their heresy, but conjure our Apostolic See to exercise its regular authority, and not to suffer to the end this innovation to make a prey of the churches. Meeting, therefore, in this Roman most Christian city, we have confirmed by our sentence the holy Fathers; we have anathematised the heretics with their most depraved doctrines, the impious Ecthesis and the most impious Typus, in order that all you who dwell over the whole earth, recognising that these things have been piously done by us for the safeguard of the Catholic Church, may carry them out together with us." "The Lord says, every kingdom divided against itself shall not stand, and every sentence, every law divided against itself shall not stand; and if the Typus destroys the Ecthesis, and the Ecthesis destroys the Typus, the one asserting that our Lord has one will and operation, the other denying it, then both are divided; and how shall the heresy stand, being shown to be invalid and empty by itself, rather than destroyed by us?" This, the neverending refutation of heresy, runs through the whole letter, and against it is set "the manifestation of God through apostles, prophets, doctors, and the five Universal Councils, whose decrees are the law of the Catholic Church". "Behold the Judge stands before the door joyfully promising crowns to those who suffer for His sake."

Thus the Lateran Council of 649, presided over by Pope Martin, who directs all the proceedings, who informs the emperor of the condemnation of the Typus, composed by this emperor's own patriarch, and issued by himself as a law, who addresses an encyclical letter to all bishops and their people, summing up its acts, who writes to various provinces, and in particular to the eastern patriarchates of Antioch and Jerusalem, appointing his vicar over them, gives us in full detail a picture of the discipline existing in the Church just at the middle of the seventh century. As to doctrine, the Lateran Council stands precisely on that set forth two hundred years before at the Council of Chalcedon by the great authority of St. Leo. In condemning the

Monothelite heresy, espoused by two emperors and three successive patriarchs of Constantinople, it alleges the tradition of the Fathers from the beginning, and the doctrinal decrees of the five Councils, then accepted as General. During these five centuries the East has been agitated almost without ceasing by the efforts of the Eutychean heresy and its last progeny, the Monothelite, to overthrow the true faith concerning the Incarnation, on which the whole economy of human salvation rests. The eastern patriarchates have utterly failed to secure the occupants of the sees of Alexandria, Antioch, Jerusalem, and Constantinople, from the prevailing error. Cyrus, patriarch of Alexandria, and Sergius, patriarch of Constantinople, are the chief patrons of this error. After them, Pyrrhus, and then Paul, are using the utmost power of the emperor from their seat in the capital to impose it by force: and the ecumenical patriarch especially is using it as a lever against the Roman Primacy, and in drawing up decrees.of doctrine fathered by the imperial power is practically denying the Roman Primacy to be the guardian of the Christian faith, and striving to transfer that guardianship to himself, always under the wing of the emperor. Had the Popes yielded to the Ecthesis or the Typus, both the faith of the Church would have been altered, and its government transferred from Old Rome to Roma Nova. St. Martin, as the first act of his pontificate, plays this most remarkable part of summoning a Council which defeats this double aggression. And the moment at which it is done may be marked as that in which the temporal weakness of Rome touches its lowest point. The subsequent treatment of the Pope, which I have now to mention, is an incontestable proof how entirely he was exposed to the machinations, the violence, and the despotic tyranny of his enemies, especially to the malevolent union of emperor and patriarch. Yet it is to be observed that neither emperor nor patriarch even affects to deny the authority of St. Peter's successor; what they attempt to do is to control and subject him in the exercise of it.

History is silent as to events in Rome from the end of the Council of 649 to 653. What the exarch Olympius, by special command of the emperor Constans II. did while it was being held, has been narrated above. Olympius was dead, but another exarch, Theodore Kalliopas, was sent from Constantinople to execute the work in which Olympius had failed. On the 15th June, 653, Kalliopas came to Rome. Concerning his purpose, Pope Martin himself wrote to his friend Theodorus in these words:[1] "Your charity has desired to know how I was carried away from the See of the Apostle, St. Peter, like a solitary sparrow from the house-top. I am surprised at your question since Our Lord foretold of evil times to His own disciples: for 'there shall be then great tribulation, such as hath not been from the beginning of the world until now; and unless those days had been shortened, no flesh should be saved. But he who perseveres unto the end shall be

[1] See the 15th and 14th letters of Pope Martin, written in his imprisonment at Constantinople. Mansi, x. 849-853.

saved.' Therefore that you may know how I was removed and carried off from the city of Rome, you shall hear no false report. Through the whole time I knew what was preparing. And taking with me all my clergy, I remained by myself in the church of our Saviour, named after Constantine, which was the first built and endowed in all the world by that emperor of blessed memory, beside the bishop's palace. There we all stayed by ourselves from Saturday, when Kalliopas entered the city with the army of Ravenna, and the chamberlain Theodorus. I sent them some of the clergy to meet him, whom he received in the palace,[1] and thought I was with them. But, finding I was not, he mentioned it to the chief clergy. Because it was our purpose to do him homage,[2] but on the next day, which was Sunday, we would present ourselves and salute him, as on that day we could not. On Sunday he sent men to that church, suspecting that there was a great multitude there, being Sunday, and he reported that, being very tired with his journey, he could not come that day, but we should certainly meet the next day, 'and we will do homage to your Holiness'. Now I myself had been very sick from October to that 16th of June. On Monday then he sent at dawn his chartular and certain attendants, and said, 'You have prepared arms and you

[1] By this we learn that the imperial palace on the Palatine was still habitable, and occupied by the exarch when he came to Rome.

[2] Quia nos eum voluimus adorare sed cras—cras omnimodis occurremus et adorabimus sanctitatem vestram. The same word "adorare" is used to express the Pope's acknowledgment of the exarch, and the exarch's acknowledgment of the Pope.

have armed men inside, and you have heaped up a
quantity of stones for resistance. This is not necessary;
do not allow any such thing.' I heard this myself, and
to remove their suspicions, thought it necessary to send
them all over the episcopal palace, that, if they saw
arms or stones, they might themselves give evidence.
They went and found nothing, upon which I suggested
to them that they had always acted thus, and proceeded
against us by intrigue and false accusation, as when,
at the coming of the infamous Olympius, they said that
I might have repelled him by arms. Now I was lying
in my bed before the altar of the church, and scarcely
half-an-hour later the army came with them into the
church. All were covered, bearing lances and swords,
shields, and bows ready bent; and they did things there
which are not to be uttered. For, as when the winter
wind blows violently, the leaves fall from the trees, the
candles of the church were struck down, and resounded
in their fall upon the pavement. And the clash of arms
sounded like a horrible thunder in the church, together
with the vast number of broken candles. Upon this
their sudden inroad, order was issued by Kalliopas to
the priests and deacons who surrounded me, that I had,
in violation of rule and law, taken undue possession of
the bishop's office, and was not worthy to be in the
Apostolic See, but was by all means to be sent to this
imperial city, and a bishop elected in my stead. This
has not yet been done, and I trust will never be done;
since, in the absence of the pontiff, the archdeacon, the
archpriest, and the first notary take his place. I have

already told you the acts which had been doing concerning the faith. But, as we were not prepared for resistance, I thought it better to die ten times over than that anyone's blood should be shed in vain. And this was done without risk to anyone, after many evils displeasing to God had been effected. So I gave myself up at once to be taken before the emperor without resistance. I must admit that some of the clergy cried out to me not to do this, but I did not listen, lest murders should instantly take place. But I said to them : Let some of the clergy necessary to me, bishops, priests, and deacons, and, indeed, such as I choose, come with me. Kalliopas answered: By all means let such as will come. We use compulsion on no one. I answered, My clergy are in my own hands. Some of the priests cried out : We live and we die with him. Then Kalliopas himself and these who were with him began saying, Come with us to the palace. I did not refuse, but on that same Monday went out with them to the palace. On Tuesday all the clergy came to me, and many had prepared to sail with me, and had already put their baggage on board ; some others also, both clergy and laity, were hastening to join us. On that same night then, preceding Thursday, the 19th June, about the sixth hour, they carried me from the palace, thrusting back all who were with me in the palace, and without even things necessary for my journey and for me when here, and they took me from the city with only six pages and a single drinking vessel. We were put on board a bark, and about four hours after dawn reached Porto.

As soon as we left Rome the gates were closed, and kept closed that no one might go out and reach us at Porto before we sailed thence. Thus we were compelled to leave at Porto all the goods of those who had put them on board, and the same day we departed. On the 1st July we came to Miseno, where was the ship, that is, my prison. Now I met with no compassion, not in Miseno only but also in Calabria; nor in Calabria only, which is subject to the great city of the Romans, but in many islands in which we were detained for our sins as long as three months, save only in the island of Naxus, for there we spent a year, I was allowed to take two or three baths, and was a guest in a house. And now for seven and forty days I have not been allowed to wash in warm or cold water. I am sick and cold through and through; for both on board and on land to the present hour my stomach has allowed me no rest. When in my hunger I am about to take something, my whole body is so shaken that I cannot take anything to strengthen nature. I have an utter disgust against what I have. But I believe in the power of God, who beholds all things, for when I am relieved from this present life all my persecutors will be called to account, so that at least they may be drawn to repent, and so converted from their iniquity. God preserve you my very dear son."

The allusion above concerning the things done as to the faith is explained in a former letter to the same friend, wherein he says: "When I left the Lateran Church, where armed men had shut me in, they cried out in the presence of the exarch, Whoever says or believes that Martin has changed or will change one iota of the faith, let him be anathema. And whoever remain not in their orthodox faith to death, let them be anathema. When Kalliopas heard this he began to excuse himself that there was no other faith than what we held, and that he had no other. And I would have you know, most dear brother, concerning the faith, and likewise those calumnies which they are putting out against the truth, that by the help of your prayers, and those of all faithful Christians who are with you, whether living or dying, I will defend the faith of our salvation, and as St. Paul teaches, 'to me to live is Christ, and to die gain'. But as to those false accusations which heretics are newly making, casting aside the truth of Christ our God, what truth can they speak to men who resist God's truth? Therefore, I make answer to you, dearest brother, by Him Who will judge this world by fire, and render to every one according to his work, I never sent letters to the Saracens, nor how they should understand a certain tome, nor ever sent money, except some alms to servants of God going thither, to whom we gave a little for their needs, by no means for the Saracens. And as to our Lady, the glorious ever-virgin Mary, who brought forth Jesus Christ our God and Lord, whom all holy and Catholic fathers call the Mother of God, inasmuch as she bore the God-man, unjust men have borne false witness against me—rather against their own souls. Whoever does not honour and worship her who is blessed above every creature and human nature save Him who was born of her, the venerable ever-virgin Mother of our Lord, let him be anathema both in this world and in the next. But men who seek occasion throw up scandals for the offence of many. God preserve you, most loving son."

In addition to these letters of the Pope himself, we also possess from the hand of a contemporary[1] "a narration of the deeds done cruelly and without respect of God by the adversaries of truth to the apostolic confessor and martyr Martin, Pope of Rome". Concerning this the writer says: "Some incidents I learnt from others; of very many I was an eye-witness". He speaks with horror of the swords drawn against the Pope as he lay sick on his couch in the Lateran Basilica; how the preacher of truth was torn from his apostolic throne by the powerful of this world who were worthy of such a ministry; how he was carried off secretly in a small vessel; how, as his ship touched at various places, the bishops and faithful brought him gifts, which the brutal guards laid their hands upon, abusing those who brought them, and saying: If you love him you are enemies of the State. "When at last that blessed man reached Byzantium on the 17th September, the guards left him from morning until the tenth hour lying in his couch on the ship, a spectacle to angels and men. For a number of men came to him—wolfish from their manners I should call them—as I conjecture hired to do against the holy Pope things which should not be mentioned to Christians. Now I remained on the shore walking up and down the whole day, mourning over him

[1] See Mansi, x. 853-862.

whom I saw in such a state; and hearing what some
heathens said against him, I was ready to expire with
grief. About sunset a certain scribe named Sadoleva
came with many warders. They took him from the
ship and carried him in a portable chair to the guard-
house, Prandiaria, and shut him up under strict charge
that no one in the city should know that he was kept in
guard. Thus the holy apostolical remained without
exchanging a word with anyone for ninety-three days.
On the ninety-third day they took him early out of
guard and put him in the fiscal's cell. They had summoned the whole Senate to meet. They had him
brought in upon his chair, for he was ill from what he
had suffered on board and the long imprisonment. The
fiscal, who presided with the other chief persons, eyed
him from a distance, and bade him rise from his couch.
Some attendant said he could not stand. The fiscal
called out in a fury, and some one of the warders, Let
him stand up, though he be supported on both sides.
This was done. Then the fiscal said: Speak, wretch,
what harm has the emperor done thee? Has he taken
anything? Has he oppressed thee? But he held his
peace. Then the fiscal said to him with imperious
voice: Answerest thou nothing? Now shall thy accusers
come in. Then many accusers were brought in against
him. But they were all sons of falsehood, and disciples
of those who killed our Lord Jesus Christ. But they
contradicted the holy man, as they had been told; for
their words were arranged and prepared. Now some of
them tried to speak the truth, but those who directed

this conflict got disturbed, and began to threaten them violently until they were induced to say what told for the death of this just man. When the Pope looked at them as they entered to bear witness, he said with a smile: Are these the witnesses? That is the rule. Some of these had been with Olympius. They were sworn on the Gospels, and so bore witness. The first of all the accusers was Dorotheus, patrician of Sicily. He swore that if Martin had fifty heads he ought not to live, since he alone subverted and destroyed all the West, and was in fact in the counsel of Olympius, and an enemy who slew the emperor and the Roman civilisation. When that just man saw them coming in and swearing unsparingly, out of compassion to their souls he said to those who presided: For God sake do not make them swear, but let them say what they please on their simple word; and yourselves, do what pleases you. Why should they lose their souls by swearing? One witness came in and said that the Pope had conspired with Olympius, and tampered with soldiers to make them take an oath. When he was asked if this was true, he answered: If you will hear the truth, I will tell you. And he began to speak: 'When the Typus was made and sent to Rome by the emperor ——' At these words he was stopped, and Troilus cried out: Do not introduce before us matters of faith; you are now on trial for treason, since we are both Romans, and Christian, and orthodox. Would to God, said the Pope; but on that day of tremendous judgment you will find me a witness in this also. As the witnesses were accusing, Troilus, the prefect, said to him : What a man art thou to have seen and heard the attempts of Olympius against the emperor, yet not to have forbidden him, but to have consented with him. To whom the Pope instantly replied : Lord Troilus, tell us when George, as you know and we have heard, who had been a monk, and was become a magistrate, entered into this city from the camp, and said and did such and such things, where were you and those with you to offer no resistance, though he harangued you and banished from the palace such as he chose ? And again, when Valentine, at the emperor's command, put on the purple and sat by his side, where had you gone ? Were you not here ? Why did you not forbid him to meddle with things not belonging to him ? Did you not all take part with him ? How was I to stand against such a man who wielded the whole force of Italy ? Did I make him exarch ? I entreat you by the Lord to do quickly what is your pleasure to do with me. For God knows that you bestow on me the greatest of gifts by whatever death you kill me. The fiscal enquired of one of the officers, Sagoleva : Are there many more witnesses ? There are many, my lord, he said. But the presidents, being foiled by the holy man standing before them, because the Holy Spirit supported him, said it was sufficient. A certain Innocentius was turning into Greek the Pope's words, and the fiscal, feeling them like fiery darts shot upon them, turned to Innocentius in a fury : Why do you translate his words ? Repeat them not. And rising with his assessors he went in to report

to the emperor what he chose. But they led the holy
apostolic man, seated in his chair, away from the cell of
judgment—I should rather say from the hall of Caiphas
—and put him in the middle of a court opposite the
imperial stable, where all the people used to meet and
await the entry of the fiscal. The guards surrounded
him, and it was a sight striking awe into the crowd.
Presently they placed him in the open, that the emperor
might look at him from his dining-couch, and see what
followed. Now there was a great multitude of people
crowded together as far as the hippodrome. So they
placed the most reverend man in the middle of that
open space in presence of the whole Senate, propped up
on both sides. Suddenly there was a great press, and
the fiscal issuing from the emperor, with the doors of the
dining-room opened, ordered all the people to make way
for him. And, coming up to the holy Martin, the
Apostolicus said to him: See how God has led thee
and delivered thee into our hands. What hope hadst
thou in struggling against the emperor? Thou hast
deserted God, and God has deserted thee. And the
fiscal calling on one of the warders standing by ordered
him instantly to take away the mantle of the chief
pastor of all Christians, who had confirmed the orthodox
confession of the holy Fathers and Councils, that is, the
Faith, and had canonically and in council put under
anathema the authors of the new error, the new heretics,
with their impious doctrines. So when the warder had
torn away his mantle and the straps of his sandals, the
fiscal delivered him over to the prefect of the city,

saying: Take him, my lord prefect, and immediately cut him in pieces. At the same time he bade all who were present anathematise him, which they did, but only about twenty souls. But all who saw this deed, and knew that there is a God in heaven who beheld what was being done, went away disturbed, with eyes cast down and in great sorrow.

"Then the executioners taking him, stripped off the pallium of the sacerdotal stole, and rending the sides of his garment, which was woven from the top throughout, put iron chains upon his holy neck, and dragging his whole body violently, did not allow him to rest a moment and recover himself, but led him from the palace, making a show of him and dishonouring him through the midst of the city to the pretorium. And the sword was borne before him. Now, that blessed one was in great and unspeakable pain. He was utterly worn out and without strength, ready to expire from the pressure of sufferings and his emaciation. Nevertheless, rejoicing in hope, he was comforted in the Lord, and the greater the affliction and violence with which he was dragged along, the more that Just One followed with serene countenance and unbroken spirit. He had but one garment, which was rent from top to bottom, and no girdle; but he was girded with faith and the grace of the Lord. You might see a man so full of God subject to such disgrace that his flesh might be seen naked. When the people saw many things which happened they groaned and sobbed. But a few of those ministers of Satan rejoiced and mocked, and shaking their heads, as is written, they said, Where is his God, and where is his faith, and where is his teaching? And when he had come to the pretorium in this dishonour, and surrounded by the executioners with drawn swords, they cast him into a prison with murderers, and about an hour later carried him thence to the guard-house of Diomedes, in the court of the prefect. But they drew him in his fetters with such haste and force that his legs and thighs were torn, and blood shed in ascending the stairs of the guard-house, which were very ragged, rough and steep. Now the blessed one was very nigh to escape the tortures of the present life by expiring before the sword came when he had no strength to mount the steps with the men dragging him. When at last they got him somehow into the guard-house, after many falls and risings again, they put him on a bench clothed in fetters. For when he was delivered by Caiphas, that is, the prefect, to Pilate[1] to be crucified, immediately when the executioners were stripping him, he suffered greatly from the cold, for it was a bitter season. They put on

---

[1] A similar outrage upon another Pope suggests to Dante a similar identification of the Disciple with the Master—both speak of contemporaneous events; as Constans II. is to Pope Martin so Philippe-le-bel is to Pope Boniface VIII.

> Veggio in Alagna entrar lo fiordaliso,
> E nel Vicario suo Cristo esser catto.
> Veggiolo un' altra volta esser deriso;
> Veggio rinnovellar l'aceto e il fele,
> E tra nuovi ladroni essere anciso.
> Veggio il nuovo Pilato sì crudele,
> E cio nol sazia, ma, senza decreto,
> Porta nel tempio le cupide vele.
> —*Purgatorio*, xx. 85.

him the heaviest iron fetters, and there was no man of his own to help him, save one young cleric, who stayed with him in custody, and stood weeping over his master, like Peter. The chief warder also was fastened to him, it being the custom that a criminal condemned to the sword should be bound to the chief warder.

"Now, there were two women, a mother and a daughter, who kept the keys of the guard-house. These witnessed the unendurable suffering of that holy man (for besides all his other punishments he was shivering with cold) and out of compassion sought to show some mercy to him and to cover him, but did not venture because of the warder who was bound to him. For they thought that the order for his execution would come at once. But after some hours when some soldiers below had summoned the chief warder he went down, and one of these women, touched with pity, came, and folding in her arms the champion of Christ and apostolic father, carried him and rested him on her own bed, carefully covering him and wrapping him. Now he remained to the evening without uttering a word. But in the evening Gregorius, the eunuch, prefect of the chamberlains, sent his majordomo with a little food to refresh him, saying, Faint not in your tribulations; we trust in God you will not die. The blessed one groaned at this increase of his troubles. Immediately they took off his fetters.

"The next day the emperor went to the patriarchal palace to visit the patriarch Paul, for he was near death. The emperor told him all that had been done to the holy man. But Paul groaned, and turning his face to the wall he said: Woe is me, this also has been done to multiply the judgments upon me. The emperor asked why he said this. He replied: Is it not miserable, my Lord, that pontiffs should suffer such things. Then he earnestly adjured the emperor that the past sufferings were sufficient, and that he should bear no more. When this was heard by that apostolical man, who did not receive what he was expecting, he was not pleased with that promise, but was made quite sad, for he was longing to finish a good fight, and to depart unto Him Whom he desired.

"The patriarch Paul died, and Pyrrhus who had been patriarch before him was trying to recover his seat, but the retractation which he had offered to the Pope Theodorus was brought up against him. The emperor sent an officer, an assistant of the fiscal, to examine Pope Martin about it. Demosthenes entering said to the Pope: See in what great glory you were, and to what you have reduced yourself. Nobody did this to you, but you did it to yourself. The Pope made no answer except, Glory and thanksgiving for all things to the sole immortal King. His majesty, said Demosthenes, has instructed you thus: inform us of what passed in the case of the expatriarch Pyrrhus here, and at Rome afterwards. Why did he go to Rome? Was it by order, or of his own accord? The Pope answered, Of his own accord. Demosthenes said, How did he draw up that paper? Under any one's compulsion? The Pope replied, Under none but of himself. Demosthenes said: When Pyrrhus came to Rome, how did

Pope Theodorus, your predecessor, receive him? as a bishop? The Pope replied with tranquillity, And why not? Before Pyrrhus came to Rome, blessed Theodorus wrote hither, that is to Paul, who had acted unfittingly, and invaded another's see. When afterwards Pyrrhus came to Rome, to the threshold of St. Peter, how should not my predecessor receive and honour him as a bishop? Demosthenes said, That is most true. But where did he get what was most needful for his support? The Pope said, Clearly from the Roman patriarchal palace. The assistant remarked: What sort of bread was given to him? The Pope said, My Lords, do you not know the Roman Church? For I tell you whoever in however poor a plight comes hither to lodge, all things for his need are given him, and St. Peter sends away none who come without his gifts; the best bread and various wines are given both to him and to his attendants. If this is done in the case of the abject, when one comes in the honour of a bishop, what treatment should he receive? Demosthenes said, We have been informed that Pyrrhus was forced to make that statement at Rome, that he bore wooden fetters, and suffered much. The Pope replied, Nothing of the kind was done. For unless some are kept in their place by fear, they cannot speak out the truth. There are many at Constantinople who were then at Rome, and know what took place there. The patricius Plato survives, who was then exarch, and who directed some of his men then to Pyrrhus at Rome. Ask him if I speak falsely about this. But why enquire further? I am in your hands. Do with me what you will. As God allows, it is in your power. If you cut me to pieces, as when you delivered me to the prefect, you ordered, I do not communicate with the Church of Constantinople. I am here : examine me, and try, and you will find by experience the grace of God and of His faithful servants." Again Pyrrhus was mentioned, who had been so often anathematised, and stripped of the sacred honour. Demosthenes and his assistant were astonished at the tranquil Pope's boldness and constancy for Christ unto death. For this his chalice of passion was ordained. The attendants also were amazed : they made a copy of all which the blessed man had said and retired.

"Now the most reverend Pope passed in that same guard-house of Diomedes eighty-five days after the first ninety-three, that is, in all one hundred and seventy-eight days. Then Sagoleva the scribe came, saying, I am commanded to take you hence, and to remove you to my house, and after two days to conduct you whither the fiscal shall command. The Pope asked whither he was to be taken ; the other refused to say. Then the holy man asked that he might be allowed to remain in the same guard-house until he was banished, and might be taken direct from it, which also was refused him. But about sunset the venerable Pope said to those who were in the prison : Approach, brethren, and let us take leave ; behold he is at hand who will take me hence. And as he said this they each drank of the chalice. And rising with serene countenance, with much firmness and thanksgiving he said to one of those present dear to him : Sir, my brother, come and give me the kiss of peace. Now the heart of that brother, as he told me himself at that very time, was, I conceive, such as the heart of that disciple who watched his Lord upon the cross. And as he was giving the kiss of peace to the most holy Pope, through the depth of their affection they shed a flood of tears. But all present broke into a terrible lamentation. The blessed man distressed at this, besought them not to do so, looking at them undisturbed. And placing his venerable hands upon his head, said with a smile : Sir, my brother, this is good, this is seasonable—should you act thus ? Is it for our peace ? Rather you should rejoice over me now. To whom the brother with deep contrition answered : Servant of Christ, God knows. I rejoice in the glory with which Christ our God has deigned that you should suffer all these things for His Name's sake ; but I am sad for the perdition of all. Then all paying him their respects retired. So the scribe coming forth at once took him away and brought him to his own house. It was said then that he was banished to Cherson, and a few days afterwards we learnt that the holy Apostolical man had been carried thither in a vessel secretly.

"Upon his arrival he wrote a letter after a few days to a most dear friend in Byzantium, one of those who loved him for the Lord's sake and for his right faith. And this our father was in banishment and great tribulation, and on account of his many and severe bodily sicknesses, and the every way defective supply of that country, where nothing was to be found, particularly bread, which they knew by name, but not in fact, asked for certain things to be sent him. Thus he wrote, attesting upon oath that a small bark touched there, carrying a little wheat in exchange for salt, and they were scarcely able to get a bushel of wheat for four coins, and that with much entreaty. That holy soul wrote that he was suffering various distresses there, not only from his own body, but through the oppression of those who ruled there, under direction from the lord in Byzantium, so that he was dying miserably. I then, your humble and sinning servant, beseech you, Fathers honourable in God, since I have declared to you what I myself saw and most carefully heard from others, that is, the trials pressing on our most blessed Pope for his right confession in Christ our Lord, and for his anathema uttered upon the new heretics. Short as is my account out of many things, but the best I could send you, do you for your part set forth these things to those who have zeal for God's worship, and beseech them to imitate him, and to maintain the traditions of the holy fathers, as he has done, and to hold no communion with those of an opposite mind. Entreat also for me, your unworthy servant, the writer, that, together with him and with you, I may find mercy from Christ our Lord for ever. Amen."

We possess two letters written by the Pope from the Crimea to his friend in Byzantium, which would seem to be the letters referred to by the writer I have just quoted. In them the Pope declares the extreme need of necessaries for life, in which he suffers. In the first he says, "If St. Peter thus supports strangers at Rome, what shall we say of ourselves, who are his proper servants, and at least for a time ministered to him, and are in such a banishment and affliction". In the second his words are still more pressing: "I am astonished at the inattention and want of compassion of all who once belonged to me, of my friends and relations who are so utterly forgetful of my misery and care not to know, as I find by experience, whether I am or am not upon the earth. Much more still do I wonder at those who are of the most holy Church of the Apostle Peter, since they have taken such pains for their own body and member— that is, for their affection to us—that we may be without solicitude. For if the Church of St. Peter possess not gold, at least, by the grace of God, it is not without wheat and wine and other necessaries whereby at least to show a moderate care of us. What fear has fallen upon men that they should not do the commands of God? Have I appeared such an enemy to the whole fulness of the Church, and an adversary to them? But may God, who wishes all men to be saved and to come to the knowledge of the truth by the intercession of St. Peter, establish their hearts in the orthodox faith, and confirm them against every heretic and person adversary to our Church, and maintain them unshaken, especially the pastor who is now declared to rule them, so that failing, declining, surrendering no whit of the things which they have writtenly professed in the sight of our Lord and his holy Angels, they may, together with my humility, receive the crown of justice belonging to the orthodox faith from the hand of our Lord and Saviour Jesus Christ. As for this my poor body, the Lord Himself will care as it pleases Him to order, whether for sorrows without end or for moderate relief. For the Lord is at hand, and for what am I solicitous? I hope in His mercy that He will not long delay to finish my course, as He has appointed."[1]

The "present pastor," whom Pope Martin thus seems to recognise was Pope Eugenius, elected at Rome in his lifetime, through dread, it is said, of the clergy there that the Emperor Constans II. would force upon them some Monothelite of his own to sit in the See of Peter.

The last scene is thus described, as appended to the foregoing narrative :—

"The most holy thrice blessed Apostolical, Martin the Pope, a true confessor and martyr of Christ our God, died in his banishment in the Crimea, according to his own petition to our Lord God, offered to Him with tears at the moment that he disembarked and trod that land— that is, that in it he might finish his life, fighting the good fight, finishing his course of martyrdom, keeping the good faith, on the 16th September, the day on which in the year's course the most precious and blessed memory is kept of the martyr Euphemia, guardian of the orthodox faith.[2] He was buried about a stadium outside the walls of the city of Cherson, in the Church of Our Lady, the most chaste, immaculate, most excellent

[1] Letters 16 and 17, Mansi, x. 861, 862.
[2] So called in allusion to the Council at Chalcedon having been held in her church.

of all creatures, the fullest of grace, the maker and giver of joy, the ever-Virgin Mary, Mother of God. By the intercessions of which Virgin and confessor may Christ our true God and Saviour, who came forth from her for the human race in a manner ineffable and without seed, guard and protect us, and all faithful hearers, and all the people whom He has acquired unto sincere faith and practice, in peace and charity, and all justice to the end."

So Pope Martin I. gave up his life for the faith of Christ and for the independence of the Church, and no less for that guardianship of both which is vested in the Holy See. For he was thus treated because he held a Council at the Lateran expressly condemning an imperial document of the reigning sovereign called a Typus, and as Pope placed it under anathema, and published his Encyclical "to the whole sacred plenitude of the Church". And he was condemned as a traitor, exactly repeating the passion of his Lord, as he sat in the seat of him to whom our Lord said, Follow thou Me. And further, he followed his great predecessor, Pope Clement I., the personal friend both of St. Peter and St. Paul, and the third successor of St. Peter, dying in the Crimea, where St. Clement died by command of the great heathen emperor Trajan, as St. Martin died by command of Constans II., a successor of Constantine, and by his office as "Christian prince and Roman Emperor" the first son and defender of the Church.

CHAPTER III.

HERACLIUS BETRAYS THE FAITH, AND CUTS HIS EMPIRE IN TWO.

WE left the emperor Heraclius carrying back the true Cross in triumph to Jerusalem from its captivity under the Persian fire-worshipper, whose empire he had wounded to death. This was in the year 629, in the pontificate of Honorius, and in that act the emperor seated at Byzantium, on the throne of Constantine, at the head of the empire which was the proper creation of Constantine, seemed to have made himself the champion of the faith which is embodied in the Cross. Had Heraclius then died it would have been with a halo not only of human but of Christian glory surrounding his head. But he survived during twelve years in which his inertness, considered by some to be unexplained, suffered the eastern empire to undergo irreparable losses. These, moreover, came from a foe of whose mere existence he was indeed conscious, but of whom he had no fear at the time of that triumphal entry into Jerusalem. An obscure Arabian raider was striving to gain a mastery among some savage tribes in that little known peninsula. The lord of the golden city, seated as queen of Europe and Asia on broad-flowing Hellespont, would hardly deign to cast his eyes upon an incursion of southern robbers, made on an empire which for three hundred years had been watching war-clouds big with tempests from the north, or matching itself with difficulty against the restored Sassanid kingdom. This at last was beaten down. Might not Constantinople hail in security the return of an emperor who had conquered Persia? But we, looking back over the ages, may think that the act of Heraclius replacing the Cross in the Holy City and in the church which Constantine had built over the sepulchre of Christ may be called with much truth the last act of the real Cæsarean empire, inasmuch as during the twelve succeeding years it lost for ever its greatest provinces to the very foe whose advent as a conqueror Heraclius had not even suspected.

We have now to follow briefly one of the greatest revolutions which has ever occurred in human affairs. It is a revolution which not merely sets up one kingdom instead of another, or alters the persons of individual rulers; but which changes human society to its very depths, provides a different standard of morals, and, so far as it succeeds, but only so far, reverses the course of Christian civilisation, and undoes in certain countries the greatest conquests which the Christian Church had obtained for the good of the human race. Not States only are changed, but fathers and mothers, husbands and wives, sons and daughters: in fine, Græco-Roman heathenism has disappeared, but instead of it arises a religion borne on the shoulders of a temporal rule, and a legislation compared with which in certain respects that old heathenism was pure and benignant. The revolution reaches in fact man's belief in the nature of God Himself: and a change of belief in the nature of God involves a change in all His relations to His moral creatures, and in their relations to each other. The creature in all action reproduces what it holds concerning the Creator. The religion of self-sacrifice springs from a God who sacrifices Himself: the religion of self-indulgence from a God from whose worship sacrifice has been expunged.

It[1] appears that even before the triumphal entry of Heraclius into Jerusalem with the recovered cross he had met in the Persian campaigns, in 622 or 623, with a certain bishop named Cyrus, then holding the see of Phasis, in Armenia. But Cyrus himself had for years before been in communication with Sergius, the powerful patriarch of Constantinople, the guide and inspirer of the emperor. Sergius had held the see of the capital since the year 610, in which the accession of Heraclius took place. It had been all along his dream to reconcile the various monophysite sects which troubled his master's empire. In the political point of view such a reconciliation could not but appear very important. In Egypt alone the Monophysites numbered about six millions, against three hundred thousand orthodox.[2] How deeply their national feeling was mixed up with their heresy is shown by the name of Melchites or Royalists, which they gave to their opponents. The patriarch Sergius and the

---

[1] See Rump, x. 121-6.
[2] Hefele, iii. 119.

emperor Heraclius fell upon the device of gaining the heretical party, not only in Egypt, but in the Eastern empire generally, to at least an outward union with the orthodox by introducing the formula " One Operation " as a theological expression for the acts of our Lord. St. John of Damascus[1] describes in his treatise on heresies the 99th as that of the Monothelites "who derived their origin from Cyrus of Alexandria, and their strength from Sergius of Constantinople. These men maintained two Natures in Christ, and one Person, but assert one Will and one Operation, by which they destroy the duality of natures, and strongly adhere to the doctrines of Apollinarius." Now Sergius, uniting great ability and strong character to his position as bishop of the capital city and minister of the Emperor Heraclius, dominated his mind. Heraclius exerted himself greatly to disseminate the formulary of these two patriarchs. His purpose was that of drawing together his own distracted empire. This purpose of Heraclius is carried back so far at least as the year 628. Nay, at the beginning of his campaign against the Persians he recommended it. How much more when by the peace of the year 628 he recovered the provinces which had been taken from him.[2] It would seem that the faltering of Heraclius in the faith, by which he was willing to subject to a deceptive compromise the doctrine of the incarnation itself, was coincident in time with the opening of the Mohammedan era, the hegira or flight of Mohammed from Mecca, which marks his assumption of the claim to propagate

[1] Vol. i. 110.   [2] Hefele, iii. 120.

by force a conquering religion. That claim was in a few years to cost Heraclius the half of his empire. It is certain that about the year 630 he promoted Cyrus to be patriarch of Alexandria. He also put a certain Athanasius of like doctrine into the see of Antioch, and thus three patriarchal sees at once were in favour of the heresy. And Sergius wrote to Pope Honorius commending it as a wonderful mode of restoring unity to the Church in the East.

Cyrus drew up nine heads of doctrine, by which he thought that he had reconciled the Theodosians and other powerful sects in Egypt. His announcement was received with exceeding joy by Sergius at Constantinople. Sergius wrote to Pope Honorius describing the action of Cyrus in these words : "Certain dogmatic heads were agreed upon between the two sides, in consequence of which those who but yesterday were parted into divisions and acknowledged the wicked Dioscorus and Severus as their ancestors, were united to the one most holy Catholic Church, and all the people of Alexandria, beloved by Christ, and besides this we may say all Egypt and Thebais and Libya, and the other dioceses of the Egyptian province, became one flock of Christ our true God. They who were until then to be seen an innumerable multitude of divided heresies, now, by the good pleasure of God and the zeal well-pleasing to Him of the most holy prelate of Alexandria, have all become one, with one voice and unity of spirit, confessing the true doctrines of the Church."[1]

[1] Letter of Sergius to Honorius, read in the 6th Council. Mansi, xi. 532.

Such was the picture set before Pope Honorius by the patriarch Sergius, then in the height of his credit as bishop of the imperial city and prime minister of the emperor, in the year 633, when Abu Bekr was elected the first of the chalifs to carry on the power of Mohammed, who had died a few months before. A few years after this supposed reunion of all, these same Egyptians welcomed submission to Omar, the second chalif and successor of Abu Bekr, as lord of Egypt, who would, as they thought, be more favourable to them than Heraclius.

And the successor of St. Peter was deceived into believing that the picture drawn by Sergius was a true statement.

But before the union described in such terms by Sergius had been completed, a man had come to Alexandria, who was to protest in the face of the whole world against this compromise to which the Catholic faith was being subjected. This was Sophronius, a monk of high repute, to whom the patriarch Cyrus showed the articles of union, while they were as yet unpublished. Sophronius threw himself at the patriarch's feet, and conjured him most earnestly not to announce them from the pulpit, as they manifestly expressed the heresy of Apollinaris. Sophronius did not succeed with Cyrus, but carried a letter from him to Sergius at Constantinople, to whom it would seem that Cyrus directed him as the chief supporter and exponent of the doctrine which Sophronius rejected.

All that Sophronius was able to obtain from Sergius was that both expressions concerning the action of our

Lord, as God-man, that is, the One Operation, or the Two Operations, should be equally avoided. Sophronius on his return to Jerusalem, was elected patriarch, and as such, presently issued his synodical letter. This is almost the most important document[1] in the whole Monothelite struggle : a great theological treatise, which embraces the Trinity and the Incarnation, and fully sets forth the doctrine of the Two Operations in Christ. Copies of it were sent to all the patriarchs. The copy sent to Sergius has come down to us among the acts of the 7th session of the 6th council. Out of the copy in the acts I will here quote some few of the very words in which the great champion of the faith states the doctrine. It is that which St. Leo defined at the Council of Chalcedon, for which Pope S. Martin offered his life in sacrifice, for which the Popes preceding and following him suffered trials and persecutions without end, which four successive patriarchs of Constantinople endeavoured to overthrow, and for their incessant quarrels over which, three eastern patriarchates, with their bishoprics, were delivered over as a prey to the hordes of the false prophet.

Sophronius[2] addressing his colleagues began with regretting that he was advanced to the pontifical throne from a very humble state against his will. Begging his fathers and brethren to support him, he

[1] Hefele, iii. 188.
[2] The synodal letter of Sophronius occupies 24 folio columns in Mansi, xi. 461-508. Its chief points are compressed by Hefele, iii. 189-145, into six pages. I have drawn my quotation partly from Hefele, and partly from the original text.

noted that it was an apostolic custom throughout the world that they who were thus advanced, should attest their faith to the colleagues preceding them. After this introduction, Sophronius threw his words into the form of a creed, in which the first part dwelt upon the Trinity. He then, at greater length, set forth his belief in the Incarnation. How God the Son, taking pity upon the fall of man, by His own will, and the will of His Father, and the divine good pleasure of the Spirit, being of the infinite nature, incapable of circumscription and of local passage, entered the virginal womb, resplendent in its purity, of Mary the holy, the God-minded, the free from every contamination of body, of soul, and of mind;[1] the fleshless took flesh, the formless, in His divine substance, took our form; the eternal God becomes in truth man. He, who is in the bosom of the eternal Father is bosomed in a mother's womb. He who is without time receives a beginning in time. Then, passing to the point in question, he went on: Christ is One and Two, One in Person, Two in Natures and their natural attributes. On this account, One and the same Christ and Son, and Only-begotten is found undivided in both natures. He worked physically the works of each nature according to the essential quality or natural property which belonged to each. This He could not have done, had He possessed, as One only Person, so One only Nature, not compounded. For then, the One and

---

[1] μήτραν εἰσδὺς ἀπειρόγαμον Μαρίας τῆς ἁγίας καὶ φαιδρᾶς καὶ θεόφρονος καὶ παντὸς ἐλευθέρας μολύσματος τοῦτε κατὰ σῶμα καὶ ψυχὴν καὶ διάνοιαν.— *Mansi*, xi. 473.

the Same would not have completely done the works of each Nature. For when has Godhead without body worked naturally the works of the body? or, when has a body without Godhead worked works which substantially belong to the Godhead? But Emmanuel, being One, and in this Oneness both, that is, God and Man, did, in truth, the works of each Nature; being One and the Same, as God He did the divine, as Man the human works. Being One and the Same, He works and He speaks the divine and the human.[1] Not one wrought miracles, and another did human works, and suffered pains, as Nestorius meant, but one and the same Christ and Son wrought the divine and the human according to each, as St. Cyril taught. In each of the Two Natures He had the two powers unmingled, but undivided. As He is eternal God, He wrought the miracles; as He was Man in the last times, He wrought the inferior and human works.

The answer to the Synodical letter of Sophronius, made by Sergius at Constantinople, was not to receive it, but to draw up his own Ecthesis, and prevail on the emperor Heraclius to stamp it with the imperial signature, and proclaim it as the faith of his empire. Before the Ecthesis was brought to Rome in December, 638, Pope Honorius had died in the preceding October. Sophronius had commissioned the chief bishop of his patriarchate, Stephen of Dor, as we have already seen,

---

[1] St. Leo's doctrine is contained in his words to S. Flavian, accepted and made its own by the Council of Chalcedon:—"Agit enim utraque forma (*i.e.* natura) cum alterius communione quod proprium est".

to carry his appeal to Honorius, in the See of Peter. And now it is time to turn to those events which were in the meanwhile happening in the eastern empire.

In the three hundred years from Constantine to his twenty-second successor, Heraclius, the empire which he had set up in the fairest city of the world had developed into a double despotism. It is difficult to say whether that despotism pressed more severely on the religious or on the civil well-being of its subjects. As to each, it is requisite to say something. The gravity of the events which took place within ten years demands it; while in their permanent effect that gravity most of all consists. The immediate result was most rapid and unexpected, yet a long train of action during the three hundred years preceding had led straight up to it, and a period of four times three hundred years has since witnessed its evolution.

Let us take first this pressure of despotism on religion. In speaking of Constantine I noted that there were in him two very distinct periods of his rule after he became a Christian. The first precedes his acquisition of the whole empire in 323; the second follows in the fourteen years from that time to his death. But in this second period the change, which dates from the moment at which he becomes sole emperor, is yet gradual. At the first General Council, in 325, the calling of which is agreed to by the Pope and the eastern patriarchs, but springs from himself, he acknowledges both in word and conduct that the Christian Church is the kingdom of Christ, and that its government lies in the hands of those who receive a divine consecration thereto from Christ. They are the witnesses of His doctrine, which they maintain and promulgate in virtue of that consecration. Upon this doctrine their judgment is final. Constantine never in thought submitted to any power but the Catholic Church. The thought of warring sects was abhorrent equally to the soldier, the conqueror, and the legislator. Yet before his reign closed, at the age of sixty-three, he had been seduced in his conduct from this high tone of action by the counsels of the Court bishop, Eusebius; he had restored Arius and persecuted Athanasius. He had selected the bishops who were to attend local councils, while he stretched the powers of such local councils beyond their competence. He had in fact advanced with his imperial sword into the Church's Council Chamber, and claimed to be a judge of her doctrine. And his kingdom was forthwith divided[1] among three sons, none of whom as rulers at all represented their father's majesty, while one, Constantius, became after not many years the sole ruler, and as such propagated the heresy of the day, and practised encroachment on the doctrinal independence of the Church. Constantius was cut off in his forty-fourth year, receiving clinical baptism from the hands of an Arian on his death-

---

[1] Compare A. de Vere, *Legends and Records*, p. 125—
                Arius since then hath died;
Since then God's Church is cloven. Since then, since then
My empire too is cloven, and cloven in five.
No choice remained. I never was the man
To close my eyes against unwelcome truth.
My sons, my nephews, these are each and all
Alike ambitious men, and ineffectual.

bed. In twenty years after his death the imperial power passes through two new families, and when a third is called in to support a falling empire, Theodosius has fifteen years given to him in which to save the empire from imminent destruction and the eastern Church from heresy. The victory of that Arian heresy during fifty years had so deranged that eastern episcopate, that no one but a saint and champion of the faith, such as St. Basil,[1] could venture to describe its condition. From the death of Theodosius, in 395, the eastern empire passed through fifteen successors to Heraclius, and in that succession there are ten changes of family. One daughter of an emperor, who was himself a successful insurgent, conferred the empire twice, both times on the most worthless of men, as much marked for their civil misgovernment as for persecution of the Church. But with every step in the succession it may be noted that the original independence of the Church, as recognised by Constantine and by his successors down to the Emperor Leo I. in a long series of imperial laws,[2] fell more and more into the background. Each general who by slaughtering his predecessor mounted the eastern throne assumed at once the bearing of the lord of the world: with the purple boots he put on the imperial pride. The Roman Primacy was indeed acknowledged by the Council of Chalcedon in 451, and no

---

[1] See the letter of St. Basil quoted above in vol. v., 231, *Throne of the Fisherman*.

[2] These may be found drawn out in eleven papers of the *Civiltà Cattolica* termed "La Chiesa e l'Impero," 1855-6.

less by the Emperor Marcian, the husband of the Theodosian heiress. But twenty-five years after that Council the western Emperor was abolished. From that moment the sole Roman Emperor was seated at Byzantium. At once an eastern schism was set up by the Bishop of the Capital. Rome was in the possession of Teuton Arians, who impaired the freedom of the Papal election, and made the imperial confirmation of it a custom. And when at last an honest general, who had entered the army as an Illyrian peasant, and risen from the ranks to the throne, had discountenanced the schism, condemned four successive bishops of his own capital, and acknowledged in amplest terms that the Pope's power was supreme, and also that it consisted in descent from St. Peter, the eastern emperor forbore, indeed, to deny the Primacy, but his endeavour was to control its action by making the spiritual subject to the civil power. This was the outcome of Justinian's long reign from 527 to 565. And the fatal conquest of Italy and Rome, making the one to be a captive province, and the other to be the garrisoned city, but not even the capital of a captive province, aided Justinian in acts to undo the reverence which in words he testified to the successor of St. Peter. In eighty-five years, from 553 to 638, the occupant of the eastern throne had advanced from holding a Council at Constantinople without the Pope's consent, to presenting at Rome a doctrinal decree for his signature. A few years afterwards, when the Pope called a Council, and condemned the decrees of two emperors as heresy, and three successive bishops of Constantinople as the heretics who supported it, the grandson of Heraclius, Constans II., tried the Pope as guilty of high treason before the Senate of Byzantium, and crowned him with martyrdom in exile. Step from Pope Vigilius a captive guarded at Constantinople in 553, to Pope Martin sentenced there as a traitor in 655, and dying in the Crimea a martyr. That step will mark the advance of eastern despotism and the peril of the Church's independence.

But it may be said that from the time Nestorius is deposed as guilty of heresy made by himself from the see of the capital in 431, to the publication of the imperial Ecthesis as a rule of faith in 638, the eastern patriarchates have been swaying backwards and forwards between the two opposing heresies of Nestorius and Eutyches : Syria is the parent of one : Egypt of the other. Through these two centuries the bishop of Byzantium has pursued under the emperor's neverfailing patronage a uniform course of self-aggrandisement. In this he was greatly helped by the extinction of the western emperor, when his master at Constantinople became the sole representative of the Roman name—that Christian king and Roman prince to whose honour so many Popes from Felix III. onward so vainly appealed. That very prince became step by step their most dangerous enemy. The first act immediately upon the extinction of the western emperor—who was the natural defender of the Holy See—was that a Byzantine bishop, Acacius, set himself up as the leader of the whole eastern episcopate. Pope Gelasius told the bishop of the day that he had no rank in the episcopate except that he was bishop of the capital: that a royal residence could not make an apostolic See. The new family of Justinian, ascending the eastern throne, was compelled by the internal state of the east, to acknowledge the Roman Primacy. Justinian never broke from that acknowledgment, but he termed his own bishop ecumenical patriarch in his laws: and every Byzantine bishop clung to the title given by an absolute sovereign. In the time of Pope Gregory the Great, a hundred years after the decree of Pope Gelasius, recording the pre-eminent rank and order of the three original Petrine Sees, of Rome, Alexandria, and Antioch, the Byzantine bishop is allowed to be a patriarch, Alexandria and Antioch have fallen under him. They themselves have been throughout all the intervening time the seats of violent party spirit, the spirit of the two conflicting heresies, striving for masterdom, disturbing succession in the sees, and ready by any obsequious act to get on their side the bishop of the capital, who dispenses the smiles of the emperor. Against all primitive order that bishop is found to consecrate his subordinate patriarchs at Alexandria and Antioch: to put down one and to raise another. When his usurpation was fresh and still incomplete, the patriarch Theophilus could persecute St. Chrysostom for the wrong done to Alexandria; but the patriarch Cyrus, made for his subserviency to Heraclius and Sergius to sit in the seat of St. Athanasius, addresses Sergius as "My Lord,[1] the thrice-blessed Father of

---

[1] See the letter in the 13th session of the Sixth Council, Mansi, xi. 561, D.

fathers, the ecumenical patriarch, Sergius, the least of his servants," and his acts are as humble as his words.

It is clear that the eastern patriarchal system had fallen from intrinsic corruption before the joint operation of Byzantine despotism and the ambition of the bishop of the capital, who bought every accession to his own power and influence by acting in ecclesiastical matters as the instrument of the imperial will. This fall was complete before the events which mark the last ten years of the reign of Heraclius as a time of unequalled and irretrievable disaster both to the Church and to the State.

Yet something must still be added to portray that civil condition of the State which led on to this disaster. In all this time the city of the emperor's residence had been exhausting of their wealth—by the terrible severity of the imperial taxation—the provinces subject to it. Egypt and Syria lived under a perpetual oppression no less than Italy and Rome. Every distinction, every favour, which Antioch, when Queen of the east, may have brought to Syria, had long migrated to the banks of the Bosphorus. All the national feeling of Egypt was aggrieved by the ruler who treated the dower of Cleopatra—the imperial gem of Augustus—as a storehouse to be plundered at pleasure. And the national spirit was intensified to fever heat by the hatred of Byzantium on the part of the Eutychean population, forming the vast majority in the whole country.

Thus the wide eastern empire instead of worshipping in union of heart and gladness of spirit that transcendent mystery in which is throned the grandeur and the mercy of the Christian dispensation, instead of falling in prostrate adoration before that vision of condescending love which the angels desire to look into, broke itself into endless conflicts in disputing about it, until the mystery of grace became a rancorous jarring of ambitious rivals. During more than 200 years this suicidal conflict was engaged in ruining the resources of a vast dominion, which in the hands of a Constantine or a Theodosius, with the spirit of a St. Leo to guide them, would have been impregnable to every enemy. Had emperor and people been faithful to the Council of Chalcedon, and to the authority which they admitted to be based on a divine promise made to St. Peter, neither the disunited hordes of the North, nor the far inferior savages of the South, nor even the impact of the great Sassanide empire would have availed to overcome the Roman power. This last and greatest enemy Heraclius had subdued. He went forth in the name of the Crucified One whom Chosroes had called upon him to disavow, and won the fight. Yet even as he was carrying back the Cross and entering the Holy City in triumph, Heraclius had become a traitor to him whom he was professing to honour. He had already conceived, under an evil influence and by the inspiration of the patriarch at his right hand, a compromise of doctrine which he thought would induce the rebellious Egyptian people to return to his allegiance. He hoped also that the same compromise would exorcise the Nestorian spirit at Antioch. They who did not agree were to be drawn into an appearance of agreement by an ambiguous formula. And the See of the Apostle Peter, last and greatest witness of the true doctrine, was to be forced into accepting the deceit, and ratifying it for the old truth by submitting to an imperial decree, which, independent of the heresy contained in it, was a violation of the Church's liberty.

The fifty years which run from 628 to 678 contain the various acts of one prolonged attempt by the Byzantine emperors to enforce their religious despotism on the Pope in the shape of the Monothelite heresy. The two standard-bearers of the heresy are two patriarchs, Sergius at Constantinople, and Cyrus at Alexandria. Precisely at this time the Mohammedan power appears upon the scene. While Heraclius is brooding over the compromise of Sergius for reuniting an empire dislocated by heresy, Mohammed is purposing the foundation of an empire resting on material force. While Heraclius is assuming the right to define the doctrine of the Church in virtue of his imperial power, Mohammed is constructing a claim to prophetic rank from which imperial power itself shall emanate. The Mohammedan claim is the exact antithesis of the Byzantine usurpation: the rise of a false prophet punishes the attempt among Christians to rule the spiritual by the civil power.

Upon the death of Mohammed in 632, his companions took counsel together and elected Abu Bekr to carry on the dominion based upon religion which Mohammed had invented. They gave him the title of "Chalif of God's Apostle". As the vicar of the new prophet, he was to exert the absolute power which belonged to the prophet's office, and of which the civil sovereignty was an offshoot. This power was rooted in the belief that Mohammed had been sent by God. The quality therefore of every act exercised by the first chalif, and by every successor, depended on the truth of such a mission.

By the choice of Abu Bekr, father of Aischa, the favourite wife of Mohammed, it was resolved that the succession to the chalifate should be elective, not hereditary. The most stirring principle of the new power was that everyone who died for its extension, which was called the Holy War, should pass at once to paradise. Paradise had been drawn by Mohammed after his own sensual imagination to suit the taste of a most sensual people. The empire sought by Mohammed and his followers was to be imposed by force. Abu Bekr stirred up the sons of the desert to this Holy War, proclaiming that he who fought for God's cause should have 700 good works counted for each step, 700 honours allotted to him, and 700 sins forgiven.

Abu Bekr held the chalifate but two years, dying in 634 at the age of 63 years. But at the very time of his death the pearl of Syria, Damascus, fell into the hands of his generals, Amrou and Khaled. From Medina the city of the prophet, and the seat of the chalif, he had sent forth three armies. Moseilama, a prophet who competed with Mohammed, was destroyed, the discontented tribes in Arabia itself were reduced to obedience. The Persian provinces on the Euphrates were attacked. The Roman empire itself was summoned to accept the new religion, or to become tributary.

Upon the death of Abu Bekr, the chief associates of Mohammed around him proclaimed Omar as chalif, and entitled him Chalif, and Prince of the Faithful. In the ten years of his chalifate, from 634 to 644, Omar made the Mohammedan empire. He had exerted great influence over Mohammed himself; he had been most powerful with Abu Bekr, who pointed him out for a successor. The man who had been of violent temper and bloody battles, now sedulously practised the administration of justice. He gave much, and used little for himself. He wore a patched dress, and fed on barley bread and water; he prayed and preached, and ate and slept upon the steps of the mosque among the pilgrims. There he received the messengers of kings. The severe chalif, a sworn foe to all effeminacy, strove to train a rude host to war. Arts he proscribed, even those of house and ship-building. When the great city of Modain, or Ctesiphon, was taken, he commanded the library of the Persian kings to be thrown into the Tigris. When some of his soldiers had put on silken garments which they had looted in Syria, he rubbed their faces in the mud and tore their garments in pieces. Such was the man under whom half-armed nomad tribes broke the armies of Heraclius, and took one after another the cities of Syria.

But on the side of the emperor were divided counsels, distrust, rankling enmities; Nestorian and Eutychean heretics hating each other, and still more the sovereign under whom they should have fought as well for a common country as for a common faith. The fate of Syria was decided in a terrible battle on the banks of the Hieromax, or Yarmuk. There, the Saracen generals, Obeidah and Khaled, "The sword of God," utterly defeated the Greek army of 80,000 men.[1] Obeidah wrote to the chalif Omar : "In the name of the most merciful God, I must make thee to know that I encamped on the Yarmuk, and Manuel was near us with a force such as the Moslem never had a greater. But God struck down that host, and gave us the victory out of His overflowing grace and goodness. God has given to 4030 Moslim the honour of martyrdom. All that fled into the desert and mountains we have put down; have beset all roads and passes; God has made us lords of their lands and riches and children. Written after the victory from Damaskus where I am, and await thy command for the division of the booty. Farewell, and the blessing and grace of God be over thee and all Moslim."

After this, city upon city surrendered in affright. In the winter of 636, Obeidah lay before Jerusalem, from which Heraclius took away the Holy Cross with himself to Constantinople. At Antioch, in his dismay, he asked the question why those miserable half naked barbarians, the Arabs, not to be compared with the Romans in armour, or art of war, beat them in the field. A veteran answered him that the wrath of God was on the Romans, who despised His commands, were guilty of every excess, allowed themselves intolerable oppression and violence.

We do not read that Heraclius made an attempt to

[1] Damberger, ii. 11.

relieve Jerusalem, which yet was besieged during a year. Obeidah wrote to the patriarch and the inhabitants: "Salutation and blessing to all those who walk in the right way. We invite you to confess that there is only one God, and Mohammed is His Prophet. If you will not make this confession, then resolve to make your city tributary to the chalif. If you delay to do this, I will set my people upon you, who all love death more than you love wine and swine flesh. Hope not that I will draw away hence, until, if God please, I have killed all your warriors, and made slaves of your children."

The patriarch Sophronius negotiated without hope of earthly aid, and Obeidah, to save the Holy City, the cradle of prophets, from being desecrated by bloodshedding, yielded to the Christian wish that the chalif in person should be asked to receive the keys of the city, and regulate the conditions of surrender. And in 637 Chalif Omar came from Medina. As the Commander of the Faithful entered the city, he rode on a camel, clothed like the poorest Bedouin, and carrying on the same rough beast a sack of dates, rice, and bruised wheat or maize, also a water-skin, and a large wooden platter, on which he took his food with his companions. The terms of capitulation which he granted to the patriarch remained for long a standard to the Moslem in the like cases. First of all was the poll tax imposed by the Koran. The inhabitants to be protected and secured in life and property; their churches not to be pulled down, nor used by any but themselves. The Christians duly to pay tribute; to build no new churches either in the city or country; not to prevent Moslim by night or day from entering the churches. Their doors to be always open to travellers. The Christian to whom a traveller comes, shall entertain him three days gratis. Christians shall say nothing against the Koran. Shall prevent no one becoming Moslem. Shall show honour to Moslim. Shall not wear garments, or shoes, or turbans, like theirs. Shall not divide their hair like them. Shall not bear surnames like them. Shall not ride on saddles. Shall bear no arms, nor Arabic writing on their seals, nor give away wine, nor sell it. They shall wear the same kind of dress everywhere, and that with a girdle. They may have no slave who has served a Moslem. No crosses on the churches; nor ring bells, but only strike them.

The chalif Omar caused himself to be led into all the holy places in the garb of a pilgrim by the patriarch Sophronius, even to the church of the Resurrection. There he placed himself on the floor, and the patriarch was most anxious lest he should practise his own acts of devotion there. With breaking heart the patriarch quoted to those around him the words of Daniel, "The abomination of desolation in the temple".

Twelve hundred and fifty years have borne witness to the truth of that sorrowful word, and still, "the desolation continues even to the end,"[1] and the soldier of the false prophet keeps order among Christians before the sepulchre of their Lord.

Hardly could the chalif Omar be induced to put off

[1] Daniel, ix. 27.

his rough garment long enough for it to be washed, and to take another. But when the time of Moslem prayer came, he would not say it in the church, lest the Moslim should seize a church in which their chalif had prayed, but he went to the steps of the eastern portion of Constantine's church and prayed there. He resolved to build a mosque on the spot where Jacob had seen in vision the ladder, or on which the temple of Solomon stood. He gave a hand himself to sweep away the rubbish from it. The structure, built in haste, disappeared suddenly. Theophanes relates that Omar was much confused at the disappearance of his new mosque. Some Jewish teachers came to him and said that the structure would only remain if the cross on Mount Calvary, not that on the Mount of Olives, were removed. Omar did what these men suggested. Some of his fanatics, in spite of the compact, broke all the public crosses, destroyed holy images, attacked various churches and chapels. He gave a special writing to protect the church at Bethlehem wherein he had prayed, but the Moslim afterwards took possession of this church and of the portico at Jerusalem, and made them mosques.

Omar returned to Medina. His armies received command to take Ctesiphon, Aleppo, Antioch. In the summer of 638, Heraclius retired from Antioch to Constantinople, and as he left, says Abulfeda, cried out, "Farewell, Syria, farewell for ever". When Antioch in August, 638, surrendered, Mesopotamia as well as Syria fell into the hands of Omar, and all

Roman land up to the Taurus belonged to the chalif, no imperial force could meet him any longer in the field. Egypt and Persia were open to him.

It was the year when Heraclius published the Ecthesis at Rome. In three years more came the doom of Egypt. Amrou was one of the most valiant and able among the generals of Omar. He asked for leave to attack Egypt, and meanwhile marched to its borders. When the chalif's answer came, he first passed the borders, and then opened it. He found written, "If this letter reaches thee before thou treadest the soil of Egypt, go back; if thou art already on it, go forward". Amrou went on. Battles he fought, especially at Babylon, near Cairo. But the Copts throughout helped him, and the Greek forces were beaten.[1] Amrou had travelled as a merchant in Egypt, and knew the dispositions of its inhabitants, and that the vast majority were so fervent in the Eutychean heresy that they were inclined to look with favour on the new Mohammedan unity of the Godhead, rather than to defend their country against the Saracenic invasion for the good of the hated Melchites, and their emperor at Constantinople. Omar sent Amrou a reinforcement of 12,000 men, and the Copts, being monophysites, made peace with the Arabs, and promised the tribute of a moderate poll tax of two drachmas, from which old men, women, and children, were exempt. There are said to have been six millions to pay this tax.

To Mukankas, a Copt, the governor under Heraclius,

---

[1] Damberger, ii. 18-20. Weiss, ii. 517-519-521, for the narrative. See also Weil, *die Chalifen*, Omar, 144.

his spies reported the life of the Arabs in the camp of Amrou. "We were among men to whom death is dearer than life; who trouble themselves little about earthly greatness or worldly enjoyments. They sit on the ground, and eat kneeling; their commander is in no way distinguished from the rest. Especially they do not distinguish between great and little, nor between masters and slaves. When the time of prayer comes, no one remains behind. Each washes himself and prays with the deepest devotion." To the reproaches of Heraclius his governor, Mukankas, answered : " It is true the foe is not near so numerous as we are, but one Mussulman outweighs a hundred of us. They yearn after martyrdom, since it leads to paradise, but we hang upon life and its joys, and fear death." The Copts in general accepted the terms made by Mukankas; the Greeks did not. At length Amrou, after four engagements, in which the Copts assisted him with provisions and the building of bridges, advanced upon Alexandria, whither the Greeks had retired.

Alexandria is said to have been besieged during fourteen months, and to have cost the lives of 23,000 Arabs. It was never cut off by sea from assistance. The Arabs had neither besieging engines nor a fleet. But Heraclius, who was dying of dropsy, instead of sending a fleet to save the last hold which he had upon Egypt, sent a bishop to make terms with Amrou for his retirement. "Bishop," said the Saracen leader, "do you see that obelisk? When you have swallowed it I will retire from Alexandria." The city fell in 640, and since Omar had the library of the Persian monarchs at Ctesiphon thrown into the Tigris, there is no reason to doubt the fact recorded that he fed the 4000 baths of Alexandria during six months with the treasures of Greek literature. An uninterrupted peace since the destruction of the Serapeium, 240 years before, had allowed that city in the world which was most devoted to literature and the richest in commerce ample time to collect the greatest of libraries. The double destruction suits exactly the character given to Chalif Omar by Arab historians.

Amrou was not allowed, by Omar's prudence, to live as governor of Egypt at Alexandria. Fostat—that is, the Tent—where he had dwelt during his siege of Babylon, developed from being the seat of his government to the present Cairo. But to the west Amrou extended the Saracen dominion over Barca and Tripolis.

Omar reigned ten years, a Chalif at whose words of rebuke his strongest commanders quailed, and he ruled a kingdom which he stretched in these ten years from Tripolis to the Indus; from the Caspian Sea to the Cataracts of the Nile. He destroyed the Sassanide empire; and the sword of Mohammed, wielded by his second chalif, cut in two the empire of Heraclius. With the loss of Syria, Mesopotamia, and Egypt, the successor of Constantine was reduced to shelter himself behind the walls of Byzantium from the Saracen host, which perpetually plundered his provinces from the Bosphorus to Mount Taurus. During the Roman dominion of many hundred years that vast territory had been in climate, as Herodotus a thousand years before had said of it, the garden of the earth. It had, further, been studded with cities rich in monuments of Greek civilisation. Afterwards these came to be ruled by bishops, many of whom descended from the preaching of St. Peter and St. Paul. Now all this territory lived in anguish at the thought of Moslem incursion. Only the invention of the Greek fire, kept a secret, saved Byzantium itself from suffering in the latter half of the seventh century the doom which fell upon it in the fifteenth.

Chalif Omar had pressed his captive provinces with heavy tributes. A Christian artisan, who was made to pay four drachmas a day for taxes in Kufa, journeyed to Medina to plead for remission before Omar in person. It was refused. He followed the chalif to the Mosque, and dealt him, as he prayed, a deadly blow. Omar died, having named, when mortally wounded, the six eldest companions of the prophet to choose his successor.

Heraclius died at Constantinople in 641. The chalif Omar reigned from the death of Abu Bekr, in August, 634, to November, 644. Before him had died the most cruel of Arabian commanders, Khaled.[1] He who buried alive captive enemies murmured on his sick-bed, "I have been in so many battles, and received so many wounds, that there is scarcely a whole place in my body; and now I must die on a bed as an ass dies on his straw". Jezdeberg, the last of the Sassanide princes, was hopelessly beaten, and in 651 closed, under Mussulman extinction, the dynasty which since 226 had renewed the battle of Persia for empire with its old rival Rome. The

[1] Damberger, ii. 22, for the following paragraph.

great city of Madain or Ctesiphon was destroyed, and Mohammed, the chalif's governor in Persia planted Kufa as a military city on the right bank of the Euphrates, three days journey from Bagdad. Omar learnt that his governor Mohammed had built himself a stately palace over against the chief mosque at Kufa. This he had adorned with a magnificent gateway taken from the palace of Chosroes at Ctesiphon. In wrath Omar wrote: "the kings of Persia have gone down from their palaces to hell: the Prophet rose from the dust of the earth to heaven. I have ordered the bearer of these lines to burn down thy palace at once, lest thou miss the way of the Prophet for that of the corrupt Persian." The palace was burnt. Omar knew how to destroy, and they record of his ten years that thirty-six thousand cities, villages, or castles were taken and wasted, and fourteen thousand Christian churches burnt or changed into mosques. History, I believe, has not recorded how many thousand Christian women were delivered over as a prey to the Arabian savages, to whom he promised paradise as a reward for dying in battle against the unbelievers. This was the Mohammedan martyrdom. Omar sought to impress a holy character upon the savage deeds which the hordes marshalled by him to victory or martyrdom practised without scruple. In setting up the colossal kingdom which he founded during the ten years of his chalifate he covered the earth with heaps of slain in the name of the most merciful God. He is said to have established judges in the chief cities of his empire, who should administer justice according to the written or traditional precepts of Mohammed. He had great care for the security of all the lands subject to him. "If," he said, "a shepherd on the banks of the Euphrates or the Tigris have one of his sheep stolen, I fear that I shall one day have to give an account for it."[1] He is praised by Mussulmen for his great qualities as sovereign. But he cared less to spread Islam from Arabia over all the world than to enrich Arabia at the cost of all the world. Foreign nations were to be put in chains, but not ennobled and bettered. They were to encounter not preachers, but tax-gatherers. His rulers might inflict any oppressions on those who were not Mussulmen, provided they sent the fruits of their oppression to him at Medina. At the same time he fed on barley bread, and had but one cloak for the summer and another for the winter, both well darned. But let us turn to his family life. Little of it is known, but that he had seven marriages—three in Mecca, four after the exit to Medina, one of them being with a daughter of Ali—and that he had two slave concubines who bore him children. Two other wives he tried to get. A daughter of Otba refused him because he kept his wives jealously shut up. But Asma, a daughter of Abu Bekr, disliked the barley bread and camel's flesh of his household. He sought her in vain by the help of Aischa. Not obtaining her, he turned to Amm Kolthum, a daughter of Ali and Fatima, and granddaughter of Mohammed. Ali said to him, "My daughter is too young to marry". Omar would not believe it, upon which Ali sent his daughter to him

---

[1] Weil, *Geschichte der Chalifen*, i. 139-141.

in a single vestment. Omar drew back her veil, and wished to draw her to him. But she escaped, and fled to her father, and told him of Omar's conduct. Ali then said to him, "If thou wert not chalif, I would tear out thine eyes". But Omar sought her again before comrades of the highest rank, grounding his proposal on what Mohammed had once said : " Every relationship and connection ceases at the Day of Judgment, except one contracted with me". Ali went home, and said to his daughter : "Go back to Omar". She rejoined : " Wilt thou send me again to this old voluptuary?" Ali replied, "He is thy husband".[1]

But though in the last years of Omar Ali became his father-in-law, no friendly relation seems ever to have existed between them. Ali had been the first in all Mohammed's battles ; by Omar he was made neither commander nor governor. But in Mussulman remembrance Omar stands as the greatest of their rulers, because of the vast power and extension to which under him Islam attained.

Let us see what Omar in his chalifate did to Constantine's empire and the Christian faith.

When in 610 Heraclius was drawn from his father's governorship of Northern Africa to end the cruelties of Phocas, the great mass of the eastern empire still stood, threatened indeed by Avar Chagans on the north, and by the restless Persian empire on the east. But the whole coast of Northern Africa, Egypt and Syria, the realm from Antioch to the end of the Euxine on the

[1] Weil, *Geschichte der Chalifen*, i. 144.

east, and to Stamboul on the west, as well as the great country south of the Danube, stretching from the Euxine to the Adriatic and down to the south of the Morea, each of which last would make by itself a noble monarchy, remained intact, and if the eastern despot held his head a little lower than Justinian's head had been held, it needed still but a Constantine or a Theodosius to breathe conquering force as well as maintaining power into that vast body which still called itself Roman. Instead of a true life and a royal will directing that life it had nothing but Greek arts wielded by Oriental despotism. In ten years the sons of the desert, half clothed and fed on barley bread, invoking the God of Mohammed, discomfited the disciplined hosts of the Lord of the world, and carried into dishonour and apostacy the women and children of great provinces. Egypt since the battle of Actium had been the most carefully-guarded province of Augustus and the emperors who came after him. It ceased at once and for ever to be Roman. Not only was there a change in the civil power, but its six millions of Monophysites preferred the crescent under Amrou, as Omar's lieutenant, to the cross enthroned with Heraclius at Constantinople. Antioch ceased to be Roman, and with it Syria and Mesopotamia. Beyond these the vast regions of Persia fell into the hands of Omar, and were ruled for the present from an Arab city Medina, unknown till then beyond Arabian limits. The outposts of Omar were at Mount Taurus, looking thence with desire over the vast historic region sprinkled with stately cities up to the banks of the Bosphorus.

These immense regions were lost suddenly but they were also lost permanently. In ten years they were forfeited by possessors who had held them for seven hundred, and after twelve centuries and a half they remain in the hands of the false religion which took them by force and keeps them against recovery by Christians.

Wonderful besides the suddenness of the stroke was the inadequacy of the instrument to the effect produced, the blindness of the time before the coming revolution. Neither St. Gregory among the saints one generation only before it came, nor Heraclius returning a conqueror over the Great King within ten years of the Saracenic catastrophe, anticipated that there were southern hordes extreme in ignorance, devoid of art, and without political sense or experience, but lying in the hand of Providence to take possession of lands with ancient culture and a thousand years of civilised history. St. Gregory indeed had witnessed himself such ruin, and followed two centuries of such disasters, which had stripped Italy of her crown of cities, that he thought the world itself was coming to an end. But the establishment of a great southern empire, founded by vagrant tribes till then known only as robbers, never presented itself to his mind. That they would go forth and conquer with a new war-cry, directed especially against the Cross of Christ, was as little in his thoughts.

By the year of Omar's death there was a new empire ruled by a man from an unknown Arabian town, in the name of a man who had died twelve years before, and claimed to be a prophet, the special herald of one God.

In the belief thus set up, it was no other than this God who had invested not the prophet only, but the chalifs who came after him with supreme power, not civil only, but religious, and supreme simply because it was religious, and exercised in the name of this new God. And the empire so set up included already the vast dominions of the Great King, and fully one half of the empire which Justinian had left.

But greater yet was the difference which separated this empire from all that had preceded it. Omar ruled with absolute power as chalif of Mohammed, whose right to power of any kind, civil or religious, lay only in his office of prophet. The Roman emperor ruled because he was lord of a subject-confederacy of nations, which the Roman arm and the Roman mind had, bit by bit, subdued and wrought together, and which, when so constituted, had been deposited entire by secular warranty in his single hand. But Mohammed ruled, and after him the chalifs, because he was "the Apostle of God," by a divine commission, whole and entire, from which civil and religious authority equally emanated, but in which the religious was the root of the civil. Such was the power which the companions of Mohammed in the first election of Abu Bekr, launched upon the world, and which, as second chalif, Omar received. And in the spirit of this, he ruled the huge empire of conquest, which stretched from the African Tripolis to the end of Persia, and from the southernmost point of Egypt to the Cilician Taurus, engulphing Alexandria, Antioch, and Jerusalem. No portion of this power did

Omar wield without assuming to represent the person who made himself, or was made by others, his followers, the last and highest of the prophets; who was willing indeed to acknowledge Jesus, the Son of Mary, in the number of prophets, but only on the condition that the prophetical list was closed in himself, that it pointed to himself, and was crowned in himself. The Mohammedan war-cry, to die for which was to be a martyr, "There is no God but God, and Mohammed is his prophet," was at once the denial of the Christian Trinity, and of Christ's Redeemership. All those who bore it, fought for it, died for it, proclaimed an absolute hostility to the Christian faith, and a definite substitution of another faith for it, and another person on whom that faith rested. This was the empire personified in Omar; and this, in the ten years from 634 to 644, seized upon the southern half of what had been the inheritance bequeathed by Constantine to his successors. The new realm was ruled by Omar with singleness of purpose and unbending resolution to make the Mohammedan standard victorious over the cross, to dethrone Christ for Mohammed.

Was the blow to the empire equally a blow to the Church? The severance of provinces so vast, so populous, so rich in natural productions, from Heraclius, was in itself depriving the lord of the world of legs and arms; but more dangerous than any material privation was the setting up an empire with a definite creed, in which religious conquest was by far the most powerful ingredient. The war-cry, "There is no God but God, and Mohammed is his prophet," meant the earth and all that is in it, its fruits, and above all, its women, belong entirely to the followers of Mohammed. They who do not either become his, or pay tribute to him, have no rights. Their children become slaves, their wives and daughters captive. These begin to be the absolute possession of the Mohammedan conqueror; if he dies in battle, rewards of martyrdom, so won, for his successors: if he lives, adornments of his life, which he pleases God by accepting.

As to the treatment of Christian countries, Omar, in the capture of Jerusalem, had supplied a rule and standard which for the present was followed at least in profession. Christians were not treated as idolaters: they were taken into covenant. We are told that the tribute was so moderate that the first Egyptians and Syrians who accepted it, thought that they had made a favourable transfer of themselves from Byzantine to Mohammedan lordship.[1] The Byzantine had perpetually interfered with their religious convictions, and domineered over their ecclesiastical appointments. Mohammedans, in the disdain of superior power resting on their exclusive possession of truth, kept entirely aloof. Once their own lordship established and acknowledged, they allowed their subjects a certain freedom of action within the lines of Omar's covenant. It is probable that they began by so doing, nor is it easy to account for the rapid and continued submission of provinces, such as Syria and Egypt, without the willingness of

[1] Weil, *Geschichte der Chalifen*, i. 103-5.

their inhabitants to accept the change be taken into account. But it is certain that the Christian religion drooped more and more under the shadow of Mohammedan domination.

Antioch fell under it in 637. From that time forth, the so-called patriarch began often to live at Byzantium. The patriarchate, which, down to the heresies of the third and fourth centuries, had probably, in Christian population, in learning, in the distinction which its bishops enjoyed each in their own city, been the most flourishing portion of the Church, began to decline. The deposition of St. Eustathius, in 330, cost its capital a schism of nearly a hundred years. The partisanship of its patriarch with its countryman, Nestorius, prejudiced both its rank and its unity. What proportion of its once eleven provinces and 161 bishops belonged to it at the time of the Mohammedan invasion might be difficult to ascertain. But how great and wide its circuit was is shown by the instance of Theodoret, bishop of Cyrrhus, which, though an undistinguished see, contained in it no less than eight hundred parishes,[1] and was under Hierapolis, as seat of the Metropolitan.

After 638, the Antiochene patriarch never more lifted his diminished head as the holder of one of the three great Petrine Sees, whom St. Innocent I. and St. Gregory I. had acknowledged with themselves as representatives of St. Peter.

In all this, we behold the consummation of a fearful history, and I will take the words of one who witnessed the

[1] Newman's *Theodoret.* Page 318.

northern wandering of the nations to illustrate, rather perhaps, to account for, the much more terrible wandering of the nations in the south. It was more than two hundred and forty years before this new kingdom arose that St. Jerome, from his solitude at Bethlehem, addressed a friend. It was in the year immediately succeeding the death of the great Theodosius. His rapid view of the generation which had just passed will inspire many thoughts. He is consoling the bishop, Heliodorus, for the loss of his nephew, the priest, Nepotian, a dear friend of his own : "and why," he says, "am I trying to heal a wound which time and thought, as I believe, have already soothed? Why do I not rather bring before you the miseries of royalty so near to us? Our time has such calamities that it were well not so much to mourn one on whom this light has ceased to shine as to congratulate the escape from such misfortunes. Constantius, the patron of the Arian heresy, in the midst of preparing for the enemy's onset, and rushing to the fight, dies in the village of Mopsis, and, in great sorrow, left his empire a prey to his foe. Julian, betrayer of his own life, and slaughterer of an army that was Christian, acknowledged in Media the power of that Christ whom he had first denied in Gaul. Striving to extend the Roman frontiers, he lost what they had already gained. Jovian had but a taste of imperial power, and died suffocated by charcoal fumes : an instance to all men of what human dominion is. Valentinian laid waste his own native land, and, leaving it unavenged, broke a blood-vessel and died. His brother, Valens, in the war with the Goths, was defeated in Thrace, and found a tomb on the spot of his death. Gratian, betrayed by his own army, and not received by the cities which he approached, suffered the mockery of enemies: and thy walls, O Lyons, bear the impression of the blood-stained hand. The young Valentinian, scarcely beyond boyhood, after flight, after banishment, after recovering the empire with great blood-shedding, was slain near the city, guilty of his brother's death: and his lifeless body suffered the ignominy of the halter. Then there was Procopius, and Maximus, and Eugenius, who, when they were in power, struck their opponents with terror. All stood captives before their conquerors: and suffered that utmost misery of those once powerful: to be reduced to slavery, and then slaughtered.

"Some one may say, this is the lot of kings, and lightnings strike high summits. Pass to private ranks, and only within the last two years. Let us take but the different ends of three lately Consuls. Abundantius is in poverty and exile at Pityuns. The head of Ruffinus was carried on a pike to Constantinople; his right hand was cut off, and, to mark his insatiable greed, taken begging from door to door. Timavius, hurled suddenly from the loftiest ranks, thinks it an escape to live nameless at Assa. It is not the calamities of the miserable which I relate, but the frailty of man's condition. It strikes with horror to follow out the ruins of our times. It is more than twenty years since Roman blood is shed daily between Constantinople and the Julian Alps. In Scythia, Thrace, Macedonia, Dardania, Dacia, Thessaly, Achaia, Epirus, Dalmatia, and all the Pannonias, Goth and Sarmatian, Quade, Alan, and Hun, Vandals and Marcomans, waste, drag away, and plunder. How many matrons, how many consecrated virgins, how many free and noble persons, have fallen a prey to these brutes! Bishops captured; priests and the various ranks of clergy slain; churches ruined; horses stabled at Christ's altars; relics of martyrs dug up. Mourning and death in every shape on all sides. The Roman world falls in pieces, but our stiff neck is not bent. What spirit, think you, have Corinthians, Athenians, Lacedæmonians, Arcadians, and all Greece, in the gripe of barbarians? I have named few cities which were not formerly strong powers. The East seemed free from these scourges: bad tidings only terrified it. When lo! last year, from the farthest heights of Caucasus, wolves, not of Arabia, but of the North, were let loose upon us. They overran at once great provinces. How many monasteries were captured! How many rivers changed into human blood! Antioch was besieged, and the cities which the Halys, Cydnus, Orontes, Euphrates traverse. Crowds of captives carried away. Arabia, Phœnicia, Palestine, Egypt, trembling with fright. Had I a hundred tongues and mouths, and a voice of iron, I could not enumerate all the tortures suffered. I did not propose to write a history; but in few words to lament our miseries; otherwise, adequately to set forth these things. Thucydides and Sallust would both be mute." The whole period of two hundred and forty years, between the time when St. Jerome, as a spectator, wrote thus, and the time of the Mohammedan inroad, is expressed in the words which follow. "It is long since we felt that we are offending God, but we do not appease Him. It is by our own sins that the barbarians prevail. It is by our own vices that the Roman army is conquered. And, as if this was not enough for our losses, our civil wars have consumed almost more than the edge of the enemy's sword. Unhappy we who are so displeasing to God that His wrath breaks forth on us through the fury of savages. The greatness of the reality surpasses language: all words are less than the truth."

For, indeed, the time was come, through the extraordinary wickedness of two hundred years, when the very sanctuaries from which St. Jerome was writing, the sanctuaries of the birth and death of Christ, Bethlehem and Calvary, were to fall, not by a sudden inroad, but a permanent occupation into the hands of His chief enemies. The time was also come when the see of the great confessor whose name we identify with the battle of faith against the world, the see of Athanasius himself, the Pope of the East, the next in hierarchical order to the Universal Pope, was to fall, and to fall for ever, from its high estate. "Almost from the death of Athanasius began the spiritual declension of his see and Church."—

"Pride is not made for man; not for an individual bishop, however great, nor for an episcopal dynasty. Sins against the law of love are punished by the loss of faith. The line of Athanasius was fierce and tyrannical, and it fell into the Monophysite heresy. There it remains to this day. A prerogative of infallibility in doctrine, which it had not, could alone have saved the see of Alexandria from the operation of this law."[1]

During the ten years of Omar's chalifate the great patriarchates of Alexandria and Antioch, and the smaller patriarchate of Jerusalem, which contained the places of pilgrimage dear to every Christian heart, visited by the faithful from all lands, not only the birth-place in Bethlehem, not only Nazareth consecrated by the angel's announcing of that birth, and by the secret life of the divine Boyhood and Manhood, but—

> The sepulchre in stubborn Jewry
> Of the world's ransom, Blessed Mary's Son.[2]

fell together into bondage under the special enemy of the Cross. In this bondage the hierarchies of the three patriarchates, as distinct wholes, almost disappear from history. It is well to consider here the condition in which they had been even from the time of the Arian heresy.[3] The declension of Antioch had been of as long standing as the declension of Alexandria. At the end of the fourth century St. Chrysostom bore witness to its

---

[1] Card. Newman, *Theodoret*, p. 340, 342.

[2] *Richard II.*, ii. 1.

[3] Card. Hergenrother's articles in *Kirchen-Lexicon* i. 946, 7, upon Antioch, and on Alexandria, i. 519-521, have supplied me with the following facts.

hundred thousand Christians. But in the course of the fifth the great third see of the Church lost much of its reputation and power. Partly it fell into weak hands, as John I., from 428 to 441, who held but a poor position in the Nestorian conflict, while Domnus II. took part in the robber council of 447. Then, at Chalcedon, the elevation of Jerusalem to a patriarchate took from its jurisdiction the three Palestines. But especially the encroachments of the see of Byzantium told upon it. The bishops of the royal city claimed to consecrate the already-named patriarchs. Anatolius ordained Maximus, who was substituted for Domnus II. when deposed in spite of his subservience to Dioscorus. In this he disregarded the rights of the bishops of the Antiochene patriarchate, and the Byzantine bishops forthwith turned that precedent into a right. Maximus was followed by Basilius, Acacius, and Martyrius. The Monophysite Peter Fullo formed such a party against the last that he resigned in despair. This usurper resisted the Emperor Zeno's condemnation to banishment, and put himself, first secretly, then openly, as patriarch against Julian. He so persecuted the Catholics, that Julian died of sorrow. The Emperor Zeno banished the heretical Peter Fullo to Pityuns. He was succeeded by the equally heretical John II., Kodonatus. But this patriarch was deposed in three months by the exertion of the bishops. The Monophysites already prevailed. They murdered in the sacred place itself the new Catholic patriarch, Stephen II., and threw his mangled body into the Orontes. The emperor punished the crime, and Acacius, Bishop of Constantinople, put in his place Stephen III. Pope Simplicius censured this violation of the canons, and prohibited it for the future, which did not prevent Acacius renewing his encroachments when, after the death of Stephen in 482, he consecrated Colendion. Colendion was afterwards banished by the Emperor Zeno, and had to yield to the old heresiarch, Peter Fullo, who kept his patriarchate to his death in 488, and was succeeded by the equally heretical Palladius. Almost all Syria rose against the Catholic patriarch Flavian; the monk Severus got hold of the patriarchate, and kept it for six years. He fled in 519, under the Emperor Justin I., to Egypt. His successors, Paul II., who resigned in 521 through fear of an accusation, and Euphrasius of Jerusalem, could no longer secure superiority to the Catholics. Patriarch Ephrem followed from 526 to 545. He held a Synod against Origenism. Patriarch Domnus III. took part in the Fifth Council in 553. He was followed by the distinguished Anastasius I., and after St. Gregory I. by Anastasius II. The See remained a long time vacant. Those who then followed, Athanasius, Macedonius, and Macarius, were Monothelites. The two latter from the time the Saracens took Antioch, in 637, resided in Constantinople for safety. After George, who is said to have subscribed the Trullan Council in 692, the See was vacant forty years, and the patriarchs had often to endure extortions, ill-treatment, and banishment.

How well Alexandria had prepared itself for the Mohammedan captivity may be seen by the following facts. Under the violent Dioscorus the see of St. Mark not only declined from its distinction when ruled by St. Cyril, but threw the whole of Egypt into wild confusion by espousing the Monophysite error. The Catholic patriarch, Proterius, was murdered in 457 : and the heretical Timotheus Ailouros set up by his party instead. He, though condemned by the emperor, Leo I., to banishment, maintained himself stubbornly against the Catholic patriarch, Solophakialos. After his death, Peter Mongus was able to expel the Catholic, John Talaia : and then, from 490 to 538, Alexandria had a succession of five Monophysite patriarchs. Under Justinian, from 538, during forty years, we find four Catholic patriarchs. So, again, in Eulogius, the friend of St. Gregory, and John the alms-giver. But during this time the Monophysites also had their patriarchal succession, and that even from different sects of the heresy. The end of it was that the bitterest enmity arose between the Melchite or Royalist, and the Monophysite party. The former, being a small minority, held by favour of the Byzantine emperor and his troops in Egypt the possession of authority. The Copts, being a great majority, considered themselves oppressed, and welcomed as deliverers, in 638, the conquering Arabs. The Melchite party sunk so low that their patriarchal place was vacant during eighty years, and the number of their bishops greatly sank. After 750, the Christian inhabitants of Egypt were more and more exposed to Mohammedan brutality. Sharp laws against them were issued : distinguishing marks and clothes prescribed.

And here not only is the fall of the three patriarchates under conquerors who strive to destroy the Christian faith to be noted as following upon two centuries of incessant heresy, but another divine judgment also. No sooner have the three patriarchs lost their original position, the two elder as second and third bishops of the whole Church in virtue of their descent from Peter, and taken definitively a position subordinate to the upstart at Byzantium, who in the last decade of the fifth century, in the time of Pope Gelasius, was proclaimed in his Council at Rome no patriarch at all, than they fall under a domination which is not merely infidel but antichristian. The aim of the chalifate is to supplant Christ by Mohammed. The patriarchs, who accepted as superior one who rose above them simply because he was bishop of the imperial residence, had from that time forward to live under a despot who reigned in the name of the false prophet. From being subjects of the Greek Basileus, who, by means of the bishop exalted by him in successive generations, strove to hamper in the exercise of his office the successor of St. Peter, even to the point of making him subject to the guidance of the Byzantine crown in spiritual matters, which was the meaning of the Ecthesis of Heraclius, they passed to be subjects of the Mohammedan chalif, who claimed the supremacy of both powers in the name of the falsehood just invented.

In the diminished territory of Byzantium, which during the rest of the century after Heraclius could but just keep the Mohammedan conqueror outside its walls, the bishop of the royal residence became in fact the sole patriarch. Sergius and Pyrrhus, Paul and Peter, the first four of those so exalted, were branded as heretics by the Sixth Council. Those who still bore the names of Alexandria, Antioch, and Jerusalem appeared at times, or were deemed to appear, at a Byzantine Council, but the hundred bishops of the Alexandrine, and the hundred and sixty bishops of the Antiochene waned and wasted more and more with every generation miserably spent under the absolute rule of the Prophet's chalif, who had for Christians only two modes of treatment, the one a noxious patronage of their heresy, if such prevailed; the other, persecution of their faith, if they were faithful and zealous.

From the accession of St. Athanasius to the See of Alexandria in 328 to the placing Cyrus in that See by Heraclius in 628, exactly three centuries elapse. In this time the great revolution begun by Constantine, when he took for his counsellor the court-bishop Eusebius, has full space to work itself out. His own son, Constantius, "patron of the Arian heresy," in St. Jerome's words, inaugurates in full force the attempt of the Byzantine monarchs to extend their temporal power over the spiritual. Valens so persecutes the eastern Church that when Theodosius is called in to save the empire, he finds the eastern episcopate in the state of ruin described by St. Basil. Unfortunately, he saw no better means of restoring it, when, in 381, he invited the bishops of his empire to anxious deliberation, than by laying the first stone of the Byzantine bishop's exaltation. An eastern Council, at his prompting, strives to make that bishop the second bishop of the whole Church on a false foundation, because Constantinople is Nova Roma. Every Byzantine monarch adds his stone to the Byzantine bishop's pillar of pride. St. Leo exposes and censures the assumption. Pope Gelasius does not reckon him among the patriarchs. Justinian enacts him to be ecumenical patriarch, which St. Gregory pronounces to be a title of diabolical pride: being, in fact, the building of spiritual power on temporal lordship. In thirty years after St. Gregory, the act of pride denounced by him receives its full interpretation. The patriarch Sergius attempts to mould the doctrine of the Church under the authority of Constantine's successor: and Constantine's empire is cut in half by the chalif of the man who claims all temporal power on the pretence that he has been invested by God with spiritual power. And two conflicting heresies, the Nestorian and Eutychean, the latter making its last development in the Monothelite, have severed the eastern empire into rivalities so bitter, that the Christians of the several parties hate each other more than they hate the new Mohammedan pretender. The episcopate, seen in all its glory and grandeur when first assembled by Constantine in 325, sinks ingloriously under the successors, in Alexandria and Antioch, of the very prelates who maintained the faith at Nicæa: sinks before Mohammed, who is seen to complete the work of Arius. The successor of St. Peter has done his utmost during two hundred years to preserve the eastern sees of

Peter: and in them the whole ecclesiastical constitution formed for herself by the Church in the ten generations preceding Constantine: but Alexandria and Antioch have no prerogative of infallibility: they perish by their own folly: heresy pollutes their sees for generations, and at last the false prophet's chalif alternately blights them with the favour which he shows to their heresy, or wastes them with the oppression which he has always ready for the faith. As to the great eastern patriarchate, from its capture by the Saracens in 638, its host of bishops, at the head of Hellenic cities descending from Alexander's empire, becomes, sooner or later, the prey of the Moslem. From the capture of Alexandria, Egypt becomes Monophysite under what the Copts fancy to be protection from the chalif, with the ultimate result that the country of the desert Fathers becomes the heart of the religion denying Christ: and, with Omar's entry into Jerusalem, upon his rough camel, with his wooden platter and his bag of barley, begin the 1260 years of the Holy City's treading down by the Gentiles.

Thus the southern wandering of the nations came upon the northern. When it came, three hundred years of such times as St. Jerome saw and described had already spread over the earth, sufferings too great for words, changes, as he says, such as neither Thucydides nor Sallust could express. But the southern wandering was much more rapid in time, and in effect far more complete. The ten years of Omar's chalifate had changed the whole aspect of the world, had shifted the centre of political power. It had been at Constantinople: it was shifted to Medina. From Constantine to Heraclius the empire had taken and enrolled in its armies unnumbered men of Teuton race. Alaric had been a Roman general: Stilicho and Aetius, saviours of Rome. This race had also fed the Church with converts of more stalwart nature than the enfeebled races who needed the infusion of northern blood even to till their fields, as well as to guard their frontiers, or to guide their polity. But the southern wandering gave no soldiers to the empire, and no converts to the Church. There would be no greater contrast than the two races from which these two great movements came. The northern barbarian, with all his wildness, could take the impress of the Church. He had in his woods and marshes, in his transmigrations and encampments, kept, in no small degree, the original tradition of the human race. Already Tacitus had noted his regard for woman as the companion of his life, for the sanctity of marriage, for monogamy, in the practical guarding of which he put to shame the degenerate Roman, and still more corrupted Greek. The heroic courage, natural to him, was an omen of the point which, as Christian martyr, he might reach. The self-government shown in the original habits of the tribe was a soil whereon princes and bishops might sit in council to form governments in which "liberty and empire," unknown to Byzantine, might dwell together. These qualities were elements of the social, the political, even the ecclesiastical life. Far otherwise was the Saracen type. Savage, rude and ignorant, with no tincture of art or learning: with habits of unlimited polygamy: with leanings to unmitigated despotism: with no regard to human life. In courage only was the southern a match for the northern barbarian. The outcome of his whole character as to the rest was different: and the religion invented for him was but the barest development of his natural temperament.

At the death of Chalif Omar, this new antichristian power had taken from the empire of Heraclius every yard of land formerly under its dominion from Tarsus to Tripoli: and stood in most threatening attitude over against all which remained to it: indeed, to the whole Christian name. Mohammed was its watchword against Christ. The northern wandering had no such counter watchword. It respected Roman laws and customs when it seized on Roman lands. It had understanding enough, not only as shown in its princes, Ataulph and Theodorich, but in a race of officers surpassing not only Roman courage, but Roman fidelity in the civil and military administration, to venerate as unapproachable by any wisdom of its own, the political fabric of which, in so many lands, it confiscated the resources.

But Omar's treatment of Greek learning in the library of Alexandria was the expression of his whole mind towards Christian civilisation. And Omar's powerful hand had not only maimed Byzantium, but absorbed Persia. All this had been done since Heraclius carried back the Cross in triumph to Jerusalem. The Persian had kept it in its shrine during its captivity with the seals untouched. The Saracen scorned all which it represented. The contest of those whom Heraclius would leave in his place was to be with the Saracens, Omar, Osman, and Ali.

After the Chalif Omar was mortally wounded in the mosque at Medina, he at first named Abd Errahman for his successor, who declined the chalifate. Whereupon Omar named six of Mohammed's companions, together with the same Abd Errahman to choose a new chalif. They were engaged during three days in heated contest, since each of the six wished to become the chalif, and were at last induced with great difficulty by Abd Errahman to accept one of their number named by him. Thus Osman, at the age of seventy, was chosen as successor of Omar. His chalifate lasted from November, 644, to June, 656: during the whole of which, eleven years and a-half, the Saracen realm was disturbed by internal struggles. Yet external wars continued. Governors, appointed by Osman, were decried, but they did many successful deeds of arms.[1] In North Africa, the boundaries of the realm were extended on from Tripolis as far as Kairawan. In Persia, a governor, afterwards removed, gained a province. The whole of Persia, which had been overrun rather than subdued under Omar, was finally conquered under

---

[1] Weil, *Islamitische Völker*, 58.

Osman. An attempt of the Greeks to recover Alexandria and Egypt succeeded for a moment, but was frustrated by the aid given to the Moslim by the Monophysite Copts. Parts of Armenia and Asia Minor were taken, and the island of Cyprus. The Moslim carried their conquering arms to the Oxus, and slew, in his retreat from a lost battle, the last heir of the kings of Persia.

In 656, the discontents produced by Osman's favour of his own family culminated in an insurrection at Medina, in which the dwelling of the chalif, after a siege of several weeks, was at last broken open, and the third Commander of the Faithful, also, like Ali, a son-in-law of Mohammed, was slain by the eldest son of Abu Bekr, the first chalif. A week after his death, the third chalif, Osman, was succeeded by Ali, the fourth, widower of Mohammed's favourite daughter, Fatima. But the six and a-half years of Ali's chalifate were occupied with a violent struggle between him and Muawiah, cousin of Osman, and governor of Syria.[1] There had ever been enmity between the family of Haschim, from which Mohammed descended, and the family of Abd Schems, from which Osman and Muawiah descended. In the course of the struggle Egypt fell away from Ali to Muawiah; and, in 660, Medina and Mecca paid him homage. Ali's power, then, was seated only in Irak and Persia. Civil war pressed so heavily on Islam that three men resolved to rid it in one day of Ali, Muawiah, and Amrou, as the causers of all the

[1] Weil, *die Chalifen*, i. 165.

trouble. Ali was to be assassinated in the mosque of Kufa; Muawiah in that of Damascus; Amrou in that of Fostat, to terminate a war carried on, not only in the field, but by mutual imprecations from the pulpit. But of the three, Ali alone was mortally wounded, Muawiah escaped with a light wound, and Amrou's representative was killed instead of him. Ali died, three days after, on the 24th January, 661. He is said to have surpassed not only Muawiah, but Abu Bekr and Omar in abhorrence of all falsehood, in love of justice, in valour and eloquence. In simplicity of life and generosity, Ali resembled his two predecessors: but, like them also, the severity which he practised by no means included moral restraint. He died at sixty-three; after Fatima's death, and, therefore, in the latter half of his life, he contracted six or eight marriages, besides maintaining nineteen slave women, with whom also, after the custom of that time, he lived.

So the second, third, and fourth chalifs—Omar, Osman, and Ali—perished by assassination within seventeen years of each other, in 644, 656, and 661. Let us turn to see what has been doing at Constantinople in these seventeen years. We have already seen how Omar, in his ten years, had built up an empire from the spoils of Byzantium and Persia, which, during the civil wars of his two successors, was yet increased. The seat of its sovereign power was transferred from Medina to Damascus as soon as Muawiah was acknowledged as chalif, in the year 661. But during the four chalifs, from the death of Mohammed in 632 to 660, the immense Mohammedan realm was governed from Medina.

When Heraclius died in 641, he was covered with defeat, and the chief provinces of his empire were, day by day, falling away. He left a son, Constantine, twenty-eight years old, who had been named emperor from his birth : and, by his second marriage with his niece, Martina, a son, Heracleonas, nineteen years old, who had been named emperor two years before, and two younger sons, David and Marinus, named Cæsars, besides two daughters, who, like their mother, had been named empresses. In his will he directed his two sons, Constantine and Heracleonas, to reign together with equal power, and to acknowledge Martina as empress-mother. Constantine III. was not Monothelite, but orthodox. At his accession he received a letter[1] from Pope John IV., maintaining the true doctrine, and also that his predecessor, Honorius, answering a question put to him by the patriarch Sergius, " taught concerning the mystery of the Incarnation, that there were not in Christ, as in us sinners, opposing wills of the mind and the flesh: and for this, certain persons, trusting to their own meaning, threw out the suspicion that he had taught there to be the only one will of the Godhead and the Manhood, which is altogether contrary to the truth ". This the Pope proceeds to prove at length. And he ends by saying that he finds a certain document, contrary to Pope Leo, of blessed memory, and the Council of Chalcedon, has been issued, to which bishops are

---
[1] See this letter in Mansi, x. 682-6.

compelled to subscribe. This was the Ecthesis of Heraclius. And he entreats the new emperor, as guardian of the Christian faith, to command this document to be torn down, and, as a first sacrifice to God, to scatter from His Church every cloud of novelty. So, if he regard the things of God, may the Lord, whose faith is preserved in purity, preserve his empire from the nations trusting in their ferocity.

But the emperor, Constantine III., died 103 days after his father, poisoned, as eastern historians say, by his step-mother, the empress Martina : with which crime they also inculpate the patriarch Pyrrhus. She then reigned with her son, Heracleonas ; but not for long. An insurrection deposed her : both she and Heracleonas were maimed and banished, and Constans II., son of Constantine III., and grandson of Heraclius, at twelve years old became emperor, under tutelage of the council. The answer given to the letter of Pope John IV. was that the Ecthesis affixed to the door of churches should be removed.

But the empire was torn to pieces by the strife of the various heresies contending for mastery. The patriarch Pyrrhus, who had succeeded Sergius in the see of Constantinople, and in the patronage of his heresy, found it expedient on the deposition of Martina to leave his see. He appeared in Africa, and had a great controversy with Maximus in the presence of the African episcopate in 645. He acknowledged himself to be defeated : and went to Pope Theodorus at Rome, where he renounced the Monothelite heresy, and was received by the Pope as bishop of the capital. But he returned presently, at the instance of the exarch of Ravenna, to the errors which he had renounced.

In due time the emperor, Constans II., produced the Typus to take the place of his grandfather's Ecthesis. And, when Pope St. Martin held his great Council at Rome in 649, Constans burst into fury, and, as above recorded, afterwards caused the Pope to be kidnapped, to be tried at Constantinople, and to be condemned for high treason; finally, to perish of want in the Crimea.

With Pope St. Martin, Maximus had been the great defender of the faith. It is time to give some record of his life, his labours, and his reward.

Maximus sprung about the year 580 at Constantinople from an old and noble family. There were few of rank superior to his relations. He had great abilities, received an excellent education, and became one of the most learned men in his time, and the ablest theologian. The emperor Heraclius drew him against his wishes to the court, and made him one of his chief secretaries. But, in the year 630, his love for solitude, as well as his observance of the wrong bias which the mind of Heraclius was taking, led him to withdraw from court. He resigned the brilliant position which he occupied, became a monk in the monastery of Chrysopolis, that is, Scutari, and, on the death of its abbot, was chosen unanimously to succeed him. Henceforth to the end of his life, at the age of eighty-two, he became, by word and deed, a champion of the Catholic faith against the Monothelite heresy. In 633, he went with Sophronius, then a simple monk, to Alexandria, and joined him in entreating the patriarch, Cyrus, to desist from promulgating the new heresy. Against this, Sophronius, having become patriarch of Jerusalem, published his synodical letter quoted above. Maximus went on to the west, visiting Rome and Carthage, and rousing the African bishops against the heresy. He showed his great dialectical skill in a contest with Pyrrhus, then the deposed successor of the patriarch Sergius. Pyrrhus even accompanied him to Rome, and renounced the heresy before Pope Theodorus.

Maximus continued at Rome to use all his efforts against the heresy, and counselled Pope Martin to call the Lateran Synod, and formally condemn it. As the Ecthesis of Sergius had been composed against Sophronius, and then the Typus—drawn up by the patriarch Paul, and imposed by the will of the emperor Constans II.—had been substituted for it at Constantinople, the Council of the Lateran which in 649 condemned both, excited the bitterest wrath of the emperor. Three men had especially in his mind counter-worked all his endeavours to impose his will as the standard of faith upon the Romans and the bishops. These three men were Sophronius, patriarch of Jerusalem, who had died shortly after the surrender of his city to Omar, Pope Martin, and the Abbot Maximus. How he avenged himself on the Pope St. Martin has been already described.

About the same time at which the Pope was carried off to Byzantium, in 653, Maximus also was seized, with his two disciples, both named Anastasius, one a monk, the other a Roman priest, who had been a nuncio. They were carried also to Byzantium, and thrown into prison. After the Pope had been judged by the senate, and condemned to death for high treason, Maximus and his disciples were also brought to trial.

Maximus had distinguished himself by a great number of writings. He is considered the greatest theologian of the seventh century. He has kept a very high rank through all the centuries which have followed him. After the death of Sophronius, the intellectual combat against the Monothelite heresy rested mainly upon him. The very high rank which he had held as a minister of Heraclius, conjoined with his scientific defence of the truth, made him the most conspicuous person in the Church after the martyrdom of Pope Martin, whose friend, counsellor, and supporter he had been, and his unbending constancy under the severest tortures has given him among the Greeks the name of "the Confessor".

Part of a letter[1] is extant from him to a certain Peter, a man of high rank, who had entreated him to meet and resist the patriarch Pyrrhus in the African conference. With regard to him Maximus says: "if Pyrrhus will neither be heretical, nor be so-called, let him not satisfy this or that individual. That is superfluous and unreasonable; for just as when one is scandalised in him all are scandalised, so when one is satisfied all surely

[1] From the letter "ad Petrum illustrem," Gallandi, vol. xii. p. 38.—Rump, x. 267.

will be satisfied. Let him then hasten to satisfy before all the Roman See. When this is satisfied all men everywhere will accept his religion and orthodoxy. In vain he speaks who would gain me and suchlike as me : and does not satisfy and implore the most blessed Pope of the holy Roman Church, that is, the Apostolic See, which has received and holds the government, the authority, and the power of binding and loosing over all the holy Churches of God in the whole earth in all persons and matters from the Incarnate Word of God Himself, and likewise from all holy Councils according to the sacred canons. For with him the Word who rules the celestial virtues, binds and looses in heaven. For if he thinks that others must be satisfied, and does not implore the most Blessed Pope of Rome, he is like the man who is accused of homicide, or any other crime, and maintains his innocence not to him who by law is appointed to judge him, but without any use or gain strives to clear himself to other private men who have no power to absolve him."

Yet more remarkable, if possible, is another testimony which this great martyr, born and bred at Constantinople, and up to the age of fifty a minister of the eastern emperor, who bears the greatest name among the theologians of the seventh century, has left behind him. It was apparently written at Rome after the completion of the Lateran Council in 649, which he mentions in it, and numbers with the five preceding ecumenical Councils. It runs thus :—

"All[1] the ends of the world, and all therein confessing the Lord with pure and upright faith, gaze stedfastly upon the most holy Church of the Romans, its confession and faith, as upon the sun of eternal light. They expect the brightness which ever lightens from it, in the doctrine of Fathers and Saints, as, guided by a divine wisdom and piety the six Councils have set it forth, drawing out with greater distinctness the Symbol of the Faith. For from the beginning when the Incarnate Word of God descended to us, all churches of Christians everywhere possess and hold as the only basis and foundation that greatest of churches, as against which, according to the promise of the Saviour, the gates of hell never prevail: as which possesses the keys of the right faith and confession of Him: as which discloses the real and only religion to those who approach it religiously, while it shuts up and stops every heretical mouth loudly speaking iniquity. For they are seeking without labour and apart from suffering, O wonderful patience of God which endures it![2] by two words to pull down what has been established and built up by the Creator and Ruler of all things, our Lord Jesus Christ, by His disciples and apostles, by all the sequence of holy Fathers, Teachers, and Martyrs, who offered themselves up by their words and deeds, their struggles and labours, their toil and blood-sheddings, and lastly, by wondrous deaths, for that Catholic and Apostolic Church of us who believe in Him. They

---

[1] S. Maximi confessoris Græcorum theologi, tom. ii., Combefis, 672.
[2] That is by attributing *One Will* to the Two Natures of Christ.

would annul that mystery of right Christian worship with all its greatness, its brightness, and its renown."

Pope Martin, who held this great Council, at which Maximus was present, supporting the Pope with all his learning, had been seized, as we have seen, in his own city and church, in the year 653, four years after it. At the same time, Maximus, being about 73 years old, was seized at the same place, and deported to Constantinople, and upon his arrival was taken straight from the ship, naked and without sandals, together with his two disciples and companions, and they were put into different prisons by five officers and their attendants. Later, when the proceeding against the Pope had been closed, Maximus was brought into the palace before the whole senate and a great crowd.[1] He was placed in the middle of the hall, and the fiscal angrily addressed him with the words, "Art thou a Christian?" Maximus replied, "By the grace of God I am". "That is not true." "Thou mayest say so, but God knows that I am a Christian." "And if thou art a Christian, how canst thou hate the emperor?" asked the judge. "But," replied Maximus, "how is this known to thee? Hatred, like love, is a secret affection of the spirit." "It is become plain by thy deeds that thou hatest the emperor and his realm, for it is only thou who hast delivered Egypt and Alexandria and the Pentapolis, Tripolis and Africa into the hands of the Saracens."

These accusations fell to the ground, as the false witnesses brought could not maintain them. But the

---

[1] Anastasius, in Gallandi, tom. xiii. 50.

end of this trial was to condemn Maximus and his two companions to a separate and severe exile.

The Pyrrhus whom Maximus had so far prevailed over in the famous conference held in Africa in 645, that he had renounced his heresy to Pope Theodorus, and been received by him in St. Peter's, who had then fallen back through the influence of the exarch, and been excommunicated, had succeeded in regaining the see of Constantinople, upon the death of Paulus, the author of the Typus. After a few months, he had died in the summer of 655. He was followed by Peter, whose synodal letter, sent to Rome to Pope Eugenius, is said to have been so dark on the subject of the heresy that the clergy and people would not suffer the Pope to celebrate Mass in the Church of St. Mary until he had promised not to accept this letter.

Later in the summer, Maximus was again brought into the judgment hall of the palace, where the two Monothelite patriarchs—Peter of Constantinople and Macedonius of Antioch, then living in the capital—were present. "Speak the truth," said Troilus to him, "and the emperor will have mercy on thee, for if one of the accusations be proved juridically against thee, thou wilt be guilty of death." Maximus declared they were all false: that he had submitted the Typus to anathema, not the emperor. The Lateran Council was asserted to have no force, for he who held it has been deposed, "Deposed he was not," said Maximus, "but expelled." Maximus and his companion, Anastasius, were sent to different banishments.

A year later, a fresh attempt was made to break down his resolution. Paul and Theodosius, two men of consular rank, and Theodosius, Bishop of Cæsarea, the latter as commissary of the patriarch, Peter, the former two of the emperor, reached the imprisoned confessor on the 24th August, 656. Every effort was made to induce Maximus to accept the Typus, and enter into communion with the see of Constantinople.

The terms which Maximus required were reported to the emperor, and fresh commissaries, the patricians, Troilus and Epiphanius, and the same bishop, Theodosius, sent again to Maximus.[1] "The Lord of the world sends us to thee," said Troilus, "to inform thee what it pleases him to require. Wilt thou obey his command or not?" Maximus requested that he might hear the command. They required that he should first answer the question. Maximus said, "Before God and Angels, and you all, I promise, what the emperor commands me, in respect of earthly things, I will do". At length Epiphanius said, "The emperor by us informs thee: since all the West and all the perverse-minded in the East look to thee and make contention because of thee, since they will not submit to us in faith, the emperor wills to move thee that thou enter into communion with us on the basis of the Typus issued by us. We will then personally go out to Chalce, and embrace thee, and offer thee our hand and, lead thee to the cathedral with all honour and pomp, and place thee by our side where the emperors are wont to sit, and we will then

[1] Gallandi, xiii. 71, translated.

partake of the life-giving Body and Blood of Christ, and declare thee again for our father: and there will be great joy not only in our own residence, but in all the world. For we are well assured that if thou enterest into communion with this holy see, all who have divided themselves from our communion on thy account will unite themselves to us again."

Then Maximus turned to the bishop and said to him with tears:—" My good lord, we are all awaiting the Day of Judgment. You know what we drew out, and agreed upon respecting the holy Gospels, the life-giving Cross, the image of our God and Saviour, and the all-holy ever-virgin Mother who bore Him." The bishop cast down his eyes, and said to him, in a lower voice:—
" What can I do, since the emperor has chosen something else?" Maximus said, " Why did you and those with you touch the holy gospels, when you could not bring about the promised issue? Indeed, the whole power of heaven would not persuade me to do this. For what answer shall I give, I say not to God, but to my own conscience, that for the glory of men, which has in it no substance, I have forsworn the faith which saves those who cling to it."

At this word they all arose, their fury overmastering them: they pushed and scratched and tore him: they covered him with spittle from his head downwards, so that his clothes reeked, until they were washed. And the bishop, rising, said, this ought not to be done, but his answer only should be heard, and then be reported to our lord. For religious matters are done in different fashion from this. The bishop could scarcely induce them to desist. They took their seats again, and reviled him with indescribable insults, and imprecations. Epiphanius said furiously, "Malefactor and cannibal, speakest thou thus, treating us and our city and our emperor as heretics? We are more Christian and orthodox than thou art. We confess that our Lord and God has both a divine will and a human will, and an intellectual soul, and that every intellectual nature has by nature, Will, and Operation, since motion belongs to life, and will to mind : and we know Him to have the capacity of Will not only in the Godhead, but also in the Manhood. Nor do we deny His Two Wills and Two Operations."

The abbot, Maximus, answered :—" If you so believe, as the intellectual Natures and the Church of God, why are you compelling me to communicate on the terms of the Typus, which merely destroys those things?" "That," said Epiphanius, "has been done for accommodation, that the people may not be injured by these subtleties." Maximus said :—" On the contrary, every man is sanctified by accurate confession of the faith, not by its destruction, as put in the Typus". " I told thee in the palace," said Troilus, " that it did not destroy, but bade silence be kept that we may all live in peace." Maximus answered :—" What is covered in silence is destroyed. The Holy Spirit says by the prophet :—' There are no speeches nor languages, where their voices are not heard ' : a word not spoken is no word at all." Troilus said : " Keep in thy heart what thou wilt; no one prevents thee". Maximus answered, "But God did not limit salvation to the heart when He said:—'He that confesseth Me before men, I will confess him before My Father in heaven,' and the Apostle, 'With the heart we believe unto justice, but with the mouth confession is made to salvation'. If then God, and God's prophets and apostles bid the great and terrible mystery which saves all the world to be confessed by holy voices, there is no need that the voice which proclaims it be in any way silenced, in order that the salvation of those who are silent be not impaired."

Then Epiphanius, speaking most harshly, said, "Didst thou sign the writing?" he meant the Lateran Council. Abbot Maximus said, "Yes, I signed". "And how didst thou dare to sign, and anathematise those who confess and believe as the intellectual Natures and the Catholic Church? In my judgment thou shalt be taken into the city, and be put in chains in the forum, and the actors and actresses, and the women that stand for hire, and all the people shall be brought, that every man and woman may slap thee, and spit in thy face." Abbot Maximus replied:—"Be it as thou hast said, if we have anathematised those who confess Two Natures of which the Lord is, and the two natural Wills and Operations corresponding to Him who is both God and Man. Read, my Lord, the acts and decree, and if what you have said is found, do all your will. For I, and my fellow-servants, who have subscribed, have anathematised those who, according to Arius and Apollinarius, maintain one Will and Operation, and who do not confess our Lord and God to be intellectual in each of those Natures of which, in which, and which He is: and, therefore, in both of them having Will and Operation of our salvation."

They said, "If we go on treating with this man, we shall neither eat nor drink. Let us go, and take food, and report what we have heard. For this man has sold himself to the devil. They went in and dined, and made their report, it being the eve of the Exaltation of the life-giving Cross in the year 656."[1]

The next day, Theodosius, the Consul, came out early to the aforesaid Abbot Maximus, and took away all that he had, and said, in the emperor's name:— "Since thou wilt not have honour, it shall be far from thee. Go to the place thou hast thought thyself worthy of, suffering the judgment of thy disciples, him at Mesembria, and him at Perberi." The patricians Troilus and Epiphanius had said:—"We will bring the two disciples, him at Mesembria, and him at Perberi, and put them, too, to the proof, and see the result. But learn, Sir Abbot, that, when we get a little relief from this rout of heathens (that is, the Saracens), by the Holy Trinity, we will bring you to terms, and your Pope, who is now lifted up, and all the talkers there, and the rest of your disciples: and we will *cook* you all, each in his own place, as Martin has been cooked". And the Consul Theodosius took him and committed him to soldiers, and they took him to Perberis. It is not known how long what is called the second exile of

[1] Hefele, iii. 323

St. Maximus lasted, which ensued after he had thus resisted the offers of the emperor.

At a later time, he was brought from Perberis, with his disciple, Anastasius, back to Constantinople.[1] A Synod, there held, excommunicated them both, as well as Pope St. Martin, St. Sophronius, and all the orthodox.[2] The second Anastasius, who had been a Nuncio, was also brought, and the Synod passed on all three the sentence:—" As the Synod has passed against you its canonical sentence, it only remains that you be subject to the severity of the civil laws for your impiety. And though no punishment could be proportionate to your crimes, we, leaving you to the just Judge in respect of the greater punishment, grant you the indulgence of the present life, modifying the strict severity of the laws. We order that you be delivered to the prefect, and by him taken to the guard: that you be then scourged; that in you, Maximus and Anastasius, and Anastasius, the instrument of your iniquity, the blaspheming tongue be cut out to the roots, and then your right hand, which has served your blaspheming mind, be cut off: that thus deprived of these execrable members, you be carried through the twelve quarters of this imperial city, and then be delivered to perpetual banishment and prison, to lament for the remainder of your errors."

This sentence was carried out by the prefect. St.

---

[1] Not from Anastasius, the Librarian, but from another source, in Gallandi, xiii. 74. See the narrative of Maximus in Hefele, iii. 215-224.
[2] Held under the patriarch Peter, Photius, i. 206.

Maximus was then transported to Lazika, in Colchis: the other two to different castles. As Maximus, from weakness, could neither ride nor bear a carriage, he was borne on a sort of bed made of branches to the Castle of Schemarum. St. Maximus foretold the day of his death, which took place on the 13th August, 662, when he was eighty-two years old. At that moment the chalif Muawiah had about completed the first year in which he had fixed the seat of the Saracenic empire at Damascus: and the "rout of heathen" from which the Byzantine Consul had anticipated deliverance, held in peril during the whole of Muawiah's reign to 680 the imperial city on the Bosphorous, where "the lord of the world" usually resided.

CHAPTER IV.

CHRISTENDOM AND ISLAM.

WE are now come to the greatest of contrasts and oppositions in human history—to the Church of Christ, the foundress of nations, and to Islam, her counterfeit and opponent; to the law which went forth from Jerusalem and struck its perpetual root in Rome, and to the force which went forth from Mecca, tarried for a while in Damascus and Bagdad, and then encamped in the city of Constantine. Two reigns which never have ceased and never can cease to counterwork each other, the reign of the Word and the reign of the Sword.

In the twenty-eight years which run from A.D. 632 to 661 of the four chalifs, Abu Bekr, Omar, Osman, and Ali, the sword has severed from the throne of Constantine its fairest provinces, and conquered besides a territory, the whole mass of which exceeded the Roman empire at its greatest extension. The sword of Mohammed's successors in doing this has inflicted deadly wounds on the Christian patriarchates and dioceses subjected to the new dominion. It has also reduced the unsubdued portion of the eastern empire to tremble for its future existence: it has made the whole West, already in possession of the Teuton family of races, gather itself together, and prepare for a death struggle with the advancing enemy.

It is necessary to consider in his personal life the man who gives name to this immense movement, who raised the banner which flouted the Cross and wrote upon that banner the symbol of human enjoyment against that of divine abasement. The facts of his life which I wish to note are especially those which are reproduced in his religion. They pass beyond the sphere of the individual because they reappear incessantly in the history of twelve hundred and fifty years, and affect nations of the south and east which dwell from the Atlantic Ocean to the extremities of China.

Mohammed[1] was born in April, 571, in the city of Mecca, of a family possessing spiritual rank in that home of ancient pilgrimages for the Arabian tribes. But the branch to which he belonged was poor. His father, Abdallah, died about the time of his birth. His mother, Aminah, born in Medina, was so poor that she could scarcely support a nurse for him. His mother died when he was six years old. His grandfather then took care of him, but died also after two years. From that time his uncle, Abu Talib, provided for him, but was so poor likewise that the orphan child was presently reduced to tend sheep, whereas the rich class at Mecca was largely engaged in traffic with their caravans, which visited Abyssinia, Southern Arabia, Syria, Egypt, and Persia.

[1] Weil, *Islamitische Völker*, p. 2. I have taken from this distinguished Orientalist and German historian, who spent thirty years in the study of eastern documents, the chief details concerning the events of Mohammed's life, which follow.

Mohammed is said in his youth to have twice visited Syria, probably as a camel driver. But it is said with greater certainty that at twenty-five he entered the service of a rich widow, Chadidja, and journeyed for her in South Arabia. He afterwards married her, and then for the first time became sufficiently rich to turn the thoughts which slumbered within him to higher subjects than procuring his daily bread.

His marriage with Chadidja lasted till he was fifty years of age, when he lost her and at the same time his uncle Abu Talib. During the whole period of his marriage with Chadidja, who was much older than himself, he lived in close union with her—what seems to have been, at least in regard to this relationship—a virtuous and religious life. Mohammed's education had been much neglected. His country at the time was in a most uncivilised condition, destitute of science, arts, and letters. Bardship alone was in repute, and for this Mohammed had no gift, though he had a great gift of oratory. The art of writing was little diffused; it is doubtful whether Mohammed even in his later years possessed it. He was acquainted with Jewish and Christian doctrines only by oral information. The great authority of St. John of Damascus says that he lighted upon the Old and New Testaments by conferences with an Arian monk, and thus drew up his own religion. He was about forty years of age when he began to carry out a design to restore what he thought the religion of Abraham, and to destroy the idolatry into which his countrymen had fallen. He met with small success and much opposition in this attempt until in the eleventh year of the mission which he claimed as prophet, and the fifty-first of his life, a most marked change in his personal conduct and in the conditions of his life took place.

The chief men at Mecca had generally refused to receive him as a prophet and to accept the reformation of religion which he proposed to them. In his first years he had confined his revelations to his nearest relations and friends. He had gained Abu Bekr and his young cousin Ali, an uncle Hamza, named for his valour "the Lion of God," and above all, Omar, at first his opponent, but when converted the most energetic character among all the companions of the prophet, and the strongest support of Islam. On the whole, however, things had gone so far against him that he retired secretly, together with Abu Bekr, from Mecca to Medina. This event, termed The Flight, took place in September, 622, from which year his followers count their time. It may be taken as indeed the time in which his full character as prophet came forth to light. Henceforth he appeared rather as the preacher of a new religion than as the restorer of what he called the religion of Abraham.

The most important principle laid down by him from the time of his migration from Mecca to Medina was that he then first permitted in the name of God war against unbelievers. He afterwards made this a holy duty. It was considered the first of virtues to fight the enemies of Islam. To those who fell in such a battle he promised the highest joys of paradise; to those who rejected him he threatened a shameful death by the disposition of God.[1]

Upon his first settlement in Medina, which afterwards changed its original name of Jathripp into this new name, signifying the city, he built a mosque and arranged worship, in which a short prayer was offered five times a day. He sought at first to gain over the Jews residing there, and marked Jerusalem as the *Kiblah*, that is, the point to which the face should be turned in prayer, and the tenth day of the first month as a fast day, and allowed Jewish converts to keep the Sabbath.[2] But when he found that the Jews would receive a Messias only of the race of David he became their bitterest enemy. Later he appointed Mecca instead of Jerusalem as the Kiblah, the month Ramadhan as fasting time, and Friday as the day of rest.

His first campaigns, when he could scarcely bring a few hundred men into the field, for the inhabitants of Medina had not yet joined him, but had only granted him protection, were but predatory attacks on the caravans of Mecca, which came near Medina. But when the Meccans grew prudent, and either defended their caravans with a strong escort, or sent them round by bye-paths to Syria, Mohammed planned a plundering attack in one of the holy months, when every Arab deemed himself secure. This is the beginning of a number of actions which, though he was not endued with a delicate moral sense, he must have known to be

[1] Weil, p. 7-24, from whom I have taken the facts which follow.
[2] Weil, *Islamitische Völker*, 8.

bad, and only ordered, or at least approved, for the sake of the end aimed at, chastisement of the heathen, and breaking in upon their commerce. What Mohammed did was to call his follower Abdallah, to give him a sealed packet, and instruct him to go to South Arabia with twelve companions. He was not to open the packet before the third day, and then fulfil the order it contained. Abdallah obeyed, broke the seal on the third day, and found only the words: Go with thy companions to the valley of Nachlah (south-east of Mecca), and there wait for the caravans of Mecca. Words which Abdallah interpreted to mean that he should fall upon these caravans. This he accomplished without difficulty. Two men were taken prisoners, one killed, and the whole lading carried as plunder to Medina. Mohammed had plainly used this short and sealed packet to cut off all explanation with Abdallah respecting an act of rapine in the sacred months, so as to be able to put away the responsibility from himself, as might be needed. Even the Moslim at Medina had but one cry of reprobation over this desecration of the sacred months. Mohammed at first disavowed Abdallah as having gone beyond his command, for he had not told him to attack the caravans in the sacred months. But when he found himself considered no less the author of this deed, and as he did not mean for the future to secure to Mecca four tranquil months for its commerce, Koran verses were published in which war against unbelievers was excused at every time, because they committed the much greater sin of driving the prophet out of his country.[1]

The attempt to exculpate Mohammed from the guilt of the blood murderously shed in falling upon this caravan is made the more difficult because his biographers speak of many other murders ordered by him even in the case of women, and extol him for such things. It may be noted that in the last time before his flight he was no longer true and sincere. Thus he recorded the whole history of the Old and New Testament prophets, adorned with many Jewish and Christian legends, which he maintained, as was his wont, to have been revealed to him by the angel Gabriel. This did not impose upon the inhabitants of Mecca, who were right in ascribing his knowledge of these things to intercourse with foreign informants less illiterate than himself.

The first proper fight between Mohammed and the Meccans took place in the second year of the Hegira at Bedr, a station between Medina and Mecca. Mohammed had gone out with somewhat more than 300 men to surprise and plunder certain rich caravans on their return from Syria. Abu Sofian, the head of the Omeiad line, led these caravans, and had notice of Mohammed's purpose. He sent an express to Mecca inviting his townsmen to despatch an armed escort to defend their property. Before these, 900 strong, arrived, Abu Sofian, knowing that Mohammed lay in wait for him at Bedr, succeeded in passing round this place by directing

---

[1] Weil, p. 10.

his caravans in security along the coast road. When news that their goods were safe reached the Meccan camp, a portion of the escort, which had taken arms only through fear of losing their property, wished to return. The rest, bitter enemies of Mohammed, and also fighting men, preferred to advance upon Bedr. This was resolved upon, but many in the force persisted in returning to Mecca. The same hesitation prevailed in the prophet's camp : which had come out intending to plunder, not for a fight with an enemy still continuing to be in number. But yet greater was the fear of showing cowardice, and so striking the new faith with the hardest blow. So they came to a bloody conflict, in which the disciplined Medinese prevailed over the Meccans whom their commercial habits had partly enfeebled. They carried off rich plunder. Mohammed did not himself fight : he was praying in a hut until he sank exhausted, and when he recovered consciousness, announced a victory to his friends obtained by the aid of celestial warriors. This first deed of arms laid the basis for a rapid increase of Mohammedanism. It gave the poor community spoil in arms, in horses, and in camels, and in no little ransom for the prisoners taken. It strengthened their confidence, increased their following, and encouraged them to further enterprise. The Jewish tribe Keinuka was their first prey. It was compelled to unconditional surrender, and would probably have been entirely massacred if a free retreat had not been obtained for it by Abd Allah, the head of an Arabian clan dwelling in Medina, with whom these Jews had been in former alliance. But all their goods went to the Moslem. At this time occur many slayings of particularly hated or dangerous enemies of Islam. So Mohammed inflicted a great terror which reduced to silence individual opponents, and carried waverers into the bosom of Islam, which promised them security.

But, in the meantime, the Meccans were not idle. Both interest and honour required them to avenge the defeat at Bedr. Abu Sofian, in the year 625, the third of the Hegira, appeared at the head of 3000 men, and occupied a camp to the east of Medina. Mohammed wished to confine himself to the defence of the city, but his more fanatic followers denounced this conduct as cowardice, and he was compelled to march out with about a thousand men, of whom nearly a third were commanded by Abd Allah : This man, a secret enemy of Mohammed, returned back into the city. The Moslim, however, in spite of their small number, fought with effect at Mount Ohod, north of Medina, until the bowmen, who were ranged against the enemy's horsemen, deserted their post, and the impetuous Chalid fell upon their retreat. A panic seized the believers, so that they sought safety in flight. Mohammed himself was wounded, and sank to the ground, so that a report of his death was spread, which added to the discomfiture of his host. But a faithful henchman recognised him by the eyes alone, in spite of mailcoat, helmet, and visor, and brought him to safety, while the Meccans, believing his death, cared not to pursue the other fugitives, and were retiring. Only after the battle was ended, Abu Sofian learnt that he was still alive. Mohammed, the day after the battle, in which he lost 70 men, pursued the enemy for some distance, only to show that he was not discouraged. The defeat at Ohod lessened Mohammed's reputation as much as the victory at Bedr had raised it. The only considerable gain which Mohammed, in the fourth year of the Hegira, could offer to his believers to make up for the losses suffered, was the expulsion of the Jews of the clan Nadir, who had lands and many strong castles near Medina. They surrendered these, and as there had been no battle, Mohammed confiscated their property, and bestowed it on his party of fugitives from Mecca. At the end of this year he appeared near Bedr with a larger force, to show that he was not afraid to defy Abu Sofian, who had threatened a fresh attack after the battle at Ohod. But the Meccans were not ready, and, moreover, would not fight on a bad year. Towards the end of the fifth year, in 627, they appeared again under Abu Sofian, about ten thousand strong, with their allies, out of various Bedouin clans before Medina. The Medinese could hardly set 3000 men against them, and were, in general, down-hearted, fearing an attack besides from the Jewish clan, Kureiza. This time Mohammed maintained his plan not to meet the enemy in the open field, but only to defend the town. By the advice of a Persian he drew a broad trench about it. Slight as this defence was, it sufficed, in the Arab ignorance of the art of siege, to keep the enemy from an attack in force. Bad weather ensued, and Mohammed succeeded in sowing distrust of each other among the confederates, so that they retired after doing nothing. But, though the siege of Medina had cost Mohammed little material loss, his reputation as warrior and as prophet had suffered greatly, as at Ohod. Instead of following the Arabian custom, to offer battle, he had cowered behind walls and trenches. Again he turned first against the Jews, who had entered into negotiations with the Meccans. After a few weeks, he compelled them to surrender. These were of the clan Kureiza, formerly confederates with the second large Arabian clan domiciled in Medina. They hoped, through the mediation of this clan, to get as good conditions as the clan Keinuka had obtained through Abd Allah. But the head of this clan had been wounded during the siege of the city, and when Mohammed appealed to his judgment, he condemned to death the men whose number ran from 600 to 900, and their wives and children to slavery. Mohammed had this hard sentence executed immediately in the marketplace of Medina. This expedition was followed by others against hostile Bedouin clans. Thus the bad impression left by the siege was gradually effaced. So at the end of the sixth year of the Hegira, 628, Mohammed was able to resolve, at the head of his friends, as well believers as heathen Arabs in alliance with him, on a pilgrimage to Mecca. He issued a solemn invitation to join this pilgrimage. It met with small acceptance. He had issued it in the name of God, and so was obliged to carry it out, though it was attended by an inconsiderable number, as to which the accounts vary between 700 and 1400 men. He had to trust to the Arab reluctance to shed blood in the sacred months, though he had himself violated one sacred month by murder and robbery. Finding the Meccans resolute to forbid him entrance into their city, he had to halt on the border of the holy territory. After long treating, agreement was made that he should retire for that year, but should be allowed in the following year to pass three days in Mecca on pilgrimage. The Meccans, for the sake of their commerce, were as anxious for peace as Mohammed, and so a truce for ten years was struck, which yet had this favourable condition for them, that, while their fugitives were to be given up, those of Mohammed might be secure in Mecca.

This repulse of the prophet and his companions from the holy city and its temple was deeply felt, yet there were advantages obtained by this seemingly dishonouring truce. Mohammed appeared at least to be recognised by the proud city as an equal power. Now he might send out his missionaries into every part of Arabia, make proselytes and conclude alliances, and the right to enter Mecca the next year with those who believed in him was something gained which perceptibly advanced his claim among the Arabians. To increase his strength, enrich his followers, and so enlarge their numbers and efface by a new victory the bad impression which the failure of the pilgrimage had caused, he attacked the Jews of Cheiber, who had lands and several castles four or five days' journey north-east of Medina. These were successively stormed and sacked, and all that the rest could do was to surrender to the conqueror on condition that they should serve him for the future as tenants who should give him half the produce of the land. So by the conquest of other Jews he was able to increase the number of his troops.

In the year 628-629 which passed between the failure of the pilgrimage to Mecca, and the subsequent pilgrimage carried out according to the treaty, several attacks on the Bedouins took place. The number of his believers and allies increased, and the thought was more and more developed in Mohammed that Islam must by degrees be accepted as the only true religion not only by all Arabians but by all the nations of the earth. Even before he had obtained possession of Mecca he sent messengers to the neighbouring princes of Persia, Byzantium, and Abyssinia, as well as to the Christian governor of Egypt, and to several Arabian chiefs subject to Byzantine or Persian sovereignty, inviting them to be converted to his faith. These embassies had no result, and were rejected with more or less harshness. Only the Greek governor of Egypt gave them a friendly reception, and without being converted to Islam sent the prophet costly presents, among them two slave women, of whom one, Mariam, so greatly charmed Mohammed that for her company he neglected his wives.

For the man who had been faithful to his old wife Chadidja until her death, when he was past fifty years of age, had from the time that he came forward, not merely as the restorer of a primitive religion which had suffered corruptions, but as the herald of a new religion, say from the date of the Hegira itself, espoused about a dozen wives,[1] some for love and some for policy, to make alliance with families of repute. Among these was Aischa, daughter of Abu Bekr, whom he took when scarcely out of her childhood, a daughter of Omar, and a sister of Abd Allah, who had been disgraced by the violation of a sacred month. The Koran limits the number of lawful wives to four, but Mohammed himself was to be an exception. At the time polygamy in Arabia had no restriction, and as public opinion was not shocked, his wives had to submit. But when Mariam, the Abyssinian slave, assumed the position of a dangerous rival, they complained to their families, and showed their contempt to the faithless husband. He promised to quit the favoured slave, but he dwelt with her for a month apart from his wives and then produced verses of the Koran, dispensing him from his promise respecting Mariam, and threatening his wives that if they continued in their disobedience he would take instead of them more submissive wives and virgins.

But a more important incident in the domestic life of Mohammed was to occur, which showed how entirely he was led away by sensual passion.[2] He had fallen in love with Zeineb, the wife of Zeid, formerly his slave, then his adopted son, and one of the most attached among

[1] Weil, p. 16.
[2] Weil, p. 17.

his followers. Zeid perceived this and was willing to cede her to the man who was not only his prophet but his benefactor. The prophet took her, and added her to the number of his wives. But the Arabians, though they practised unlimited polygamy, did not allow to marry the wife of an adopted son, whom they considered in the light of a real son. Mohammed felt the scandal, and produced a passage from the Koran. In it he declared in the name of God the custom hitherto entertained of treating adopted children as really children to be foolish, and for the future even sinful. Then he spread the belief that Zeid's divorce from his wife had taken place against his own advice ; he makes God remind him in a following verse how notwithstanding his own love for her he had counselled Zeid to keep her ; and how even after the divorce, he had shrunk, through fear of men, from espousing her until God had expressly commanded it,[1] and this for two reasons, first, to shew that he who acts after the will of God should not heed the tattle of men ; and secondly to give by his own example the more force to the newly-enacted law in regard of adopted sons ; a law, he added, which earlier prophets, whom he takes care not to name, had promulgated.

But this marriage [2] also led to further revelations in the Koran, which entirely severed the wives of Mohammed from the male world : and also separated the other believing women by a thick veil from the eyes of

[1] Sura 33. Sale, p. 317.
[2] Weil, p. 18 ; see the 33rd Sura.

strangers. Mohammed's jealousy stretched even beyond the grave, and he forbade second marriage to his wives even after his death. The object was to restrict them from all life in public to their own homes, and even there, to intercourse with their own sex, or only their nearest male relations. In spite of their polygamy, the wife had hitherto among the Arabians been the companion of their life : Mohammed reduced her to be a house-slave. She became in Islam a holy thing, indeed : but a holy thing kept under veil and bolt, and guarded not by her own virtue, but by eunuchs, from desecration.[1]

Mohammed's invitation to the governor of Egypt, followed by the gift of the slave woman to Mohammed, led to disastrous consequences in Islam to woman's position. The prophet called in God to sanction man's lordship over woman : the first time in history that such a corruption claimed a divine sanction.

In the eighth year of the Hegira, January, 630, Mohammed obtained possession of Mecca. To avenge a rupture of the existing truce, he broke with 10,000 men into the neighbourhood of the city, which admitted him both as its temporal lord and as the prophet of God, without a fight. He received the homage of its inhabitants on one of the city's hills, and their oath to follow him in all wars against unbelievers. At the same time, he declared Mecca to be again a holy city, in which God had allowed

---

[1] Weil, p. 18.

him alone to shed blood, which, for the future, was never to be.[1]

After gaining this possession of Mecca, Mohammed issued in the ninth Sura of the Koran what amounted to a new law of nations, and a new practice of war. From that time forward none but Mohammedans were to enter the holy city of Mecca and its circle: but likewise, outside of this, idolaters were to be exterminated, Jews and Christians were only to be suffered, when they paid tribute, and humbled themselves.[2] "O true believers, verily the idolaters are unclean: let them not therefore, come near unto the holy temple after this year. And if ye fear want by the cutting off trade and communication with them, God will enrich you with His abundance, if He pleaseth, for God is knowing and wise. Fight against them who believe not in God, nor in the Last Day, and who forbid not that which God and His Apostle have forbidden, and profess not the true religion of those to whom the Scriptures have been delivered, until they pay tribute by right of subjection, and they be reduced low. The Jews say Ezra is the son of God, and the Christians say Christ is the Son of God. This is their saying in their mouths: they imitate the saying of those who were unbelievers in former times. May God resist them. How are they infatuated! Besides God, they take their priests and their monks for their lords, and Christ, the Son of Mary; only they are commanded to worship one God

[1] Weil, p. 19.
[2] Sale's Koran, Sura 9.

only. There is no God but He. Far be that from Him which they associate with Him. They seek to extinguish the light of God with their mouths: but God willeth no other than to perfect His light, although the infidels be averse thereto. It is He who hath sent His Apostle with the direction and true religion, that He may cause it to appear superior to every other religion, although the idolaters be averse thereto."

This Sura was the last in time of those issued. "It[1] bears the stamp of much reflection and careful execution." In March, 631, Mohammed had sent the greater pilgrimage to Mecca, under guidance of Abu Bekr. This Sura was published on the chief day of the pilgrimage, and "its promulgation committed to Ali,[2] who rode for that purpose on the prophet's slit-eared camel from Medina to Mecca, and, standing up before the whole assembly at Al Akaba, told them that he was the messenger of the Apostle of God unto them". Thus it establishes the definitive position of Mohammed in regard to all other religions, and the exclusiveness of his own claim.

In the last days of Mohammed, when the religious capital of Arabia had been taken by him, and this new law of war had been published, embassies from all parts of Arabia streamed to him, for to the Arabians there remained no choice between the Koran and the sword. He may be considered as the lord by conquest of Arabia, and moreover as one who pretended to issue in

---

[1] Weil, quoted by Rump, x. 88.
[2] Note in Sale's Koran, 9th Sura, p. 128.

the name of God and as His sole apostle a new world-religion. Scarcely more than a year after this proclamation of war against what he chose to consider idolatry he died on the 8th June 632, at the age of 63 lunar or 61 solar years.

When we review the ten years which elapsed from the Hegira to the death of Mohammed, the following points are salient.

The imposition of religious belief by force becomes more and more the main principle of Mohammed. As he increases in power the principle is set forth with greater distinctness. He began as a citizen of Mecca by trying to persuade his relations and friends. With some he succeeded. His kinsmen gave him a partial support rather of clanship than of faith. But he found it expedient to fly from his native city, and the flight marks to all future time the beginning of his assumption not only to be a prophet, but in that character to publish a new religion. The Flight is the Mohammedan era as the birth of Christ is the Christian. At the end of the ninth year the proclamation against idolatry in the ninth Sura, the last in time of the whole series, marks the completion of the parent idea. Mohammed declares himself the apostle of God, as such alone charged " with the direction and true religion," while Christians, though they are commanded " to worship one God only, associate Christ the Son of Mary with Him ". Whereas Mohammed declares Christ to be indeed one in the series of prophets, the last before himself; but himself to be the prophet who completes the chain. Thus he enacts that Christians can be safe before his people only in one of two ways, either by forming part of them, that is, by taking Mohammed instead of Christ, or by submitting to pay tribute, and to the humiliations which accompany tribute. Thus the parent idea is the messiaship of force.

It may be noted that it comes out in a profession of faith drawn especially to exclude the association of the Son of Mary with God. Thus Mohammed crowns the work which Arius attempted three hundred years before. After the restless heresies in which the Greek mind had fluctuated during these three centuries, the greatest enemy to the Greek empire and faith was set up on that very negation of the godhead of Christ with which those heresies had begun. Fifty years of Arian success, in which the emperors, Constantius and Valens, take a large part, inspired and supported by Eusebius, Macedonius, Eudoxius, and Demophilus, four successive bishops of Byzantium, cause that disorganisation of the eastern Church which St. Basil described as its ruin. Fifty years of patronising the Monothelite heresy, in which the emperors Heraclius and Constans II. bear the largest part, supported by four Byzantine patriarchs, Sergius, Pyrrhus, Paulus, and Peter, beginning in 628, mark the rise and accompany the establishment of the Mohammedan empire and creed. Honorius dies before the heresy is presented for acceptance in Rome in the imperial Ecthesis. Ten Popes succeeding Honorius, in spite of the temporal distress which surrounds them, oppose to the utmost the Byzantine heresy and despotism in the midst of whom one gloriously lays down his life and is martyred by the eastern emperor as guilty of high treason. This is the connection between Arius and Mohammed, who appears as the divine punishment and remedy for Byzantine successors of Constantine who would confiscate the liberty of the church, and for state-made patriarchs who foster and formulate heresy.

Secondly, the revelations which Mohammed professes to receive from God he professes also to be brought to him by the Angel Gabriel. Nor is he ashamed to make this angel serve him in actions of the utmost turpitude. Thus when the governor of Egypt bestows on him the slave-girl Mariam, he falls so desperately in love with her that his proper wives, including his favourite, the girl-wife Aischa, the daughter of his chief adherent, Abu Bekr, revolt. The prophet is embarrassed and summons the Angel Gabriel to his aid. Forthwith a passage of the Koran preaches to the discontented wives obedience in the name of God, and the prophet threatens that if they continue to be insubordinate he will dismiss them and find others more obedient and submissive. Nor is even this the lowest depth of infamy. For when he violates even the customs of the Arabs around him, loose as they were, and favourable to the selfishness of the stronger sex, and takes the wife of his most faithful follower and adopted son, he calls in Gabriel to justify the adultery in the name of God, and to enlarge to any extent which the prophet may choose his exclusive privilege of taking wives. It would be difficult to say how the stamp of imposture could be fixed on the Koran with more convincing force than by this association of an angel and of God himself with acts which are contrary to the universal natural law.

Thirdly, it may be remarked that as to polygamy, since it was the custom of the Arabians in his time to practise it without restraint, Mohammed might be considered as neither better nor worse than his countrymen, who had so corrupted the purity of the original law of marriage. This might be allowed if we were considering Mohammed simply as a Saracen of that time. But we are considering him in the light in which he put himself forward as the apostle of God, the one apostle who was to set forth the one God : " there is but one God and Mohammed is his prophet ". It is in this character that he did what no one had ever done before. Polygamy had crept in, " through the hardness of men's hearts," but Mohammed attempted to set by his appeal to God and his use of the Angel Gabriel a divine sanction upon this great corruption, and upon the unlimited concubinage which he practised himself, and authorised in others. Thus St. John Damascene a hundred years after his time used of him these indignant words : " This Mamed put together many foolish things. Thus in the writing entitled ' Woman ' he lays down the law that a man may openly take four wives, and a thousand concubines if he can, as many as he can subject to himself[1] besides the four; and he may divorce when he pleases and take another. And he made this law for the following reason." Then St. John narrates the case of Zeid and his

[1] See Sura 33.

wife in these words: "Zeid had a handsome wife; Mamed fell in love with her. As they sat together Mamed said, God has charged me to take thy wife. Zeid answered: Thou art the apostle, do as God told thee. Or to go further back, he said: God charged me that thou divorce thy wife. Zeid divorced her. After some days Mamed said: God also charged me to take her. So he took her and made her an adulteress, and then he enacted that every one who will may divorce his wife, and after the divorce, if she return to him, another must marry her first."[1]

Patriarchs and prophets have sinned, as well as common men; but Mohammed is the only legislator who has called in God to sanction his sin, and propagate it among others in the name of God: and he did this under the title that he was the special apostle of God, sent to propagate the only true religion. The terrible sin of David stands out as contrary to all his previous life. He sought pardon for it, and after it became the great penitent, and humbly bowed his head beneath chastisements as awful as his own sin. Mohammed exulted in his sin, as deserving of praise and exceptional privilege.

Fourthly, throughout the ten years, from the Hegira to his death, Mohammed carried out his own principle of propagating religion by force in his utter disregard of human life. As soon as he had left Mecca he practised robbery upon its caravans and killed without scruple those who resisted the robbery. He tried to make

[1] St. John Damascene, on the 101st heresy. Vol. I. 114.

friends with Jewish clans around him, and when they rejected him for their Messias, slew them by hundreds. He slew even for private revenge those who stood in his way : and women as well as men.

These alleged revelations become in Mohammed's hands the enactments of a sovereign legislator. He claims them to be words of God delivered to him by the angel Gabriel. The personal character of Mohammed as developed in them is, therefore, of the greatest importance. He speaks not only of his " brother Moses " in the Jewish legislation which he closes, but of the Son of Mary as the Word and Spirit of God, on whose work he sets the superior seal of his own mission ; and as a matter of fact, those who took his name had his personal character and actions before them for a standard, as the Christians had the Son of God. From the moment of his death this fact is brought out by the conduct of his followers. His chief companions meet and elect a head whom they call the chalif or successor of the prophet. That title is the sole source of his authority, which is both religious and civil, supreme in each, but supreme because it is the transmitted authority of the Prophet who is not a prophet only, but the "Apostle of God ". The four points above noted, the propagation of religion by force, the imposture in the use of the name of Gabriel, the enacting of polygamy with the superadded license of unbounded concubinage, and the employment of murder as means of success, mark the intense antagonism between the character of Mohammed and the character of Him whom he charged the Christians with associating to God. Instead of the Man, meek and humble of heart, who said to His disciples that in following His meekness and humility they should find rest for their souls, we have the man who ordered the believers in him to beat down all idolaters that did not profess, "There is one God, and Mohammed is His prophet," and made death in battle against them to be the martyrdom which he chose for his people. Instead of the Man who said, "If I had not done among them the works which no other man hath done, they would not have sin," we have the man who answered the appeal made to him for miraculous works in testimony of his mission, by disclaiming the power to do them. Instead of the Virgin's Son who set up the virginal life, and propagated His faith by the teaching and example of those who followed it, we have the man who forged a divine permission for the grossest polygamy and an unlimited concubinage obtained by successful war. Instead of the Man who reverenced above all men the sanctuary of human life, we have the man who murdered without scruple those who did not accept his mission.

As to the nature of the kingdom which each of these two set up, the One in His last words to His disciples on the night of His sacrifice said, "The kings of the gentiles lord it over them, and they that have power over them are called beneficent, but you not so: but he that is the greatest among you let him become as the younger, and he that is the leader as he that serveth". In accordance with this precept, just as Mohammed was preparing to appear as the prophet, the greatest among Christians took as the symbol of his spiritual rule for his title, Servant of the servants of God : and so Chalid, the chief fighter, under Mohammed, Abu Bekr, and Omar, was termed "the sword of the swords of God". The prophet in the Sura proclaiming his religion pronounced force to be the instrument of spreading it, and in doing this blood was to be shed like water : and from his time his chalifs have practised the slaughter of as many as they chose. Nor is this confined to enemies, but his religion has considered his own subjects thus slaughtered as witnesses of the prophet's claim. To be killed by order of the chalif is to the believer a title of honour, and the sacrifice of so many a day to his order a sacrifice to his religion.

The pretension put forward by Mohammed in the ninth Sura has been fully accepted by his people from the beginning. He is their apostle, and accordingly from his life they have taken and woven into their own in every age the employment of force, the imposture of a man's invention put in an angel's name, the right to take away life at the pleasure of the ruler, but above all, polygamy and concubinage. The sensual life of Mohammed began exactly at the time when, discarding persuasion as the instrument of converting unbelievers, he began to propagate by force his pretended mission as a prophet. The deterioration in the moral life coincides with the time when he passed from the character of one who sought to restore the religion of Abraham to the very different character of one who sought to introduce a new and universal religion. Moreover, this sensual life of the founder has likewise infected with a moral pestilence all those parts of Asia, Africa and Europe, wherein his followers have prevailed. The man who from fifty to sixty years of age was multiplying young wives, moving them to jealousy with a slave concubine, seizing the wife of an adopted son, in virtue of a feigned divine decree, and making a special license to himself as the prophet of God to marry as many wives as he pleased, and whose wives he pleased, has corrupted all the generations of those who profess his religion. But more than in any others this corruption is apparent in those who rule in the prophet's name. Omar, Osman, and Ali, the second, third, and fourth chalifs, followed Mohammed closely in this corruption of domestic life. Ali, the husband of his favourite daughter, equalled her father in his wives, as likewise Osman, the husband of another daughter. Every Mohammedan prince, as a rule, follows the founder of his dynasty and creed, and thus, as the race of the Virgin Mother reproduces in every age the example of her whom all generations call blessed, and her Divine Son has planted in her the tree of chastity, of which He is Himself the first fruit, and which takes root in an honourable people, and as every work of superhuman charity grows upon that tree, and the sex lost in Eve is glorified by Mary, so the Mohammedan line is equally true to its origin. To the very end of the long night of heathenism, on which the coming of our Lord dawned, monogamy still survived in the noblest descendants of Eve. The German had it and the Roman, and there were ages in which those races, heathen though they were, honoured woman, and maintained the sanctity of marriage, before it was exalted into a sacrament, and before the foundation of human society was consecrated by the blessing of the Redeemer, given in the touch of His Blood. The degradation of woman in every age and every people during the 1250˙ years of Mohammedan domination, is the special stamp of the various peoples who have borne his name. I take the example highest in position and worst in character. To the precept of Mohammed, enforced by his own conduct, we owe it that in Constantine's own city the very chalif who represents him continues without marriage to practise an unbounded concubinage. Thus from generation to generation the race of Othman— which can scarcely be called a family—has been continued, and enabled to reign over the fairest countries of the globe, Christian during many hundred years, for a period almost as long as the long descended lines of Capet and Hapsburg have subsisted in honourable marriage. Concubinage has provided it with children, and fratricide has prevented rivals down to the time of Sultan Mahmoud. When he succeeded to the throne, stained in every generation with such crimes, he was the only survivor of his race. Out of the previous history a Turkish annalist[1] records without astonishment, for it was an ordinary incident, that in a tumult which had taken place at the funeral of Sultan Murad III.,

[1] Quoted in *Mohammed's Religion*, p. 23. The annalist is Raima.

nineteen brothers of the Sultan Mohammed III., all innocent and guiltless, were strangled and added to the company of martyrs. From the life of Mohammed himself has sprung a despotism without limit, a cruelty which scorns natural affection, and a sensuality without example. As the personal life on earth of the Son of God is seen in the religion which He planted, and in the history of the people which He formed and maintains, so the personal life of the man Mohammed is seen in the religion which bears his name, and in the people which have carried it on. It is only to elucidate this thought that I have selected these particulars of the Arabian's life, and as a prelude to the contrast which the religions themselves present.

A few months after his return from the great pilgrimage to Mecca in 632, Mohammed was preparing a third campaign against the Byzantines, which however could only be executed after his death. A word must be said as to his exact position at the moment of his death. In the ten years which follow immediately the Hegira, the original camel driver, who became husband of Chadidja, and lived with her virtuously to her death, pursued the life of a freebooter, which had many alternations of failure and success. In his character of prophet, "the apostle of God," he aimed at material power, and scrupled not to pursue it by deceit, robbery, and murder, all exercised as means of converting men to the worship of one God, the almighty and "most merciful". He had fifteen months before his death so far prevailed as to obtain mastery over the city which he had left as a fugitive. It was in a certain sense the capital of Arabia, and he was claiming and in a great degree receiving the homage of all Arabians. But other men who also called themselves prophets, such as Moseilama, were his rivals. The subjection of Arabia was by no means complete at the time of his death. The German historian—himself of the Jewish race and religion—from whose careful study of Mohammedan writers I have taken many of the incidents above recorded, says that with the exception of his weakness in his relations to the female sex, in regard to which he claimed the privileges allowed to him as a special favour from God, he gave a fair example to his people. There was the greatest simplicity as to his dwelling, his clothing, and his food. He was so unassuming that he not only refused every external mark of honour from his companions, but declined every service even from his slaves which he could perform himself. He was often seen in the market place buying food, mending his clothes in a miserable little room, or milking a goat in his court. Every one could approach him at all hours, whether in the street or in his dwelling. He visited all the sick, and showed sympathy to every sufferer, and was also magnanimous and indulgent where policy did not otherwise require. His generosity and benevolence, and also his care for the common good were boundless, so that in spite of the many presents which he received from all sides, and the rich plunder which came to him from his wars, he left little property behind him, and treated even this as belonging to the State. After his death it was not given to his daughter Fatima, his only heiress, the wife of Ali. He had other sons and daughters besides Fatima, on the number of whom tradition varies. They all died before him. We may name only Rukejja and Umm Kolthum, whom the future Chalif Osman successively espoused, both by his first wife Chadidja; and also Ibrahim son of the Coptic slave Mariam, whose early death the prophet sorely lamented. But this historian treats the bringing in the Angel Gabriel as the bearer of his revelations to have been a deceit throughout.

The power which Mohammed claimed rested entirely on the truth of his assertion that God had committed to him a prophetical office, carrying with it the promulgation of a new and universal religion. The absolute falsehood of this assertion is contained in the invention of the Angel Gabriel. The Jewish historian whom I have quoted fully admits this imposture, just as St. John Damascene made it a reproach a hundred years after Mohammed's time. The virtues above mentioned, what are they but the beautiful spots of the tiger's skin veiling the ferocity of the beast? Mohammed by the confession of his friends would appear to have had two intense passions, one for sweet odours, the other for women. Thalebi commenting on the 5th Sura records how ten zealous disciples used often to meet and pray in the house of Osman.[1] They watched through the night and had resolved to prepare themselves for

[1] From Damberger, i. 394.

paradise by chastity and mortification. Mohammed did not approve of it, and preached to the people that it was no way his mind that those who professed Islam should abstain, like Christian priests and religious, from women and from eating flesh, and from sweet odours; should debar themselves from sleep, and practice hardships. Fighting was his monkhood. Abulfeda says he openly confessed as to himself, "Two things attract me and carry me away: women and sweet odours. My joy is in these two pleasures, and they make me more prayerful." In fact Mohammed was never so pious as when he took a new wife; while he deserted them all for the Coptic slave-girl Mariam. And the Koran told him that he was right.

What were pharisaic prayings in the market place to the devotions of Mohammed? He called upon all with whom he came in contact to accept the one God, and Mohammed as his prophet, on pain of being exterminated, and he delivered up to the pleasure of the Mohammedan fighter as many female captives as any one could take, over and above the four wives whom he allowed to all. These captives were not the victims of angry passions in men maddened by a furious conflict, but the avowed and justified reward of those who might, if slain in battle, have been martyrs, but instead were victorious. The very worst corruption [1] which we meet with in the idol worship and demon worship of Greeks and Romans was the shamelessness which pandered to all lusts of the flesh under cover of religion. But Mohammed added to this

[1] Damberger, i. 395.

corruption. In virtue of his Koran the most infamous passions were allowed not in belief of false gods, themselves models of impurity, but in worshipping the one holy God. In all this the example as well as the word of the religious founder had gone before, and his people followed it from age to age.

Mohammed then at the time of his death was a successful robber in a country wherein the tribal life was in a state of great confusion and incessant changes, and the ancestral religion had degenerated into a rude and senseless idolatry. The race which occupied Arabia—the whole people which claimed Ishmael the son of Abraham for their ancestor—was devoid of order and of culture, of art or science, and had not affected the history of the world beyond its own boundaries. That the lord of Byzantium on the one hand or the lord of Ctesiphon on the other contemplated permanent danger to their realms from the incursions of such a race can as little be supposed as that Europe now is in fear of subjugation from a host of Caffres or Zulus, people, in personal bravery, resolution and bodily strength, equal probably to what the Saracens then were.

In Omar's chalifate[1] he had sent an army of 30,000 men, under one of Mohammed's eldest companions, to compel the Persians on the Euphrates to become Mohammedans. They had placed themselves under the last heir of the royal race, the young and valiant Jezdejerd. When the embassy requiring them to accept Islam or tribute came, the heir of the great

[1] Weiss, *Lehrbuch der Weltgeschichte,* ii. 516.

king said to them mockingly: "You came hither as traffickers and beggars. Your food was green lizards; your drink salt water; your dress rough camel's hair. Now you would force upon us a hateful religion. Hunger pushes you on; so I forgive you. Go back and I will load your camels with corn and dates. If you disdain a generous offer, punishment shall find you in Persia." Then the old sheick Mughira answered undismayed: "What thou sayest of our misery is true. So great was our poverty that we fed on worms, snakes, and scorpions. The hair of our camels and our goats we worked into a covering for our nakedness. Our faith consisted in perpetual war and robbery. We put even our daughters to death to escape supporting them. Then God took pity on our miserable state, and sent us through His holy prophet the book of the true faith. It commands us to make war against the heathen, to change our poverty and our misery for riches and power. Take then our religion which binds you to no other burdens than all the faithful bear. Or pay the tribute of the heathen. Will you do neither, arm yourselves to fight."

Such was the people among whom Mohammed arose. The spirit which he wakened speaks in the words of the poetess Chansa, with which she sent her four sons to battle. "By God, the only one, ye are the sons of a man as ye are the sons of a woman. I have not deceived your father; I have not brought your uncle to shame, nor stained your race. Ye know what rich reward God has promised to Moslim for war against the unbelieving.

Bethink you that the eternal dwelling is better than this place of sojourn." All her four sons fell in battle. Chansa cried : " Praise be to the Lord who has made me a name through the martyr-death of my sons ". The words of this mother breathe the whole spirit which made Islam a conquering power.

Mohammed had died without leaving any indication as to whom he wished for his successor. His chief adherents, Abu Bekr, father of his wife Aischa, in whose residence he had died, his sons-in-law Ali and Omar, with their several parties, met together. Omar put aside his own claims, and had influence sufficient to procure the election of Abu Bekr, and to frustrate that of Ali. Severe as the struggle to obtain the chalifate was, at the moment it brought with it greater burden than dignity.[1] Mohammed had spread his belief more by bribery, deceit, and violence than by conviction. Many provinces of Arabia after his death were shaking it off. Aischa's own words were, " when the apostle of God died, the Arabs were deserting him; the Jews and Christians raised their head; the hypocrites no longer concealed their hypocrisy, and the Moslim were like an abandoned flock on a cold winter night ". Abu Bekr's prudence and Omar's energy put an end to the rivalry of pretending prophets and Bedouin reluctance of taxation. In March, 633, revolt in Arabia was overthrown, and the first chalif could execute the injunction of Mohammed to spread Islam beyond the Arabian peninsula.

[1] Weil, *Islamitische Völker*, Abu Bekr, p. 42.

The choice of a chalif not in the family of Mohammed to carry on his newly made realm and religion with armed hand was of the utmost moment to both. In idea realm and religion were one and the same thing. And the choice indicated that force was the power which ruled both. Abu Bekr had not only been chosen by the influence of Omar, but during his short chalifate of two years had that most resolute of all Mohammed's companions behind him to support, inspire, and perhaps control him. When the companions met upon his death in 634 Omar's star was in the ascendant; and in the ten years of his chalifate he won in the opinion of his people the highest name which any Mohammedan ruler has attained. In truth, he made the empire. At the first choice of Abu Bekr for chalif it was but a horde of robbers in a province hitherto without name in history; when twelve years later Omar died by the hand of an assassin, it already rivalled the greatest empires of the world. To feel the profound contrast between the kingdom of Christ and the kingdom of Mohammed, we need but to consider the course of the first twelve years from the death of each founder. When the sword of Herod fell upon St. James, the son of thunder, the first of the apostles who was to seal his faith with his blood, and so fulfil his acceptance of his Lord's chalice, the kingdom of Christ had been preached among labours and trials innumerable. No one had yielded submission to it but in obedience to the inward dictate of conscience, and every one who so accepted it had suffered loss so far as this world is concerned. It was from imminent peril of death that when St. James, probably then the second in rank and influence of the apostolic band, was put to death, the first of all escaped from prison under angelic guard and went into another place to found the Roman Church. A martyrdom undergone by one apostle and a martyrdom postponed by another marked the setting up of St. Peter's pastoral staff in the capital of the Cæsars. The Christian people were everywhere then a poor, distressed, and praying people; hardly distinguished by the imperial Roman from the provincials of Judea, whom among all his subjects he most disliked. When Omar died, Antioch, Jerusalem, and Alexandria had fallen beneath his arms; the sepulchre of Christ was in his power; the patriarch of the holy city trembled lest the chalif of Mohammed should desecrate it to be a mosque by praying in it. Every Mohammedan convert received honour and wealth; everyone not converted to Mohammedanism risked honour and life, wife and child. The Christian martyr shed his blood on the scaffold; the Mohammedan martyr died in the heat of battle, and his companions received for the danger which they had risked and overcome the persons and goods of the conquered. Omar's empire stretched for thousands of miles over Africa and Asia; his authority was that of the prophet, who wielded civil power as an appendage of the spiritual, because, as he held, there could not be two swords in one sheath. The chief apostle exercised one of the greatest of his acts—that of choosing the capital of the Christian faith —when he was flying from a tyrant put in Jerusalem by the caprice of a Roman emperor. The arms were spiritual in one kingdom and material in the other; exercised with the long suffering of an apostle in one, with the unquestioned despotism in the other of a ruler who triumphed over souls by destroying bodies. The fundamental opposition which marks the two kingdoms is seen in strongest evidence during the first twelve years in each.

Hitherto, in human history, there is one man and one man only, who has matched himself with the Son of God: and not only matched himself, but declared that he was the superior; that the commission given to the Son of Mary was subordinate to the commission given to the Son of Abd Allah: that the prophet Jesus led up to the prophet Mohammed. It is certain that in the Mohammedan religion its prophet occupies the place which in the Christian religion is occupied by our Lord. But when this is said, it must be said with the understanding that "Mohammed's religion is a Judaism built stiffly on an abstract unity of God, stripped of its Messianic character, and of all the deeper spiritual elements which belong to that character".[1] When it is said that Mohammed has matched himself with Christ, it must be added that he has first stripped Christ of the divine Sonship, and placed Him simply as a prophet in a series of prophets, the last and greatest of whom is Mohammed himself. He has denied the Blessed Trinity: he has termed the honour paid by Christians to the Son, idolatry; he ranks Christians as idolaters for offering it,

[1] *Mohammed's Religion*, p. 4.

as being, incompatible with the unity of God. He denies the Incarnation on the Arian ground, that it is impossible for the one only Nature to generate or be generated. He has denied the fall of man, equally as he denies his restoration. He denies the passion of Christ, for unfallen man needs no such sacrifice as that of the Son of God offered upon the Cross. In the system set up by him there is no sacrifice. In that point of singular meaning it stands alone among the religions of the earth. Accordingly there is no priesthood. Mohammed claimed to exercise the prophetical and in it the regal power; but not the sacerdotal. There is none such in his religion. Such as it is, on an infinitely lower level than the Christian, Mohammed is the centre of it. From the Jewish and the Christian religions he took prayer, fasting, and almsgiving, likewise the doctrines of primary import, the unity of the godhead, the resurrection of man in body as well as spirit, to a final and eternal judgment of reward or punishment. That which came from himself is purely bad; a corruption affecting all the relations between the sexes, and reducing all those who live in his religion to a far worse condition, as respects those relations, than experienced by those who lived in Greek, or Roman, or German heathenism, at their worst. As the personal life of Mohammed, from the time of his claim to be the prophet of a new religion, was in this respect infamous, so is his religion. All that the Christian faith and Church, by the sufferings of unnumbered martyrs, and the wisdom of great pastors, who are the honour of human nature, had done in 600 years for the restoration of marriage, the creation of woman's worth and dignity, the whole fabric of the Christian home, the whole offspring of Nazareth, Bethlehem, and Calvary, Mohammed, by word and example, strove to overthrow. He embodied in his religion the revenge of Asia and Africa upon Christian purity: and the hand which established a pure Arian doctrine, as to the Godhead, destroyed the Christian wife and child, husband and father, so far as its malignant influence extended. So it was at the beginning: so it has been through the 1260 years: so it is now.

The whole movement of Mohammed was to establish a counter kingdom to that of Christ, of which he who lived as a sensualist from fifty to sixty years of age is the standard. His chalifs were its continuators. And while his instrument was conquest, the bait which keeps each successive generation, and defies the approach of the Christian faith, is the indulgence of those sensual enjoyments which marked the life of the founder from the time of the Flight, which has equally marked the conduct of the ruler and the rich during all the twelve centuries. The Mohammedan peasant may have a virtuous home, for the harem is beyond his means: he may be sparing, sober, and honest: but where is the Mohammedan ruler or rich man whose inner life will bear inspection? As Roman law stopped before entering the slave apartment, Mohammedan law stops before entering the women's apartment: while the mark of the chalif's supreme dignity is to have no wife, but concubines, in the very words of St. John Damascene, a thousand if he please. Has any false religion ever shown such a mark of imposture? or is any opposition to the Son of God so deep as this, so universal in its effect upon the whole character?

About a hundred years after the time of Mohammed there lived at the court of the chalif of Damascus the man who ranks as the last great Father of the eastern Church : who, indeed, anticipated in some degree in that Church the position afterwards held by St. Thomas Aquinas, in the West.[1] His father, Sergius, though a fervent Christian, held high office in the Syrian court. He purchased and set free captive Christians, and among them was a Thalian monk, named Cosmas, learned in theology and philosophy. Cosmas became teacher of his benefactor's son, John: and gave him such an education, that upon the death of his father the chalif made him one of the chiefs of his council, while Peter, bishop of Damascus, charged him to defend by writings the Christian truth against unbelievers.

He must have known well the religion of the chalif, in whose court he was a high officer. He thus speaks of Mohammed. "Down to the time of Heraclius the Saracens were avowed idolaters. Afterwards a false prophet arose among them, named Mamed. He lighted upon the Old and New Testament, and as the result of confabulations with a certain Arian monk constructed a heresy of his own. He gained by the appearance of piety influence with his people, and pretended that a

[1] Nirschl, iii. 612.

Scripture was brought down to him from heaven. Having put together in his book certain most absurd statements, he delivered to them a worship.

"He says there is one God, the Creator of all things, who is neither begotten nor begetting. He says that Christ is the Word and Spirit of God, a creature and a servant: and that He was born without a father from Mary, the sister of Moses and Aaron. For, says he, the Word and Spirit of God entered Mary, and she bore Jesus a prophet and servant of God. The Jews wickedly wished to crucify Him: they seized and crucified His shadow. But Christ Himself, he says, was not crucified, nor did He die. For God took Him to Himself into Heaven, for He loved Him. And this, he says, that when Christ ascended into Heaven, God asked Him: 'Jesus, didst Thou say, I am the Son of God, and God?' And he says, Jesus answered, 'Lord, pardon me. Thou knowest that I never said it, nor am too proud to be Thy servant. But men that were transgressors wrote it, that I said this word, and they lied against Me, and are in error'. And God answered and said to Him: 'I know that Thou didst not say this word'. Now he said many other portentous and ridiculous things in this Scripture of his, which he pretends to have been sent down to him from God. Now when we allege, who is the witness that God gave him a Scripture? Which of the prophets foretold that such a prophet was to arise? Moses received the law from God in the sight of all the people, when he appeared on Mount Sinai, in cloud, and fire, and darkness, and storm. And all the prophets from Moses onwards foretold the coming of Christ, and that Christ is God, and that the Son of God would come in the flesh, and would be crucified, and die, and rise again, and that He is the Judge of the living and the dead. And when we ask, why did not your prophet come so, others bearing witness to him. Why did not God, as He gave the law to Moses in the sight of the people on the smoking mountain, give the Scripture which you speak of to him in your presence, that you also may be assured. They answer, God does what He will. We reply, that we know well. But we ask how the Scripture came down to your prophet. And they answer, the Scripture came down upon him when he was sleeping.

"Again we ask, how is it, when in this Scripture of yours he enjoined to do nothing, and to receive nothing without witnesses, that you did not ask him, first show by witnesses that you are a prophet, and have come forth from God, and what Scripture bears witness to you? They are mute through shame. Since you may not marry without witnesses, nor market, nor possess, nor take an ass or beast of burden without witness. Wives, indeed, you have, and possessions, and asses, and all the rest through witnesses. Faith alone and Scripture you have without a witness. He who gave you this has no security whatever. No witness preceding him is known: but he received it asleep. They call us associators, because we bring in an associate to God, when we say that Christ is the Son of God, and

God. We reply, prophets and Scripture have handed this down to us. You, as you assert, acknowledge prophets. If we are wrong in saying that Christ is Son of God, it is they who have taught it and delivered it to us."

The objection here made in general, that Mohammed had no witness to his mission, and none to the assertion that his Scripture came from God, has received no answer. Indeed, not only is there no witness that the Koran was given by God, or by the agency of the prophet Gabriel, but the condition in which it was left by Mohammed at his death supplies the strongest internal evidence that the Scripture was an imposture. This is the account given by the historian of the present day, who has used thirty years of his life to study, and compare Mohammedan writers on their prophet.[1]

"The Koran is the Arabic name for the Mohammedan Bible, or collection of discourses held by Mohammed in the name of God, in his quality as inspired prophet, which, as he asserts, were partly communicated through the angel Gabriel, partly revealed to him immediately by God through dreams or visions. But the Koran is not, like the Bible, a book drawn up in chronological order, or according to the variety of its contents, but a mixing up of hymns, prayers, dogmas, sermons, casual writings, narratives, legends, laws, and orders of the day, with many repetitions and contradictions. This comes because Mohammed himself made no collection of the revelations given singly to him during a course

[1] Weil, *Islamitische Völker*, 26-29, *der Koran*. Translated.

of twenty-three years. It is probable that it was not even his wish that all of them should be kept, since a great number of them had only a transitory meaning. Likewise he had undertaken so many alterations in his doctrines and laws that he had reason to shrink from handing them all down to posterity. In fine he certainly wished to retain up to his death free room for modifications and additions which might be necessary. But after his death all fragments of the revelation were thrown together, even when they had been repealed by others, or were already issued in different form. All portions of the Koran, scattered in different hands, inscribed on parchment, palm-leaves, bones, stones, or other rough materials for writing, were collected—or even such as lived only in the remembrance of his companions and disciples—and were divided, mostly without regard to their contents, or the time at which they had been revealed, into greater or smaller chapters, Suras; and thus the actual Koran, with all its defects, was made. It is only by an accurate knowledge of the circumstances of Mohammed's life, and the language of the Koran, in some degree possible to restore the chronological order of its several parts. By the help of Mohammed's Arabian biographers, some of whom go back so far as the second century of the Mohammedan era, it is possible to determine the date of such sections as relate to historical events. Where this is not the case, the character and form of the revelation serve to direct. Mohammed in his first time appears more as a reformer, later as the founder of a new religion, at last

as prince and legislator. In the first period he was
carried away by inward enthusiasm: his language has a
rythmical movement, with true poetic colouring. In
the second period a calmer consideration takes the place
of excited fancy; he is more rhetorician than poet: his
words spring rather from an understanding wide awake,
not sparkling, as before, with warmth of heart. In the
third period the language sinks to sober prose, not only
in ordaining laws, issuing injunctions, or narrating campaigns, but when he paints, as before, God's Almightiness, the wonders of creation, the terrors of the last
judgment, or the joys of paradise.

"The Koran was first collected by the chalif Abu Bekr.
This collection is said to have been occasioned by the
death of many acquainted with the Koran in the war
against the rival prophet, Moseilama, and the fear that
there would soon no longer be men who had learnt it
by heart and understood it. A certain Zeid who had
served the prophet as secretary was charged to collect
the revelations, and when he had completed his work,
he gave it over to the chalif, from whose hand after his
death it passed into that of his successor, Omar. Omar
left it to his daughter Hafsah, widow of Mohammed.
Zeid's work aimed merely at providing a copy of all the
scattered fragments. No thought seems as yet to have
been taken to arrange them in order or to divide them
into chapters. This collection had as yet no public
authority, for other fragments were in circulation, which
varied from it more or less, so that there were often
disputations about the true reading of particular pas-

sages. To meet this state of things, so dangerous to the unity of the faith and the law, Chalif Osman caused a new edition of the Koran to be prepared. The collection made by Abu Bekr formed the basis of this. Osman sent copies of this edition to the chief cities of the subject provinces, and caused all versions varying from it to be destroyed. The division of the Koran into 114 chapters dates from Osman. In this, however, as above remarked, neither subject nor order of time was sufficiently considered. The sequence was generally determined by the size of the chapters, the larger being put at the head, and the smaller at the close. The Koran of Osman now stood for the ground text of the divine revelation. If later further copies led to variations of the text, they spring from the incompleteness of the Kufish writing, which continued in use for several hundred years. In this not only were the vowel marks wanting, but the diacritic points which served to distinguish from each other several similar letters.

"The Koran contains subjects of highly mixed character. It embraces not only the whole doctrine and legislation of Mohammed, but likewise a considerable portion of his life, of his mental and material struggles, as well as the history of prophets preceding him, and the legends concerning them."

Thus in the year 632 a robber who was compelling the whole Arabian people to submit to his authority had somewhat suddenly died. His companions, robbers like himself, met together after his death. They proclaimed the dead chieftain " to be supreme teacher of religion, and, in that capacity, law-giver over the whole extent of the social, civil, and political domain ".[1] They elected one of themselves to continue this authority by the name of chalif, or successor. In this act I note four things. The successor is not taken out of Mohammed's family, but by free choice of the faithful. Secondly, he is chosen as a spiritual head : but this headship carries in itself the whole temporal power. Thirdly, the place of Mohammed among his own faithful, corresponds to the place of Christ in his Church, if we bear in mind all the differences which distinguish the two communities. Fourthly, the chalif in the Mohammedan community corresponds to the Pope in the Christian. He is the successor of Mohammed, God's Apostle, as the Pope is the successor of St. Peter. The chalif is the bearer of Mohammedanism, as Mohammed's vicegerent : the Pope is the bearer of Christendom, as the vicegerent of Christ, and the spiritual Peter. As Christ and Mohammed answer to each other in religions radically antagonistic to each other, so Pope answers to chalif, with the same requisite differences.

It is to be noted that Christendom and Islam coincide as to the time of their rise. A Catholic Church there had been through all the six preceding centuries. But the allegiance of different bodies politic to one Christian faith and legislation was only beginning when Mohammed arose. The various kingdoms which the Teuton races were forming in all the countries of the West drew their common spiritual life from the Pope in Rome.

[1] Döllinger, *Mohammed's Religion*, p. 7.

The eastern emperor was becoming one of many sovereigns who acknowledged the authority of Peter. If Heraclius thought himself to wield the one sovereignty displayed by Justinian, he was undeceived before his death. If his grandson kidnapped a Pope out of his Lateran Church and Palace, and then martyred him as a traitor to his absolute power, the isles of the West were looking upon him at the same time as the bestower to them of the Christian faith, and of all the blessings which that faith brought with it to their civil life. St. Wilfrid spoke to the Northumbrian king concerning the doorkeeper of the kingdom of heaven. The king listened and obeyed. Thus the roots of Christendom were sprouting in France and Spain and Britain at the moment that Omar guided the suffrages of Mohammed's companions to choose the aged Abu Bekr for his successor. From that time these powers are formed over against each other in perpetual contrast and antagonism. The union of the two powers in Islam becomes the centre of a complete despotism. The distinction of the two powers in Christendom—which Pope Gelasius had marked with so much emphasis to the encroaching emperor Anastasius a hundred and forty years before—which St. Martin exercised at the cost of his life in the time of the third chalif—was the pledge and guarantee to Christendom of authority, supreme but temperate, of spiritual rule protecting civil liberty. A long succession of Popes—at the mercy of eastern despots as to civil matters—maintain their spiritual independence and their guidance of that new assemblage of nations in a common Christendom through the terrible seventh century. At the same moment Northern Africa, and Egypt, and Syria fall passively into the hands of the chalifate, and Byzantium loses the half of its power and trembles for its own existence.

How vast in its importance for future ages the establishment of the chalifate upon the death of Mohammed was, may be seen from the following considerations.[1] It cannot be denied that the absolutely despotic form of government in lands under the sway of Mohammed has been created by the influence of the religion. It has indeed often been maintained that the genius of Asiatic peoples specially produces this form of rule. But states which are not Mohammedan rest on quite a different basis: and their rulers are or were subject to great and essential limitations. A Hindu king who reigned under the laws of Manu could not break through the immunities of the Brahmins, or the separation of the castes. An emperor of China, though he be called the son of heaven, and his throne be approached only with forms of the deepest submission, can name no officer except according to the list of candidates provided by the learned order. Not so the Princes of the Faithful. Two elements here concur to produce the most complete form of despotism: the mixing together or more properly unification of the spiritual and the temporal power; and the military power resting on conquest. According as the theocratic or the military principle prevailed, the sovereignty would take a distinct colouring: the

[1] Döllinger, *Mohammed's Religion*, 38-40.

despotism assume a milder or a sterner aspect. When, as in the case of the Arabian chalifs, and in a certain degree of the Turkish sultans since Selim, the religious character prevailed, and the political power, in accordance with the original spirit of Islam, appeared only as an issue and endowment of the spiritual, the unconditional submission would take more of a religious and conscientious devotedness. Then the dynasty, clothed in the divinity which hedges a king, could enjoy greater stability and security : the ruler himself, reminded ever of his consecrated character, of the duties and the higher responsibility which lay upon him, would make through regard for the prescriptions of religion a more moderate use of an authority in itself unlimited. Where, on the contrary, the spirit of an arbitrary military lordship prevailed, as in most of the kingdoms formed after the overthrow of the chalifate in Central Asia, the blind obedience of the subject would rather be the result of fear and custom. An attempt to overthrow the possessor of supreme power, with the self-same violence by means of which he had raised himself to it, would appear at once as allowable and attractive. Thence would follow more frequent change of dynasty, indifference to it on the part of the population, continual suspicion, and tyrannical exercise of even the bloodiest means to put down every opposing force.

Thus the government of the Ottoman kingdom did not take that character of brutal tyranny which marks the history of Persia. The Persian king is so absolutely lord of the life and property of his subjects, that a sentence even issued in a drunken revel without the least formality receives immediate execution. A Persian proverb truly says : To be near the shah is to be near a burning fire. The general view that a king is naturally tyrannical and unjust has passed into the very language, so that a complainant for the strongest expression of the wrong which he has suffered says : He played the king over me. Thus the learned in the law maintain that the king's commands are superior to the right of nature, they only yield to a positive divine command. The lordship of the Ottoman sultans, though resting on the same principle of unlimited power, appears on the whole milder and more moderate. Here too, as the founder of the line declared, all property belongs to the sultan ; here also " the slave's neck is thinner than a hair," and all subjects rank as the sultan's slaves, and even call themselves so : here too the sultan's mother calls her son " my lion " or " my tiger," and Moslim name the sultan not only " the Shadow of God," or " the Refuge of the World," but also " the Executioner, the Slayer," since he alone possesses the absolute right over the life of all. Turkish doctors ascribe to him also a holy character not to be effaced by any immorality. If his actions shew a scorn of all admitted conceptions of justice or prudence, yet in force of a Mohammedan fiction it is assumed that he does much or most of this in consequence of a divine suggestion, and therefore that his motives can neither be discerned nor judged by men. In the same spirit the learned in the law maintain that the sultan can put to death every day fourteen persons, without giving reason, or lying under imputation of tyranny. Whoever receives death without resistance from his hand or by his order becomes thereby a martyr, and many of his servants are said to have striven after the honour of such a death as a secure pledge of eternal happiness. A tyrannical power such as this as a rule naturally strikes those only who stand near the throne. The members of his own family, the higher officers of state, fall victims to it. The mass of the people seldom feels such direct effects of their despot. Here the principle holds, the higher the dignity, the more perfect the confidence, the greater the danger. The grand visiers, the other selves of the sultans in temporal matters have experienced this. A hundred and eighty statesmen have held this highest office of the kingdom from 1370 to 1789: most of them therefore scarcely more than two years. Many have been executed after a short time. One of the most esteemed Mohammedan princes, Soliman the Magnificent, executed during his government, one after the other, most of the men on whose shoulders he had laid the most important works and the highest offices of his kingdom. An instinct of obedience, an inclination to unconditional absolute subjection under absolute authority prevails among Mohammedans, to which the utmost cruelty appears endurable, the utmost perversity natural.

It must be added that the Sultan of Morocco unites the spiritual, and the temporal power, as sheriff, that is descendant of the prophet through Hosein and Ali. He is a despot as absolute as the king of Persia. All depends upon his will. He makes, alters, suppresses, and restores laws. He changes them according to his humour, convenience, or interests. Here there is no body of Ulema, no Mufti clothed with an authority independent of the sovereign, no divan, colleges, or ministerial departments. All follows the single command of the ruler.

The nature of the supreme authority in these three Moslem empires speaks at the present day of its origin in the person of Mohammed.

What we see is this. The misuse of Cæsarean power in applying to the Church of God, which from the beginning by divine order was independent, a supremacy in spiritual things not belonging to the civil ruler, is allowed by Divine Providence to call forth a far more terrible despotism, in the guise of a false prophet who invents a religion of which he is to be the apostle, and then claims all power, spiritual and temporal, as belonging to him in the character of apostle, and the use of force as the means of propagation. That despotism is allowed to seize for permanent occupation the richest provinces of the eastern empire, and to make its capital in fear of perpetual subjection. But it is also used to check the imperial usurpation over the Church, and to begin an era, now lasting for twelve centuries and a half, in which two religions, and two forms of government springing from these religions, stand over against each other in perpetual and irreconcilable opposition.

The structure of the Church was vehemently shaken by the earthquake[1] which attended the pouring out of

---
[1] *Mohammed's Religion*, p. 141.

Islam upon the south-eastern and southern countries of the former Roman empire. It had to be seen whether the whole fabric would maintain itself upon its foundation of rock when such mighty portions of its structure were torn by main force away. Moslem writers say, when the locust swarm darkened vast countries, they bore on their wings these Arabic words:—" We are God's host, each of us has nine and ninety eggs; and if we had a hundred we should lay waste the world with all that is in it ".

The hundredth egg has never been granted, but if the assassin's stroke had not carried off Chalif Omar in 644, and again Chalif Osman in the year 656, and again Chalif Ali in the year 661, perhaps the desolation might have been fully accomplished; as also if the chalifate, created by election in 632, had not become within thirty years a mere hereditary kingdom, in which rival pretenders and rival families exhausted the strength of Islam by perpetual conflicts. The empire of the sword has also illustrated the divine decree: "All that take the sword shall perish with the sword ".

CHAPTER V.

OLD ROME AND NEW ROME.

THE seizure of Pope St. Martin in his Lateran Church by the exarch of Ravenna, Kalliopas, under order from the Emperor Constans II., his secret deportation to Constantinople, his trial before the Senate as guilty of high treason, his condemnation to death, and subsequent death in the Crimea from hardship or starvation, with the election of Pope Eugenius during his lifetime by the Roman clergy through dread of a Monothelite being forced upon them by the Byzantine; all this marks probably the lowest point of civil depression and helplessness to which the Papacy was ever reduced in those momentous three centuries which run from Genseric to Aistulf, from 455 to 755. The emperor who committed acts so mean, perfidious, and cruel was reigning over an empire already cut in two by the sword of Mohammed's chalif. How little he had heeded the chastisement we learn from an incident in the trial of the great eastern confessor, St. Maximus, which I have already recorded, but to which I recur that I may exhibit the full insolence of the eastern despot, as well as his blindness. Theodosius, the consul, coming straight out from the emperor's cabinet, with the condemnation of Maximus in his hand, addressed him in these words :[1] " Learn, Sir Abbot, that when we get a little relief from this rout of heathens (that is, of the Saracens who had stripped Constans of Syria, Egypt, Mesopotamia, and North Africa as far as Kairowan), by the Holy Trinity we will bring you to terms, and your Pope, who is now lifted up, and all the talkers there, and the rest of your disciples ; and we will *cook* you all, each in his own place, as Martin has been cooked ".

These words were spoken on the 14th December, 656.[2] The Pope Eugenius was the Pope alluded to in them, and it is inferred from them that he rejected those terms of union which the emperor was seeking to impose and which the nuntios were willing to accept. The martyrdom of St. Martin had taken place on the 16th September of the preceding year, 655.

It was the providence of God that the chalif himself never allowed the sworn protector of the Church who sat on the eastern throne to execute this threat. Rather he was all through this century in dread lest the Mohammedan, having fixed his throne at Damascus, should advance it to Constantinople. It was again the providence of God that Constantinople itself should not fall during this time of its utmost weakness, and so open

[1] πλὴν ἵνα ἰδῇς κύρι᾽ ᾽Αββᾶ, ὅτι μικρὰν ἄνεσιν ἐὰν λάβωμεν ἐκ τῆς συγχύσεως τῶν ἐθνῶν, ἁρμόσασθαι ὑμῖν ἔχομεν μὰ τὴν ἁγίαν τριάδα, καὶ τὸν Πάπαν τὸν νῦν ἐπαιρόμενον, καὶ πάντας τοὺς ἐκεῖσε λαλοῦντας, καὶ τοὺς λοιποὺς σου μαθητὰς καὶ πάντας ὑμᾶς χωνεύομεν ἕκαστον ἐν τῷ ἐπιτηδείῳ αὐτοῦ τόπῳ, ὡς ἐχωνεύθη Μαρτῖνος.—Gallandi, tom. xiii. 73.

[2] Hefele, iii. 223.

the whole of northern Europe to Mohammedan domination. The city of Constantine was then the material rampart which stopped the impetuous current of Saracen invasion to the north. The chalif Muawiah, who reigned over the immense Saracen empire from 661 to 680, was strong enough continually to beat the Emperor, to ravage his Asiatic territory, to advance towards his capital, but he was never able to take it. The advance of the seat of the Saracenic empire from the remote Medina to the near and beautiful Damascus, the paradise of eastern cities, dwelling in its perpetual garden among ever-flowing waters of Abana and Pharpar, was itself a sign how the empire had fallen. A religion founded on the denial of the Christian faith, of which it was, moreover, the special rival, had full possession of the once Roman and Christian East. Muawiah became chalif on the death of Ali in 661. He had conducted the civil war against Ali, which distracted for five years the Saracen power, with the forces of Syria, as its governor; and when he became supreme made it the capital of his empire.

Constans II., having crowned with martyrdom the greatest confessor of the West, Pope Martin, and the greatest confessor of the East, St. Maximus, resolved in the year 662, to visit the West. The tyranny of Constans in regard to the Pope was not completed even by his treatment of St. Martin. When he had condemned this Pope, but before he had caused his death he is supposed to have compelled the Roman clergy to elect another Pope. This was Eugenius, who was recognised in the year 654 for Pope, while St. Martin was yet alive.[1] Whether the urgency and threats of the imperial ministers overcame at length the constancy of the clergy, or whether, as is more probable, they feared to see some heretic sent by the emperor to occupy the throne of St. Peter, they elected Eugenius, by birth a Roman, a person of great goodness and holy life, who held the See two years and eight months. The synodical letter of Peter, the fourth Monothelite patriarch of Constantinople in succession was sent to him, but being obscure in its expressions about our Lord, was sent back with indignity.[2] It would seem that the exceeding danger of the time caused the election and consecration of Pope Eugenius in the lifetime of St. Martin, to pass for legitimate. Eugenius died in 657, and was succeeded by Pope Vitalian, after a vacancy of a month and 29 days.

Pope Eugenius had not acknowledged either of the patriarchs Paulus or Peter by writing to them, but Vitalian sent his nuntios to Constans to announce his accession to the papacy by his synodical letter. Constans received them graciously, acknowledged the privileges of the Roman Church, and sent by them to St. Peter at Rome a copy of the gospels bound in golden covers and studded with diamonds. Vitalian, says Anastasius, preserved in all respects the ecclesiastical rule and vigour.

Constans had a brother named Theodosius, whom he

[1] Muratori, *Annali d'Italia*, A.D. 654.
[2] Muratori, *Annali d'Italia*, A.D. 655.

forced to become a deacon, and he had repeatedly
received from his hands the chalice of the Lord's Blood.
Afterwards he caused him to be murdered. He was
said to have often dreamt of his victim, offering him a
chalice full of blood, with the words : " Brother, drink ".
The stings of conscience and the hatred of the people
for his cruelty and his protection of heresy, were supposed
to drive him from his capital.

The book of the Popes under its notice of the life of
Vitalian says :[1] " In his time the emperor came from the
royal city by coast to Athens, thence to Tarentum,
Beneventum, and Naples. At Rome he arrived on the 5th
July. The Apostolical went out with his clergy to the
sixth milestone from the city to receive him. The same
day the emperor went to pray at St. Peter's, and offered
his gift. On Saturday he went to St. Mary's and also
offered his gift. On Sunday he went in procession
with his army to St. Peter's. All went out with wax
candles to meet him, and he offered on the altar a golden
woven pall, and Mass was celebrated. Again on Saturday the emperor came to the Lateran, took a bath, and
dined in the Julian basilica. On Sunday there was a
station at St. Peter's, and after celebration of Mass the
emperor and the pontiff took leave of each other.
Twelve days he remained in the Roman city. Every
bronze statue which ornamented the city he took down,
nay, and he unroofed of its brazen tiles the Church of
Blessed Mary at the Martyrs, and sent all things which
he had taken to the royal city. Then on Monday he

[1] Mansi, xi. 13.

left Rome and returned to Naples. Then he went by land to Rhegium and entered Sicily. He lived in the city of Syracuse, and caused much affliction to the people, the inhabitants or proprietors of Calabria, Sicily, Africa, and Sardinia, by his exactions during many years such as had never been.[1] He separated even wives from their husbands, and sons from their fathers, and they suffered many other unheard of things, so that a man had not hope of life. They took even the sacred vessels and ornaments of God's holy churches, and left nothing."

The visit of Constans to Rome casts a strong light upon the condition of things in a century concerning which we are singularly destitute of detailed information.

When Constans landed with a certain force at Tarentum, he found the Lombards in possession of the duchy of Beneventum. A legend said that their king Autharis after a bold march through the Peninsula to the Straits of Messina, had spurred his horse into the sea and exclaimed, "This shall be the Lombard boundary". But his successors had never made good the words of Autharis. Naples and Amalfi, Sorrentum, Gaeta, and Tarentum had imperial governors. Alboin however made a duchy of Beneventum which then included the ancient Samnium and Apulia, and portions of Campania and Lucania. It was a stronghold of Lombard robbers in southern Italy. Constans tried to expel the young duke Romuald. But he failed, and hearing that King

---

[1] See Muratori, A.D. 665, who quotes from Paulus Diaconus, lib. 5, ch. xi. p. 336 and 366.

Grimoald was approaching to aid his son, he went to Naples, left at Formiæ, the present Mola di Gaeta, 20,000 men, and marched on Rome by the Appian Way.

Pope Vitalian went out to meet him as legitimate Roman emperor. It was true that ten years before he had seized Pope St. Martin in his church, and carried him off by stealth to trial, suffering, and ultimate martyrdom in the Crimea. It was true likewise that while holding St. Martin in prison, he had repeated the evil deed committed by Justinian's empress Theodora, a hundred and sixteen years before, and compelled the Roman clergy under threat of worse things to elect a new Pope while the Pope was living, though in this case the elected was himself blameless and excellent. It is true, also, that later still he had treated the great confessor Maximus with equal cruelty. But these crimes did not prevent his being the actual emperor to whom loyal submission was due from the great throne of justice in the earth. It would seem also by the mode in which Constans had received the nuntios who bore Pope Vitalian's synodical letter, announcing his accession, and by the superb present which he sent back in acknowledgement, that somehow a better spirit prevailed at the moment towards the Pope. We are met indeed by the fact that the Monothelite patriarch Peter held the see of Constantinople for twelve years from the death of the re-established Pyrrhus in 654, to his own death in 666, being the fourth heretic in succession from Sergius in the see of the royal city. Constans approached Rome at the head of an army. He made his offerings as emperor to the three great churches of Rome, the Lateran, St. Peter's and St. Mary Major. The Pope was completely at his mercy. He lodged in the imperial palace on the Palatine, which, however great its desolation, was able at least to receive him. In his twelve days sojourn he laid his hands upon every bronze statue which he thought worth plundering: and he stripped of its costly roof the church which his predecessor sixty years before had given to the Pope, dedicated to the Mother of God and all Martyrs.

Such a visit accompanied by such acts give a lively picture of the regard entertained by a Byzantine emperor for the city which gave him his title. It sums up the hundred and ten years of abject servitude into which all Italy had fallen since the capture of the city by Narses under Justinian. We have the contemptuous despot, the long-suffering Pope, the half-ruined powerless city. Three hundred and six years had passed since the degenerate son of Constantine, when he came to Rome in 357, was amazed at the beauty of its great buildings, the forum of Trajan, the theatre of Pompey, the unequalled Flavian amphitheatre. But in Constans the memories of Rome were dead: he robbed the last relic of its grandeur, Agrippa's pantheon, nor was he ready to reverence the protection of the Blessed Virgin over the Church dedicated to her by the Pope on receiving it as the gift of a preceding emperor. These last spoils he had embarked for his royal city, but they were detained at Syracuse, and on its capture shortly afterwards by the Saracens fell into their hands.

But before this event the life and misdeeds of the emperor Constans II. had come to a sudden end. He was living in Ortygia, the sole remaining quarter of that once princely city, wherein Achradyna, Tyche, Neapolis, and Epipolæ lay desolate. He had entered his bath one day, and received in it a blow on his head by his attendant, whether a slave, or a conspirator. His courtiers when they at length came in found him dead. The Greek chronologist Theophanes alleges as a reason for this event that after his murder of his brother he became greatly hated at Constantinople, both for his persecution of Pope Martin and Maximus, "that most wise confessor, whose tongue he cut out, and whose hands he cut off, and condemned many of the orthodox with tortures, banishments, and confiscations, because they would not submit to his heresy". In his dread he had wished to transfer his residence to the West, but this his counsellors prevented. His treatment of the Sicilians was so bad that some in despair went to settle at Damascus, though it had become the capital of the chalif.

So lived and so died the grandson of Heraclius, Constans II., "Roman emperor and Christian prince"[1] from 642 to 668, in the times when the chalifs of Mohammed, Omar, Osman, Ali, and Muawiah carved the Saracen realm out of the empire which Heraclius had possessed, and out of the kingdom of the "Great

---

[1] The words in which Pope Felix III. addressed Zeno, the first who became sole ruler after the cessation of the western empire. See above Vol. vi. p. 80.

King," whom Heraclius, when bearing the standard of the cross had brought low. If Heraclius treated Syria and Egypt as Constans treated Rome and Italy, is not the wonder diminished that in the ten years of Omar the structure of Roman power which had lasted seven centuries was overthrown, and those provinces had received a Mohammedan instead of a Byzantine master? Muawiah at Damascus cherished the Syria which at Antioch the lord on the Bosphorus had ground down with taxes. The Rome also which Constans, when he had been welcomed as its emperor, left stripped of its last ornaments was regarded with veneration by the farthest isle of the West, which it was winning at once to civilised and to Christian life. An English authority tells us that five years after the visit of Constans, Pope Vitalian, in the twelfth year of his pontificate, on the 26th March, 668, consecrated a monk of Tarsus, then living at Rome, learned both in secular and divine literature, speaking both Greek and Latin, of holy life, and venerable in age, being sixty-six years old. Thus Theodore was sent to be Archbishop of Canterbury. He was received in his passage through France by the Archbishop of Arles, and the bishop of Paris. He reached his see in the following year, 669, and sat in it full twenty-one years.[1] St. Bede's account of him says that he went over the whole island, wheresoever there were English, was received by all most cordially, and obeyed, when he gave them a right order of life, and the canonical celebration of Easter, which he spread

[1] Hist., iv. 1-2.

abroad. St. Bede adds that he was the first among the archbishops whom the whole Church of the English consented to obey. His friend Adrian, who had recommended him to the Pope, and accompanied him from Rome, attended him in England: they had a large number of disciples, whom they instructed not only in theology, but in music, astronomy, and arithmetic. St. Bede wrote forty years after the death of Theodore, and says, " Even at this day there survive persons taught by them, who know the Greek and Latin languages as well as their own. Nor from the time the English came to Britain were there ever happier times, since, possessing kings most valiant and at the same time Christian, they were a terror to all barbarous nations; and the vows of all men tended to the joys of the heavenly kingdom but newly revealed to them; and all who wished to be instructed in the sacred lessons had masters ready to teach them."

Constans was succeeded by his son Constantine IV. after he had put down in Sicily a short-lived rebellion. He did not imitate his father's violent deeds: he did not wish to maintain by force the Typus, which was still in legal existence. Pope Vitalian had done him service in his struggle with the usurper, and made use of his favourable sentiments to proceed with more decision against the Monothelites.

The Monothelite patriarch Peter had died in 666, two years before Constans. The three following patriarchs, Thomas II., John V., and Constantine, inclined to orthodoxy. They occupied together only nine years, from 667 to 676. The Sixth Council left their names in the diptychs. Yet so great was the power which the Monothelites possessed in the capital that Constantine Pogonatus, though not a Monothelite, and much wishing to be reconciled with the Roman Church, thought it dangerous at the beginning of his government to alter the state of things ; and the Typus, as law imposed by the State, was not abrogated. The next patriarch, Theodore, in 676 was again Monothelite, and he was, though moderate himself, induced by Makarius, patriarch of Antioch, to erase from the diptychs the names of all the Popes since Honorius.

Pope Vitalian, after an admirable pontificate of fourteen years and a half, had died in 672, and was succeeded by the Roman, Adeodatus, who sat four years, and he by Pope Donus, also a Roman, in 676. Donus died in 678, and was followed by Agatho, a Sicilian of Palermo.

During seven years, which end in 678, the Emperor Constantine was fighting a battle of life or death with the Saracen chalif Muawiah for Constantinople itself. Every year during several months the Saracen fleet was in the waters of the Bosphorus. They had taken the city of Cyzikus and wintered there, renewing the contest in the spring. During seven years they continued to do this. Had they taken the city the whole Christian empire in the East would have fallen. It is hard to limit the ruin which would have ensued to the Christian Church. But in weighing the events of this century the extreme peril in which the Church lay through the furious outburst of the Saracens should not be forgotten. On this occasion the Greek fire is said to have been first used. By it, as water would not extinguish it, many ships and their crews were destroyed. After this conflict of seven years, the Saracens having lost a great multitude of men, at last retired, owning that they were defeated. Their fleet in retiring met with a great tempest, and in a battle also which took place with three imperial commanders the Saracens lost 30,000 men. Muawiah, the chalif, treated for peace with the emperor, and it was concluded on glorious terms for the empire. This victory led the northern Avars also to treat the emperor with deference.[1]

Thus the emperor was enabled to execute his wish for the restoration of communion with the West. He addressed a letter to Pope Donus on the 12th August, 678, requesting him to send commissioners to Constantinople to make arrangements for a Council to be held there. Pope Donus had died in 678 and this letter was received by his successor, Agatho. He desired the whole West on this occasion to be called to council, and for that purpose caused particular synods to be held everywhere. During this year Theodore, the patriarch of Constantinople, was deposed, it is not known on what grounds, but he was indisposed to union with the West. In his stead George was chosen, who at first was on the Monothelite side, but, instructed by the testimonies of the Fathers and the synods at Rome, which were read in

---

[1] The facts from Photius.

the Sixth Council, he attached himself strongly to the orthodox.

Pope Agatho, waiting for many bishops, among them English, to come to Rome, only held in March, 680, his synod of 125 bishops in preparation for the Council to be held in Constantinople, and to name legates to attend it. This was a great Council of the western patriarchate, which had been preceded by smaller Councils in the several provinces, as, for instance, Milan. Agatho and the council sent two letters to the emperor, which developed the creed of the Church according to the Lateran Council of 649, and signified its acceptance as necessary to all believers. The priests Theodore and George, the deacon John, and the sub-deacon Constantine were appointed legates for the Roman Church; the Bishops Abundantius of Paterno, John of Porto, and John of Reggio as deputies for the Council; and the priest Theodore to represent Ravenna. Agatho described these commissioners, not as learned theologians, for the confusion of the times made such very rare. His words run, "How can perfect knowledge of the Scriptures be found in men who live in the midst of heathens and get their support by manual labour with the greatest difficulty? but we maintain whatever has been defined by our apostolic predecessors and the Five Councils in simplicity of heart as the unambiguous faith descending from our fathers".[1]

Theodore, Archbishop of Canterbury, had been invited by the Pope to attend his Council at Rome, but was un-

[1] Jaffé, p. 167, who refers to Mansi, xi. 179.

able to come. In the preceding year, 679, St. Wilfrid, Bishop of York, was heard at the Lateran on his appeal in a Council of 16 bishops and restored to his see.[1]

The legates were honourably received in the capital and lodged in the Placidia Palace. After their arrival on the 10th September, 680, the emperor invited the patriarch George, of Constantinople, and through him Makarius, of Antioch, to call to council the metropolitans subject to them. At first the court had not thought of the sees of Alexandria and Jerusalem, which were under Saracen domination. But before the Council entered on deliberation two regular priests, Peter and George, were found, the first to represent Alexandria, the last to stand in the place of Theodore, vicar of the patriarchate of Jerusalem. It would seem that it was as well through this representation of the other sees, as also because of what Pope Agatho had done, that the Council which now met, though it had not been the original purpose of the emperor, from its beginning was marked as ecumenical, and afterwards took rank as the Sixth of these with the Five preceding.

The Council was held from the 7th November, 680, to the 16th September, 681, in the hall called the Dome of the Imperial Palace, under the presidency of the papal legates and the imperial presidency of honour. The Emperor, with many officers of State, was present at the first eleven sessions, and with them directed the external order of business ; but both he and they were carefully distinguished from the members of the Council, whose

---

[1] See Hergenröther, *Kirchen-grochichte*, i. p. 365.

numbers did not at first reach a hundred, but afterwards rose to 174.

In the first session, the 7th September, the Roman deputies, in an address to the emperor, desired that those who represented the Byzantine Church would declare the origin of the innovation which had existed in it for more than forty years. Macarius and his associates appealed to the earlier General Councils and to the Fathers. Thereupon the acts of the Council of Ephesus were read. There was found in them nothing in favour of the Monothelites, for the words of Cyril, that the will of Christ was almighty, could only be referred to His divine nature. In the second session, on the 10th November, the acts of the Council of Chalcedon were read, which were entirely unfavourable to the heresy. Macarius in vain attempted to insist on the words "theandric operation" without determining their meaning. On the reading the acts of the Fifth Council, at the third sitting, the 13th November, the writing of Mennas to Vigilius and two alleged letters of the latter were admitted to be spurious. The Monothelites could show nothing for themselves out of the General Councils. They had now to seek proof from the writings of the Fathers. They begged for time, and, on the proposition of George of Constantinople, the letters of Agatho and the Roman Council were ordered to be read, which occupied the fourth session, on the 15th November. In the fifth and sixth sessions, of the 7th December, 680, and the 12th February, 681, Macarius proposed passages from the writings of Fathers in behalf of his doctrine, but it was shown that they were mostly falsified or imperfectly quoted or indecisive. At the seventh session, 13th February, 681, the Roman collection of passages from the Fathers in support of the doctrine of Two Wills and Two Operations was read against the others. George and Macarius received copies of them. While Macarius remained obstinate, George was convinced of the correctness of the doctrine set forth in the papal letters, and on the 17th February he gave in a confession to the Roman legates in which the Two Wills and the Two Operations were expressly acknowledged. When, then, the emperor at the eighth session, on the 7th March, questioned the bishops on their accession to the letters of Agatho, not only George of Constantinople admitted this, who requested and obtained from the emperor the reinsertion of Pope Vitalian into the diptychs of his Church, but also Theodore of Ephesus, Sisinnius of Heraklea, Domitius of Prusias, and other bishops, mostly in the jurisdiction of Byzantium, five also from that of Antioch. On the contrary, Macarius put in a confession directed against "the godless heresy" of Maximus. The examination of the patristic passages put in by him began, which was continued in the following session of March 8, wherein Macarius took no more part. He and his pupil Stephen were deposed as falsifiers of the faith and teachers of error. At the tenth session, the 18th March, the testimonies put in by the Roman legates were, after collation with the manuscripts of the patriarchal archives, found correct, and a confession agreeing with the declaration of

Agatho was delivered by Theodore, Bishop of Melitene, and others. As the close of the eleventh session, the 20th March, in which at the instance of the representative from Jerusalem, the letter of St. Sophronius to Sergius, and, at the instance of the Roman legates, four passages of Macarius and his pupil Stephen were read, the emperor announced that as he was prevented from further attendance at the sessions by state business, four officials of rank would henceforth represent him. But, besides, the chief matter was already settled. Old and New Rome were again united in belief.

At the twelfth sitting on the 22nd March a number of writings were read which Makarius had transmitted to the emperor, but the emperor sent on to the Council unread. Among them were contained the letters of Sergius to Cyrus and Honorius, and the answer of the latter. These documents were collated with the manuscripts of the patriarchal archive, and found to agree. Thereupon in the thirteenth session, on the 28th March, condemnation was passed upon the heads and favourers of Monothelitism, on Theodore of Pharan, Cyrus of Alexandria, Sergius, Pyrrhus, Paul, Peter of Constantinople (the three patriarchs next following, of whom nothing heretical was found, were spared), as likewise upon "Honorius of Rome, who followed Sergius and confirmed his teaching". The synodal letter of Sophronius was acknowledged as orthodox. In the fourteenth session, on the 5th April, at which also the newly-elected Catholic patriarch of Antioch, Theophanes, was present, the falsifications in the Fifth Council, the writing ascribed to Mennas and the two suppositious letters of Vigilius, were laid under anathema. On the octave of Easter, the 14th April, John, bishop of Porto, celebrated Mass in the emperor's presence at Sancta Sophia according to the Latin rite. The monk and priest Polychronius, who already in the fourteenth session had been accused by Domitius, bishop of Prusias, as a deceiver of the people, was brought before the Council at its fifteenth session on the 26th April. He desired in confirmation of the Monothelite doctrine to raise up a dead man. He was allowed to try in order to undeceive the people. He laid his confession of faith upon a dead body which was brought in, and whispered for two hours long into his ears, of course without effect. As he was not shaken in his attachment to the heresy, he was deprived of his rank as priest, and excommunicated. In the sixteenth session, which was held, after a long interval, on the 9th August, a Syrian priest, Constantine of Apamea, wished to get the doctrine recognised that there were in Christ two operations belonging to the Natures, but only one personal Will of the Word: that besides this Christ had once indeed also a natural human Will, but that He laid aside this at the crucifixion together with flesh and blood. The Council condemned this doctrine as savouring of Manichean and Apollinarian heresy, issued anathema against those whom it condemned, and resolved to publish a confession of faith, which was considered at the seventeenth session of the 11th September, and solemnly proclaimed at the closing session on the 16th September, in presence of the emperor. In this, after agreement declared with the five preceding General Councils, it was proclaimed that there are to be received in Christ Two Natural Operations and Two Natural Wills undivided, inseparable, unchangeable, and unmixed, which are not contrary to each other, since the human will follows the divine and is subject to it, is indeed deified and exalted, but not removed or extinguished. Neither of the Two Natures can be without operation or without will. The Council thanked the emperor in a special address for his labours to bring about the peace of the Church, requested that five accredited copies of the decree of faith should be provided for the five patriarchal sees, and in a special letter to the Pope besought the confirmation of their decrees by him.[1] Besides this very brief summary of the eighteen sessions of the Sixth Council, it is requisite to take notice of certain documents which were either presented to the Council by the legates, as their commission from the Pope, or proceeded from the Council or the emperor at its conclusion.

Pope Agatho had committed to his legates a long letter to the emperor. One passage from it may shew how plainly he set forth the authority of the Apostolic See and its inerrancy in matters of faith. He lays down the doctrine which opposes the Monothelite heresy, not as a matter for discussion, but as absolutely determined. "St. Peter," he says, "received the charge to feed the spiritual sheep of the Church by a triple commendation from the Redeemer of all Himself. By

[1] Translated from Hergenröther's *Kirchengeschichte*, i. 365-8.

his help this apostolical Church of his never turned aside from the way of truth to any error. The whole Catholic Church and General Councils followed in all things his authority as that of the chief of the apostles. This is the true rule of faith, which in prosperity and adversity the spiritual mother of your empire, the Apostolic Church of Christ, has kept unswervingly, which, by the grace of Almighty God, will be proved never to have erred from the path of apostolic tradition. It has never yielded to the corruption of heretical novelties, but as from the beginning of the Christian faith it has received from its authors the chief apostles, it has continued spotless according to the divine promise of the Lord our Saviour Himself, which He spoke to the chief of His disciples in the gospel: 'Peter, behold Satan has sought to sift you, but I have prayed for thee,' etc. Let your clemency consider how the Lord and Saviour of all, whose the faith is, who promised that the faith of Peter should not fail, charged him to confirm his brethren, which it is known to all that the apostolic pontiffs, my predecessors, have ever confidently done."

A more peremptory assertion cannot be made than this, and it is made by a Pope to an emperor, on the occasion of calling a General Council. It is carried by his legates, as ambassadors carry the commission of their sovereign. The answer[1] which the Council sent at its conclusion to the Pope shows how it was received. It ascribes to the Pope in fullest terms the position

[1] Letter of the Sixth Council in answer at its conclusion to the Pope. Mansi, xi. 684-688.

which he claimed, beginning in these words : " Greatest diseases require the greatest remedies, as you, most Blessed, know ; and therefore Christ our God, whose power created, whose wisdom provides all things, has appointed your Holiness as a skilled physician to meet the contagion of heresy by the force of true belief, and to impart the vigour of health to the members of the Church. We then, having read through the letters of a true confession sent by your paternal Blessedness to the most gracious emperor, leave to you what is to be done ; to you who hold the first see of the universal Church, standing on the firm rock of faith. We recognise your letters as written from the supreme head of the apostles. By them we have cast out the heretical sect which has lately set up its manifold error. According to the sentence previously passed upon them, we have cast out Theodore, bishop of Pharan, Sergius, Honorius, Cyrus, Paul, Pyrrhus, and Peter. We have sent what we have done, and these things will be learned from those who represented you, Theodore and George, priests; John, deacon ; and Constantine, sub-deacon. They state accurately the doctrine which they have approved, which we beseech your paternal Holiness to set your seal upon by your honoured rescript."

Is it possible to accept in more express terms the authority claimed by the Pope in his letter to the emperor, including that descent from Peter, to whom the promise made by our Lord is made the source and the guarantee of the authority? Is it possible more fully to acknowledge his right to confirm, in their own words, "to set his seal" on their proceedings?

But the Council also congratulated the emperor on the work over which as sovereign he had presided. Its success they attribute to the Pope in these words: "The highest of all,[1] the first apostle fought with us; for we had for our supporter, who by his writing set forth the mystery of theology, his imitator and the successor of his chair. The city of Rome the elder presented to you a confession dictated by God, and caused the daylight of belief to rise from the West. Paper and ink it seemed, but Peter spoke by Agatho."

This address is signed first by the three legates, Theodore, George and John, "holding the place of most Blessed Algatho, universal Pope of the City of Rome," next by "George, by the mercy of God bishop of Constantinople, New Rome"—thirdly by Peter, a priest, holding the place of the Apostolic See of Alexandria; fourthly by Theophanes,[2] by the mercy of God bishop of Antioch, Theopolis; fifthly by George, the priest, representing Theodore, not bishop but representing the See of Jerusalem.

Thus these two patriarchates could only shew two priests to record their agreement.

The emperor issued an edict[3] in which he set forth a

---

[1] Address of Council to emperor, Mansi, xi. 665, C. ὁ δὲ κορυφαιότατος ἡμῖν συνηγωνίζετο πρωταπόστολος· τὸν γὰρ ἐκείνου μιμητὴν καὶ τῆς καθέδρας διάδοχον εἴχομεν ὑπαλείφοντα.

[2] Theophanes had been put in the place of Macarius, deposed by the Council.

[3] Mansi, xi. 697-712.

most carefully drawn creed. He also addressed a letter[1] to Pope Leo, who had succeeded Agatho. He mentions how the legates of the Pope had been received, how every authority of Scripture and the preceding Councils had been carefully examined ; "moreover we beheld as it were with the eyes of our mind the chief of the apostolic choir, the Peter of the first see, setting forth the mystery of the whole dispensation, and addressing us in the words of Christ : Thou art Christ the Son of the living God. For his sacred letter portrayed to us the whole Christ, which we joyfully and sincerely received and folded him in our arms as Peter himself." God has done glorious things and preserved to us the faith entire. How should He not in that rock in which He founded the Church Himself, and foretold that the gates of hell, the snares of heretics, should not prevail against it ? Act therefore as a man and be firm, gird thyself with the sword of the word, and sharpen it with divine zeal. Be the firm champion of the right faith ; study to cut short every heretical talk or attempt as of old Peter struck off with the sword the sense of Jewish hearing, prefiguring the deafness of the legal and servile synagogue. The condition of the whole Roman polity is tranquillised with the tranquillity of the faith. We exhort therefore your most sacred headship[2] to send at once your nuntio to our royal city, that he may dwell here and in all emergent matters, dogmatic, canonical,

---

[1] Mansi, xi. 716 B.
[2] προτρέπομεν τὴν ὑμετέραν πανίερον κορυφήν.

or simply ecclesiastical may express the person of your Holiness.

"Farewell in the Lord, most blessed, and pray the more earnestly for our realm."

We have, therefore, on this great occasion a complete concurrence of three authorities; of the Pope in addressing an eastern emperor in prospect of a General Council, of that Council itself answering this address of the Pope; of the emperor in his letter to the Pope by his legates returning to him from the Council ; and it is to be noted that the Pope does not assert the nature of his authority as descending by a divine grant to Peter and exercised in virtue of it during six centuries with any greater emphasis than the emperor and the Council acknowledge it.

In the meantime Pope Agatho had died on the 10th January, 681. The see remained vacant eighteen months, during which the Council ended. Leo II. was consecrated the 17th August, 682, and his short pontificate ended the 3rd July, 683. To him the letter of the emperor was carried, and he discharged the office of confirming this Council, as St. Leo had confirmed that of Chalcedon, and of bringing it to the knowledge of the West.

The letter to the emperor, in which Leo II. confirms the Sixth Council, is a document extending over nearly six folio columns.[1] It shows throughout the Pope's great anxiety for the exact maintenance of the faith, and how severe had been the struggle with the heresy which had been upheld by two emperors and by four successive

[1] See Mansi, ii. 725, etc.

patriarchs of the imperial city. The Pope draws out in it a creed of the utmost minuteness in regard of the contested doctrine, the Person of our Lord in His Two Natures. He repeats his acknowledgment of the Five preceding General Councils as handing down one continuous doctrine from the beginning, and joins with them the Council just held as witness of the same doctrine; and he likewise joins the heretics during several hundred years from Arius, in one anathema, which closes with the inventors of this new error—that is, "Theodore, Bishop of Pharan, Cyrus of Alexandria, Sergius, Pyrrhus, Paul, and Peter, who lurked like thieves in the See of Constantinople rather than sat as guides;[1] nay, and also Honorius, who did not set himself to hallow this Apostolic Church by the teaching of the apostolic tradition, but allowed it, being spotless, to be stained by a profane betrayal". These words, by which St. Leo expressed how far he assented to the condemnation of Honorius by the Council, have a light thrown upon them by the words which he used in making known the condemnation of the Monothelites to the Spanish bishops, when among the condemned he included Honorius, "who did not extinguish the flame of heretical doctrine when it first arose, as was the office of the apostolic authority, but by neglecting fostered it".[2] And, again, in announcing the confirmation of the Council to the Spanish king, Erwig, he says of Honorius, "who allowed the spotless

[1] τοὺς τῆς ἐκκλησίας κωνσταντινουπόλεως ὑποκαθιστὰς μᾶλλον ἤπερ καθηγητάς.

[2] Mansi, xi. 1050-1055.

rule of the apostolic tradition, which he had received from his predecessors, to be stained ".[1]

It may be noted that St. Leo II. does not enter into the matter contained in the letters of Honorius ; does not express agreement with words which passed in the Council that " they were opposed to apostolic belief, to the declarations of Councils, and of all the approved fathers," that " they agreed with the false doctrines of heretics " ; he does not repeat the reproach that Honorius, by proof of his letter to Sergius, agreed in all respects with his meaning, and confirmed his godless doctrines. " Be it sufficient for us to know that if the name of Pope Honorius appeared in those sentences it certainly was not because he really taught or held the Monothelite heresy, but solely because with too great allowance he did not rebuke it, nor set himself to strangle it at its beginning, insomuch as undoubtedly that manner of action had given great encouragement to the favourers of those errors."[2] I quote two further judgments of the present day, that "the letters of Honorius contain nothing heretical," and that " in fact no error of faith whatever is found in those letters of Honorius ".[3] The anathema which lies on the memory of Honorius, who lived in renown and was buried in honour in St. Peter's, is a warning given by the Holy See itself to everyone who sits in that chair to weigh well both words and conduct, and guard both from the slightest negligence

[1] Rump, x. 465.
[2] Muratori, *Annali d'Italia*, A.D. 681.
[3] Hergenröther, *Kirchengeschichte*, i. 369.—Jungmann, *de Causa Honorii Romani Pontificis*, p. 430.

in matters of doctrine. Honorius died before the Exposition of Sergius was published or presented for his acceptance. Had he lived to judge of it those who study the history of the time succeeding down to the Sixth Council cannot doubt that he would have censured it as his successors censured it.

The Sixth Council closes a crisis of danger to the faith of the Church than which no greater is to be found in all history. The years from 638, in which Honorius died, to 682, in which his successor St. Leo II. approved the doctrinal decision of the Council, and further, allowed the conduct of a predecessor to be condemned, are occupied by ten successors of Honorius, every one of whom with the utmost zeal condemned the heresy which was supported by two emperors, wielding absolute power, and by four successive patriarchs of Constantinople, besides patriarchs of Alexandria and Antioch. All these put ecclesiastical authority at the service of these emperors to carry out their will. Heraclius and Constans II. were not theologians, and it required theological skill to construct concerning the Person of our Lord a heresy which could present itself to the fastidious Greek mind, clothed in proper expressions of a language lending itself with unsurpassable accuracy to every variation of thought. Cyrus, made for his first suggestions, by the grateful monarch, patriarch of Alexandria, was so good as to provide Heraclius with doctrinal decrees intended to make the disloyal sects of Egypt believe that they could express their own false doctrine in words which might pass for an assent to the Council of Chalcedon and the doctrine of St. Leo. When the patriarch Sophronius denounced the error and appealed to Rome and Pope Honorius in words which after twelve hundred years sound like a trumpet's call, Sergius being patriarch of Constantinople, the bosom friend and most trusted counsellor of Heraclius, holding the see of the Golden City for eight and twenty years, living and dying, too, in the greatest renown as an orthodox bishop, approached Pope Honorius with insidious language, totally disguising the real state of things in the East. He wished the Pope to believe that Cyrus of Alexandria was winning the proud and tumultuous sects of Egypt to Catholic union with the doctrine of St. Leo, which Honorius held with the utmost fidelity. Not only did he write letters, but he constructed a document to which he induced the emperor to set the imperial seal and require it to be signed by all bishops, and especially by the bishop of Rome. The document was intended to introduce that heresy formulated by Cyrus, which Sophronius exposed and refuted. Pope Honorius died in October 638, and never saw this document. Sergius got it passed by his Council at Constantinople, but died himself in December of the same year. Pope Severinus was elected to succeed Honorius before the end of the year 638, but his consecration was delayed by Greek intrigues for nineteen months, in the hope of obtaining his assent to the document drawn up by Sergius. This was found to be hopeless. The exarch then contented himself with plundering the Lateran treasury. Pope Severinus was at length consecrated, and sat for two months and six days, in which time however he condemned the Ecthesis. He was succeeded by two Popes, John IV. and Theodore, who behaved with the same decision and fortitude. But a new emperor had succeeded, after a frightful revolution, at twelve years of age ; and a new patriarch of Constantinople was ready to draw up a new document for the heresy. It was met by another Pope, whose first act was to call a great Council at the Lateran, to condemn the heresy under anathema, and the two documents, of which the first was fathered by Heraclius, and the second by Constans II. For this act of courage St. Martin four years afterwards was stolen from Rome, judged at Constantinople as a traitor by the senate, and sent a prisoner to die of famine, as is believed, in the Crimea. The emperor, having Rome in full possession, used such means that Eugenius was put into the see while St. Martin was still living as a condemned criminal. But Eugenius could not be compelled to accept the heresy of the Byzantine monarch and patriarch. There follow five Popes, Vitalian, Adeodatus, Donus, Agatho, and Leo II. At length, when Constans had perished miserably in his bath at Syracuse, his son Constantine broke the line of heretical emperors. But he found in truth the heresy so embedded in his capital that he was obliged to act with great caution. After repulsing a Mohammedan attack upon his capital which lasted seven years, and was overcome only by the aid of the Greek fire, when if the city had been taken the Greek empire would have ended, and the patriarch of Constantinople have shared the lot of his brethren at Alexandria and Antioch, the emperor was enabled to invite Pope Donus to hold a Council at Constantinople which should terminate this long struggle. It was a struggle in which the whole West followed the Pope, but much of the East was in favour of the heresy. Pope Agatho had succeeded Donus; he accepted the request of the emperor, he had Councils held through the West, and a full patriarchal Council at Rome. So he appeared by his legates at Constantinople, and was welcomed with the words, 'Peter has spoken by Agatho,' as 230 years before they cried, 'Peter has spoken by Leo'. But Agatho also died before the Council had finished its work, and the tenth successor of Honorius, Leo II., during his short pontificate of ten months, set his seal upon the Council, and endured to censure a predecessor for neglect of his office, and for allowing by that neglect a heresy to obtain a temporary success. Ten Popes in succession, one of them actually martyred, all of them vassals of absolute sovereigns, had during all this interval of forty years alone prevented the heresy being forced upon the Church. Four patriarchs of Constantinople in succession had fostered it; and four were together condemned. They were condemned, not for negligence in allowing others to spread the heresy, but as its originators; as advisers and mouthpiece of emperors, all whose power had been bent by them to extort approval of it from Popes, who in their civil position were helpless subjects in a "servile" province, but in their religious character were successors of St. Peter.

Now at the time the western emperor ceased to exist seven Popes succeeding St. Leo defended his doctrine against two emperors, Zeno and Anastasius, and foiled all the efforts of Acacius to use the eastern jealousy and the pride of the royal city, and exalt his see above the control of St. Peter's successor, until the seventh Pope, Hormisdas, then a subject of the Arian Gothic king, Theodorich, compelled the eastern emperor, the patriarch, the bishops, and the court, to confess his supreme authority, as successor of St. Peter. Seven Popes then stood neither hesitating nor fluctuating : over against them in that time stood seven bishops of Constantinople, one originator of the whole schism, others yielding to the emperor's will even against their own wishes. It was a contest of 44 years with an oriental despotism, waged by Popes the subjects of Arian Goths. They alone maintained the faith of the Church, as embodied in the decrees of the Council of Chalcedon, and saved the East.

Now, again, there has been a struggle for 44 years, in which ten Popes, subjects of the eastern emperor, and liable as such to be summoned by him to his capital, where one of them was indeed condemned to death, stood likewise as one man. They dwelt in a Rome no longer recognised as the head of the empire. Of this whole seventh century the special historian of the city says that for Rome it was " the most frightful, the most devastating of all ".[1] Civil power was not in their hands. Their election itself had to be confirmed by the exarch

[1] Gregorovius, ii. 112 (3rd edition).

as representing the emperor, or by the emperor himself. The first of the ten, Pope Severinus, had to wait nineteen months for it, after which he sat two months. The last of the ten, St. Leo II., began to sit eighteen months after the death of his predecessor, St. Agatho, and then only sat ten months. During the whole of this period, from the death of Honorius in 638, to the ratification of the Sixth Council in 682, the yielding of any one of these ten Popes would have carried with it the subjection of the whole church to the Monothelite error. They saved the East, they saved the Royal City, the seat of all power, in spite of its four patriarchs condemned as heretics. That Heraclius and Constans did not destroy the faith in the seventh century is as much their work and merit as that Zeno and Anastasius did not destroy it in the fifth. Perhaps the test which by the force of circumstances was applied to the Popes from the time Rome was governed from Constantinople as a captive city in the second half of the sixth and the whole of the seventh century was even more severe than that applied to them in the fifth. Their condition was more helpless, inasmuch as the Byzantine subjection was heavier than the Arian Gothic control, while the pillaged Italy of the exarchs was wretched, and the prosperous realm of Theodoric guarded jealously the last remains of imperial grandeur. He at least was a king in Italian Ravenna and Verona, and Rome was both great and dear to him. But Justinian and those who followed him were task-masters on the Bosphorus, who placed a tax-collector at Ravenna to wring out the last drop of Italy's blood, and plunder, as occasion served, the treasury of the Church in the Pope's Lateran Patriarcheion.

In what consisted the power by which twenty-nine Popes from Pelagius I. in 555, to Gregory II. in 715 bore so fearful a strain? Solely in one thing: in the belief that the throne of St. Peter had been fixed at Rome, and that St. Peter had received by a direct gift from Christ, and his successor had inherited, the charge to feed and govern the universal Church. The five times captured Rome lived on in this belief, and was become the city of the Popes. The eye of a conqueror, legislator and ruler, had chosen with a wisdom which all posterity has acknowledged the fairest and the strongest of cities for the seat of his power. He made it a royal residence; he could not make it an apostolic see. When at length his city fell, the empire fell with it. In the day of its pride it sought to trample on the elder Rome by the privileges of new Rome. The second of these attempts was foiled by the ten successors of Pope Honorius.

The danger to the Christian faith in these fifty years which begin, it is to be noted, at the death of Mohammed and the election of a chalif in his stead, has been touched upon; but the danger to the empire must not be dissociated from it. All the tyranny, the extortion, the spiritual encroachment of the empire could not sever the links which bound it to the Church. Heraclius had been warned by his former minister Maximus how perilous to his empire his meddling with the creed would be.[1] "It is not a time for such things," he said. "It is a

[1] St. Maximus, vol. ii. p. 106.

time of blood on account of our sins, not of theologising ; a time of lamentation, a time of imploring God's mercy, not of sophistical contradiction, moving Him to greater indignation." The Greek[1] chronographer in the ninth century marks the rise of the Arabian enemy as a scourge of Christian sins. He traces the whole calamitous series of events to the seduction of Heraclius, by a certain Athanasius, full of native Syrian guile, whom he promised to make and did afterwards make patriarch of Antioch : Heraclius was confused by his use of new terms. He consulted Sergius, and also Cyrus, then bishop of Phasis. He found the three agree. He followed them. He translated Cyrus from Phasis to Alexandria. Then Heraclius issued an imperial edict on doctrine. When Constans had succeeded as emperor another imperial edict on doctrine, drawn up by another bishop of Constantinople, appeared, which St. Martin condemned in his Council at Rome. Then the emperor Constans, full of wrath, carried St. Martin and St. Maximus to Constantinople, tortured them and banished them to the Chersonese, and punished many of the western bishops besides. But Agatho, being elected Pope, and moved by the zeal of God, also summoned a holy Council and put under ban the Monothelite heresy. Upon all his narrative the conclusion of Theophanes is : " The Church being thrown into disorder by emperors and impious bishops, Amalek the child of the

---

[1] Theophanes, see the passage p. 506-511 ; ending with the words quoted. It has inaccuracies which prevent citing the whole passage ; but the spirit of it is both true and of great importance.

desert rose up to scourge us, the people of Christ. The Roman army met with a great defeat on the Yarmuk. There followed the capture of Palestine, of Cæsarea, of Jerusalem, then the loss of Egypt, then the captivity of inland and islands, and all Romania; the utter destruction of the Roman force in Phœnicia, the dissolution of all Christian peoples and places, which did not cease till the persecutor of the Church perished miserably in his bath in Sicily."

Thus when the Sixth Council met at Constantinople not only had the emperor Constantine the Bearded declined far from the position held by Justinian, at the time in which he made Rome a garrison city in a servile province, a hundred and thirty years before, but his empire was not half so great as that of his great grandfather Heraclius, after the triumph of the Persian war. Not only were Syria and Egypt, and all Roman land on the side of Persia, and northern Africa as far as Kairowan, lost to the empire, but it had just escaped utter destruction by repelling the fleet of Muawiah after a conflict of several years from the waters of the Bosphorus. And the great and abiding difference to the eastern monarch was that he had lost this vast amount of territory to an enemy who had put the propagation of a different creed, antagonistic in its first principles to the Christian faith, into the hands of a single man. That single man, a chalif, wielding an absolute civil power, appertinent to the prophet's spiritual authority, had fixed the seat of his dominion in the heart of Rome's former domain in the East. The Mohammedan now moved upon Constantinople from his basis at Damascus. He had advanced upon Sicily likewise, and had taken Syracuse in 669, and from that time forth southern Italy had to dread his descent upon its coasts. By his union of spiritual and civil power in his person as chalif, he had now the whole Saracen force by land and sea at his command.

What were the Avars of the North or the Persians of the East compared to this new enemy, whose war-cry was, "There is no God but God, and Mohammed is His prophet"; whose meaning was, "There is no Christ, and no Mother of God, and no saints and no sacrifice, no kingdom in heaven to be gained by penance and humility. But there is the reign of a prophet on earth; receive his successor and you shall be our equals, refuse him and you, your wives and your children will be the captives of his sword."

These were the wounds struck by the Monothelite heresy on the Christian Church and the eastern empire in the first fifty years which ran from the death of Mohammed.

Constantine IV. died in 685, leaving the throne to his son Justinian II. He had reigned since the murder of his father in 668, and the whole course of his reign showed a very favourable contrast with that of Constans II. But greater still, if possible, was to be the contrast presented to his government by that of his son, who succeeded at a most immature age, and showed himself without counsel, self-command, and reason in all that he did. He was the first of several bad and incapable rulers. His tyranny deprived him of the throne after ten years. He was deposed with the Byzantine penalty of an amputated nose. Upon this deposition, in 695, the following twenty-two years produced seven revolutions, putting the imperial power into new hands and new families. One of these violent changes replaced Justinian II., maimed and dishonoured as he was, after a banishment of ten years. But he had learned no prudence, and the inhumanity of his last six years in his second reign exceeded that of his first reign.

In those first ten years from 685 to 695 events happened of importance to the Church, which also illustrate the spirit dominant at Constantinople. The condition of the empire required the strictest union with the West. It was pressed severely by the Mohammedan advance. To meet this effectually the reconciliation which had taken place at the Sixth Council was needed to be wisely and temporately maintained. But Justinian II. summoned a Greek Council to meet in the same hall of his palace, called the Dome, in which that Council had been held. It passed a number of canons on discipline, many of which were injurious to the West and only calculated to increase the mutual estrangement. Inasmuch as the Fifth and Sixth General Councils had passed no canons of discipline, this Council held in 692 was to complete that omission. It called itself the Quinisext. The later Greeks even confounded it with the Sixth Council, others contented themselves with saying that "it was held five or six years after it, and by nearly the same Fathers". It issued a hundred and two canons on discipline. "It seemed as if the bishops of this Council in their disgust at the undeniable superiority of the Roman Church in matters of faith, in which its authority had always at last prevailed and determined the issue, were bent on making good their right of autonomy at least in matters of discipline, and sought to avenge themselves by disapproving Roman customs for that superiority burdensome to Greek vanity."[1] As a matter of fact these canons had the effect of widening the breach between Latins and Greeks. It is true that in the eighth century all Greeks did not yet count them ecumenical, but in the Iconoclast contest they gained great consideration, and in the ninth century scarcely a Byzantine doubted any longer that they were ecumenical.[2]

The chief value of this Council now lies in the picture which it presents to us of the actual state and temper of the eastern Church at that time, the closing ten years of a century about which we possess so little detailed information. I am here concerned especially with two things—one, the position of the emperor as regards both the Pope and the Church; the other, the position of the patriarch of Constantinople; on both this Council casts light.

As to the emperor, not only was it convoked[3] by his command and assembled in a hall of his palace, but its

---
[1] Döllinger, *Lehrbuch der Kirchen-geschichte*, sec. 69, quoted by Hergenröther.
[2] Photius, i. 217.
[3] Hefele, iii. 313.

canons were subscribed by the emperor first with the imperial vermilion, and the second place was left vacant for the Pope's signature.[1] Then followed the subscriptions of Paul of Constantinople, Peter of Alexandria, Anastasius of Jerusalem, George of Antioch; on the whole, of 211 bishops, or their representatives, all Greeks and Orientals, including Armenians. It styled itself ecumenical, and the emperor tried to impose it as such. In its address to the emperor it said by that it was called[2] by him "to restore to order the Christian life, and root out the remains of Jewish and heathen perversity," while it ended by addressing to him the words, "as thou hast honoured the Church by convoking us, so also be pleased to confirm what we have decreed".

As to the Bishop of Constantinople, this Council said in its 36th canon, "renewing the decrees of the Second and Fourth General Councils, we decree that the see of Constantinople enjoy the same prerogatives as that of old Rome, and in ecclesiastical matters be as great as it, counting as the second after it. After it comes the see of Alexandria, then that of Antioch, then that of Jerusalem."

In order to comprehend what this canon gave to the see of Constantinople, it is requisite to bear in mind the actual condition of the eastern Church at the time. We are now at the year 692, that is full fifty years since the other eastern patriarchates fell under Saracen domi-

---

[1] The pretention shown in this by the emperor Justinian II. is noted by Le Quien, *Oriens Christianus*, i. 140.
[2] Hefele, iii. 300-331.

nion.[1] They had become more and more powerless. They depended upon the alms and the support given to them from Constantinople. In fact at this time the archbishop of the Grecian capital was the only real patriarch in the diminished empire. The courtiers of Constantinople, as we have seen thirty years before in the persecution of St. Maximus, affected to consider the conquests of the Saracen barbarians as transitory. Since then Constantinople itself had only been saved by hurling the Greek fire on the assailing Saracen fleet. A shadow only of their old right remained in the Saracen provinces of Alexandria and Antioch; they had still their old names. These were put down for them, if, as is supposed, they were not present at this council, because there were none at the moment. Four years later Carthage was taken by the Saracens; within eight years the whole Roman domination in Africa to the Atlantic was at an end. The empire had not yet lost everything in the West, for there were still some Byzantine troops and possessions in Italy. The Pope still acknowledged the emperor as his sovereign; and to Pope Sergius the emperor Justinian II. sent these canons, with the request that he would sign them. It is obvious that the position given in them to the bishop of Constantinople was no longer mere rank as in the first step taken in this direction by the Council of 381 under the great Theodosius. It was a higher jurisdiction similar in the East to that which the Pope held in the West. The Byzantine conception, as shewn in this Council, is clearly that the

[1] Photius, i. 221.

emperor was head of the Church, who, as he did it the honour to call it together, so he did it the further honour to confirm its decrees. Not, as in the case of the first Constantine, that he should make them laws of the empire, over and above their intrinsic spiritual force, as canons of those to whom Christ had committed the government of His Church, but that the emperor's signature, in the same way as he created a law in civil matters, made a canon in spiritual.

So ten years after the emperor Constantine IV. in the Sixth Council and the Council itself asked from the Pope for the confirmation of its decrees, his son Justinian II. required the Pope as his subject to accept as one of five patriarchs, three of whom it may be said were nonentities, a position of subjection to himself in the spiritual domain. The place left for the Pope's signature *after* that of the emperor and *before* that of the bishop of Constantinople graphically represents the idea which Justinian II. was seeking to impose. The Pope was to sign as patriarch and first of the five, not as the successor of St. Peter, who in virtue of his Primacy "set his seal," according to the expression of the Sixth Council, on the whole. In the Trullan canons, the Byzantine idea having evolved itself with undeviating encroachment during three centuries, appears complete. Its completeness is shewn in two things. Constantine IV. asked the Pope to confirm the Council; his son Justinian confirms it himself, and the council which he would confirm exhibits an eastern primacy seated at Constantinople. It admits not only the priority, but in a certain sense the superiority of the Roman primacy; but it would keep both the eastern and the western primacy under the imperial control. The eastern primacy would make itself the chief instrument of this control, and so practically put itself above the western.

As has been seen above, the emperors through four patriarchs of their capital tried during forty years to force the Monothelite heresy on the Popes. In like manner from the Trullan Council they tried to force the Greek discipline and the eastern primate upon the Popes. Had they succeeded the ambition of the Byzantine prelates would have reached its full success.[1] The imperial residence on the Bosphorus would have taken the place of old Rome. The city of Constantine, fighting for very existence with the ever-advancing Mohammedan, tried this last stroke in its hour of greatest weakness.

Turning to Rome at this time we find a very rapid succession of Popes, for which we have no information enabling us to account. They are also frequently Greeks or Orientals; and here the suspicion arises that the exarch of the emperor had influenced the election in the hope that some national feeling might affect them in the administration of their office. St. Agatho, who died in January, 681, was a Sicilian of Palermo, St. Leo II., who succeeded in 682 and died 683, was likewise a Sicilian. The next, Benedict II., a Roman, sat only from June, 684, to May, 685; his successor, John V., a Syrian, of Antioch, only from July, 685, to August, 686, and

[1] Photius, i. 223.

Conon, a Thracian, from October, 686, to September, 687. The following election was remarkable. There were two parties among the electors[1]—one for the archpriest Theodore, the other for the archdeacon Paschalis. Both were in the Lateran palace. Here both sides agreed to elect the priest Sergius. One of the rival candidates, Theodore, did him homage at once; the other, Paschalis, very unwillingly, and he secretly called in the exarch from Ravenna to his aid. The exarch, John Platina, came suddenly to Rome. He convinced himself that the choice of Sergius was canonical and that of the large majority, but as Paschalis had promised him a donation of a hundred pounds' weight of gold, he insisted upon being paid this sum from the Church's treasury. Sergius was obliged to submit, and thereupon was consecrated in December, 687, and sat till 701.

Pope Sergius was born at Palermo, of Syrian parentage, his father having settled there from Antioch. He had come to Rome in the time of Pope Adeodatus, had recommended himself by his ability, and had passed through the various ranks of the clergy. His eastern parentage did not prevent his offering as strenuous an opposition to the heretical suggestions of the Greek emperor as his predecessors had shewn.[2] One and the same spirit lived in all the Popes: the will and the genius of government. The natural quality of the old Romans had been transfigured by the supernatural gift belonging to the Church. The restless spirit of Byzan-

---

[1] From Anastasius and Gregorovius.
[2] Gregorovius, ii. 205 (1st edition).

tium, inexhaustible in the production of new theological doctrines, which at least maintained a continuous interest on the popular mind, tried in vain all the arms of Greek sophistry and dialectic skill against the rock of Peter. They recoiled from the sturdy Roman understanding and only helped the Popes in their work of massing the western fabric of concentrated discipline.

The rank of Rome [1] as the holy city, reverence for the head of the universal Church, veneration of the apostle Peter, had mounted higher and higher at this time in the West. If St. Peter had already enjoyed, at the period of the Gothic denomination, a worship which impressed the Greeks, his influence now had become more decided, characteristic, and world-wide. It dwelt not so much on his martyrdom, on his high rank as an apostle, but rather on his being the founder of the Roman Church and its see. The invisible saint in heaven was the possessor in title of many domains and patrimonies on earth: the theocratic king of Rome. He had begun to consider its people as his own, he counted upon its political government, which he transmitted like a celestial fief to the Popes his successors. His golden tomb at Rome in a Basilica radiant with gold had gradually become the symbol of the Church and of the salvation which the world received from this his institution. Pilgrims from the furthest lands now streamed to venerate it. The Anglo-Saxons especially, in the glow of their first conversion, were impelled by a passionate

---

[1] Gregorovius, i. 209, 1st edition translated: in the 3rd edition he has made omissions and alterations.

yearning to Rome. At the moment that the East sent its pilgrims to Mecca and Medina, swarms of pious pilgrims from Gaul, Spain, and Britain descended the Alps to cast their eyes upon eternal Rome and prostrate themselves before St. Peter's tomb, which had become the sanctuary of the West.

In the year 689 the young king of Wessex, Cadwalla, excited the greatest admiration. After many battles at home, he sheathed his sword and undertook the long journey to Rome to receive baptism from Pope Sergius himself. There on Easter eve the long-haired barbarian king was seen in the white dress of the illuminated at the porphyry baptismal font of the Lateran, with the wax candle in his hand, and received the name of Peter. He lived but eight days after, and was buried in the atrium of St. Peter's, with a long inscription, still extant. It said how King Cadwalla, for the love of God, left his throne, his family, his country, all that the valour of his ancestors and his own had gained him, coming far over land and sea as a royal guest to behold Peter, and Peter's see. He died at thirty years of age, in the reign of the Lord Justinian, in the second year of the pontificate of the apostolic man, Pope Sergius.

Cadwalla's appearance at Rome was a prelude to those long centuries wherein the Teutonic West would bow before the spiritual authority of the Pope. Twenty years later two other Anglo-Saxon kings, Conrad of Mercia, and Offa of Essex, came to Rome, not to be baptised, for they were already Christians, but to change the royal robe for the monkish cowl. Their long hair was cut off and dedicated to the apostle, and after living as monks under the shadow of the Vatican, they received a grave in the atrium of the Basilica, as a pledge that they had entered the company of the saints. It was not long before Rome had a Saxon colony in the neighbourhood of the Vatican.

Sergius raised a monument to St. Leo the Great in St. Peter's itself. It was the first example, as hitherto the Popes had either been buried in the cemeteries outside the walls or in the atrium of the Basilica. But from the time that in 688 Pope Sergius had translated the body of St. Leo into the transept itself, and raised an altar over it, other very distinguished Popes received the like honour.

But Pope Sergius also received a special messenger from his lord Justinian II. He had sent the canons of the eastern Council of 692, held in his palace, to the Pope, requesting him to sign them on the line left vacant between his own signature and that of his patriarch. The Greeks were above all things anxious to obtain their acceptance by the Pope. This was refused by Pope Sergius, who forbade the acts of the Council to be published. Upon this the emperor sent a high officer to Rome, who carried off to Constantinople John, bishop of Porto, and Boniface, counsellor of the apostolic see. But he did not stop with this. He sent likewise the captain of his guards, Zacharias, with orders to seize the Pope and deport him to Constantinople.[1] But by the mercy of God, and help of Peter, prince of the apostles,

---

[1] Anastasius.

who guarded his own Church, the heart of the army of Ravenna, and also of the duchy of Pentapolis (that is the five cities, Ancona, Umana, Pesaro, Fano, and Rimini), was moved not to allow the Pontiff of the Apostolic See to go up to the royal city. And when the soldiers had assembled in a multitude from all sides, Zacharias the guardsman, in fear and trepidation lest he should be killed by the angry crowd, besought the Pope that the gates might be closed, but he himself took refuge with the Pope, and besought him with tears, that he would take pity on him and not suffer him to be killed. Now the army of Ravenna had entered by St. Peter's gate, and reached the Lateran palace in its ardour to catch sight of the Pope, who was said to have been taken away in the night, and put in a vessel. The gates of the palace, both upper and lower, had been shut. They threatened to tear them down unless they were opened. The guardsman Zacharias, in his extreme terror and despair, had crept under the Pope's bed. He had lost his senses, but the Pope comforted him, and came out and seated himself on the basilic of St. Sebastian, in the seat called "under the apostles," where with mild words he turned away the wrath of the soldiers and people, but they would not leave the palace until with mocks and gibes they had turned the guardsman out of Rome.

So after forty years Justinian II. had repeated the worst deed of his grandfather Constans. Had Pope Sergius been taken to Constantinople the same lot awaited him there as had befallen his martyred predecessor Pope Martin. Yet in the interval the emperor's own father had acknowledged in the amplest terms the authority of St. Peter's successor. But the people of Rome as well as the emperor's own army at Ravenna and in central Italy had learnt rather to defend the Pope than to yield to an unjust outrage.

Justinian, at this time beaten in the field by Saracens and Bulgarians, was anxious to improve the beauty of his palace, by constructing a magnificent fountain and esplanade, from which he could better view the party of the Blues which he favoured. Now a church stood in the way of this enlargement, and he called upon Callinicus, who had succeeded Paul as patriarch in 693, to use the prayers customary when a church was pulled down. The patriarch replied that he had prayers for the building of churches, but none for their demolition. The emperor insisted, and Callinicus so far yielded as to use the prayer, "Glory be to God, now and for ever more, who allows and endures even this". After which the church was pulled down.

Three years afterwards the tyranny of Justinian met with its reward. He had prepared a massacre, in which also the patriarch would have been included. The patrician Leontius, a general of merit, had been imprisoned for some years. He was set free and ordered to Greece. On his way he lamented his fate to some friends. They advised him to rise against the emperor. He presented himself at the prætorium, gained admission in the emperor's name, overpowered the officer in command, set free the prisoners under his charge, some of the best men in the city who had been confined there for six or even eight years. Leontius then with his friends marched through the streets, inviting all Christians to Sancta Sophia. He went to the patriarch who knew that he was involved in the sentence of death intended by Justinian. The patriarch accompanied Leontius to the baptistery where a great multitude had assembled and uttered these words: "This is the day which the Lord has made". It became the signal for a general insurrection. The people rushed to the hippodrome. Thither in the morning Justinian was brought. His nose and tongue were both maimed, and he was banished to the Crimea. And Leontius reigned in his stead.

But Leontius was not fortunate in war. He had dethroned by this sudden revolution the fifth sovereign in the line of Heraclius. In three years an army which dreaded punishment because it had not saved Carthage from the Saracens rebelled against him; he was deposed by another officer, Apsimar or Tiberius II., who lasted seven years from 698 to 705. At that time the banished and maimed Justinian was enabled by help of the Bulgarians to recover possession of Constantinople.[1] Then began the time of vengeance not only on the two usurpers, as he deemed them, who had sat between them ten years on his throne, but on all who had supported them. Leontius and Apsimar were carried in chains through all the streets. Then, as the games in the circus were proceeding and the people crowding to them,

[1] Theophanes, 574.

they were thrown prostrate before the emperor who was seen seated with a foot on the neck of each, while the crowd as they went by shouted, "Thou hast trodden upon the asp and the basilisk, and trampled on the lion and the dragon". When the games were over Justinian removed his foot from the necks of his fallen rivals, and dismissed them to be beheaded. The patriarch Callinicus he deprived of sight, and banished to Rome, and put in his stead Cyrus, a monk, who had foretold his restoration. He slew a vast multitude of civilians and soldiers. He tied men up in sacks, and threw them into the sea. He invited men to a great banquet, and as they rose from it had them hung or beheaded In the meantime, while these events took place at Constantinople, Pope Sergius had closed in honour his pontificate of thirteen years and eight months, in September, 701. The native soldiers of Italy had defended him against the attempt of Justinian, and during all his pontificate he refused to recognise the Trullan canons. He was succeeded in less than two months by another Greek, Pope John VI. At the time Tiberius Apsimar was emperor, having dethroned Leontius. He ordered his exarch Theophylact to proceed to Rome. He was supposed to come with a bad intent against the Pope. Italian troops from the provinces flocked to Rome, and the city also rose against him. The Pope again, as in the time of Pope Sergius, ordered the gates to be closed; induced the Italians to retire from Rome, and saved the exarch. Without troops himself he possessed a greater influence over the Italians than the exarch. This Pope also induced the Lombard Duke of Beneventum to retire from an attack on Campania, in which he had done much harm. Pope John from the treasury of the Church redeemed his captives. We hear nothing of the exarch giving help either to defend or to ransom the emperor's subjects.

After little more than three years John VI. was succeeded by another Greek, John VII. He was consecrated in March, 705. In the autumn of that year Justinian II. regained his throne. He sent at once two Metropolitans to Rome, to urge the Pope to accept the Trullan canons. The Pope returned the canons in silence. He did not accept the Council of 692 any more than his predecessors. He died in 707, and was followed by Sisinnius, a Syrian, who sat but 20 days, and his successor Constantine, also a Syrian, was consecrated in March, 708, the seventh Pope in succession who came from Syria or the Greek empire.

In the year 709, Justinian II. wreaked his vengeance on Ravenna, stored up during the ten years of his banishment, whether it was that their opposition with that of Pope Sergius had rankled in his mind, or that they had rejoiced at his fall, or, at anyrate, that they had not been faithful to him. Now, at length, he sent the patrician Theodore, who commanded the army in Sicily, with a fleet against them. The chief people of the city, including the archbishop Felix, were enticed by the general to his ship, where they were received by twos in his tent. They were then seized, gagged, and put into confinement below. The Greeks landed, burned and plundered the city, and killed many. The chief captives were carried to Byzantium, and brought before the emperor, who sat on a throne studded with emeralds, and wore a diadem of pearls embroidered with gold. As soon as he saw them, he ordered them to execution, contenting himself with only blinding archbishop Felix, and banishing him to Pontus.[1]

Intense was the hatred of Byzantium kindled in Italy by such deeds.[2] It was at this time that Justinian II., by an imperial letter, summoned Pope Constantine to his capital. The Pope obeyed the command, and set sail from Porto on the 10th October, 710, accompanied by a considerable attendance. After he had left Rome, the exarch, John Rhizocapus, came, in the emperor's name, to Rome, and put to death four of the chief officers of the papal court, and " going to Ravenna, there for his most foul misdeeds perished by a most ignominious death ".

Pope Constantine passed by Naples and Sicily, and wintered at Otranto. Here he received an imperial order, requiring the magistrates to treat him wherever he went with the same honour as the emperor himself. When he reached Constantinople, the young son of the emperor, the highest nobility, the patriarch Cyrus, with the clergy, and a great multitude, came out seven miles to meet him. The Pope, wearing the dress which he wore at Rome in great ceremonies, entered the city with his train, riding the imperial horses richly capari-

---

[1] Muratori, *Annali d'Italia*, A.D. 709. Niehues, i. 485.
[2] Anastasius, *Life of Pope Constantine*.

soned. They were taken in triumph first to the royal palace, and then to the Pope's own abode at the Placidia palace. Justinian, being at Nicæa, sent him a letter full of thanks, and begged the Pope to meet him at Nicomedia. When they met, the emperor, wearing his crown, threw himself at the Pope's feet, and kissed them. They then embraced to the great joy of the people.

It appears that the Deacon Gregory,[1] the next successor of Pope Constantine, was attending on him, and that he answered with great ability certain questions put by the emperor. They are supposed to have referred to the Trullan canons. They were not confirmed. The later practice[2] of the Roman Church, with regard to these canons, continued to be to suffer those only to hold, which were not contrary to the decrees of the Popes and the western discipline. On the Sunday, the Pope celebrated Mass before the emperor, who received Communion from him; besought him to pray that his sins might be forgiven, renewed all the privileges of the Roman Church, and left the Pope free to return home. That return was delayed by the frequent sicknesses of the Pope. At length, however, he reached Gaeta in safety, where a great number of clergy and of the Roman people met him, and he entered Rome in joy in October, 711.

But the Pope had left behind him, and counselled in

---

[1] Anastasius, *Life of Gregory*, iv.

[2] Anastasius, in his letter to Pope John VIII., prefixed to the Seventh General Council, quoted by Photius, i. 223.

vain, an emperor bent on his own destruction. Justinian had conceived a furious hatred against the town of Cherson. He had sent a large fleet against it. Its chief men were taken away and cruelly tortured. The fleet itself was afterwards utterly wrecked by a tempest: upon which Justinian prepared another, under fresh commanders, who were instructed to inflict fresh cruelties. In the end the people of Cherson was driven into revolt. They proclaimed emperor Bardanes, one of the commanders of the fleet. Another officer, a chamberlain of Justinian, whom he had frightfully injured, and who expected to be killed by him, joined in the revolt. He was sent by Bardanes to seize Justinian, persuaded the soldiers to desert him, fell upon him, and, with his sword, cut off his head, which he sent at once to Bardanes, who forthwith despatched it by the same soldier to Rome. And thus the extinction of the race of Heraclius was signified to the West by the exposure of his head. His only son, Tiberius, a boy of ten, had already been slaughtered like a sheep.[1]

Thus it was that Pope Constantine, three months after his return to Rome, received tidings that Justinian was killed, and that Philippicus Bardanes had taken his place. In these days[2] theology had so penetrated every relation of life that every emperor, on his accession, was accustomed to send his profession of belief to the highest bishops of his empire. That of Philippicus

[1] From Theophanes, p. 574-584. I have shortened as much as possible a narrative in its details too horrible to repeat.
[2] Gregorovius, ii. 198.

unhappily signified to the Pope that he was a Monothelite. Thereupon Pope Constantine, in council, refused to accept his letter.

In fact, the Armenian officer who had at length put an end to the life and crimes of Justinian II., had no sooner obtained recognition as emperor, than he resolved to overthrow the Sixth Council, and establish the heresy which it had condemned. In the year and a-half, during which he reigned, he caused a council to meet at Constantinople. He deposed the patriarch Cyrus, who would not yield to his wishes : and put in his place the deacon, John, who was more submissive. This council, whose Acts were buried with the emperor, and whose numbers are not known, ordered the Monothelite heresy to be subscribed by all. Most of the bishops, with miserable cowardice, gave way to the will of the court. Among the number is said to have been even Germanus, then archbishop of Cyzicus, and afterwards, as patriarch of Constantinople, a firm defender of the faith. Only a few bishops, like Zeno of Sinope, resisted. The copy of the Acts of the Sixth Council, kept in the palace, was burnt. At Rome, the Pope's rejection of the new emperor's creed was taken up by the people with the utmost zeal. They would not receive his image in the church, nor bear the mention of his name in the Mass, nor tolerate his coin.

But, in eighteen months, his own profligate life caused him to be deposed. Two officers of high rank, one of them commanding the forces in the neighbouring provinces, determined to rid the empire of such a master. An emissary of theirs, entering on Whitsun-eve suddenly by the golden gate, with a company of soldiers, gained admittance to the emperor's chamber, and carried him off unconscious from the effect of a drunken carouse on his birthday. They took him to the hippodrome, and there blinded him. On the next day, being Pentecost, the people were assembled in the great church, and Artemius, the first secretary, was crowned, and his name changed to Anastasius. On the following Saturday, he punished with blindness the two conspirators who had so treated his predecessor.[1]

Thus Rome and the East were suddenly delivered from a revolution which had fallen upon them with equal suddenness, a fresh domination of the Monothelite heresy. All acts done by the government of the fallen Philippicus were annulled, and the Sixth Council solemnly proclaimed afresh by clergy and people at Rome. There was great rejoicing at the fall of Philippicus, and the rise of Anastasius, who sent to the Pope a letter containing his orthodox belief.

It is to be noted also that the patriarch of Constantinople, John VI., who had been put into the place of Cyrus by Philippicus, had joined in the emperor's acts against the Sixth Council, and led the council which rejected it, now wrote to Pope Constantine to excuse himself for having yielded to force. He began the letter with these words :—[2]

"God, who has constructed the magnificence of visible

---

[1] Theophanes, p. 588.
[2] Mansi, xii. 196.

things as a mark of His own Godhead and power, has specially in the formation of man, the most honoured of the sensible creation, shown His glory and wisdom, so that the prophet cried out, 'Such knowledge is too wonderful for me'. Now, the Maker of our nature, designing the head to be over the whole body, placed in it the most important of our senses, and caused all the movement and perfection of the other limbs to spring from it, and be preserved in it. If one of these meet with loss or injury, it is not left without care, but the head shows a natural sympathy even to the extremest parts of the body, and heals the local suffering by the hand's ministry and the eye's guidance, the aid of which it does not refuse as useless. With this we can compare your own apostolical pre-eminence, counting you, according to the canons, as the head of the Christian priesthood.[1] And so with reason we ask of you to be released from the discouragement which has fallen on the body of the Church by the pestilent exercise of tyrannical power."

The patriarch further beseeches the Pope to pardon his fault that under this stress he had rejected the doctrine of the Sixth Council, in the words : "Since you are the disciple and the successor of him who heard from the Lord, 'Simon, Simon, behold Satan has sought to sift you as wheat, but I have prayed for thee that thy faith fail not : and thou when thou art converted confirm thy brethren,' you are a debtor to supply what is

---

[1] τούτοις δὴ τὰ κατὰ τὴν ὑμετέραν ἀποστολικὴν προεδρίαν ἔχομεν παραβάλλειν, ἁγιώτατοι, καὶ κεφαλὴν τῆς κατὰ Χριστὸν ἱερωσύνης κανονικῶς ὑμᾶς λογιζόμενοι.

needed for the correction which confirms, and also to show a sympathetic kindness ".

Pope Constantine is the fifth and also the last Pope who paid a visit to Constantinople. As these visits cast an important light upon the condition during two hundred years under which, being acknowledged as successors of St. Peter, they exercised as subjects in the civil order their supreme authority in the Church, I think it belongs to the matter now treated to refer to the facts and results of each visit. Pope John I., who sat from 523 to 525, was a subject of King Theodorich, and was summoned by him to Ravenna. There he was compelled, much against his will, to go with three senators on an embassy to the emperor Justin I. Theodorich was most indignant that the emperor had required Arians in his empire to give back their churches to the Catholics. He threatened the Pope that if this treatment was not reversed he would drown Italy in blood.[1] So the Pope, being sick, went with the senators to Constantinople. On their arrival the whole city went out with wax lights and bannered crosses in honour of the blessed Apostles, Peter and Paul, for the Greeks testified that from the time of Constantine and St. Silvester they had never merited to receive a successor of St. Peter. Then the emperor Justin, doing honour to God, threw himself to the ground upon his face and worshipped the most blessed Pope John. Pope John and the senators besought him with many tears to accept

---

[1] Rex Theodoricus hereticus hoc audiens, exarsit in iram, et totam Italiam voluit gladio extinguere.—*Book of the Popes*, Mansi, viii. 599.

their legation. The emperor rejoiced that he had been found worthy to see in his kingdom a successor of St. Peter and was gloriously crowned by his hands.

When they returned with success to King Theodorich at Ravenna they found that he had imprisoned the two illustrious senators, Symmachus and Boethius ; he put the Pope likewise in prison, and so the bishop of the first see suffered affliction in ward, and died of want. Ninety-eight days after his death in prison the heretical King Theodorich by the will of God suddenly died.

Ten years after this, in 535, the same Book of the Popes records that Pope Agapetus, being the subject of Theodatus, King of the Goths, was sent by him on embassy to the emperor Justinian. Theodatus had put to death the Queen Amalasunta, daughter of Theodorich, who had herself given him the crown. He hoped that the Pope might save him with the emperor. The Pope was received with all distinction. But he found a heretic seated on the see of the capital, whose orthodoxy the emperor defended. And the emperor said to the Pope, " Either agree with us or I will have you banished ". The Pope replied : " Sinner that I am, I came to Constantinople to see the most Christian Emperor Justinian. I find instead a Diocletian. But I do not fear your threats. But that you may know that your bishop does not belong to the Christian religion, let him confess there to be Two Natures in Christ." Then the Bishop Anthimus, being cited by the emperor, would never confess in answer to the question of Pope Agapetus that there are Two Natures in our Lord Jesus Christ. So the Pope prevailed.

The emperor with joy submitted himself to the Holy See, and worshipped Pope Agapetus; he expelled Anthimus from his communion and banished him, and besought the Pope to consecrate Mennas in his stead. This was done. The Pope was taken ill, and died after two months at Constantinople. He was buried with a greater concourse of people than had ever attended the funeral of emperor or bishop. His body was carried back in triumph to Rome and buried at St. Peter's.[1]

Shortly after Justinian added the direct sovereignty of conquest to that respect, whatever its extent may have been, with which Rome and the Popes regarded the sole emperor who since the abolition of the western emperor in 476 represented the Roman name, though seated on the Bosphorus. Pope Vigilius in 547 was his subject, and as such summoned by him to Constantinople, whither he went with the same reluctance as his two predecessors at the command of Theodorich and Theodatus. The emperor's purpose was to force the Pope to set his seal upon a doctrinal edict of his own. At first Justinian humbly besought his blessing, and embraced him with tears. But this soon turned to persecution, and seven years of perpetual humiliation for the Pope followed. Deceived, isolated, imprisoned, deserted, he did not surrender the faith. St. Peter in his person was not overcome, but he was discredited, and it required forty years, crowned by the wisdom and fortitude of St. Gregory, to restore the full lustre of the Holy See.

[1] *Book of the Popes* given in Mansi, viii. 845.

After a hundred years and a succession of fourteen Popes, St. Martin held a great Council at Rome in 649, in which he passed anathema upon the heresy of two eastern emperors, grandfather and grandson. In requital for this the grandson had him seized in his Lateran Church itself, carried secretly to Constantinople, judged by the senate there for high treason, condemned to death, and finally suffered him to die of starvation in the Crimea. As Pope John I. gained his crown of martyrdom by the first visit of a Pope to Constantinople, so Pope Martin gained the like crown by the fourth.

About thirty years after this a General Council was held in which the heresy which St. Martin had placed under ban was condemned afresh ; and it was called by the wish and command of the then reigning emperor, son of the very man who had persecuted St. Martin to death, and in it the largest acknowledgments of St. Peter's succession at Rome were made to St. Martin's successors.

Yet, ten years afterwards, this man's son, then emperor, tried to repeat upon Pope Sergius the crime of the grandfather committed on Pope St. Martin. That his attempt was baffled, the life of his messenger saved by Pope Sergius, and the messenger dismissed in most ignominious flight, was owing to the Italian troops of the emperor rising in defence of the Pope. They would not allow him to be taken to the capital on the Bosphorus.

In another ten years the usurper Apsimar had despatched another exarch, Theophylact, to carry Pope

John VI. to Constantinople that he might be induced to give the consent which Pope Sergius had refused to the canons of the Trullan Council. This attempt also was frustrated by the flocking of Italian troops to Rome in defence of the Pope.

Last is the visit of Pope Constantine, in which two things are remarkable. The very emperor who had attempted to kidnap Pope Sergius in 693, being on the eve of the extinction which was to fall on the line of Heraclius, in 710 invited Pope Constantine to visit him, ordered him everywhere to be received with royal honours; when they met, fell, though crowned, at his feet to kiss them, and sent him back in highest honour. And presently the patriarch of Constantinople, begging of him to be condoned for a grievous fault, drew a picture of his supremacy the functions of which he compared to those which the Creator in His wisdom has given to the head in the human body. I will venture to say that no western mind has expressed with greater force or tenderness the office which belongs to him who sits in the see of the chief apostle than was done by the tenant for the time of that see of New Rome, which for more than three centuries had been striving to rival and depress the elder Rome.

The emperor Anastasius, so strangely chosen from a first secretary to succeed a fallen usurper, and undo his establishment of heresy, was both orthodox and blameless in conduct, and strove to defend his much endangered empire. He had armed a fleet, but it rebelled and killed its commander. The end of a civil war, lasting six months, was that Anastasius retired of his own accord on condition that his life should be spared: he became a monk and priest and was banished to Thessalonica. He had reigned two years and a half.

Anastasius, some time after his retirement, made, when Leo III. was established on the throne, an attempt to regain it. For this he was publicly executed at Constantinople. So he was added to his predecessors, Leontius, Apsimar, and Justinian II., making the fourth of the seven emperors reigning from 685 to the accession of Leo III. in 717, to whom the throne was a scaffold.

Theodosius III., a good man but an incapable ruler, had in vain tried to escape the crown imposed on him by the rebellious fleet. After a year the general of the army of the East, a soldier of great capacity and vigour, was advancing to dethrone him. The senate and patriarch advised him to resign. His private property was secured to him on condition that both he and his son became priests. Theodosius III. yielded possession of a throne from acquiring which he had fled, and lived in peace at Ephesus. He gave himself up to good works, and when he was buried in St. Philip's Church he had ordered the single word *health* to be engraven on his tomb: a silent intimation that he was the sole among Leo's six predecessors who had escaped unhurt, and no less that he found in death the healing of all sorrows.

In the year 717 Leo the Isaurian mounted the throne thus vacated, and entering by the golden gate on the 25th March, 717, was crowned in Sancta Sophia by the patriarch Germanus, after he had taken before him the oath to maintain the faith of the Church intact.

On the 8th April, 715, Pope Constantine died, after a pontificate of seven years, "a strenuous and successful defender of Rome's orthodox faith, and a worthy predecessor of greater successors, under whom Rome was delivered from the Byzantine yoke".[1] After forty days St. Gregory II. became Pope on the 19th May, 715.

Between the two Popes St. Gregory I. and St. Gregory II. lies a period of 111 years, marked with disasters to the Christian people and religion such as no preceding century can show. At the death of St. Gregory I. in 604, all the shores of the Mediterranean were in possession of Christians. The authority of the eastern emperor extended from Constantinople over Asia Minor, Syria, and the region up to the Euphrates, Egypt, and the long range of Northern Africa, embracing the present Tripoli, Tunis, Algiers, and Morocco, to the Atlantic. The beginning of Christian kingdoms, looking up with filial affection to their spiritual Father in Rome, was apparent to the eye of the first Gregory. Gaul and Spain and Africa, lately recovered by Justinian, had a network of spiritual provinces, in which each Metropolitan received from Rome the pallium, the token of apostolic authority and unity. St. Gregory himself had added to these by the mission of Augustine, and the chair of unity founded at Canterbury. Full as these countries were of violence, mutual aggression, and unsubdued ferocity, the Teutonic invaders had nevertheless

---

[1] Gregorovius, ii. 240 (1st edition).

accepted the law of Christ from Rome, and the first principles of human order had been fused with their natural traditions of freedom. Above all, the Arian heresy had been dispossessed, and there was no appearance of a religion counter to the Christian arising. In every city of a vast region the bishop was regarded by his people with veneration, the very source of which lay in a power which he held by imposition of hands. A spiritual head to those around him, he was himself a link in the chain of that universal hierarchy the head of which was at Rome.

At the accession of Gregory II. the whole coast line from Cilicia at least to Mauritania on the Atlantic, had been lost to the Roman empire, and in a very great degree to the Christian Church as well. It was all now in the occupation of a single power, the head of which was termed the successor. The successor that is of the Arabian who had set himself in the place of Christ, who had conquered the Christians in this vast range of territory, and would allow them to live only on tenure of subjection. Instead of the remnant of primeval tradition which formed the mythology and influenced the customs of the northern tribes at the time of their descent on the western empire, the Arabian prophet and his successors had impregnated their people with a furious and fanatical belief to be imposed by force. It was a chief part of that belief that it ought to be imposed by force on all outside. And they who fell in such a holy war were held to be martyrs, as indeed they witnessed and imitated the life of Mohammed from the time of the Hegira. Thus the possession of the world was attached to the profession of one God and Mohammed as his prophet. In the century next after the death of the prophet those who retrace the deeds of his followers must admit that every possible disregard of human life and of the things most hallowed in Christian society had been shown by them in the construction of a kingdom now stretching from the Atlantic to the Indus. The religion under whose inspiration all this had been done, was framed in essential antagonism to the Christian faith. For indeed the mystery on which the Christian faith rested, that the Son of God had assumed human nature for the redemption of man, was denounced by it as derogatory to the very conception of God. Mohammedans proscribed Christians as associators of a creature with the Creator. This association they called idolatry. The northern wandering of the nations might receive Christian belief and be formed into a Christendom. The southern wandering of the nations, since it rested on a prophet the personal antagonist of the Christian founder, could only substitute Islamieh for Christendom.

This it had done over the empire which as we have seen was constructed at the time St. Gregory II. became Pope, and Leo III. after six revolutions became emperor at Constantinople.

Between the two Gregories twenty-four Popes occupied the throne of St. Peter, from Pope Sabinian to Pope Constantine. Of these three only, Honorius, Vitalian, and Sergius, sat over ten years each ; the three together occupied forty-one years, leaving seventy years in the gross for the remaining twenty-one pontificates. But a considerable portion of these years must be deducted for the time which intervened between their election, and the allowing of their consecration by the consent of the emperor or the exarch as his viceroy. In that interval Greek arts were applied, to induce the Pope elect to consent to some thing desired by the emperor. Thus Pope Severinus on the death of Honorius was kept out of his see for nineteen months and sixteen days, to obtain, if possible, his consent to the doctrine put forth by Heraclius in the Ecthesis. In this manner the pontificate of Severinus was reduced to two months and three days, in which he found time to condemn the emperor's Ecthesis. So again on the election of St. Sergius in 687, the exarch hurried down from Ravenna to prevent it if possible; but he was too late, and could only plunder the Church's treasury of one hundred pounds weight of gold. These are samples, but the action continued over the whole period. Historians remark that the seven last Popes who sat during it were all Greeks, and conclude that the emperors thought compliance might be hoped for in such cases. This series of seven began with John VI. in 685. The seven Popes were all faithful not to the exacting demands of emperors, but to the charge of St. Peter, and during the thirty years in which they occupied the Holy See seven revolutions of emperors took place at Constantinople. Three emperors perished by public execution; a fourth was only blinded; a fifth having become a priest, and attempted to regain the throne was then executed as a traitor by its actual tenant. The worst of the six was the fifth emperor in the line of Heraclius, whose head was sent to Rome as a ghastly but indisputable witness that Italy was delivered from his tyranny.

During the whole one hundred and eleven years Italy was governed as a province which had no civil rights. I recur to the words of St. Agatho in his letter[1] to the Sixth Council for the importance of his acknowledging the sad condition of learning, as a result of the miserable danger and uncertainty of the time. Not often does a Pope say of his own legates, "How should they who gained their daily bread by manual labour with the utmost hazard, possess accurate and abundant learning?" But he gave assurance that "with simplicity of heart and without faltering they maintained the faith handed down from their fathers, making their one and their chief good that nothing should be diminished, nothing changed, but the words and the meaning both kept untouched".

Whatever pomp and glory remained to the empire was centered in Constantinople. Rome and the Pope were powerless as to material strength. So St. Martin, when accused at his trial of favouring an enemy of the emperor, replied: "What was I to resist an exarch, without any force of my own?" At that time Constantinople was probably the greatest as well as the richest city in the world. When Constans II. eight years after visited Rome he swept away whatever works of art pleased him

[1] The letter *Consideranti mihi*, Mansi xi. 234.

for the further adornment of his capital. In the four centuries down to Leo III. which elapsed since the consecration of the capital by its founder, every successor had made it a point of honour to improve the beauty and increase the strength of the imperial residence.

Thus those twenty-four Popes from the first to the second Gregory were dwelling in a Rome which continued to exist only as the seat of their own primacy, drawing successive generations to it, and visited year by year through the pilgrims who came to it from all parts of the world, since they sought the tomb of the chief apostle when the sepulchre of the Master was enthralled by the Saracen. Beside that tomb they stood with Roman fortitude against Byzantine fluctuation. Heraclius published an Ecthesis, and Constans II. a Typus. Ten Popes condemned both, and then Constantine IV. humbly admitted that both were worthless. He further undid the heresy of four successive patriarchs by putting them under anathema. He received as the living Peter the successor of one whom his father had stolen from Rome and martyred in the Crimea; just as his son Justinian fell at the feet of Pope Constantine, after he had tried to repeat the crime of his grandfather Constans on the person of Pope Sergius. So in 680 Theodore, then patriarch of Constantinople, urged on by another patriarch who lived at Constantinople since his own Antioch was become a spoil of the Saracen, expunged from the diptychs the names of all the Popes after Honorius to his own time. Theodore was himself deposed while the Sixth Council sat, and Macarius, his adviser, was deposed by that Council, but Theodore lived to be restored and to die as patriarch with a sounder faith than he had shown at the beginning. It is remarkable that after the four Monothelite patriarchs, Sergius, Pyrrhus, Paul, and Peter, who were condemned at the Sixth Council, three patriarchs, Thomas II., 667-8, John V., 669-674, and Constantine I., 674-6,[1] "leant to orthodoxy," and so escaped the censure of the Council, while Theodore was heretical from 678 to 680, and orthodox when restored from 683 to 686.

Thirty years after the Sixth Council the patriarch, John V., after presiding at the council summoned by the Emperor Philippicus, who attempted by it to re-establish the Monothelite heresy, besought pardon of Pope Constantine as the head whose function it was to heal all the wounds of the body. I know not what proof of the Roman primacy surpasses in force, to those who have eyes to see, this proof arising from the alternate persecution and confession of Byzantine emperors and patriarchs, compared with the unbending fortitude and unalterable faith of the twenty-four Popes in that long century when Rome served as a slave in the natural order, and was worshipped in the spiritual kingdom as a sanctuary.

[1] Photius, i. 207.

CHAPTER VI.

AN EMPEROR PRIEST AND FOUR GREAT POPES.

THE Sixth General Council had been held in 680, and on the union of the East and West the long and obstinate Monothelite heresy had seemed to be extinguished with all the authority wielded by the Pope at the head of a General Council. Yet thirty years after this event the fifth emperor of the line of Heraclius was dethroned and beheaded by a usurper; and the first act of the insurgent when seated on the throne of Constantine was to call a council of his own eastern bishops at Constantinople, which at his command attempted to abrogate the Sixth Council and to set up again as the proper faith of the Church the heresy which it had condemned. And this act of Philippicus Bardanes met with nothing like an adequate resistance from the eastern bishops. It is true that the patriarch Cyrus, refusing to comply with the wishes of the new emperor, was deposed by him, and a more obsequious successor, the deacon John, put in his place. But even Germanus, then archbishop of Cyzicus, yielded to the storm, and thus a bishop of imperial blood, who four years afterwards was himself placed in the see of Constantinople, who held it during fifteen years, and then was deposed because he would not yield to the heretical measures of another emperor, is said to have been subservient to the will of Philippicus Bardanes.

No incident can show more plainly the pretensions of the eastern emperor and the weakness of the eastern bishops than the fact that the first act of an Armenian officer when he had, by the murder of his sovereign, put on the imperial buskins on which the eagle of the Roman power was embroidered, consisted in an attempt to alter the faith of the Church, and that the alteration was supported by the bishops whom he had convened. Philippicus himself was a worthless sensualist, whose reign was put an end to in eighteen months by another revolution. Two more transient emperors passed to the dishonoured throne, and then appeared a third, who reigned twenty-four years, and has left his mark on history.

Leo III. was a soldier of great courage and considerable skill. He was of low birth in the province of Isauria, but worked his way through the various grades of the army until he became the most highly reputed of its generals at a moment when a succession of seven revolutions had seemed to portend the coming extinction of the empire. Besides its internal dissensions, it was hard pressed by the chalif Solomon, who was making every preparation for the final conquest of the capital. When by the cession of the good but impotent Theodosius III. the Isaurian officer obtained the crown, sodden as it were with the blood of three successive emperors, it might have seemed that the last hour had come of the great city whose ramparts had served as the only sufficient bulwark against the Mohammedan torrent of conquest. Leo III. thought not so. His first act was to defeat the chalif and cast back his invading host. The eastern empire breathed afresh under his resolute spirit and strategic skill, and learnt to meet not ingloriously the Saracen in battle. Ten years of success had given to its ruler some rays of the glory which had shone upon the older emperors.

It is of the year 726 that the most learned of Italian historians [1] speaks in these words: "This year Leo, the Isaurian, began a tragedy which convulsed the Church of God and laid the foundations for the loss of Italy to the Greek emperors. Theophanes, Nicephorus, and other historians tell us that a submarine volcano had broken out in the Ægean Sea and cast up a quantity of pumice stone on the adjoining coast. This natural incident had produced the greatest alarm. Moreover, a perfidious renegade named Bezer,[2] who had embraced the Arabian superstition, had nestled himself in the imperial court, and succeeded in making the emperor believe that God was enraged with the Christians on account of the images which they had in their churches and venerated. No doubt abuses did exist in the veneration of these images, as have since appeared among the Moscovites, united to the Greek Church. But such abuses neither were nor are a reason to abolish these images, for, as men of

---

[1] Muratori, *Annali d'Italia*, anno 726.

[2] Beserem tot malorum auctorem atque incitamentum. *Historia Concilii Nicæni II.*—Mansi, xii. 955, a.

great knowledge have proved, the use of images and a well-regulated veneration of them is not only lawful, but greatly fosters piety in the Christian Catholic people. Now the emperor Leo, infatuated by his own great penetration of mind and seduced by this evil counsellor, practised a usurpation upon the rights of the priesthood, and published an edict ordering that from that moment all the sacred images should be forbidden and removed through the territory of the Roman empire. He called the kissing them or venerating them idolatry. This was the beginning of the Iconoclast heresy. This rash and iniquitous prohibition excited great commotion among his subjects. The larger part detested him as heretical, as holding Mohammedan sentiments, and the more because it was known that he held in abomination the sacred relics, and denied the intercession of the saints with God—that is, attacked beliefs established in the Church of God. He also impugned thereby the profession of faith which he had made when he assumed the imperial throne, refusing to listen to the judgment of bishops who are chosen by God for guardians of the doctrine which belongs to the faith. Though we have not the letters written by him to Pope Gregory II. about abolishing the sacred images, and the pontiff's answers to him, yet the sequel plainly shows that he sent to Rome the above-named edict, and that the holy pontiff not only opposed it, but wrote with kindled feelings to the emperor about it, inducing him to give up this sacrilegious design."

Though the letters thus mentioned no longer exist, we

possess letters from Pope Gregory II. to the emperor Leo shortly after, which present to us the clearest and most authentic picture of the Iconoclast contest. Both the contention of the emperor and the censure of the pontiff are there expressed in the words used at the very moment of the struggle. I shall follow them accurately and in so much detail as to show the interests which were then at stake.

In the person of St. Gregory II., after several Popes of eastern descent, a Roman had again reached the pontificate.[1] He was acquainted with Constantinople, to which place he had accompanied his predecessor, Pope Constantine. His experience in political things was as great as his grasp of theological knowledge was firm. He had dealt with Greeks and Lombards, not only in ecclesiastical affairs, but as counsellor, as arbitrator, and as party concerned in disputes. He adorned the churches of Rome, but he likewise strengthened her fortifications on the Esquiline. When, in the year 717, a considerable portion of the city had been dangerously flooded, and in the quarter of the Via Lata the water had risen eight feet high, the poor people found support and consolation in the Pope. During many years there had been peace between Church and Empire as also between the Roman See and the patriarchate of the imperial capital. The first years of Leo III. promised nothing but good. Born of low birth in the mountains of Isauria, and destitute of education, he had risen by his valour step by step, and was in command of the Anatolian army when called to

[1] See Reumont, ii. 101.

succeed Theodosius III. His reign of four and twenty years would have been fortunate had not the dogmatising fancies which seemed to be inherited by the most various natures on the Byzantine throne taken possession of him. Through them he kindled a conflict which set East and West in commotion, and completed the rent between them.

It was about the year 727, the twelfth year of his own pontificate, and ten years after the accession of Leo III., when the acts of the eastern emperor caused St. Gregory II. to address the following letter to him.[1]

"The letter of your God-protected majesty and fraternity we have received by the augustal officer of the Guards, and we likewise keep it securely in the holy church close to the confession of the holy and glorious Peter, prince of the apostles, where likewise are kept the letters of your predecessors who reigned in the love of Christ. In this letter you well and piously, as befits a Christian emperor, professed that you would keep without fail the injunctions of our holy fathers and teachers. It is first, and remarkable, that the letter is yours and not another's, sealed with the imperial seal, and subscribed within in vermilion, by your own hand, as is the wont of emperors to subscribe. Therein you professed with the clearest piety our blameless and orthodox faith. You wrote, ' he who moves and pulls down the boundaries of the fathers is execrable '. On receiving this we uttered hymns of thanksgiving to God, for God assuredly has given you the throne. You were running well. Who

[1] Mansi, xii. 960-974, as read in the Seventh Council.

then has rung an alarum in your ears, and perverted your heart like a twisted bowstring, and turned your eyes backwards? During ten years by the grace of God you went well. You never spoke of the holy images. Now you say they take the place of idols, and that those who worship them are idolaters. And you are bent on sweeping them away, and clearing the land of them. And you fear not the judgment of God in bringing scandals into the hearts of men, not of the faithful only, but of the faithless too. Christ charges you not to scandalise one of the little ones, and for a small offence to depart into everlasting fire, and you have scandalised the whole world, as if you could not endure death, nor make an evil confession. You have written that 'we should not worship things made with hands, nor any kind of likeness, as God said, neither in heaven nor on earth'; and show me, if you please, who has charged us to reverence and worship things made with hands. Then I will confess that is God's command.' And why, you that are emperor and head of Christians, did you not enquire of those who had the knowledge of experience? You might have been satisfied by them concerning what things made by hands God spoke, before stirring up, confounding, and disturbing humble people. But you thrust away, and denied, and cast out our holy fathers and teachers whom, with your own hand and in writing, you professed to obey and follow. The holy and inspired fathers and teachers are our scripture, our light and our salvation. The six Councils held in Christ have commanded us, and you do not accept their testimony.

We are compelled to write to you in rude uncultured words, since uncultured and rude you are. But truly they carry the power and the truth of God. We entreat you in God's name to cast aside the haughtiness and pride which beset you, and gently and humbly give us your attention. May God lead you to the truth of what He has said. He was speaking of idolaters who had possession of the promised land. They worshipped animals in gold and silver and wood; they worshipped the whole creation, and all winged birds. Their cry was, 'These are our gods and other god there is not'. It was for these devilish things, made by the hand, injurious and execrable, that God condemned their worship. For since there are things made with hands to the service and glory of God, whose will it was to introduce His own holy people of the Hebrews, as He foretold to Abraham, Isaac and Jacob, to give them the land of promise, and to make the Israelites possessors and inheritors of the possessions of idolaters, and to crush and utterly wipe out those generations because they had polluted the land and the air by their transgressions, God warned His people beforehand not to fall into their modes of worship. He selected two men of the Israelite people, blessed and hallowed them for the execution of works wrought by the hand, but for the glory and service of God, as a memorial to those generations, Bezaleel and Eliab, of the first tribe of Dan. God said to Moses, 'Cut out two tables of stone and bring them to Me'. He brought them, and God, with His own finger, wrote upon them the ten life-giving and immortal words. Then God said : ' Make cherubim and seraphim, and a table, and cover it within and without with gold: and mark an ark of incorruptible wood, and put thy testimonies into the ark for a memorial to your generations, that is, the tablets, the urn, the rod, the manna'. Are these fashions and resemblances made by hand, or are they not? But they are for the glory and service of God. That great Moses, full of fear, in his desire to see a likeness and resemblance, not to be deceived, besought God, saying, 'Lord, show me Thyself manifestly, that I may see Thee'. And the Lord answered, 'If thou seest Me, thou wilt die. But pass into the hole of the rock, and thou shalt see My hind parts.' God showed to him in a vision the mystery hidden from the beginning of the world. But in our generations, in the last days, He showed Himself to us manifestly, both His front and His hind part, entire. When God saw the race of men perishing to the end, taking pity on His own creation, He sent forth His Son, begotten before time. And, coming down from heaven, He entered the womb of the holy Virgin Mary. The true Light shone forth in her womb, and, instead of human generation, the Light became flesh. And He was baptised in the River Jordan, and us also He baptised. He began to give us pledges of knowledge, that we might not be deceived. And, entering into Jerusalem, into the Upper Chamber of holy and glorious Sion, to the mystical supper, He delivered to us His holy Body, and gave us to drink His precious Blood. There also He washed our feet; we drank with Him, and we ate with Him, and our hands felt Him, and He became our companion. And the Truth was manifested to us, and the error and the mist which encompassed us fled away and vanished. And their 'voice went forth into all the world, and their words to the end of the earth'. Then men from the whole world came flying as eagles to Jerusalem, as the Lord said in the gospels, 'wheresoever the body shall be, there shall the eagles also be gathered together'. Christ is the Body: the high flying eagles are men who worship God and love Christ. Those who saw the Lord, as they saw Him, drew His portrait. Those who saw James, the Lord's brother, as they saw him, drew his portrait. Those who saw the proto-martyr, Stephen, as they saw him, drew his portrait. In a word, those who saw the faces of the martyrs who poured forth their blood for Christ, drew them. And men in all the world, beholding, gave up the worshipping of the devil, and worshipped these not with absolute, but with relative, worship. Which of the two seems to you, O emperor, right, to worship: these images, or those of the devil's error? When Christ was present at Jerusalem, Augar, then king of the Edessenes, hearing of His wonderful works, wrote to Christ: and Christ, with His own hand, sent him an answer, and His own holy and glorious face. Send to that not made with hands, and behold it. Multitudes of eastern peoples flock thither, and worship. Many other such things not made with hands exist, which the hosts of Christian pilgrims possess, whose daily worship you overlook.[1] Why do we not examine and depict the

---

[1] The reading here is doubtful.

Father of our Lord Jesus Christ? Because we know Him not, and it is impossible to examine and depict the nature of God. Had we beheld and known Him as we did His Son, Him also we might have examined and depicted, and you might call His image, too, an idol.

"We entreat you, as brethren in Christ, enter again into the truth, which you have left. Cast aside pride, destroy your self-assurance, write to all and everywhere, raise up again those whom you have scandalised and blinded, though, insensible as you are, you hold this for nothing. The charity of Christ knows that, when we enter the church of the holy Prince of the Apostles, and behold his portrait, compunction comes on us, and, like rain from heaven, a flood of tears comes down. Christ made the blind to see; you have blinded those who saw well, and have made them stumble, little as you think of it. You have reduced men to ignorance, stopped their fair running, deprived them of their prayers. Instead of vigils, prayerfulness, and zeal to God, you have dissolved the poor population in sleepiness, slumbering, and carelessness. They have lost their head. And you say that we worship stones, and walls, and boards. Not so, O emperor. But to rouse memory and feeling, to raise up the dull, rude, and untaught mind, by their names, their invocation, their features. Not as gods, as you assert: far from it: for we do not place our hopes in these things. If it be a picture of our Lord, we say, 'O Lord Jesus Christ, Son of God, help us and save us'. If it be of His holy

Mother, we say, 'Holy bearer of God, Mother of the Lord, intercede with thy Son, our true God, to save our souls'. If it be of a martyr, 'Saint Stephen, who didst shed thy blood for Christ, by thy confidence as proto-martyr, intercede for us'. So we say, in the case of every martyr who suffered martyrdom. Suchlike are the prayers which we address through them. It is not, as you assert, O emperor, that we call the martyrs gods. Put away those evil thoughts of yours. I charge you, save your own soul from the scandals and the imprecations which you receive from all the world: for even the little children make a mock of you. Go to the children's schools, and say, 'I am he who pull down and drive away pictures'. They will answer by throwing their slates at your head: and what you have failed to learn from the wise, you will be taught by the simple.

"You write, 'Ozias, the Jewish king, took out of the temple, after eight hundred years, the brazen serpent: so have I, after eight hundred years, expelled the idols from the churches'. Truly, Ozias was your brother, and had your self-conceit, and tyrannised over the priests of that day, just as you do. For holy David carried that serpent into the temple with the sacred ark. What was it but a brazen work consecrated by God for those who were then suffering from the bite of serpents: that an image might be shown to the people of the prime suggester of sin to the first creature formed by God, Adam and Eve, this was set up for the healing of sins. But you, as you boast, after eight hundred years, have cast out from the churches the blessing and consecration of the martyrs, and, as you fairly confessed at first, of set purpose and without necessity, and, lastly, by the subscription of your own hand, put upon your own head their curse.

"Now we, as holding supreme and undoubted authority from St. Peter the chief, were minded to rebuke you, but since you have brought the curse upon yourself, keep it and share it with your advisers. See to what extent you have broken in upon the edification and good course of others. The charity of Christ knows this. When we enter a church ourselves and behold the picture of our Lord Jesus Christ's wonderful deeds and of His holy Mother bearing in her arms and nursing our Lord and our God, and the angels standing round them and chanting the Holy, Holy, Holy, we do not leave that church without compunction. And, again, who is not touched with compunction and moved to tears when he beholds the baptismal vessels and the circle of priests surrounding, and the mystical supper, and the blind recovering their sight, and the raising of Lazarus, and the healing of the leper and the paralytic, and the multitude reclining on the grass, the baskets and the remnants taken up, and the fragments, and the transfiguration on Mount Thabor, the Lord's crucifixion, His burial, His resurrection, His holy ascension, and the descent of the Holy Spirit? Who that beholds the history of Abraham, and the knife approaching the throat of his son, is not moved to compunction and tears? In a word, all the sufferings of our Lord. It

were better for you, emperor, if the choice were offered
you, to be called a heretic than the persecutor and
destroyer of the histories, the pictures, the images, the
sufferings of our Lord. Yet to be called a heretic would
be thy misery and thy loss. Let me tell you the difference. The heretic is said to be known, when he is
known only to few. The scandals he gives are dark, the
thoughts perplexed and hard to discern. Those who
enforce them and are destitute of humiliation soon fall by
their own ignorance and confusion of mind. Their condemnation is not so great as yours. You have openly
pursued things well observed and conspicuous as light.
You have stripped naked the churches of God. As the
holy fathers clothed and adorned them you have left them
bare and tattered. And that, too, when you had no less
a pontiff than the lord Germanus, our brother and fellow
priest. You should have taken his counsel as that of a
father and teacher, as aged and experienced in matters
both of Church and State. He is ninety-five years old ;
he has served one after another patriarch and emperor.
He was never dispensed with, for his utility in both
these services. You disregarded him and called to your
side that transgressing fool the Ephesian, the son of
Apsimar, and his like. For the lord Germanus and the
then patriarch George, having informed and persuaded
Constantine, the son of Constans, the father of Justinian,
to write to us at Rome, he wrote to us under sanction of
an oath, and proposed to us fitting men that there should
be an ecumenical Council. 'Nor will I,' said he, 'sit
with them as emperor, nor speak as having control, but

as one of them; and as the pontiffs enact I will execute. And those who hold the right we will receive, and those who hold the wrong we will cast out and banish. If my father perverted anything in the pure and blameless faith, I will be the first to lay him under anathema. For it was by the grace of God that we sent to you; and the Sixth Council was held in peace.' O emperor, you know that the dogmas of holy church belong not to kings but to pontiffs, and require to be infallibly determined. For this reason pontiffs have been set over the churches, who abstain from secular matters, and kings equally abstain from matters of the Church and take charge of what is in their hands. The agreement of Christ-loving kings and of faithful pontiffs is one power when their administration is ruled by peace and charity.

"You have written in favour of an ecumenical Council being held. To us it seems unadvisable. You are he who prosecutes, insults and destroys the images. Give way, and grant us silence, and the world will be at peace, and scandals will cease, Suppose that we listen to you, that bishops have met together from all the world, that the Senate and Council have sat. Where is the devoted Christian emperor who is wont by custom to sit at the Council, to honour those who speak on the right side, to reject those who err from the truth, when you, the emperor, waver, and speak with the tongue of barbarians? Know you not that your attack upon the holy images is a work of contention, arrogance, and pride? At a moment when the churches of God enjoyed unbroken peace you raised up dissensions, enmities, and scandals.

Be quiet, rest, and there is no need of a Council. Write to every one and everywhere throughout the world which you have scandalised by saying that Germanus, patriarch of Constantinople, and Gregory, Pope of Rome, have erred respecting the images, and we will bear you scatheless for the sin of your mistake, as having received from God authority to loose things in heaven and things on earth. God is our witness that we have presented all the letters which you have written to us to the ears and hearts of the kings of the West, pacifying them in respect of your soul, praising and magnifying you in respects of your former government. Hence they welcomed your imperial letters with the honour due from kings when they had not yet heard of your evil attack upon the images. When they heard and were assured of this, that you had sent Jovinus, your officer of the guards, to destroy the statue of our Saviour, called the Witness, by which many miracles have been worked, many women of fervent zeal, such as the ointment-sellers, were present, beseeching the guardsman not to do it. He heard them not, but planted a a ladder, and mounted it, and with three blows of his axe shivered the face of the Saviour. The women could not bear that impious act. They drew away the ladder, clubbed him, and put him to death on the spot. You, zealous for evil, sent and slew there I know not how many women, in the presence of competent witnesses from Rome, from France, from the Vandals, from Mauritania, from Gothia, and generally from all the countries comprising the interior of the West. When these returned each to his own land and told the story of your revolutionary and childish deeds, they tore down your laurelled letters and defaced your countenance. Lombards and Sarmatians and other peoples towards the north overran unhappy Decapolis, they took your very metropolis, Ravenna, deposed your magistrates, and appointed their own. And they are minded so to do to imperial possessions adjoining us, and to Rome, while you are not able to defend us. These are the results of senseless folly. Yet you frighten us and say 'I will send to Rome and break in pieces the image of St. Peter, nay, and bring up in fetters their bishop Gregory, as Constans did to Martin'. And yet you should know and be assured that the pontiffs who in series sit at Rome for the sake of peace are as a middle wall and a fence to the East and to the West, the arbitrators of concord. And the emperors, your predecessors, struggled hard to maintain this peace. And if you bluster and threaten us, we have no need to fight you. Let the Bishop of Rome retreat twenty-four stades into Campania and go you, pursue the winds. Our predecessor, the pontiff Martin, sat for peace-sake exhorting. Thus it was that the evil Constans, erroneous in his belief as to the Holy Trinity, and throwing in his aid to the then heretical pontiffs, Sergius and Paul and Pyrrhus, sent and kidnapped him and tyrannously brought him up to Byzantium. After many cruelties inflicted he banished him, as he inflicted many on Maximus the monk also, and his disciple Anastasius, and banished them to Lazika. And Constans, their banisher, was murdered, and died in his sin. And the count, who was the chief of his household, being assured by the bishops of Sicily that he was a heretic, buried him secretly in the church, and his course was ended in his sin. But for the blessed Martin, the city in which he was banished bears witness to him, Cherson, and the Bosphorus, and all the North, and the dwellers in the North, by flocking to his tomb and receiving cures.

"May the Lord think us worthy to go the way of Martin, but for the help of the many we are willing to live, and live on. For all the West has its eyes fixed upon our humility, if we be not such, but they have a great faith in us, and upon him whose statue you threaten to destroy and sweep away, the blessed Peter, whom all the kingdoms of the West look upon as a god upon earth. And if you venture to try the truth of this, the kings of the West are ready even to avenge the easterns whom you have wronged. But, we beseech you in the Lord, turn away from these revolutionary, childish actions. You know that you are not able to defend Rome, the very head of your royalty, unless perhaps the mere city from its nearness to the sea and a fleet. As I said before, if the Pope go two miles and a half out of Rome, he fears nothing from you. One thing is our grief: savages and barbarians are civilised; you that are civilised become savage and barbarous. In full assurance of faith the whole West makes its offering to the holy Prince of the Apostles. And if you send to pull down the statue of St. Peter, look, we tell you beforehand, not on us be the bloodshed which will follow. On thy neck and head let it fall. We have just received an entreaty from the far West, from one called Septetus, desiring by the grace of God to see our face, that we may give him holy baptism. To avoid the reproach of neglect and slackness we are preparing for the journey.

"May God cast his fear into your heart and bring you back to the truth after the evils which you have inflicted upon the world. Let me receive your letter announcing your conversion. May the God who came down from heaven, and entered into the womb of the holy Virgin, the Mother of God, for the salvation of men, dwell in thy heart and cast out at once those who dwell in thee and have put in scandals; and may He bestow peace upon the Church of all Christians for ever and ever. Amen."

To this letter of Pope Gregory II. to Leo the Isaurian must be added a second, written at some time between the date of the first, in 727, and the date of the Pope's death in 731. Indeed from some expressions in the second we may infer that it was sent very shortly after the first.[1]

"We have received by our legate Rufinus the letter of your God-defended Majesty and Brotherhood in Christ. Indeed it is a burden to my life that you have not changed, but persist in the same evils—not having a Christian mind, nor being a follower and imitator of our holy and glorious wonder-working fathers and teachers. Indeed, foreign teachers I do not bring into the field, but those of your own city and country. Are there

[1] Mansi, xii. 975-981. This letter also was read in the Seventh Council.

wiser than Gregory the wonder-worker, and Gregory of
Nyssa, and Gregory the theologian, and Basil of Cappadocia, and John Chrysostom? not to speak of thousands
upon thousands like to them of our holy fathers and
teachers inspired by God. But you have rather followed
your self-assurance, and the passions of your own heart,
when you wrote, 'I am priest as well as emperor'. This
indeed, the emperors before you showed both in word
and deed by planting and caring for the churches; in
conjunction with the bishops seeking out the truth with
the desire and zeal of orthodoxy. Such were the great
Constantine, the great Theodosius, the great Valentinian,
and Constantine the father of Justinian II., the man of
the Sixth Council. Those emperors governed in the
spirit of religion, assembling councils in unity of mind and
purpose with the bishops, searching out truth of doctrine,
and so establishing and adorning the holy churches.
These are priests and emperors; they showed it by their
action. But you from the time you took the empire
have not kept to the end the boundaries set by the
Fathers. You found the churches arrayed in embroidered
robes, fringed with gold; you stripped off their ornaments and left them in nakedness. For what are our
churches? Are they not things made with hands—
stones, wood, straw, at best? But they were adorned
by pictures and histories, portraying the wonders of
the saints, the sufferings of our Lord, and of His holy
and glorious Mother, and of the holy Apostles. On
these histories and pictures men spend their substance.
Fathers and mothers, bearing in their arms little children

fresh from baptism, leading the youth and those who have come in from the heathen, point with their finger to the histories, build them up in faith, and carry their minds and their hearts aloft to God. You have deprived the poor of these things, and have plunged them into idle talk, gossip, songs, castanets, pipings, and trifling. Instead of thanksgiving and glorifying you have taught them to babble. Have your portion with the speakers of idle words.

"O emperor, listen to our humility, and cease. Follow holy Church as you found and received it. Dogmas belong not to emperors, but to bishops. It is we who have the mind of Christ. One is the discipline of the Church's commands; another, the perception of secular things. That military, ill-omened, rude mind, which you have for secular management, you cannot use for the spiritual treatment of doctrine. I point out to you the difference between palace and church, between emperors and pontiffs. Acknowledge it, and save yourself, and be not contentious. Were any one to take from you the royal robes, the purple, the diadem, the mantle, the several marks of rank, you would seem, in the sight of men, unseemly, shapeless, worthless; so you have made the churches. As you would then be, you have stripped the churches, and reduced them to tatters. For, just as the pontiff has no authority to enter the palace, and to make royal appointments, so the emperor has no authority to enter into the church, to make elections of the clergy, to consecrate and handle the symbols of the sacred mysteries, nor even to participate in them without the priest. Let each of us remain in the vocation wherein he was called by God. O emperor, do you see the difference between bishops and kings? If any one sins against you, O emperor, you confiscate his house, and leave him naked of all but his life, and, at last, you hang or behead him, or banish him, and make him a stranger to his children, and all his relations and friends. Pontiffs do not this. But if any one has sinned and confessed, instead of hanging and beheading, they put upon his neck the gospel and the cross, they guard him in their treasury, banish him to where the deacons and catechumens attend, put fasting on his stomach, vigil on his eyes, thanksgiving on his tongue. And when they have well disciplined and chastised him, they set before him the precious Body of the Lord, and give him to drink His holy Blood. And having restored him to be a vessel of election, cleansed from sin, they help him forward, pure and blameless, to the Lord. Emperor, do you see the difference between church and palace? Emperors who have reigned piously in Christ have neither disobeyed nor afflicted pontiffs. You, O emperor, transgressor and perverter, wrote with your own hand and subscribed, that he who removes the boundaries of the Fathers is accursed. Therein you condemned yourself, and separated the Holy Spirit from you: you punish and tyrannise over us with the soldier's arm of flesh. We, unarmed and undefended, having no earthly and carnal armies, invoke the sovereign ruler of all creation, Christ, whose seat is in heaven, who leads the hosts of the heavenly powers that He may send to you a demon, according to the Apostle's words, to 'deliver over such a one to Satan for the destruction of the flesh,' that the spirit may be saved. See, O emperor, into what a depth of shamelessness and inhumanity you have thrust yourself. You have cast your soul into abysses and precipices, because you would not humble yourself, nor bend your stubborn neck. For, when bishops, by good instruction and teaching, are able to present kings to God blameless, and exempt from errors and faults, they lay up a store of praise and glory before Him for the great Resurrection, when God will make manifest our hidden deeds in the presence of His angels. We, the humble, will then be ashamed, not to have reclaimed you through your disobedience. The pontiffs, before us, who each, in his own time, present their emperors to God, shame our poverty, in that we do not, in our days, present an emperor in honour and glory, but one disgraced and counterfeit. Once again we invite you: repent and be converted: enter into the truth: maintain what you found and received: give honour and glory to our holy and renowned fathers and teachers, who, following God's guidance, opened the blindness of our hearts and eyes, until they recovered sight. Your letter said, 'Why was nothing said about images in the six Councils?' Most true, O emperor, neither was anything said about bread and water, eating or not eating, drinking or not drinking. From the very beginning these things were given for the life of man. So, too, were images handed down. Bishops carried them into councils. No traveller, loving Christ and God, went on a journey without pictures, as men of virtue, and in God's favour. We pray you become bishop at once, and emperor, as you wrote. If, as emperor, you are ashamed to call yourself to account, write to all the countries which you have scandalised, by saying that Gregory, the Pope of Rome, has erred in the matter of images, and also Germanus, the patriarch of Constantinople. Then we take upon ourselves the guilt of your sin, as those who have received from the Lord authority and warrant to loose and to bind things on earth and things in heaven. And we will make you without charge as to this. You refuse. We, as those who shall give account to Christ our Master, have exhorted, have instructed you, as we were taught by the Lord. You recoiled : you refused to obey us, weak as we are : and Germanus, your bishop : and our fathers, the holy and glorious wonder-workers and teachers. You followed men perverse and rotten, erring from truth of doctrine. Take your portion with them. As we wrote to you before, we, by the grace of God, are following the road to the interior of the West for those who seek baptism. I have sent thither bishops and clergy of our holy Church. Their princes have received them, and bow their heads to be illuminated. They ask for me in person to receive them. On this path, by God's grace, we are bent : that we may not be condemned for neglect.

"May God grant you understanding and repentance to return to the truth which you have deserted, and restore the humble populations to Christ, the One Shepherd, and to the one fold of orthodox churches and priests. And may our Lord and God grant peace to the whole world now and for ever and ever. Amen."

These letters, which I have given entire, were written at the end of the third decade of the eighth century. They mark the breaking out of the Iconoclast persecution. They seem to me to give a complete picture not merely of the personal character in the two great factors of the time, Pope St. Gregory II. and the Isaurian emperor, Leo III., but of the power and influence of the Pope and the bishops in the spiritual life, and of the eastern ruler in the civil commonwealth. What the Pope claims, he puts forth in the most distinct language, and through all his letters it comes out that his predecessors have ever both possessed and exercised it. It is matter of simple history. Again we see incidentally from the words which he uses regarding the images and pictures, that, when he wrote, they were as much part of the Church's ritual as the prayers. To expel them from the Church was at once a complete interference with the inner life and conduct of Christians, and also had the effect to make at least in appearance the sacred places themselves synagogues and mosques, instead of habitations wherein Christ, His holy Mother and the saints had a dwelling. The conjunction of tyranny with impiety in Leo's attempt is made manifest.

Again, the relation between kings who rule the secular commonwealth, and the Pope, who, with the bishops throughout the world, presides over the one fold of Christ, is marked as simply and also as decisively as words can mark it. The Pope recognises in the amplest terms the temporal king as God's minister in his own domain, not a mandatory appointed by the people, who might be called to account by the people, and be deposed at its will, but the image of God, and one who administers the authority of God for the government of human society. As simply and as distinctly he mentions himself as holding, by express grant of God, power to bind and to loose things in earth and things in heaven. The king has no more power to enter the Church and touch the things of God therein than he himself has to enter the palace, and make appointments in matters of State. But there is this great difference—he has to answer for the conduct of kings in spiritual matters. Kings have to answer for how they treat him; but cannot call him to account for his adminstration of the divine power committed to him. In all things that concern sin the spiritual supremacy is complete. Its giver is God alone, and to God alone it is subject. This root of the spiritual power is brought out by the whole tenor of his words, in which the exact mediæval relation of the two powers is implicitly contained. The supreme minister of God in temporal things is the first son, but likewise the subject of the Church in spiritual things. In all this Pope Gregory II. in the year 727 may be said exactly to repeat what Pope Gelasius said in the year 494, both unarmed Popes speaking to emperors, lords of armies and absolute in civil power.

The relation between East and West is also very distinctly stated. The East lies crouching almost helpless beneath an unalloyed despotism, whilst all the nations of the West look up to St. Peter in Rome "as a God upon earth". When this was written just ninety years had passed since the sepulchre of Christ had fallen into subjection to the infidel and no less anti-Christian Saracen. The pilgrims who could no longer go to the sepulchre of Christ went to the sepulchre of the fisherman, and saw in the statue of St. Peter in his own Basilica the symbol of Christ reigning. But likewise all the kings of the West looked upon the successor of St. Peter as no less seated on the throne of justice, of peace, of concord, of charity, than as the supreme oracle of the Christian faith. What the patriarch Sophronius had said of him in the agony of the holy city before the impure Omar, the nations of the West knew and felt him to be. As Leo III. threatened to destroy the statue of Peter, so they went to him for baptism, so their kings were already buried in peace beneath the shadow of the Vatican. In 716, the year before the accession of Leo III., Theodon, Duke of Bavaria, came to Rome, being the first German prince who made a pilgrimage to the tomb of the apostles, as later on in 726, the very year in which the nefarious proceedings of Leo III. began, Ina, king of Wessex, with his queen Ethelberga came and began the school of the English in Rome, and made his land tributary to the Romescot.[1] So Constantine the Bearded had acknowledged the authority which his

[1] See *Brunengo Origini*, p. 32, Mansi, xii. 227.

successor was trying to diminish, while he sought to reduce the Christian Church, instinct with the presence, the miracles, the sufferings of our Lord, His Mother, and His Saints, to the bareness of the Jewish synagogue and the Mohammedan mosque.

It may be observed also that the Pope associates his own office with that of bishops throughout the world, especially with that of Germanus, as bishop of the imperial city. In his mind the bishops belong to the Pope, and the Pope no less to the bishops. There is no jealousy of them in his supremacy, nor of him in their subordinate jurisdiction. He censures Leo III. for not consulting his patriarch, Germanus. The authority which he so clearly describes is one and the same in the whole episcopate, where St. Gregory II. himself according to the language used three centuries before of St. Leo the Great is " princeps episcopalis coronæ ".

All these things come out not in the way of controversy but in an uncontroversial and authoritative exhortation of a Pope to an emperor. The Pope is clad in spiritual armour only in the midst of a captive province; the emperor is the master of fleets and legions behind the walls of Constantine.

No history written afterwards at a distance of time could set forth these things with so great a force as the words of a Pope issued to the chief actor in a desperate struggle at the very beginning of the conflict. The immediate result is to be noted. In the year 730 the emperor, finding that he could not make Germanus, the nonagenarian patriarch of Constantinople, further his design in stripping the churches of their ornament, deposed him and put a compliant instrument in his stead, Anastasius, a priest and officer of the great Church, who held the see three and twenty years to the time of Leo's son Kopronymus, with what effect and what ending will be afterwards seen. St. Gregory II. died in 731. In the four years which elapsed from the first letter to his death he was rewarded for it by the emperor Leo in five attempts to have him murdered. All these attempts were frustrated by the fidelity of those about the Pope, and by the awakened solicitude of the Italian people, who saw in Leo the most cruel and remorseless of tyrants, in Gregory not only the champion of their faith, but the defender of their temporal well-being, of every moral as well as religious liberty.[1]

The Greek chronographer, Theophanes, the main part of whose life belongs to this same eighth century, calls Pope Gregory II. "the most holy apostolic man, the assessor[2] of Supreme Peter in his chair, conspicuous in word and deed". His resistance to the rude soldier on the eastern throne won him great praise from the subjects of that throne. The rude soldier met him only with scorn and violence, as he met the murmuring of his people. Greece itself had taken arms in defence of its violated churches. Leo, by means of the Greek fire, destroyed the fleet of the insurgent Cyclades, and punished with the utmost severity his opponents in the capital. He carried on with greater violence the attack

---

[1] See Photius, i. 234, for the authorities presently quoted.

[2] Πέτρου τοῦ κορυφαίου σύνθρονος. Theophanes, p. 628.

on the images. In many cases it passed on to the relics. The patriarch Germanus made one more attempt to persuade the emperor. He reminded the emperor of the oath taken at his coronation to maintain the faith of the Fathers. This brought matters to an open breach. St. John of Damascus attests that " the blessed Germanus, distinguished in his life and his words, was scourged and banished". Another Greek historian, Cedrenus, adds that the emperor called him an idolater and struck with his own hands the patriarch of ninety years, who laid upon the altar of the great church the omophorion, the symbol of his rank, and departed into exile, with the words, " If I am Jonas, cast me into the sea, but I cannot touch the faith without a General Council be held ". Germanus had sat for fifteen years ; St. John Chrysostom and he the noblest who ever sat on that perilous throne. He retired to his paternal house, and did not cease his courageous struggle against the Iconolast. He died in most extreme old age, it is supposed in 740.

The destruction of the images proceeded with brutal violence. Leo was not content with destroying them, but likewise ruined the finest works of art. The new patriarch, Anastasius, priest and syncellus of Sancta Sophia, who had played the traitor to the man in whose place the emperor had intruded him, acted with the emperor in all his violence. Bishops were persecuted as idolaters, and above all the monks, who practised painting. The schools directed by them perished almost entirely. Leo is even said to have burnt the famous library with the twelve monks and their superior who presided over it. The imperial edict found no execution in the East only, under Saracenic domination, where the great theologian, John of Damascus, openly opposed the Iconolasts, as the Pope had; like whom he censured the imperial despotism in religious matters. "It belongs not to kings," said he, " to lay down laws for the Church. The Apostle said, 'God has placed in the Church first apostles, then prophets, thirdly, pastors and teachers for the perfection of the Church'; he did not go on to say kings. And, again, ' Obey those set over you and be subject to them, for they watch over you, as those who will give account for your souls'. And further, ' Remember your prelates, who have spoken the word of God to you, whose faith follow, considering the end of their conversation'. Not kings, but apostles and prophets, pastors and doctors spoke the word to you. When God had commanded David concerning building Him a house, He said afterwards to him, 'Thou shalt not build Me a house, because thou art a man of blood'. The Apostle Paul cried out, ' Tribute to whom tribute is due ; custom to whom custom ; fear to whom fear ; honour to whom honour'. To kings belong prosperity of the body politic; the regimen of the Church to pastors and teachers. This, brethren, is the invasion of a robber. Saul rent the mantle of Samuel. What was the retribution? God rent the kingdom from him and gave it to David, the meekest of men. Jezabel persecuted Elias ; swine and dogs licked up her blood, and harlots washed themselves in it. Herod slew John, and died eaten up of worms. And now the blessed Germanus, illustrious in life and word, has been scourged and banished with many other bishops and fathers, whose names we know not. Is not this a robber's act? 'The Lord, when scribes and Pharisees drew near to tempt Him, that they might entangle Him in His talk, and asked Him, is it lawful to give tribute to Cæsar. He answered, bring Me the coin: when they brought it He said, whose image is this? They answered, Cæsar's. And He said, Give then to Cæsar the things of Cæsar, and to God the things of God.' We yield to you, O emperor, in the things that are secular, tribute, custom, gifts. As to these our substance is in your hands. But in the regimen of the Church we have pastors who have spoken to us the word, and have formed ecclesiastical legislation; we remove not the ancient boundaries which our fathers have set us, but we hold to the traditions as we have received them. For, if we begin to pull about in the smallest thing the structure of the Church, the whole will come to pieces bit by bit."[1]

While Leo III. was thus violently proscribing and executing the defenders of the Church's rights in the East, St. Gregory II. at Rome censured his interference with the faith, but maintained his sovereignty as emperor in Italy. He had much ado to keep the peoples of Italy within imperial allegiance. When Anastasius, the intruded heretical patriarch of Constantinople, sent the letter announcing his succession to Gregory, the Pope rejected it. The personal acts of the emperor against his life did not move him from his settled

[1] St. John Damasc., *de Imaginibus Orat.*, ii. c. 12. Vol. I. p. 335.

purpose. The guardsman Marinus was sent as duke to Rome with orders to kill the Pope, or at least to take him prisoner. He could do nothing. A second attempt was made by the Duke Basil, in conjunction with the chartular Jordanes and the sub-deacon John. A third under the exarch Paul, who caused troops to march against Rome. Romans and Tuscans encountered them and made them retreat. Duke Basil had to save his life by taking refuge in a monastery. The Romans frustrated the further attempts of the exarch, and compelled the Pope to assume the full government of Rome, while the emperor intended to depose him and put a compliant tool in his place. Venice, Ravenna, and the five cities of the Pentapolis, under support of the Lombards, chose themselves dukes, renounced obedience to the exarch, and declared themselves for the cause of the Pope. The purpose of the Italians was to choose themselves a new emperor and advance upon Constantinople. Only the fidelity and the prudence of the Pope, who still hoped for the emperor's amendment, prevented the execution of this project.

The Lombard king, Liutprand, thought it was just the opportunity for which he was waiting to extend his monarchy in central Italy. Exhilaratus, imperial prefect at Naples, with his son Adrian, got possession of part of Campania, and set the people against the Pope; but the Romans attacked them, and after a furious battle slew them both. They chased the duke Peter from Rome. In the territory of Ravenna it came to a fierce struggle between the Italians on the Pope's side and the im-

perials, in which the exarch Paul lost his life. The
Lombards took many cities, especially in the Pentapolis,
and well nigh put an end to the imperial dominion
there. King Liutprand advanced as far as Sutri, took
it, but a hundred and forty days later bestowed it upon
the Apostles Peter and Paul, that is, the Roman Church.
This was in the year 727. It is reckoned by some the
first beginning of the State of the Church.[1]

Then it lay in the hand of the Pope to put an end to
Byzantine dominion in central Italy. The exarchate
was in Liutprand's possession. Had Gregory II. come
to terms with him, the Pope would have obtained a
free hand over the duchy of Rome. It already refused
tribute to the emperor; in arms repulsed his troops,
frustrated the repeated attempts upon the freedom and
life of Gregory II., and bound itself under oath to
protect him. The city of Rome expelled the imperial
duke, and seems to have given itself a municipal
government. It was the desire of the cities on the
Adriatic to substitute an orthodox for an heretical
emperor. Had the Pope put himself at the head of
this revolt, the emperor's power was at an end. He did
it not. He maintained the purity and the freedom of
the faith against imperial interference; but he urged
the population to continue their allegiance to the
sovereign. No stronger proof of this can be given than
a letter of the Pope to Ursus, doge of Venice, in these
words: "Gregory, the bishop, servant of the servants
of God, to Ursus, duke of Venice. Since by sinful

---

[1] See Reumont, ii. pp. 104-5.

action the city of Ravenna, the head of all, has been captured by that unutterable race of Lombards, and our son, the noble lord the exarch, is, as we know, sojourning at Venice, your nobility should support him, and maintain his cause, as we do, that the city of Ravenna may return to the former condition of the sacred commonwealth, as belonging to the domain of our lords and sons, the high emperors Leo and Constantine. So by the help of the Lord we may be able to remain firm, by zeal and love to our holy faith, in the commonwealth and the imperial service. God preserve you in safety, beloved son."[1]

This conduct could not fail to endanger the Pope's position with king Liutprand. In the year 728 the strangest scene of this perplexed time took place. The Lombard king appeared with his host before Rome. Pope Gregory II. visited him in his camp, and exercised such influence over him that the king desisted from the siege, went as pilgrim to the Apostle's tomb, and left as gifts there his crown, his arms, and his mantle.

Such events as these fill up the last four years of Gregory II. The result was what we might expect. Lord of Rome the emperor was called; Pope Gregory II. became in fact a glorious beginning of the papal rule. Not reckless force, not ambitious struggle and self-seeking formed the basis of this rule, but the free voice of the population in return for real protection, for duty steadfastly fulfilled, for never-failing courage, firm belief, and holy life. Put on the one hand the struggles, the

[1] Mansi, xii. 244.

fierce enmities, the treacheries, the revolts, the scenes of blood, the shifting of parties evoked by the Iconoclast storm in Italy and Rome, threatened by the two antagonists, Greeks and Lombards; and on the other hand the great activity of Pope Gregory II. in his own spiritual domain. And then estimate the Pope who repulsed Leo III. in his attack upon the Church's indefeasible rights, but maintained him as emperor; who fostered St. Boniface, enabling him by erecting a united hierarchy to lay the foundation of a Germany, one and Christian. We may fairly place the second Gregory by the side of the first for prudence, for courage, for insight, for the sagacity of a ruler in the person of a saint. The great annalist has even said of him, "If what he wrote were extant, and what he did had been more carefully recorded, he would be thought no less than Gregory the Great".[1]

On the 11th February, 731, St. Gregory II. closed a pontificate as renowned in its present action, as fruitful in its results. While the clergy and laity stood beside his coffin, they chose his successor, who was consecrated thirty-five days later, when the consent of the exarch was brought from Ravenna, this being the last time it was given by a viceroy of the Greek emperor.[2]

Concerning this Pope, Anastasius writes:—" Gregory III., a Syrian by nation, son of John. He sat ten years, two months, and twenty days. A man most meek and most wise, well instructed in the holy Scriptures, knowing both the Greek and Latin tongues. He

[1] Baronius, anno 731, 1. [2] Reumont, ii. p. 106.

knew all the psalms by heart, in their order, and was exceedingly skilful in their meaning by his long study of them. He was a polished speaker, an exhorter to all good works, a favourite popular preacher, a maintainer of the Catholic and Apostolic faith immutilate, who, by his fatherly warnings, ceased not to strengthen the hearts of the faithful, a fearless and zealous defender of orthodoxy : a lover of poverty, providing solicitously for those in want, not only with piety, but with careful pains. Redeemer of captives, generous supporter of orphans and widows : a lover of the religious life, so, by God's help, he reached the sacred order of the priesthood. Upon him the Romans, moved from the highest to the lowest by an inspiration from heaven, while he was absorbed in devotion beside the coffin of his predecessor, suddenly laid their hands and chose him for pontiff. It was in the times of the emperors Leo and Constantine, in the midst of that persecution which they set up, for the casting down and destruction of the sacred images of our Lord Jesus Christ and the holy Mother of God, of the apostles, and all saints and confessors. The same most holy man issued writings with the vigour of the Apostolic See, like as his predecessor of holy memory had done, to move them to repentance, and to put away this error."

Anastasius then records how the emperor had imprisoned his messenger in Sicily. "Whereupon the pontiff, with greater zeal, attended by the archbishops of Grado and Ravenna, with other bishops of the western part, to the number of ninety-three, held a Council at the sacred confession of St. Peter's most holy body, with all the clergy and the people, and passed a decree, that if henceforth there be any who, despising those who faithfully retain the ancient usage of the Apostolic Church, pull down, destroy, profane, or blaspheme the veneration of the Sacred Images, that is, of our God and Lord Jesus Christ, of His Ever-Virgin Mother, the immaculate and glorious Mary, of the blessed apostles, and of all saints, he be debarred from the Body and Blood of our Lord Jesus Christ, that is, from the unity and structure of the whole Church. This they all solemnly confirmed with their subscriptions." [1]

While the emperor replied to the Council's decree by imprisoning the papal bearer of it for a year in Sicily, the position of Pope Gregory III. was one of great difficulty in respect to the Lombard duchies of Benevento and Spoleto. They desired to be set free from their loose connection with King Liutprand, who, on his part, desired their complete subordination to himself. To the Pope their maintenance was of great importance. Thence arose a web of party-shiftings, treaties, and counter treaties, which encompasses the whole later history of the Lombard kingdom.

The archbishop of Ravenna had taken part in the Council at Rome, and his city was as much opposed to the emperor's godless attempts as was Rome. Leo III. resolved to be avenged upon the Pope and Italy. He put a great fleet under the command of the Duke

[1] See Rohrbacher Kellner, vol. xi. p. 175.

Manes, and ordered him to sack Ravenna, to treat the cities of the Pentapolis as rebels, to march on Rome, to destroy the images there, to treat without mercy those who attempted to defend them, to seize the Pope, and bring him in fetters to Constantinople. But storms deranged these plans. A hurricane fell upon the fleet as it was in sight of Ravenna. Part of it was sunk with all the crews: part managed to reach an arm of the Po, close to the city. Manes disembarked troops from it, and went against Ravenna. The people took arms, with the bishop at their head: whilst the women and old men went in sackcloth and ashes through the streets in supplication; the young marched out against the enemy, and drew him into an ambuscade. The Greeks flew to their ships, many of which were sunk, and the 26th June, 733, was kept as a perpetual festival in Ravenna: while, for six years out of hatred to the Greeks the conquerors would eat no fish from that arm of the river.

Leo became furious at this reverse: he redoubled his cruelty on the defenders of images, and since he could hurt the Roman Church in no other way, he confiscated all the possessions of the Church in his realm. In the words of Theophanes,[1] "That opponent of God, roused to a greater madness, and indulging further in his Arabian mind, imposed capitation taxes on the third part of Calabria and Sicily. Moreover, he ordered to

---

[1] Theophanes, p. 631. τότε ὁ θεομάχος, ἐπὶ πλεῖον ἐκμανεὶς, Ἀραβικῷτε φρονήματι κρατυνόμενος . . . ὅπερ οὐδ' αὐτοί ποτε οἱ διδάσκαλοι αὐτοῦ Ἄραβες ἐποίησαν εἰς τοὺς κατὰ τὴν ἑῴαν χριστιανούς.

be paid to the public treasury the so-named patrimonies of the holy chief apostles honoured at Rome, three golden talents and a-half, which had been paid of old to the churches, and he subjected to inspection and enrolment the male children, as Pharaoh did of old to the Hebrews: what not even his teachers, the Arabs, had done to the Christians in the East."

But he did a great deal more and a worse thing not noted by Theophanes. By an arbitrary act of secular despotism he severed from the jurisdiction of the Roman patriarch not only Calabria and Sicily, but the ten Illyrian provinces, Epirus, Illyricum, Macedonia, Thessaly, Achaia—that is present Greece—Dacia, Mæsia, Dardania, Prævalis, and attached them to the patriarchate of Constantinople. By this act its jurisdiction became co-extensive with the eastern empire, and the patriarch ecumenical in that sense of the Greek word which considered their own empire as pre-eminently the world, the land that is inhabited by men, as contra-distinguished from the land foraged by barbarians.

The patriarch to whom this honour accrued was that Anastasius who had been put by force into the place of the deposed Germanus, and was afterwards scourged and deposed by the same force under Leo's son and successor, Kopronymus.

Calabria and Sicily returned to the jurisdiction of the Pope as patriarch when the eastern emperor lost his dominion in them. The other provinces remained under the jurisdiction of Constantinople, the gift of an heretical emperor to a patriarch raised by him as his instrument to the ecumenical throne and at last deposed by his son as an instrument of little value.

In this act we see the completion of the aggression begun in the year 381, which attempted to give to the see of Constantinople the second rank in the Church. The sees of Alexandria, Antioch, and Jerusalem have sunk under it, but they have fallen into Saracen domination, and are little more than names; the diminished empire has in its capital the only real patriarch, and seeks to indemnify him for eastern losses by severing ten provinces from the patriarchal jurisdiction of Rome, under which they had been from the beginning of the Christian hierarchy. And Nova Roma, halved it is true in its secular extension, and trembling at the perpetual aggression of the Mohammedan chalif, beholds at length its patriarch standing over against the elder Rome as the chief instrument of imperial despotism in spiritual things.

Leo III. consciously completes the structure which Theodosius unwittingly began. The exaltation of the see of the capital is from beginning to end the work of imperial power, and this special character bears out to the full the denunciation of it by St. Gregory the Great in his own time, when he called the bishop's assumed title "a name of blasphemy and diabolical pride, and a forerunner of anti-Christ".[1]

Further, the acts of Leo III. in 733 are unanimously viewed by historians as having a large effect in the deliverance of Italy from the eastern sovereignty, and

[1] See above, vol. vi. p. 302.

his arrogation of the power to sever from the Pope, as patriarch, a large extent of provinces is viewed no less as a prelude to the great schism between the East and West. The remaining years of Gregory III. are filled up with his embarrassing position between the Lombard duchies of Benevento and Spoleto and Liutprand aiming at uniting Italy in a Lombard monarchy, whereby the Pope should become his subject as before he had been a subject of the Goths. From the moment when king Liutprand resumed more decidedly his plan against the Greek possessions and therefore against the duchy of Rome, he was bound to endeavour to end the independence of the two outlying Lombard duchies. But at the same time the alliance between these duchies and the papacy became a political necessity.

In the year 738 Liutprand took the field. He began with incursions into the territory of Ravenna, and invited the dukes of Spoleto and Benevento to attack the duchy of Rome. They refused, since, as Pope Gregory III. in one of his letters informs us, they had declared that they would not take the field against God's holy Church and her people, with whom they had entered into covenant. Thereupon the king made war against his disobedient liegemen. While he laid waste the possessions of the Church in the territory of Ravenna, he sat down before Spoleto in the spring of 739 with a considerable force. Duke Thrasimund could not resist and fled to Rome. In June the king entered Spoleto. He compelled Benevento to receive his nephew Gregory for duke. At the same time he drew the exarch to his interest, to whom the Pope's independence had long been odious. The confused accounts of annalists and historians make it difficult, if not impossible, to establish particular events in chronological accuracy. And the greatest uncertainty lies upon one of these events which is of particular importance, since it would secure for us an adequate reason for the Pope's conduct. Liutprand is said immediately after the taking of Spoleto to have appeared before Rome, demanding that the fugitive duke should be delivered up to him. Encamped in the meadows of Nero, beside the Vatican, he plundered St. Peter's, laid waste the neighbourhood, and made many Romans prisoners. It is certain that he took four cities in the Tuscan part of the Roman duchy, Amelia, Ortes, Bomarzo, and Bleda, as hostages for Duke Thrasimund.

The Pope was in the utmost danger of being speedily swallowed up by the encircling Lombard monarchy. Another siege of Rome, perhaps its capture, was to be immediately expected. The Lombard duchies were unable to repulse the Lombard king : for defence the emperor was impotent. He could send a fleet to ravage the imperial metropolis of Italy ; he could not defend the ancient mistress and maker of his empire: from whom he still took a title, which seemed a mockery. The Lombard threatened to dethrone Leo and make the Pope his subject. The dread of sacrificing the Church's independence drove St. Gregory III. to the last and sole remaining refuge.

The relations[1] of the Franks to Rome had been

[1] See Reumont, ii. 108.

various since the emperor Maximian had received the Salian Franks into the number of Rome's allies. After the victory over Syagrius, near Soissons, Clovis had raised up the Gallic-Frankish kingdom upon the ruins of Roman and Visigoth dominion. When baptised by St. Remigius, Clovis had become the first Catholic king in the midst of northern peoples attached to Arianism. This had brought him into manifold connection with the Holy See. In the time of Pope Gregory II., the conversion to the faith of Germany, from the Rhine as far as Saxony and Thuringia, not only relied for support, but had its root in the Frankish kingdom, and bound it still closer with the Papacy. There were also connections of another sort. As far back as the year 577, the emperor Justin II., conscious of his own impotence, had given to the messenger from Rome, soliciting help against Lombard aggression, for answer, either to seek to gain one of the Lombard dukes, or, if that failed, to draw the Franks to make a diversion by an expedition into Italy. The emperor Mauritius had himself made use of these means. From the year 584, king Childebert had been induced, by Byzantine invitation and gold, to undertake four campaigns against the Lombards. But it was reserved to a stronger family than his to co-operate in producing a great change south of the Alps. At the head of a people formed by the conjunction of various races amalgamated out of Germans, Gauls, and Romans, there grew up, in spite of sundry partial divisions, the mass of a mighty monarchy, north of the Alps. The weakness of the larger number of the kings who succeeded Clovis caused the chief officers of the crown to increase in strength. The lower the Merovingians sank, the higher rose the sons of Pipin, from the banks of the Meuse, until they equalled and outgrew the effete race. By the end of the first quarter of the eighth century, Charles Martell, Major Domus, first of the Austrasian, and then of the Neustrian-Frankish realm, had all power in his hands. In October, 732, he had won a greater merit from all the West than, perhaps, even Aetius and the Visigoth kings had gained. They had repulsed the vast Mongol mass at Chalons: he, by Tours, in a bloody battle, had set bounds for ever to the advance of the Arabians, overflooding Gaul after the conquest of Spain. He threw them back upon the uttermost south of Gaul, from which, after many a battle, they were forced to recross the Pyrenees.

To Charles Martell, shining in the lustre of that great victory which saved the West from Mohammed, as Leo III. prevented his entrance into Constantinople, the beleagured Pope turned from the cruel yet impotent tyranny of Leo, and the pretension of the encroaching Lombard. And his own words, at the moment of trial, will better express his situation than any others which can be put in his mouth :— [1]

"We have thought it necessary to write again to your Excellency for the excessive grief which is in our heart, and for our tears, confiding that you are a loving son of St. Peter, prince of the apostles, and ours also,

[1] From the *Liber Carolinus*, quoted by Mansi, xii. 184.

and that from reverence to him you will listen to our charge for the defence of God's Church, and his own peculiar people: we, who can no longer endure the persecution and oppression of the Lombard race. They have taken from us all the lights in St. Peter's Church, which were given by your relations or yourself. Next to God, we take refuge in you : for this the Lombards oppress and make a mock of us. St. Peter's Church is stripped, and reduced to utter desolation. But we have rather confided the details of our sorrows to your liegeman, the bearer of this, which he may present by word of mouth. O my son, may the Prince of the Apostles deal with thee now and in the future life before our Almighty God, as thou disposest and contendest with all speed for his Church and our defence, that all nations may know your fidelity, your pure intention, the love which you bear to the Prince of the Apostles, to us, and to his peculiar people, by your zeal and your defence of us. And by it you will also gain eternal life."

Either with this letter, or before it, the Pope had sent to Charles Martell the keys of St. Peter's Confession, together with rich presents. His messengers were received with great honour, but no actual help in soldiers came. It is supposed that Charles Martell was then engaged, together with Eudo, Duke of Aquitania, in expelling the Saracens from Southern France.

The acts of Leo III., as an open enemy of the Pope's spiritual power, by his completion of the Byzantine patriarch's usurped jurisdiction in the year 733, as above described, thus precede, by about five years, the appeal made to Charles Martell, by Gregory III., in the face of the advancing Lombard king, Liutprand, on the one hand, and the absence of any protection by the emperor on the other.

Such was the uncertain position of things when, in the year 741, the three great actors were withdrawn from this life, Leo III., on the 18th June, Charles Martell, on the 24th October, Gregory III., on the 27th November.

Of what this most noble Pope did for Rome, Anastasius gives a long account. If the Romans loved and admired him as a cardinal priest, they loved and admired him no less as Pontiff to the end. While fully acknowledging still the sovereignty of the eastern emperor, a man as unworthy of the loyalty which bound the Pope to him, as a sovereign could be, the Pope neither by his heresy nor by his tyranny was induced to renounce him. He did, indeed, one great and momentous act. He sent to Charles Martell the keys of St. Peter's Confession, conjuring him, in the name and person of the Apostle, to save his city from the Lombard robber: the city which its sovereign was neither able nor willing to save: the city on which the robber was descending with the utmost force. It is supposed that Charles Martell was engaged in battle with the Saracens in Southern France at the time. The Pope sent a second time, to the great leader, the Hammer of the infidel, the Liberator of the Christian. What took place is not exactly known: but the Lombard king, Liutprand, retired in the month of August, 739, from the siege of Rome with his army to Pavia, and helped Charles Martell against the Saracens, who had again invaded Provence. Then also Rome was saved by her pontiff from becoming a Lombard prey.

Once more towards the end of 741, Liutprand was preparing a new expedition against Rome and its duchy, when Rome lost, on the 27th November, St. Gregory III., its pontiff, prince, and champion. At Constantinople, Leo III. had been succeeded by his son, Kopronymus, whom the Greek Zonaras calls, " a cub more cruel than his sire ". Rome seemed covered by a terrible tempest : France had been deprived not a month before of Charles Martell. All minds were in fearful expectation, when a star of peace appeared on the horizon. There rose up one who, by the force of his mind and the unsparing risk of his own person, was to preserve Italy during ten years from the destruction which seemed impending.

Upon the death of Pope Gregory III., the Roman chair was filled in four days. The usual three days having been devoted to the solemn funeral of that Pope, the electors, on the fourth day, which was Sunday, the 2nd December, met in the Lateran palace, and immediately united their votes on the person of Zacharias, and he was consecrated the same day. Two things combined to bring about this rapid election and ordination, one the extraordinary merit of the elected, the other the extreme urgency of the public need, as Rome, with its provinces, was threatened by King

Liutprand. The confirmation by the exarch, that token of imperial oppression, was not waited for. Zacharias was the last of those illustrious orientals of whom a series at this time occupied the Roman Chair. Though born in Italy, being a native of the Calabrian city, St. Severina, he was Greek by lineage. Of him and of his predecessor, Photius himself, the leader of the Greek schism, has left written, "How could I pass over in silence the two Roman prelates, Gregory and Zacharias, who were eminent for their virtue, who contributed to increase the flock of Christ by their teaching full of divine wisdom, who were even conspicuous by the divine gift of miracles?" Of Zacharias, the character given by Anastasius is, "a man most meek and gentle, adorned with every goodness, a lover of the clergy and all the Roman people, slow to anger and quick to mercy, rendering to no man evil for evil, nor punishing according to desert, but from the time of his ordination made kind and tender to all: so that he returned good for evil to his former persecutors, both promoting and enriching them". During ten years, Zacharias, by his wisdom and personal influence, kept at bay the three Lombard kings, Liutprand, Rachis, and Aistulf, who seemed on the point of completing the long-fostered ambition of their people by the absorption of Rome into a barbarian kingdom. The whole time is a contest of mind against matter, of right against encroachment. We learn, by the very words of these Popes, that even in the eighth century the radical opposition between Romans and Lombards continued still as in the time of the first invasion under Alboin. The end of the Lombards was to make themselves lords of all Italy: that of the Romans, to prevent themselves passing under a barbarian yoke. True peace there could never be between them. A truce, liable at any time to be broken, was all that could subsist.

Three times at least in the ten years of his pontificate, Zacharias repeated, with Lombard kings, the action of his great predecessor, Leo, with Attila. Liutprand, after thirty years of reign, was consolidating his kingdom by the reduction of the two Lombard dukedoms, Spoleto and Benevento. Bent upon gaining Rome, when he had subdued Spoleto, free from the check of Charles Martell, secure of the East by the contested succession to Leo of his son, Kopronymus, Liutprand was at Terni. Thither Pope Zacharias resolved to go in person, accompanied by a train of clergy. Liutprand received the Pope with great honour, and the result of a long interview was that he agreed to restore to the Pope four cities of the Roman duchy which he had taken. He likewise gave back the patrimony of Sabina, which he had seized thirty years before, and made peace with the Roman duchy for twenty years. The Pope returned as it were in triumph to Rome, was received with exultation, and ordered a procession of thanksgiving from the Church of St. Mary of the Martyrs, that is, the Pantheon, to St. Peter's. This was in his first year, 742.

But the next year, 743, Liutprand broke out against

the exarchate : and Eutychius, the exarch, with the archbishop of Ravenna, and the other cities of Emilia and the Pentapolis, had no better resource than to beseech the Pope to succour them. The Pope, accepting the request, sent two legates to the king with gifts, beseeching him to cease hostility with the Ravennese. But they accomplished nothing.

Then the Pope left Rome to the government of the Duke Stephen, and, with his train of clergy, went in person to Ravenna. The archbishop met him fifty miles from the city. The people welcomed him with cries, " to the shepherd who left his own sheep to deliver us who were about to perish ". But the Pope insisted upon going on to Pavia itself, in spite of the objections of king Liutprand to receive him. Disregarding every risk, he reached the Po on the 28th June, where he met the Lombard nobles sent to attend him ; and, on the 29th, he celebrated Mass on the feast of the chief Apostle in the church of St. Peter, called the Golden Ceiling, wherein was the shrine of St. Augustine : whose body Liutprand himself had brought from Sardinia.

King Liutprand then received the Pope with great honour in his palace. The Pope pressed him not to attack the province of Ravenna, but to restore its cities. The king, after great resistance, consented to leave the province of Ravenna as it was before. The king then accompanied the Pope to the river, and sent his chief captains with him on his return, who restored the territories of Ravenna, and the castle of Cesena.

So the Pope disarmed a second time the most powerful of the Lombard kings, and saved the exarchate for the empire. From that time Liutprand lived in peace with the Romans and the Ravennese. He did not live to receive the report of the ambassadors whom he had sent to Constantinople to inform the emperor of the peace thus given to Ravenna. He closed in the next year, 744, his reign of thirty-two years, the longest in the Lombard series, and that in which the Lombard kingdom most developed its power. It must be confessed that the power of religion was great over the mind of Liutprand. He reverenced Pope Gregory II. under the walls of Rome : he listened to the voice of Pope Zacharias in the interviews of Terni and Pavia. At the bidding of the Vicar of Christ, he more than once stopped himself in the middle of his victories, and renounced the greatest desire of his heart.

Hildebrand, Liutprand's co-regent, and successor, maintained himself only a few months, and had to resign the crown before the end of the year 744 to Rachis, duke of Friuli. A good understanding seemed to be established with the Pope under a king renowned for piety, married to a Roman, who made rich offerings to the Church. Peace was assured with the Roman duchy. But after a few years Rachis also was in conflict with the exarchate. In 749 a new war burst out in central Italy. The king of the Lombards came in great wrath and with a valiant army to besiege Perugia. Then once more Pope Zacharias appeared. Attended by some clergy and chief people of Rome he went to the camp at Perugia. His gifts and his prayers so prevailed with King Rachis that he consented to raise the siege of the city and return in peace to Pavia. But the king had been so moved by the words of Pope Zacharias that after a few days he resigned his kingdom. With his queen Tassia and his daughter Ratruda he came like a pilgrim to Rome to venerate the tomb of St. Peter and to ask admission among the clergy. The Pope cut off the long hair of the Lombard king, gave him with his own hands the clerical tonsure, and vested him, as well as his wife and daughter, in the habit of St. Benedict. He retired, by the Pope's suggestion, to Monte Cassino, which had been restored by the abbot Petronax from its ruin towards the end of the sixth century. With him also retired the prince Carloman, younger brother of King Pipin, and a Benedictine as well as Rachis. Pope Zacharias greatly loved that monastery, enriched it with gifts and books, and exempted it from all episcopal jurisdiction, subjecting it immediately to the Holy See.

The three pacific victories gained by Pope Zacharias, twice over King Liutprand and once over King Rachis, victories due to the dignity of the Vicar of Christ and his Christian virtues, had raised to the highest point the estimation of the Romans for the Holy See. Is it possible to conceive a greater contrast that that presented by Leo III. and his son Kopronymus on the one hand, and the three pontiffs, the second and third Gregories and Zacharias, on the other; or between the governments of the blinding, scourging, maiming, and torturing sovereigns of the East, and the pastors ruling with beneficence and risking their lives for their flock in the West? Thus had the Popes become the protectors of desolated Italy; therefore had the Kings Liutprand and Rachis offered their royal mantles at the shrine of St. Peter. We are come now to the last and crowning incidents of this contrast.

On the resignation of Rachis the true Lombard spirit had raised his brother Aistulf to the throne. In June, 749, he was elected at Milan. Almost immediately thereupon a series of regulations showed that other political principles than those of Rachis had obtained the mastery. The presents made by the last king after his abdication were declared invalid; commerce with the Romans forbidden. The fortresses in the Alpine passes were strengthened. The army was put on a new footing. Presently Aistulf marched upon the exarchate. In July, 751, he was in Ravenna. Every imperial possession in the northern and midland Adriatic provinces fell into his power. Only Rome then was wanting to Aistulf's ambition. Hitherto no barbarian had been able to fix his seat there. His dreams were to reach all the power of the ancient emperors in Italy, and so verify the proud title of "king of all Italy" which a hundred and fifty years before Agilulf had inscribed upon his crown. He named his palace at Pavia "the palace of Italy," and an inscription has been found, " Aistulf, in the name of Christ, by God's will Imperator Augustus, in the fourth year of his reign ".[1]

No help came from Byzantium, where the emperor

---

[1] Brunengo, *Le Origini della Sovranità temporale dei Papi*, p. 106, quoting inscriptions recorded by Troya, Codice diplomatico.

Constantine Kopronymus, after putting down a pretender to his throne, was only occupied with Iconoclast troubles. For a long time no opposition was perceived; when the last exarch fell into the Lombard king's power Rome seemed to be the sure prey of him who had won Ravenna.

At that moment when the last authority of the empire threatened to disappear a new bond was knitted between Rome and the West as token of the world's changed situation. Pipin, son of Charles Martell, on the point of taking the idle sceptre from the hand of the last phantom-king of Merovingian race, turned to Pope Zacharias with the request that he would approve this great change. This is one principal mark of the immense moral power wielded by the Pope in the middle of the eighth century that the mayor of the palace in the Frankish empire sought his sanction to change his deputed into immediate royal authority. The Pope thus called upon exercised his supreme judgment in this highest secular matter. He decided that it was lawful for him who fulfilled the royal duty to be king rather than for him who only bore the name. In these words he deposed the Merovingian and recognised the Carlovingian dynasty, and the nobles of the Franks assembled in diet accepted his judgment. Pipin was proclaimed king of the Franks in 752 on the field of Mars at Soissons. Some but not all accounts say that St. Boniface, at the head of the German episcopate, three years before his martyrdom, gave the Church's sanction to the political act, in accordance with the judgment of the Pope.

This momentous judgment of Pope Zacharias, given at the end of 751, was one of his last acts. He died on the 14th March, 752. The last words of Anastasius respecting him are an epitome of his life and character. Having recorded his general deeds of kindness and munificence, he adds :—" Embracing and fostering all as a father and good shepherd, and absolutely allowing none to suffer tribulation in his times, the people entrusted to him by God lived in great security".

At once clergy and people proceeded to a new choice. but the Stephen whom they chose lived but three days, and died before consecration. " Then," says Anastasius, " the whole people of God met in the basilica of St. Mary at the Crib, and beseeching the mercy of our Lord God, and with the good will of our Lady, the holy ever-virgin Mary, Mother of God, they elected, with one mind, another Stephen, a man preserving the tradition of the Church with inviolable constancy, swift to help the poor, a firm preacher, a most valiant defender of the fold in the strength of God." Immediately a great persecution against the city of Rome and its adjoining cities broke out from the savage king Aistulf. Three months after his consecration, the Pope sent two legates, his brother, Paul, and another, with large gifts to move the Lombard king to a treaty of peace. The king made a peace for forty years, but in four months, treading oath and treaty under foot, he pretended that the city of Rome, with all its province, was subject to him, and that all the inhabitants should pay him yearly a capitation tax of a gold solidus. The Pope sent to him two fresh legates, whom the king received, but refused all conditions, and ordered them to return to their monasteries without seeing the Pope.

At the end of this year, an imperial legate came to Rome with two *sacred* letters [1] from the emperor, one for the Pope, the other for Aistulf. In it he asked the Lombard king to restore the lands of the Commonwealth, unjustly taken by him. The Pope immediately sent on his brother, Paul, with the imperial Silentiarius, to Aistulf at Ravenna. The king scorned to listen either to emperor or Pope, but he added a messenger of his own, to go to Constantinople, and make some proposition to the emperor. The two legates, John the Silentiarius, and Paul, the deacon, returned to Rome, and reported to the Pope that they could do nothing. Then the Pope, convinced of the evil purpose of the king, sent to the imperial city his own messengers, in company with John the Silentiarius, " beseeching the imperial clemency that, as he had already often written to him, he would come with an army to defend by every means all this part of Italy, and would deliver this city of Rome and the whole Italian province from the fangs of the son of iniquity ".[2]

In the meantime, " that most atrocious king of the Lombards burst into fury, threatening that he would slay all the Romans with one sword if they did not submit to his sovereignty ". The Holy Father called

---

[1] *Litteræ divales.*
[2] Anastasius, *Vita Stephani Papæ.* Mansi, xii. 521-532, from which the following quotations are taken.

all the Roman people together, and walked in procession with them with naked feet, bearing in his arms the image of our Lord still venerated in the chapel *sancta sanctorum*. This he carried from the Lateran Church to Santa Maria Maggiore, the clergy and people chanting litanies and intercessions; and Aistulf's broken treaty of peace was affixed to a lofty cross, and formed part of the procession.

This legation from Pope Stephen II. took place in the year 753. The emperor Constantine Kopronymus was not the man to save Italy from the Lombards. To the repeated requests of the Pope he sent no other help than imperial letters, charging him to induce Aistulf to restore the provinces he had taken from the empire, and to Aistulf in the same sense, calling him to undo his diabolical aggression.

The emperor also left the Pope free to unite himself with any one who could defend him. It was a natural right in such a case: but the imperial sanction made it more easy of success.

"Then," says Anastasius,[1] "the most holy man having, in vain, sought, by innumerable presents, to conciliate that pestilent king for the flocks committed to him by God, that is, for the whole army at Ravenna and all the people of that province of Italy, of which he was in possession, and seeing especially that there was no help from the imperial power, as his predecessors of blessed memory, the second and third Gregories and Zacharias, begged help from the king of the Franks

[1] Mansi, xii. 524.

against the oppressions and invasions which they had suffered in this Roman province from the abominable Lombard race ; so he in like manner, by the inspiration of divine grace, sent in his deep sorrow a letter by a foreign hand to Pipin, king of the Franks." Thus from 726, the beginning of the Iconoclastic heresy and tyranny of the emperors Leo III. and Kopronymus, the Popes acknowledged the Byzantine sovereignty until in 753 the direct attack of the Lombard king Aistulf upon Rome, and the attempt to make himself sovereign of the Popes of Rome and of the territory called its duchy, together with the impotence of the Byzantine emperor to defend his own subjects, and the Pope himself vainly entreating succour from him, compelled Stephen II. " to turn his thoughts from the East to the West".[1]

While the Lombards were pressing Rome and all its fortified places, Pipin replied to Stephen's entreaty for succour by sending the Bishop of Metz and the Duke Autchar to accompany him in his journey to France. "Then the same most blessed Pope, trusting in the mercy of our almighty God, went out of this city of Rome to St. Peter's on the 14th October, and many Romans followed him and people of the neighbouring cities, and weeping and crying, they would hardly let him go on. But he, trusting in the strength of God and the protection of the holy Mother of God and the chief apostles for the safety of all, weak as he was in body, began that laborious journey, commending all the Lord's flock to Peter, our Lord, the good shepherd and blessed

[1] Muratori, *Annali d'Italia*, 753.

Prince of the Apostles." As he drew near to Pavia that most wicked king Aistulf sent him messengers, ordering that he should on no account ask for the restoration of Ravenna and its exarchate or the other places of the commonwealth which Aistulf or his predecessors had invaded. The Pope replied that nothing should induce him not to ask it. When he reached Pavia and was received by the king he made him many presents, and ceased not with many tears to ask him for the restitution of what he had taken. He could obtain nothing. The Frank legates pressed that he might be allowed to go on to France. The king asked the Pope if he desired it. The Pope avowed it, and the king gnashed his teeth, and sent his satellites repeatedly in secret to turn him from it. The Frank legates at last succeeded in obtaining permission for him to go forward.

On the 15th November, attended by the bishop of Ostia and a large train of clergy, he left Pavia, and continued his journey. He reached the valley of the Rhone by Aosta and the Mons Jovis, where about two hundred years later Bernard of Menthon founded the monastery which has given its new name to the mountain, and he rested at length at the abbey of St. Maurice, now one of the oldest existing monasteries.[1]

Stephen II. was the first Pope who crossed the Alps. The few Popes who had up to that time travelled outside Italy had been banished, as St. Clement by Trajan to the Crimea, or St. Liberius confined by Constantius I. at Berea in Thrace, or St. Silverius banished by

[1] Brunengo, *Le Origini*, etc., p. 135.

Belisarius to Patara; St. John I., St. Agapetus, and Vigilius had by royal orders gone to Constantinople. St. Martin had been taken thither a prisoner by Constans II., and Pope Constantine, ordered by Justiuian II. to go thither, had been courteously received by him.

Now at the call of duty, but with his own free consent, Stephen II. crossed the Alps and took refuge in France, to consolidate an alliance with the most potent kingdom of the West, full of importance for that Christendom which the see of St. Peter, and that alone, was creating. As the eastern emperor had nothing for him but to impose heresy and execute tyranny, the king of the Franks, hearing news of his approach, sent a splendid train under his eldest son Charles to convoy him. That was a memorable day when Stephen and Pipin met at the royal villa of Pontigny, near Chalons, on the Marne, not far from the field of battle where Attila three hundred years before failed to make Europe a Mongol empire. Now the union of Stephen and Pipin saved it from a Mohammedan enthralment.

The long-suffering loyalty of so many Popes was at length exhausted. The deliverance of the Holy See and their flock from the intolerable Lombard yoke, a usurpation both upon their natural right and their divine commission to rule the people of God, combined with their desertion by the eastern emperor, whom, in despite of the most inhuman government during two hundred years ever practised by men called Christian, they had acknowledged and maintained, led Stephen II. to inaugurate a new political order of things. His request, accompanied with many tears, to Aistulf at Pavia to restore to "the commonwealth" of the empire the exarchate and to forbear grasping Rome, a request which the Lombard cast away in scorn, led the Pope, feeble as he was, to risk all the dangers of the Alpine passes, as well as to seek in France, where alone it could be found, an arm strong enough to save Italy both from Lombard and from Byzantine.

The king of the Franks, besides his eldest son Charles, had sent Fulrad the abbot and Rothard the duke to conduct the Pope from the monastery of St. Maurice, whom they brought with all his retinue to the king with great honour. "When," says Anastasius, "the king heard of the most blessed pontiff's approach he hastened to meet him with his wife, his sons, and his chief men. Advancing three miles from his palace called Pontigny, he dismounted from his horse, and with great humility threw himself on the earth, together with his wife, his children, and his chieftains, and so received the Pope. He also walked for some space to a certain spot guiding the Pope's horse." Then the papal train went on together with the king to the palace, rendering thanks to God in hymns and spiritual songs. It was the feast of the Epiphany, and Pope and king sat side by side in the oratory, when the Pope with tears besought the same most Christian king that by a treaty of peace he would arrange the cause of St. Peter and the commonwealth of the Romans. And the king satisfied the Pope by oath that he would to the utmost listen to all his requirements and restore the exarchate of Ravenna and the other rights and territories of the commonwealth.

"It being winter, he then caused the Pope with all his retinue to take up his abode in the abbey of St. Denys, near Paris. King Pipin, going to Quiersy and there assembling all the nobles of his royal power, inflamed them with the words of so great a father, and ordained with them to fulfil what, under favour of Christ, he had decreed with the most blessed Pope."

By this solemn compact between the Frank realm and the Holy See, the king bound himself, should he be victorious, to give over to St. Peter, and in him to Pope Stephen, and his successors, all the places of the exarchate, and of those lands which had belonged to the empire, of which the Lombards had taken possession. If we are to follow the text of the contemporaneous statements and later references, Pipin considered this act not as a donation, but a restitution. Those for whom this restitution ensued were so blended together in the view which results from Pipin's subsequent declarations that to separate them seems impossible.[1] The one party is the Roman Commonwealth, which here takes the place of the empire, without, in its essence, containing any other idea, for empire is but one form of commonwealth; the other party is the Roman Church. There is no reference here to the duchy of Rome, the territory belonging to the city according to the Byzantine departmental administration. The Pope conferred on the king the title of Roman Patricius, a title which

[1] Reumont, ii. p. 115.

Pipin accepted simply in its true meaning, understanding by it protection of the Church, as he afterwards named himself merely Defensor or Protector of the Church.

Stephen, in the meantime, was staying at the Abbey of St. Denys, near Paris, for a long time dangerously ill, in consequence of his sufferings during his journey, and also of his great anxiety. On the 28th July, 754, he anointed in this abbey Church, afterwards the resting-place of the kings of France, Pipin and his wife, Bertrada, with their sons, Charles and Carloman. So, for the first time, the hand of a Pope touched the youthful head of that Charles, who, in riper age, was destined to act with such force on the fortunes of the western Church.

When the negotiations between the king of the Franks and Aistulf led to no result, the Frank army began its march. The Lombards were defeated near Susa, at the foot of Mont Cenis, and presently Pipin stood before Pavia. Thereupon Aistulf consented to peace. He promised to surrender Ravenna, and divers other cities: he bound himself no longer to oppress Rome and her territory. But scarcely was the covenant made, and the Frank host withdrawn, and the Pope returned to Rome, which he entered before the conclusion, having been welcomed in the meadows of Nero by the exulting people, when king Aistulf repented of his concessions. Not only did he not give up a palm of land in the exarchate: he broke again into the Roman territory, took cities, laid waste the country. In this distress wore away the year 755. With New Year's Day, 756, the king began the siege of Rome. He shut in the city on three sides. On the height of the Janiculum the Tuscans were encamped. Aistulf, with his main force, lay beside the Salarian and neighbouring gates : the Beneventans shut in the southern gates. His attacks upon the walls were repulsed. Every one took part in the struggle. Abbot Warnehar, the Frankish minister, put on armour and worked day and night upon the walls. The whole country round, with its churches, villas, and dwellings, was mercilessly wasted. The Lombards made a desert round Rome. Letter after letter the Pope sent to Pipin.

The Father and Head of the Christian family was in the utmost possible danger of beholding the spiritual rights of his see and the people which he loved and cared for, subjected to the half barbarous domination of intruders, who, for nearly two hundred years, had forced themselves upon Italy. In those two centuries the possession of Rome, and lordship over it, had been the coveted prize first of their heathen, and then of their semi-Christian ambition. The rule of the Goth, much nobler in his natural character, and much less savage, had yet failed, even under the genius of Theodorich, to amalgamate itself with Roman thought, law, and usage. The strong hand of the great Gothic king had seemed to tame it : as soon as he was gone, it corrupted his grandson, and murdered his daughter and heiress, Amalasunta, too good and noble for her people. But the prospect of having to submit to an Aistulf, and his ferocious nobles, was worse than the Gothic servitude had been, which yet had subjected the free election of their Father and Pontiff by the Roman clergy and people to a foreign domination. And this domination from Odoacer to Leo III. regarded not the good of the Church, but the ends of Byzantine or Lombard.

What, in this day of terror, Pope Stephen wrote to Pipin bears so strongly impressed the inmost belief of his own heart and of the Church at the time that I quote it in part.

" Peter, called to be an apostle of Jesus Christ, Son of the living God, and in me the whole Catholic and Apostolic Roman Church of God, the head of all the Churches of God, founded upon the firm rock in the blood of our Redeemer, and Stephen, bishop of the said Church, to the most excellent kings, Pipin, Charles, and Carloman, to the most holy bishops, abbots, presbyters, monks, also to the dukes, counts, armies, and people of France, grace, peace, and valour be abundantly ministered to you by our Lord God for the rescue of that holy Church of God and its Roman people entrusted to me, from the hands of persecutors.

" I, Peter, the apostle, having been in the absolute choice of supernal clemency called by Christ, Son of the living God, to illuminate the whole earth—who hold you for my adopted children to defend from the hands of adversaries this Roman city, and the people committed to me by God, and likewise the house in which, according to the flesh, I rest, to deliver it from the contamination of the heathens : but likewise our

Lady, the Mother of God, ever-virgin Mary, adjures, admonishes, and commands you: and with her the thrones and dominations, the whole army of the celestial host; also, the martyrs and confessors of Christ join in the adjuration, that you may grieve for that city of Rome, entrusted to us by the Lord God, and for the Lord's flock dwelling in it, and deliver it with all speed from the hands of the persecuting Lombards, who are perjured with so great a crime. Hasten and help before the living fountain, whence you have been consecrated, and born again, be dried up."[1]

The siege[2] had entered into the third month when tidings came that the king of the Franks was on his way to answer the appeal of Pope Stephen. In April, 756, he passed Mont Cenis. Again the enemy did not venture to defend the Alpine passes. It would seem that Aistulf had not expected so early a movement. The siege of Rome was broken up. The siege of Pavia took its place. Pavia yielded sooner than Rome. Pipin was still in camp before the city when a mission from the Greek emperor appeared to desire the surrender to the empire of the lands which had been or were to be taken from the Lombards. Here was seen in what sense the king of the Franks had understood the word "restitution". The eastern deputies promised rich presents to Pipin,[3] if he would give back Ravenna and the other cities and fortresses of its territory to the empire. The king of

[1] Mansi, xii. 543. This letter I have much shortened: but nothing important is omitted.
[2] Reumont resumed, ii. p. 116.
[3] *Vita Stephani Papæ II*. Mansi, xii. 531.

the Franks replied that for nothing on earth would he suffer those cities to be taken from the rule of St. Peter, the jurisdiction of the Roman Church, or of the pontiff of the Apostolic see. He declared upon oath that for uo man's favour had he repeatedly entered into this conflict, but only for the love of St. Peter and the pardoning of his sins, adding that no amount of treasure could persuade him to take away what he had once given to St. Peter.

Then Aistulf, in fear of losing everything, asked for peace. The Frank nobles in the army who had previous connections with the Lombard, managed the agreement. Aistulf not only ratified the previous contract, but surrendered the third of his treasure, and promised the payment of a tribute which had been paid in the time of the dukes. Pipin presented to the Pope a solemn document respecting the gift of the conquered territory. The Abbot of St. Denys, accompanied by the Lombard Commissioner, with full powers, executed the agreement and the royal will. Upon arriving at Rome, he laid the keys of the cities ceded by the Lombard upon the tomb of the Prince of the Apostles. The exarchate and the Pentapolis, and a large portion of Umbria, were to belong to the Roman Church, and partly then, and partly later, came into its actual possession, on one side from Comacchio, in the swampy lowlands along the Adriatic coast, down to what was afterwards the mark of Ancona; on the other side as far as Narni, not far from the confluence of the Nera and the Tiber, where the duchy of Rome began. That it did not need. If the distant emperor exercised nominal authority there, the virtual authority had long belonged to the Pope, who ruled there with acceptance of the people.

It was the summer of 756. About the end of the winter Aistulf died through a fall from his horse, hunting. After his death ensued a struggle for the throne. The monk Rachis strove again for the sovereignty, which Desiderius, duke in Tuscany, contested. It is not clear how parties in the Lombard kingdom had been so transformed that he who had been compelled once to quit the throne for yielding to Rome now was unsuccessful against a competitor favoured by Rome. But this one bought his victory dearly. He renounced in favour of the Church several cities not mentioned by name in Pipin's gift, from Ferrara and Bologna down to south of Ancona. At the same time Spoleto and Benevento put themselves under protection of the Pope and the king of the Franks, as the dukes and nobles swore fidelity. "This change is of the hand of the Lord," wrote Pope Stephen to Pipin at the beginning of 757.

In the course of a few years a new State, the State of the Church, had been founded.[1] For a new State it was, even if its connection with the empire was not dissolved. Its geographical position in the centre of the Peninsula and touching both seas, enhanced its importance. The moment was great and decisive. The times of the Roman empire were fulfilled. East and West had more and more decidedly parted, as well especially on the field of theological science as on the field of political

[1] See Reumont, ii. 118.

formations. Agreement had become impossible unless the West was willing to give up its civilising mission. Italy's political formation was closely bound up with that mission. The Gothic domination had fallen inasmuch as it had been powerless to assimilate land and people. The Lombard people, inferior in energy and in warlike qualities to the Goths, in its late attempt to unite Italy under one sceptre, had failed less through the weak resistance of the last remains of the Roman empire than through the deep-lying failures of its political and military constitution. These showed themselves soon after its permanent occupation to the south of the Alps by its parting into numerous military fiefs, with slight internal connection. Moreover, the instability of relation between the two nationalities from the beginning made almost impossible the task which Liutprand and Aistulf had set themselves. Attempts to assimilate in life, custom, and law had followed a long period of barbarous oppression, when the hand of the Church had already enfolded conquerors and conquered. These attempts had there produced a reaction which threatened to undo what had been accomplished. After two hundred years of settlement the Lombards were still held to be strangers. Not to mention numerous other tokens of this, it has a deep meaning when under the successor of Pope Stephen " the whole Senate and all the people of the God-protected city of Rome" write to king Pipin concerning the extension of this province "rescued by you out of the hand of the heathen".[1] The

---

[1] "De manu gentium."

national Italian elements made their complete effect sensible in the State of the Church, and secured its establishment in opposition to that temper of aliens represented by the Lombards. The new temper was not one-sided and exclusive, but assimilating, and therefore certain of development and progress. Never has a State arisen under circumstances so remarkable, in the midst of a violent shock, yet with so general a concurrence. It was due to the consistently-pursued management of a series of distinguished men as the result of their moralising influence. This did not limit itself to the populations immediately participating in it, which had found steady advocates and actual protectors in the Popes, notwithstanding the extreme need and oppression suffered by them. It embraced the whole Christian world. The Church absolutely required secular independence in order to maintain in living energy this moralising influence, to fulfil this her great mission. This necessity must appear clear to every one if there were in the history of Italy and the Papacy no other period than that of the last Lombard times, or that following when the Carlovingian rule was falling to pieces. The foundation of the temporal power was no artificial plan devised by Gregory II. for himself and his successors when he began the great battle against the Iconoclasts. It was a necessity in the world's history, developing itself rapidly, yet step by step, out of the situation of things both in politics and religion. And as if it should not want a legitimate title also, the new formation rose at a moment when, independently of action on the part of the Popes, the whole claim of the empire practically disappeared in the centre of Italy. It was recognised by the Popes alone even when scarcely anything more remained of it than a mere form and name.

CHAPTER VII.

ROME'S THREE HUNDRED YEARS, 455-756, FROM GENSERIC TO AISTULF, BETWEEN THE GOTH, THE LOMBARD, AND THE BYZANTINE.

I PROPOSE to give a continuous review of the Roman pontiff's position in the city of Peter from the plundering of imperial Rome by the Vandal Genseric in 455 to the siege of papal Rome and desolation of the Campagna by the Lombard king Aistulf, beginning January 1, 756. This attack was followed in that year by the enfranchisement of Rome and the gift of the exarchate by Pipin, king of the Franks, to St. Peter and his successors, when he laid the keys of the cities surrendered by the Lombards on the tomb of the Prince of the Apostles.

Three hundred years of suffering unbroken and of glory unsurpassed which preceded the passage of the Roman pontiff from servitude to sovereignty.

The sun of imperial Rome set for ever when the degenerate grandson of the great Theodosius, great grandson also of Valentinian, whose name he covered with infamy, perished by the stroke of an assassin in the Campus Martius, the result of a life in which he imitated the crime of Tarquin. But Tarquin's crime led to Rome's freedom, the crime of Valentinian III. brought the end of the imperial city, and the substitution of a Rome built upon revealed truth and eternal justice for the Rome of secular pride and unjust conquest.

In these three hundred years the brother Apostles, the fisherman and the tentmaker, took the place of the robber brothers, Romulus the slayer, and Remus the slain, when the twelve centuries of augured dominion were exactly fulfilled, and in the time of St. Leo the Great the twelve vultures had had their full flight.

The three hundred years begin with the formal acknowledgement of St. Leo's primacy, as consisting in the descent from St. Peter, bearer of the keys and feeder of the flock, made to him by the Council of Chalcedon in the letter soliciting the confirmation of their decrees by him; a letter to which the eastern emperor Marcian, husband of the noble grand-daughter and heiress of Theodosius, adds his own request for confirmation, and with his wife, St. Pulcheria, in his character as the head of the temporal power, acknowledges St. Leo, the Pope, as "the very person entrusted by the Saviour with the guardianship of the vine".

The three hundred years end with the Pope emerging a temporal sovereign from the Iconoclast persecution. The eastern empire also has fulfilled its work in these three centuries, and the soldier of fortune, who, at the end of many revolutions has become the successor of Marcian, has ridden his warhorse into the Church of God, and attempted to substitute himself as its governor for the successor of St. Peter, to dictate its creed, and interfere with its worship. In recompense he is expelled from the

Italy which he and his predecessors had stripped and sacrificed during two hundred years. Then the crown of temporal sovereignty is added to the papal mitre of spiritual power, which Leo the Isaurian had sought to displace. And, moreover, the "advocate of the Church," who, "as Christian prince and Roman emperor," had used *against* the Church the very God-given power which it was his first duty to use *for* her, was on the eve of seeing the same powerful race which had enfranchised Rome and dowered the Roman See exalted to the imperial throne in the face of both the Byzantine and the Saracen. The emperor of the East had lowered his dignity to the poor ends of ambition, and the task of degrading God's Church. In Leo the Isaurian, and in his son Kopronymus we see, in fact, that the man who sits on the throne of the first Christian emperor is become the chief enemy of the Church. The deeds of Heraclius and Constans II. had given adequate cause for the Divine Providence to allow the rise of Mohammed and the severance of its eastern and southern provinces for ever from the empire of Constantine and Theodosius. Thereupon Leo and his son Kopronymus interpreted the lesson thus given as entitling them to meet the assumption of the prophet-emperor enthroned in the Damascus which had ceased to be theirs with equal arrogance in the counter assumption to be emperor-priest. The enemy from Mecca had seized Both Powers in his claim to be prophet; the enemy at Byzantium seized both as emperor. Civil power was the appendage to Mohammed, but became the root of spiritual authority to Leo the Isaurian.

Let us now retrace the period of civic disaster which the Popes encountered from the last years of St. Leo the Great. The following may be considered the main causes:—

First of all is the domination, not of barbarians only, but of heretical barbarians, as Pope Gelasius termed Odoacer.[1] In that passage of his letter the Pope says that when "Odoacer occupied the realm of Italy he had enjoined things to be done which were not lawful, but to which we, by the help of God, would, as is well known, not submit". He speaks in the name of his see, but what the acts alluded to were we do not know. The domination of Odoacer and of Theodorich after him was Arian. It lasted at least sixty years, from 476 to 536. It was the policy of Theodorich to treat Rome well, in its civil aspect. He fostered the Senate, keeping it in quiet subjection to himself. He professed to treat Italian and Goth on equal terms. As long as the Acacian schism lasted, which effectually prevented unity of action between the emperors Zeno and Anastasius and the Popes who had ceased to be their subjects, but who regarded the Roman emperor with all the consideration required by Roman loyalty to the head of the Roman name, the Gothic king observed this conduct of neutrality; but when a new emperor, Justin I., had acknowledged all the demands of Pope Hormisdas and began to act as a Catholic emperor, Theodorich dropped the mask and appeared as he was, the head and bond of the whole Arian league in the West. Pope

[1] *Epis.* xiii.; Mansi, viii. 60.

Symmachus died in 514. The Acacian schism at that time was in full force; the emperor Anastasius full of emnity and deceit against the Pope. Theodorich allowed Hormisdas to be elected Pope after a vacancy of the see for one single day. Hormisdas died in 523, and a vacancy of six days only ensued, when Pope John I. was allowed to be freely elected. In the meantime the acts of the emperor Justin I. roused the full Arian spirit in Theodorich. He allowed Pope John I. to be freely elected, which did not prevent him from compelling that Pope to go as his ambassador to Constantinople in order to gain indulgence for the eastern Arians. And he uttered the threat that he would fill Italy with blood if his demands were not complied with. And when Pope John I. came back crowned with honours rendered to him as the first Pope who had ever visited the eastern capital, Theodorich threw the Pope into prison, and he never came out alive from the royal dungeon at Ravenna.

This fact throws back a full and disastrous light upon the whole Arian domination in Italy. A poet of our day has put in the mouth of the doomed Gothic princess, the royal-hearted Amalasunta, words of her father :—

"I never loved that Apostolic Throne!"[1]

the truth of which is a striking epitome of history. No Arian ruler *could* love that Apostolic Throne. But we learn from the fact what the Popes must have gone

[1] A. de Vere, *Legends and Records, Amalasunta*, p. 278.

through from the period when Rome fell under the rule of northern condottieri to the expulsion of the Goths under Belisarius and Narses. It is impossible that one who denied the Godhead of the Master should look, with love and veneration, upon the successor of the Disciple. If the Shepherd of shepherds be not God Himself, the Shepherd, who acts in His name, will not be received, as invested with supreme and universal spiritual power.

Let us examine the connection of Arian domination over Rome and Italy, as exercised, first, by Odoacer, and, secondly, by Theodorich, with the eastern throne's position and claim.

Odoacer exercised the authority which he held in Rome and in Italy, with the approval of the emperor Zeno. He compelled the Roman Senate to send to Zeno at Constantinople the insignia of the western emperor's dignity, together with the declaration that a western emperor was no longer required; and that one emperor seated at Constantinople was sufficient. In return, he was invested by Zeno with the title of Patricius of Rome. It may be said that Zeno could do nothing else at the time: and that Odoacer's power was really the power of the sword. Nevertheless, the emperor of the East had become the sole Roman emperor. The Popes acknowledged him as such, and continually called upon him to discharge the duty of protection to the Church of God, which belonged to the head of the Roman Commonwealth. A few years later, Zeno wished to be delivered from the near neighbourhood of the stirring Gothic king, Theodorich. He commissioned Theodorich to lead his people into Italy, and take possession of it. Five years of terrible conflict ensued between the Herule and the Goth. They inflicted great sufferings on the Italian cities. The Goth prevailed. Ravenna was taken. There was a compact made between Theodorich and Odoacer. A banquet ensued, and in it Odoacer was slain. The first act of Theodorich was to send an embassy to the emperor Anastasius, who had succeeded Zeno, asking for the crown of Italy from his hands. He was acknowledged by Anastasius as the ruler of Italy, and as ruling it in the imperial name. Theodorich became more and more powerful, and if he did not expressly renounce the emperor's over-lordship, he acted, in all respects, as the sovereign of Italy, and of the great dominion which he had attached to it. But the Byzantine sovereignty in Italy was never resigned in the purpose of the emperor. When, after 33 years of rule, Theodorich expired in 526, and Justinian speedily succeeded his uncle, Justin I., the Gothic rule showed evident signs that it had been built up by the extraordinary skill and energy of a single man, but had entirely failed to assimilate the Roman and the Gothic elements in a stable union. When Justinian conquered the northern provinces of Africa, and Rome, the old seat of the empire, by the arm of Belisarius, he was, in his own mind, only recovering his own, and reassuming what Zeno and Anastasius had *lent* to Odoacer and Theodorich. This was the mind of every Byzantine sovereign from the date of the western empire's extinction in 476, or rather it was not extinguished to them, but *they* had become its lords. Herule, and Vandal, and Goth, and Frank, and Burgundian, and whatever else those northern savages called themselves, they were only encamped on the sacred Roman soil, which belonged indefeasibly to the emperor who sat at Constantinople, the heir of Constantine's Rome.

What has just been said will supply us, as I believe, with a key to the whole conduct of the eastern emperors. I will review it under three heads: first, Byzantine despotism as exhibited in secular government: secondly, Byzantine despotism as pushed into theological doctrine: thirdly, Byzantine despotism, as laying claim to the government of the Church. The three together make up the thing which has received the name of Byzantinism.

The first vacancy of the Holy See, after the extinction of the western emperor by the death of Pope Simplicius, in 483, witnessed the beginning of the Acacian schism. The connection of that schism with the making Zeno sole Roman emperor I have already traced in a former volume. It also marks the beginning of the aggression by the civil power ruling Rome with the title of Patricius bestowed by Zeno, but really with the unrestricted power of the barbarian sword, upon the freedom of Papal election.

When, on the death of Pope Simplicius in 483, they were assembled at St. Peter's for the election of his successor, Basilius, prefect of the prætorium, and patricius, representing also king Odoacer, rose and said that the late Pope had given Odoacer the most earnest charge to guard against any injury being done to the Church, upon his own death, by being present, and sharing in the election. Odoacer[1] did not go so far as to claim authority to *confirm* the election. No such power was then recognised either in the eastern emperor, or in the actual ruler of Rome. Pope Gelasius was elected in 492; Pope Anastasius in 496; they were chosen in Rome; they took possession of the chair of Peter immediately upon their election; they then informed the emperor of their accession, or received first congratulations from him.

Pope Symmachus in 498 followed Pope Anastasius. And here acts of great importance took place. The Acacian schism had then divided the East from Rome. Zeno, in order to unite the Monophysites with the Catholics, had drawn up an ambiguous formulary of union called the Henotikon. The emperor Anastasius was most desirous to maintain this formulary. He also wished to recover union with Rome. When the Senator Festus came to Constantinople on the embassy of Theodorich, he promised the emperor that he would induce Pope Anastasius to accept this formulary. But Festus, returned to Rome, found Anastasius dead, and Symmachus chosen by the greater part of the clergy to succeed. He saw that there was no chance of inducing Symmachus to accept the formulary. But Festus was able to raise a schism, and set up, as Antipope, Laurentius. After great troubles, which lasted four years,

[1] *Stimmen aus Maria-Laach*, vol. viii. 42-44.

Symmachus was established: but neither the emperor nor Theodorich exercised or claimed authority to *confirm* his election.

In 514 Theodorich, the king of Italy, allowed the election of Pope Hormisdas to take place without interference: and again the election of Pope John I. in 523. But upon the death of that martyred Pope in 526, instead of his former indulgence, a state of suspicion and anger against Rome had taken possession of the mind of Theodorich. He imposed upon the Romans the choice of Pope Felix IV. It is supposed that at this time he enacted that in future no one should ascend the papal chair without the confirmation of himself and his successors.[1] Thus only can it be explained that after this, on the death of a Pope the Apostolic Chair remained vacant sometimes for months, and a large sum had to be paid into the Gothic treasury for the deed of confirmation.

Very shortly after the death of Pope John I., and the fellow-victims, Boethius and Symmachus, Theodorich died, and was succeeded by his grandson, Athalarich, eight years old, under the tutelage of his mother, Amalasunta. During her regency Pope Felix IV. died in 530. The electors were divided into a Gothic-Roman and a national-Roman party.[2] The candidate of the former, Bonifacius II., and of the latter, Dioscorus, were both elected two days after the death of Pope Felix, and both consecrated on the following Sunday: and so without any confirmation from Ravenna. But

[1] Niehues, vol. i. p. 434.   [2] Niehues, vol. i. p. 436.

the death of Dioscorus after twenty-eight days prevented a schism, and Boniface was fully recognised as Pope. Boniface, in dread of troubles which would arise at his death, ventured to summon the clergy to St. Peter's, and laid before them a decree to subscribe : upon which he declared the deacon Vigilius to be his successor. But feeling speedily that this act was contrary to the existing laws of the Church, he called a second assembly of the clergy, the senate, and the people of Rome, declared himself to have violated the freedom and sanctity of the Papacy, and caused in their presence the paper nominating Vigilius to be burnt.

The next election took place in 532, according to the usual conditions. The young king, Athalarich, was made to defer the confirmation of Pope John II. for two months.[1] The state of Rome in the meantime was frightful. Every man sought to plunder the goods of the Church. The Senate had passed a decree strictly forbidding the alienation of church goods by candidates for the Papacy. It was disregarded : and the only resource for the new Pope was to appeal to the king and beg him to confirm the senate's decree. Athalarich decided that the decree should be inscribed on a marble tablet, and set up in front of the court of St. Peter's. But the Gothic king's help was purchased dearly, and the fee for confirming a Pope was established at 3000 gold pieces.

Such in fifty-one years was the result of Odoacer meddling with the Papal election. Not only had the right

[1] Niehues, *Kaiserthum und Papstthum*, vol. i. 437.

to confirm been allowed to the civil ruler of Rome, but a heavy money payment had been imposed for the confirmation, and delay superadded.

In that year, 534, the young King Athalarich perished at the age of eighteen by his own excesses. The Queen Amalasunta speedily lost her power. She nominated her cousin, Theodatus, of the royal blood of Amali, king. He repaid her by allowing her to be murdered. His name and character became odious to the Romans. On the death of Pope John II. in 535 he allowed the free choice of the Roman Agapetus to take place in seven days. But he exercised great tyranny over the Romans. He forced Pope Agapetus to go to Constantinople as his ambassador. When that Pope died, as we have seen, in the eastern capital, he imposed on the Romans the choice of Silverius as Pope, threatening with death any one who did not consent to his appointment.

This is the briefest possible record of how the original liberty of the Roman clergy and people to elect the Pope was treated by the foreign Arian rulers, Odoacer, Theodorich, Athalarich, and Theodatus. Then the emperor Justinian became by right of conquest immediate lord of Rome, and seized without scruple upon the appointment and confirmation of the Popes. The act of his empress Theodora, in her violent deposition of Pope Silverius, is the first specimen of Byzantine conduct when it enters by right of conquest upon Italian territory. That the Romans had every reason to wish for the extinction of foreign, which was also heretical, domination, must be clear to every one who follows history in its detail. But likewise the example with which Byzantine domination in Italy opens will suffice to represent to us in a living picture the permanent relation of the Popes to the eastern or Greek empire. If arbitrary[1] violations of the freedom of Papal election by the Gothic kings may be given as the exception, it became by frequent repetitions under Justinian the rule. As the patriarchal see of Constantinople had long been given only to select Court favourites, and taken away from the occupants at every change of imperial inclination, the same plan was pursued henceforth with the filling of the Apostolical See. The emperor issued his edict: the Romans and the Pope were expected to obey. Not even the domain of the Faith was kept free to the Pope. In this also the attempt of the emperors was to lower the chief dignity of the Church to be the echo of their commands.

From Justinian onwards the Byzantine emperors claimed and exercised the right to confirm the papal election.[2]

When the ill-treated Vigilius died at Syracuse, returning from his unhappy sojourn of eight years at Constantinople, Justinian caused the archdeacon Pelagius, who had been nuncio at Constantinople, to be elected his successor. In like manner John III. in 560, and Benedict I. in 574 were elected under pressure from the emperor. But in 568 the Lombards came into Italy,

---

[1] Niehues, p. 446.
[2] *Stimmen aus Maria-Laach*, viii. p. 48. *Die Regierungen und die Papstwahl.*

and at the death of Benedict I. in 578 they were pressing Rome so severely that no one could undertake the journey to Constantinople to ask for imperial confirmation. So the Book of the Popes says, " Pelagius,[1] a Roman, was consecrated without the command of the emperor, because the Lombards were besieging the City of Rome, and Italy was greatly laid waste by them. There was such calamity as had not occurred in memory of man." In 590 St. Gregory the Great waited six months for his election to be approved at Constantinople. What use was made by the eastern emperor of the right to confirm the Papal election from the time of St. Gregory to the breaking out of the Iconoclast persecution has already been recounted. The last instance of this degrading mark of servitude was the confirmation of Pope Gregory III.'s election in 731 by the exarch of Ravenna. From that time forth the Popes elect were no longer confirmed by the emperor or his delegate ; and in 756 the hand of a western ruler made them sovereign princes, and the much injured Italy was relieved from eastern oppression so far at least as regarded Rome and the central and northern provinces.

What took place at the death of a Pope was after this fashion. The representation of the see was vested in the three chief officers ; the primicerius of the notaries, the archpriest and the archdeacon informed of the fact the exarch of Ravenna. They addressed their letter thus : " To the most excellent and distinguished lord, long to be preserved by God for us in the discharge of his

---

[1] *Vita Pelagii Papæ*, ii.—Mansi ix. 879.

supreme office, N., ex-consul, patricius, and exarch of Italy, N., the archpriest, N., the archdeacon, N., the primicerius of the notaries, keeping the place of the holy Apostolic See ". The exsequies of the late Pope took place, and a three days' fast and prayer preceded the act of election. In this act took part the higher clergy with the whole spirituality, the more important magistrates of the city, the nobility, the deputies of the people, and such Greek troops as might be present in the city. When the election was completed the elect was conducted in solemn procession to the Lateran, where he received the first homage of the people. The electors subscribed the decree of election which in the meantime had been prepared, and laid it up for future record in the archive. A second shorter copy was sent to the emperor at Constantinople, which ended with the words :[1] " wherefore we, all your servants, in our sorrow beseech that the piety of our masters may favourably receive the entreaties of their servants, and by their grant of their permission would allow the desires of their petitioners to take effect for the good of their empire by their own command. So that in virtue of their sacred letters we, being under the same pastor, may solicit without ceasing the almighty God and the Prince of the Apostles, who has granted the appointment of a worthy governor of his Church, for the life and empire of our most serene masters."

Yet more submissive is the tone of the letter to the exarch. After the election has been fully described, it

[1] From the *Liber diurnus Romanorum Pontificum*, Tit. iii.

continues: "This being so, most exalted God-protected master, we yet more earnestly entreat that by God's quick operation inspiring your heart you would give command to adorn the Apostolic See with the perfect consecration of our father and pastor, as by the grace of Christ happily and faithfully discharging your execution of the imperial supremacy, so that we, your humble servants, seeing our desire more rapidly fulfilled, may be enabled to return unceasing thanks to God, to the imperial clemency, and to your admirable government willed by God. Thus, by the appointment of the Pontiff of the Apostolic See, our spiritual pastor, we may pour forth continual prayers for the life and safety and complete victory of our most Christian masters. For we know that the prayer of him whom by God's will we elect to the supreme pontifical dignity, will propitiate the divine power, and obtain for the Roman empire all the success which it can desire. It will also preserve your own power, under God's protection, for the ruling of this captive Italian province, for the protection of us, all your servants, and for the continuation of long deeds of arms."[1]

The three Papal officers also informed the archbishop of Ravenna, the magistracy, and the Roman nuntio there, of what had taken place, beseeching their assistance that the confirmation of the election might speedily be given. When this arrived from Constantinople and Ravenna, the Pope elect received consecration. The seven regions of Rome were represented in a procession

---

[1] Niehues, vol. i. 462-3.

which conducted him from the sacristy of St. Peter's to the Confession of the Prince of the Apostles, where he recited his profession of faith. Thereupon Mass began to the Gloria, the bishops of Albano and Porto led him to the bishop of Ostia, who was seated in an elevated chair. They held the gospels over his head, and said the first and second prayer. Then the bishop of Ostia completed the proper consecration, while the archdeacon laid the pallium upon him. After this, the new Pope ascended the papal throne, gave his blessing to all the priests, and proceeded with the sacrifice of the Mass.

A papal vacancy was reckoned from the burial of the deceased Pope to the consecration of the Pope elect.

This power of confirming the election of a Pope, in complete derogation from the original liberty, which had only once been broken by the tyranny of the first Constantius, in the year 355, down to the Arian occupation of Rome by Odoacer, appears to have been exercised from the last days of Theodorich in 526 down to Pope Gregory III. in 731. The emperor Constantine the Bearded, had, after the Sixth Council, suffered Pope Benedict II., in 684, to be freely elected : but his son, Justinian II., reimposed the yoke.

The weight of imperial pressure upon Rome had been considerably affected by the Lombard occupation of the northern provinces of Italy, beginning in 568. The capture of Italy as a province, won for Justinian by the conquest of Narses, was only completed in 555. In thirteen years the Lombards entered upon the country which the Goths had well nigh reduced to ruin.

Lombard aggression ran well nigh side by side with Byzantine oppression for two centuries. Right in the midst of both the Apostolic See was placed. In 596, the great St. Gregory complained that he had been keeping watch and ward against these new northern robbers for twenty-eight years, which is the second arm of Byzantine oppression.

The exarch, in the judgment of the despotic Justinian and his successors, was a viceroy of all Italy, planted in the fortress of Ravenna, one side of which was guarded by the sea, the other by marshes. Thence Theodorich ruled: there he was buried: and the Byzantine only felt secure in the Gothic stronghold. Defenceless Rome was stretched out beneath his feet in central Italy, or, if it had a defence, it was that the deathless spirit of the Apostolic See lived within the walls of Aurelian, and animated by its guardianship the often broken and rudely repaired towers of the world's ancient mistress. The exarch was the choice instrument of the emperor's despotism. St. Gregory, in his fourteen years' struggle with all the elements of civil dissolution, accounts the exarch Romanus as his worst enemy. He was always ready to combine with the Lombard, then in the depths of savagery and ignorance, against his own lord's liege vassals in Rome. Thus St. Gregory unbosoms himself to Sebastian, bishop of Sirmium:—" Words cannot express what we suffer from your friend, the lord Romanus. I would say, in a word, that his malice towards us surpasses the swords of the Lombards. The enemies who destroy us seem to us kinder than the magistrates of the Commonwealth, who wear out our thoughts by their ill-will, their plundering, and their deceit. At one and the same time to have the care of bishops and clergy, of monasteries and people, to watch carefully against enemies in ambuscade, to be exposed even to suspicion by the deceit and ill-will of rulers—the labour and the sorrow of this your brotherhood can the better weigh by the purity of your affection for me who suffer it."[1] These words may fitly introduce us to the Byzantine exarchate as a government. In the thirty years succeeding St. Gregory, the exarch appears as the great manager of Papal elections: from which his least hostile act would be to extort a fee as great, at least, as that laid down in the last Gothic time as 3000 gold coins. Now and then, as opportunity offered, he would enjoy the greater luxury of plundering the Lateran treasury of the Church at his leisure: as done by the exarch Isaac in 638, who was immortalised for the deed in the inscription of his tomb at Ravenna, as the most faithful servant of his most serene masters at Constantinople. The exarch Olympius, in 648, received from his master, Constans II., the higher commission to murder St. Martin, as he was giving holy Communion. But the attempt was frustrated, as was believed at the time, by a divine intervention. However, the exarch Theodore Kalliopa, sent for the special purpose, succeeded in carrying off Pope St. Martin, as he lay ill before the altar of the Lateran, five years later in 653, and placing him in the

[1] *Ep.*, v. 42.

hands of Constans II., to be condemned for high treason, in that he had not waited for the confirmation of his election by Constans, but, instead, had condemned his heresy in the great Council which he summoned at Rome. In the interval of twenty-five years, from the death of St. Martin to the opening of the Sixth Council, the exarchs were faithful to the imperial tradition until Constantine the Bearded renounced the heresy of which his father, Constans, and his grandfather, Heraclius, had been the chief supporters, while they were nursed in it by a succession of Byzantine patriarchs. But when Justinian II. had followed, the exarch John Platina, in 687, hurried from Ravenna to Rome to hinder the election of the great pontiff, Sergius. Finding it accomplished, he was obliged to content himself with fining the new Pope to the extent of a hundred pounds' weight of gold, that being the bribe which the unsuccessful candidate had promised him if he would come to Rome to secure his election. Four years afterwards, Justinian II., unable to induce Pope Sergius to accept the decrees of his Council in Trullo, or to accept the place for his signature of them which the emperor had provided in a line between his own signature and that of his patriarch, sent Zacharias not an exarch, but a guardsman, to repeat, if possible, in the person of Pope Sergius, what had been done forty years before in the person of Pope St. Martin. But, instead, the emperor's own troops caused the guardsman to tremble for his life. His only place of refuge was under the bed in the Pope's own chamber : the Pope's intercession alone saved the imperial emissary from a fatal outburst of Italian wrath. Yet ten years later, under the upstart emperor Apsimar, in his short reign, another exarch, Theophylact, was again repulsed from his execution of an intended attack on the Pope by Italian soldiers. Once more, when Pope Constantine, obeying an imperial letter of the restored Justinian II., had left Rome for Constantinople, several chief Papal officers were summarily executed at Rome. Thus the five attempts on the life of the Pope Gregory II. made by exarchs or guardsmen, at the bidding of the emperor Leo III., in his Iconoclastic fury, were but the consistent continuation of the spirit shown by the exarchs, and fostered and supported by the emperors, from the time of St. Gregory's adversary, the Lord Romanus.

During these two hundred years, from the first inroad of the Lombards, nothing could be more embarrassing than the civil position of the Popes. Beside the main body of the Lombards, occupying the great plain of North Italy, with their capital at Pavia, there were two duchies, one of Spoleto, immediately to the north of Rome and its territory, and another of Benevento, holding a considerable portion of Italian territory near Naples. This city, with other seaports, continued in possession of the empire. The Lombard kings were evermore trying to bring their outlying duchies into closer obedience to the royal power. Again the fortress and territory of Ravenna, the imperial metropolis, lay further to the north, touching the Lombard possessions. The Lombards, when they came into Italy, were so little

advanced in political science of government, so little
coherent among themselves, that at one time they were
divided among thirty-six chiefs, so many heads of
robbers and devastating bands, barbarous and un-Christian.
There can be no doubt that the aim of the Lombard
kings from the beginning had been to make themselves
masters of Rome, and to rule the whole of Italy
as a kingdom. The example and success of Theodorich
was fresh before them. Justinian's success under his
generals Belisarius and Narses was even younger than
the glory of the great Gothic king. Gregory the Great
had laid a foundation for christianising the Lombard
people in his friendship with the great and good Queen
Theodelinda. In process of time they had become
Catholic. Their king, Liutprand, had caused the relics
of St. Augustine, which had been carried from Africa to
Sardinia during the Vandal persecution, to be brought
to his capital city, Pavia, where the shrine of the greatest
of the fathers still abides in honour. Pope Zacharias,
by his personal dignity, prevailed over both Liutprand
and Rachis. But the contest for the dominion of Italy
went on in spite of reverence for the Apostolic See. The
people were Catholic, but tumultous and stubborn.
After a long-continued struggle of various success, the
king Liutprand seemed to be on the point of incorporating
the Spolentine and Beneventan duchies, of closing
upon Rome, and expelling the emperor from Ravenna.
Upon his death, and the retirement of Rachis, Aistulf
was uniting all the Lombard force for the attainment of
their purpose from the beginning, to expel the emperor

from Italy, and to make the Pope a Lombard subject. He went so far as to put a poll-tax on the Roman duchy, and to style himself king of Italy. There the Carlovingian hand arrested him: and the keys of the cities which the Lombard had won from the Byzantine, and Pipin from the Lombard, laid by the gift of Pipin on the tomb of the chief apostle, signified to all men that his successor had become a temporal prince, after forming Rome in the centre of a captive province from a heathen city into a spiritual capital during the unceasing calamity of three centuries. We have scarcely any record of the indescribable sorrows which the Lombard in his aggressive policy, and the Byzantine in his continuous resistance, made up of treachery and bribery added to insufficient military power, inflicted on the cities and the people of Italy: nor of what the Popes endured in their loyal acknowledgment of their duty as subjects, and their unbroken tenacity in maintaining the faith and government of the Church against the succession of adventurers who mounted the Byzantine throne. These culminated in the seven revolutions terminated by that of Leo III. Then the strong man, armed, rode his charger right into the Church of God and strove to add the Popes of Rome to the number of patriarchs whom he raised, deposed, blinded, and executed as he pleased. He made them ecumenical and trod upon them when so made, with the heel of the imperial buskin. And now we come from the first oppression in confirming the Pope, and the second in reducing him to a captive vassal, to the third of subjecting him as the chief teacher of the Church to the lay power of the emperor.

As we look back we see the whole mind of Justinian photographed in his imperial legislation. When he had to speak to the bishop of his capital his language ran : " To the most holy and blessed Archbishop of this Imperial City, and Ecumenical Patriarch "—the core of the title was "Bishop of this Imperial City," its corollary " Ecumenical Patriarch ". To him the bishops of Alexandria, Antioch, and Jerusalem were to submit any appeal from the provinces subject to them. Rome was not to be deposed from the prior rank acknowledged once for all by the eastern monarch and episcopate at the termination of the Acacian schism, in which act Justinian himself, as the ruling nephew, had taken notable part : but there was to be at Constantinople a similar patriarch, whom the whole eastern world should obey. From him the eastern bishops were to learn the mind of the emperor, just as, when they attended the court, he introduced them to the imperial presence. The emperor would honour him by using him as his chief ecclesiastical minister, who held the portfolio of doctrine. The laws which all the world was to receive bore this exaltation of the imperial bishop in their bosom. And it must be confessed that in St. Gregory's time the patriarchal title which Pope Gelasius had utterly refused to the Byzantine bishop a century before, had been conceded to him in St. Gregory's practice : the patriarchal title, but not the ecumenical. Of the patriarchs, when speaking of a fault to be condoned, he wrote, "if any of the four patriarchs had done this we could not pass it over," and Constantinople must be added to Alexandria, Antioch, and Jerusalem to make up this number of four: but of the assumed title of ecumenical, he wrote that it was diabolical, and the forerunner of anti-Christ.

But another part of Justinian's conduct is no less salient. He is not the first, indeed, but he is the chief of the theologising emperors. The disastrous assumption of dictating doctrine, and deciding in theological controversies, which, at the moment of the fall of the western empire, the insurgent Basiliscus had begun during his short-lived reign, and Zeno continued, and Anastasius reinforced, was taken up with far greater force by Justinian. He laboured during eight years just at the middle of the sixth century to exhibit Pope Vigilius at Constantinople as the first of *his* five patriarchs: he made the bishop of his capital hold a General Council without the Pope: he imposed his own doctrinal lucubrations upon that Council. He raised in the minds of the western bishops suspicions and fears as to Pope Vigilius being forced to become his instrument. The patriarch Epiphanius, who had weakly yielded to him, he afterwards deposed. Pope Vigilius escaped at last to die at Syracuse on his return to Rome worn out with the "contradiction of sinners" which he had experienced. In his person St. Peter had been a captive; seeds of schism and distrust had been scattered by Justinian in the West: which it required all the wisdom, the energy, and the patience of the great St.

Gregory a generation later to overcome and root out. The following theologising emperors, Heraclius, Constans II., Justinian II., the poor phantom Philippicus Bardanes, and lastly Leo III., were only completing and crowning Justinian's double work, of making an ecumenical patriarch, and an emperor behind him, the ultimate judge of doctrine.

But had Leo III. succeeded in his attempt to grasp spiritual and temporal power in one hand, the Church of God would have come to an end. The whole future of the world was touched by the issue of this conflict.

It is to be remarked how immovable the Popes were, not only in the maintenance of Christian doctrine pure and proper, but likewise in the maintenance of that relation between the Two Powers which Christian doctrine requires as one of the conditions of its own action in the world. What on this subject Pope Gelasius in the last decade of the fifth century had said to the emperor Anastasius, now after two hundred and thirty years Pope St. Gregory II. was saying to the Iconoclast emperor Leo. In the interval Italy had been governed by the Byzantines, so far as they possessed it, during two centuries as a subject province, the captive of its spear; Rome had lived through it only in virtue of the Pope's primacy. The eastern empire having been false to the faith in its emperors and in many of its bishops, but especially in four successive patriarchs of Constantinople, had been cut in two, and one half of it given over to an anti-Christian religion to rule with unrestricted violence. And now the diminished emperor, who had just saved his capital from the Mohammedan chalif, had been seduced by Jewish aud Mohammedan principles to sweep the Christian churches in his remaiuing dominion, from Sancta Sophia to the least country church, free of Christian symbols, beginning with the most sacred image of the Redeemer[1] which adorned the gate of his own palace as the witness for the need of the oppressed. Then St. Gregory II. stood up against Leo III. exactly as his predecessor, Pope Gelasius, had resisted the emperor of the former day. Syria and Egypt and North Africa, and, still greater shame and peril, Spain had become Mohammedan. The Pope stood, in 727, where he had stood in 495. Iu the interval all these countries had fallen: but St. Gregory II. could tell a furious tyrant that all the nations of the West looked to St. Peter as "a god upon earth"—that he could not execute his threat to pull down the statue of St. Peter, which the Christians of that day reverenced in his basilica at Rome, which the Christians of eleven centuries have reverenced since in the same place, and put their head under the Apostle's foot as the acknowledgment of the dignity with which Christ invested him.

St. Gregory II. told Leo, the Isaurian, that his own imperial dignity was itself of divine institution, as the organ of human government: while the ecclesiastical dignity was of divine institution, in virtue of that divine intervention by which alone men become sons of God. The answer of the tyrant was five times to

---

[1] The statue called 'Αντιφωνήτης, the Answerer, as having miraculously answered the appeal of a friendless stranger.

attempt the Pope's life, as that of a rebellious vassal whom he was entitled to put under ban, and efface as a *natura ferina*. But the issue of this contest was that three Popes, St. Gregory II., St. Gregory III., St. Zacharias, equally great, wise, and prudent, maintained intact their Primacy: that their successor, Stephen II., was the first Pope who crossed the Alps ; that he consecrated the Carlovingian dynasty, and was accepted in Rome triumphantly as her king. In this series of acts he had also broken the chains of Italy, and a Pope presently following, who had ceased to be an eastern vassal, was to create a counterpoise to the chalif of Mohammed in an emperor, not Byzantine, but Roman, not grasping illicit power in the spirit of Saracenic pride, but as a type of Christian monarchy placed at the head of lawful government, not a perversion of Constantine and Theodosius, but the loyal spirit of both embodied by a divine consecration.

During the reigns of Leo III. and his son, Constantine Kopronymus, and the times of the Popes Gregory II:, Gregory III., Zacharias, and Stephen II., certain events take place in the East and the West respectively, which, by their striking contrast with each other, while they coincide in the time of their happening, remarkably express and sum up the course taken by the three centuries which we are considering. Despotism matures in the East, and barbaric savagery triumphs : freedom, order, the majesty of nations growing into one faith, dawn upon the West.

In 727 the yet existing letters of Pope Gregory II.

to the emperor Leo exhibit that monarch as thoroughly possessed with the claim to govern the Church as he governs the State. In this he is as thoroughly encountered by the Pope, who calls up against him the unbroken tradition of the Church during the seven centuries, and reminds him of the sad misfortunes of those emperors who had attempted to carry their civil authority into the domain of revealed truth. The great eastern teacher, St. John of Damascus, then living in the Syrian court of the chalif, lays this down in language as peremptory as that of the Pope. The guilt of Leo III. is heightened by the fact that he had before him in the history of his own realm during the hundred years preceding him the rise of a religion essentially opposed to the Christian faith, which he was professing himself to purify. Its force, ever exercised against Christians with the utmost virulence and cruelty, was centered in the fact that its chief deduced all civil authority from the prophetic office of its founder. But while the kingship of Mohammed, as inherited by his chalifs, began with his attempt to found a religion, Leo, in continuing and advancing to their utmost tension the interferences of Justinian with the spiritual order, was undoing the ancient laws of the empire for a hundred and fifty years, from the time of Constantine to that of Zeno. His own patriarch, Germanus, chose rather to lay his omophorion on the altar, and depart into exile than sanction and accept Leo's usurpation in sacred things. The whole liberty, and with it the whole existence of the Church, were comprehended in the resistance maintained by Pope Gregory, and attested by patriarch Germanus as a victim. Gregory II. followed, in giving to Cæsar the things of Cæsar, but to God the things of God, the whole line of his predecessors. Leo III. imitated wrongly the chief antagonist of the Christian name; but Mohammed was at least consistent with his original falsehood. In this his religion itself was contained. Likewise the whole work of Christendom was embodied in the victorious defence of Gregory against the consummation of eastern despotism.

The acts which followed by Pope and by emperor agreed with their several principles. Gregory III. on his accession at once endeavoured to bring the emperor to a better mind. But Leo had already deposed Germanus, and put Anastasius, a docile instrument, in his stead. The Pope called a council at Rome, which entirely supported the freedom of the Church. Leo turned to brute force. He sent out a great fleet with the commission to destroy his own metropolis, Ravenna, then to advance upon Rome, seize the Pope, and carry him away captive, as eighty years before St. Martin had been taken. Five years after this violent act of despotism, which the winds and seas had frustrated, Pope Gregory III., pressed hard by the advancing arms of the Lombard king, Liutprand, besought the great conqueror, Charles Martell, to take up his defence. He appealed to the piety of the Frank leader in behalf of St. Peter, a piety extinct in the Roman emperor's breast. Two years later Pipin had succeeded to the power of Charles Martell, and intimated in the strongest manner the veneration for the Apostolic See felt by the Frank people, in asking Pope Zacharias to pronounce as Pope that Pipin might duly be elected king of the Franks. Zacharias gave his decision : and the diet of the kingdom at Soissons bore out to the full the sentence of Pope Gregory II. in his letter to Leo III., that all the nations of the West looked to St. Peter as a god upon earth. Pipin became king of the Franks by the diet of the Franks accepting the decision of Pope Zacharias in 752, when in 733 the rough Isaurian soldier thought only of subduing the predecessor of Zacharias, Gregory III., by a dungeon in Byzantium after the mode of Constans II. with St. Martin. But even yet the contrast is not complete.

Not only had Leo III., in his wrath at being foiled by the elements, confiscated the patrimonies of the Church in the southern provinces of Italy which he possessed, and in Sicily, and in his realm generally, but he interfered with the immemorial spiritual jurisdiction of the Pope as patriarch, and assigned to his own patriarch at Constantinople the privileges which by the appointment of St. Leo had been given to the great metropolis, Thessalonica. This jurisdiction the patriarchs of Constantinople had coveted for centuries. Theodosius II. had tried to give it them by an imperial decree : but it was rescinded. Anastasius, who had been substituted for Germanus in 730, received the ill-omened gift in 733. The giver's son, Kopronymus, afterwards punished by blindness this unhappy man, but sent him back thus blinded to occupy his see during ten years ; made him crown his son, and only in 753 Anastasius, becoming once more a servile persecutor of images, terminated the episcopate which he had so ingloriously received in 730. On the other hand, Pope Stephen II., successor of Zacharias, in spite of bodily weakness and continual danger, crossed the Alps, crowned Pipin, his wife and his sons, in the Abbey of St. Denys, in 754, and so consecrated the Carlovingian race. The rising monarchy of the Franks exulted in that very dignity of St. Peter's successor, which the Byzantine monarch was striving to subject to his own will.

But this contrast had a yet further and even more striking issue. Pope Stephen II., hard pressed by the resolute attempt of king Aistulf to make himself temporal king of Rome, applied for defence to the man he still recognised as sovereign, Constantine Kopronymus, and received for answer only the words that he might get it where he could. He beheld the Lombard destroying and trampling on every thing outside the walls of Rome. In the utmost bodily weakness he had taken the road to Pavia: he resisted every effort of Aistulf to detain him. He had been received by Pipin with joy and admiration. Protection against the Lombards was promised him. The Lombard king gave way to his fear of the Frankish kings, but presently broke through every engagement. On 1st January, 756, he had promised himself Rome, and all which it contained. By the end of the year he had surrendered the exarchate to St. Peter, and Rome had accepted her Pontiff Stephen as her king. And the name of Stephen II. is numbered with that of his three predecessors as the maker of pontifical liberty. Kopronymus ventured to ask Pipin to restore to him the cities which Pipin had conquered. He received for reply that not for earthly reward or wealth, but for the love of St. Peter, the king of the Franks had bestowed on the Pope, his successor, the cities which he had delivered from the Lombard, and restored Rome to him by delivering it from Lombard aggression.

Constantine Kopronymus had succeeded his father Leo III. in 740. An insurrection arose against him in his own house. It was put down with terrible severity.[1] These were his doings in Constantinople in the same year 754, when Pipin was crowned by the Pope. He had surpassed his father in the cruelty with which he attempted to alter the existing worship of the Church. He had obtained some advantage in war against the Saracens, who were divided by the contest between the Ommaiads and the Abbassides, but he thought not the least of saving Italy from the Lombards, much more he desired to deliver the churches from the sacred images. For this purpose he caused many assemblies to be held and addressed the people, moving them to destroy the images. At last he held a Council at Constantinople of 338 bishops. At their head stood Gregory, bishop of Neocesarea, Theodosius, archbishop of Ephesus, a son of the emperor Apsimar, Sisinnius, bishop of Perge in Pamphylia. There was no patriarch, no representative from the sees

[1] Kellner, vol. ii. p. 863, in the German edition of Rohrbacher's History.

of Rome, Alexandria, Antioch, and Jerusalem. The see of Constantinople was vacant, as Anastasius had just died. The Council met on the Asiatic side, opposite Constantinople, on the 10th February, 754, and sat six months. Then on the 8th August it passed over to the Church of Blachernæ. There the emperor presented himself at the ambon holding by the hand the monk Constantine, bishop of Sylæum, and cried with a loud voice, " Many years to the ecumenical patriarch Constantine ". At the same time he invested him with the patriarchal robes and the pallium. The Council ended that day, and nothing of it remains to us except a so-called confession of faith in the acts of the Seventh Ecumenical Council, the second of Nicæa, in 787, where it was refuted and rejected.

The Council of 787, called in the time of another Constantine, the grandson of Kopronymus, when the eastern emperor had returned for the moment to the orthodox faith, has denounced this Council of 754 as claiming most unlawfully the title of ecumenical. Being confirmed by Pope Adrian I., it enjoys that title itself, and its utter condemnation of the Council of 338 bishops which met at the request of Kopronymus can be trusted. Here it is sufficient to say that this Council of 754 covered Kopronymus and his little son Leo with acclamations for having destroyed idolatry. When the emperor and the new patriarch Constantine and the rest of the bishops appeared in the square at Constantinople they published the decree of the Council, and renewed their anathemas against the patriarch Germanus and St. John

Damascene. When the decree reached the provinces, Catholics were everywhere dismayed; the Iconoclasts began to sell the holy vessels and disorganise the churches. The images were burnt, the pictures torn down or whitewashed; only landscapes and the figures of birds and beasts were retained, especially pictures of theatres, hunts, and races. To bow before the images of Christ and of the saints was forbidden; to bow before the emperor was retained, and any insult to his figure upon a coin punished with death.

In 754, Kopronymus, holding Constantine by the hand, presented him to the assembled bishops as his own choice for ecumenical patriarch. Not only was the individual his choice, but his father, Leo, twenty years before, had made the office by constituting the spiritual jurisdiction of the bishops of the capital conterminous with the empire, in that he deprived the Pope in his quality of the first patriarch of the ten provinces which from the beginning had acknowledged his patriarchal superintendence.

We may follow to his end the ecumenical patriarch who had this beginning.

It seems that neither a bishop nor a secular priest in the eastern empire ventured to oppose the decree of this Council. But monks suffered the most fearful persecution.[1] They were driven away and their monasteries destroyed. Nor were these the worst blows which the emperor dealt upon their institution. He invented truly devilish means to make them contemptible and abhorred.

---

[1] The following four pages are taken from Kellner, p. 407, who has drawn the facts from Theophanes, p. 371.

Some who had been banished from Constantinople yielded to his will, subscribed the edict against images, quitted their dress and married. Thereupon they returned to the city, recovered all their civil rights, were marked with favour, received the emperor's personal attention. But those who remained true to their faith and their habit experienced his utmost severity. A month after his return from the war, the 24th August, 766, on which day he had appointed a chariot-race, he caused the monks in the neighbourhood of Constantinople to be brought together into the racecourse. There, as the rows of seats were crowded with people, he compelled each monk to pass in procession with a woman of bad life beside him. Thus they suffered every indignity which an excited populace could put upon them. The bad courtiers saw that it was an evil stroke of the emperor. Those who had not the secret thought that they had been taken in company with these women.

This spectacle so pleased the emperor that, four days afterwards, he repeated it with nineteen of his chief officers, whom he charged with a conspiracy against him. The real offence was the maintenance of the right belief, the having had relation with the banished Stephen in his exile at Proconnesus, and more than once to have praised his constancy in suffering. He caused them to be led round the racecourse, and made the crowd spit on them and revile them. The two of highest account were beheaded: two patricians, brothers, Constantine, who had been controller-general of the posts, and Strategius, officer in the life guards ; the rest were blinded and banished to an island, nor did Kopronymus forget every year that he lived to send thither executioners to inflict on each a hundred strokes of oxhide. When he found that the people grieved over the execution of Constantine and Strategius, had not forborne tears, and even murmured, he put down this to the fault of the prefect Procopius, who ought to have suppressed these seditious cries; he had him scourged and deprived.

The patriarch Constantine had received from the emperor extraordinary and unfitting honours. They were followed by public disgrace. The emperor learnt that he had had intercourse with one of the accused for conspiracy. He put up witnesses who declared that they had heard expressions from him against the emperor. This the patriarch absolutely denied, and proof was not forthcoming. The emperor caused them secretly to confirm their statement by an oath taken on the holy Cross. Thereupon, without further proof he set seals upon the door of the patriarchal palace, and banished the patriarch to Prince's Island. Constantine was thus deposed on the 30th August, 766, and on the 16th November the emperor, without regarding any canonical form, named Nicetas to his place. The new patriarch was yet more unfitted for so eminent a rank, being a eunuch and slave by birth. From his youth he had only been accustomed to attend on women, had scarcely learnt to read; but the emperor, on recommendation of certain ladies of the court, had caused him to be made a priest and given him a post in the Church of the Apostles. Upon entering the patriarchal palace Nicetas showed himself worthy of the imperial choice, for he caused the magnificent mosaics on the walls to be destroyed, These his two predecessors had spared for their beauty.

By similar services the highest dignitaries of the kingdom were obtained. A zealous Iconoclast was in the eyes of the emperor qualified for every civil or military post. Thus Michael of Melissene, brother of the empress Eudocia, was made governor of Phrygia, Lachanodracon of Asia, and Manes of Galatia. At the beginning of 767 Constantine sent these new and yet more severe governors into the provinces, having just before imposed an oath on all his subjects not to honour images. Then began a general persecution of the orthodox. Those governors showed themselves in the provinces obedient instruments of their emperor's rage. They profaned churches, persecuted monks, and destroyed pictures. They tore relics of the saints from their sanctuaries, and cast them into rivers or drains. They mixed them with bones of animals, and burnt them together, so that the ashes might not be distinguished. The relics of the martyr St. Euphemia, in whose church at Chalcedon the great Council had been held, were its chief treasure. The emperor had the shrine cast into the sea, changed part of the church into an arsenal, and made the other part a place where all the rubbish of the city might be shot. The waves carried the shrine to the Isle of Lemnos, whose inhabitants fished it up. Twenty years after the death of Kopronymus, Irene, then reigning with her son Constantine, caused this treasure to be brought back to

Chalcedon, the church to be purified and restored to its former condition.

The deposed patriarch Constantine had endured the hardest treatment at Prince's Island during thirteen months. The emperor had learnt that this unhappy prelate had told to others an impious remark concerning the Mother of God, which the emperor had made, and enjoined silence about it. Furious in his wrath he ordered him to be brought to Constantinople; he had him beaten till he could not stand, and had him carried in a litter to Sancta Sophia to be degraded. He was cast down on the steps of the sanctuary. A court-secretary read in presence of the whole assembly, called together by the emperor's order, a detailed accusation with loud voice, and as he read each detail struck him with it in the face. In the meantime Nicetas had mounted the patriarchal chair, and presided over each insult which his benefactor suffered. When the reading was finished, Nicetas took the act of accusation, had Constantine carried to the tribune, where he was held upright by several, that the people might see him, made one of his suffragans go up to pronounce the anathema, to take off the episcopal robes, and with insulting expressions to expel him from the church, from which he had to go backwards.

The next day, a day of games in the circus, his beard, eye-brows, and hair were torn out; he was dressed in a short woollen smock without sleeves, put backwards on an ass, and led through the circus by a nephew whose nose had been cut off. The parties of the circus reviled him and spat on him. At the end of the circus he was thrown down, trodden under foot, and put upon the stone which terminated the circus to be exposed there, so long as the games lasted, to the jeers of the riders as they passed. He was then thrown into prison, where he lay almost forgotten to the 15th August of the following year, 768. That day was the last of his sufferings. The emperor sent two patricians to him to ask what he thought of the emperor's belief and the doctrine of the council. The sufferer, to the last a courtier, thought by a submissive answer to alleviate his punishment. He replied : " The emperor's belief is holy, and the council has issued a holy confession ". The patricians said at once: "That is just thě admission which we wished to have from thy godless mouth. Nothing more remains for thee but death." They then pronounced his condemnation, and led him into the amphitheatre, where his head was struck off. It was fastened by the ears to the mile-stone, where it served the mob three days for a spectacle. The body was dragged to the Pelagium, a spot where the church of St. Pelagia had stood, which the emperor had pulled down, to make a court where the bodies of the condemned were thrown after execution ; in the same way as on the other side the water he had pulled down St. Andrew's church to make a place of execution. The body was also said to have been dissected for the good of science.[1] This was the reward which the patriarch received for having

---

[1] Photius, p. 242, with note 97 from George Hamartolus.

sacrificed his faith and conscience in giving sanction to his master's impieties.

This degradation by Kopronymus of the man whom he had made and called ecumenical patriarch, and to make him had persisted in his father's overthrow of the Church's order from the beginning, by an act of despotic power breaking into her constitution, is it not also a token of the condition into which the most ruthless tyranny had reduced the episcopate of that eastern realm? Those bishops who, at the bidding of an adventurer, successful for the moment and presently swept away, had met at Constantinople in 710 to overthrow the Sixth Council and the faith of the Church; and again, the three hundred and thirty-eight who had met at the same place at the bidding of Kopronymus to make the whole order of divine worship subject to his will, did the spirit of St. Basil, St. Athanasius, St. Chrysostom, St. Cyril of Alexandria live in them still, or were they in possession indeed of unquestioned episcopal rank and all the powers which belong to consecration, but in fact the most abject minions of the most debased human will — the will of a Byzantine despot? The will of one fined already of one half his empire by the divine Hand which raised up the most abject of savages to punish a debased Christian realm. Yet ruler after ruler had not received the lesson which faith derives from chastisement. Leo III. surpassed his predecessors, and his son surpassed the father, in imitating the arrogance of a false theocracy. He carried his civil autocracy into interference with the doctrine and the worship of the

Church. This interference the laws of his own empire warned him against, as cited by St. Gregory II. in the examples of the greatest emperors.

It is not too much to say that the despotism wielded by those who occupied the Byzantine throne from Justinian to Kopronymus had eaten out the courage and dulled the sense of divine things which we admire in the Fathers of the fourth century. Athanasius denounced a Constantius, and Basil a Valens, but the eastern bishops of the eighth century crouched before Leo and Kopronymus, and if there had not been a succession of Popes, in whom the spirit of St. Leo lived on, and the doctrine of St. Leo was maintained, the Church herself would have yielded to the most debasing despotism ever seen. But it must not be forgotten that the bishops of the West were faithful to the teaching and emulated the stedfastness of the Popes. A despotic patriarch, nominee and instrument of a despotic emperor, made a servile episcopate. A martyr Pope, such as St. Martin, likewise made an army of martyrs. The several character of bishops in the East and West completes the contrast which we have been drawing out.

In the patriarch Constantine the ecumenical patriarchate received its completed form. Kopronymus chose him; took him by the hand, presented him to the 338 bishops who held an illicit and heretical council at his bidding; having used him for his purposes, deposed, beheaded him, treated his lifeless body with extreme dishonour.

In the same Kopronymus, the two hundred years of secular lordship begun by Justinian's conquest of Rome came to an end. He had disregarded the appeal of Pope Stephen to defend his own dominion from the Lombards. Pipin had deprived them of that dominion, and then bestowed it upon St. Peter. Kopronymus asked Pipin to give it back to him. Pipin refused, and after thirty-four successive Popes had endured a dominion which began with the deposition of St. Silverius by a shameless woman, and perhaps cannot show a single act of generous defence in return for loyal service during two centuries, the attempt inaugurated by Justinian, and finished by Kopronymus, to reduce the successor of St. Peter to a patriarch whom they might treat as the patriarch Constantine was treated, failed finally and for ever. Stephen II., an infirm old man who had crossed the Alps at the risk of his life, deserted by Kopronymus and threatened by Aistulf, sat at the grave of the chief Apostle, Prince as well as Bishop of Rome, and the Christian faith was not left to be determined by soldiers of fortune on the throne of Byzantium, but saved by and for the guardianship of the living Peter.

From Metrophanes,[1] the first recorded bishop of Byzantium, not yet Constantinople, in the time of the Nicene Council to Methodius, in the year 842, when the Iconoclast contest came to a final end, fifty-eight bishops sat on the chair of the Greek capital. The first was simple bishop of a suffragan city to the Thracian metropolis of Heraclea. As soon as Constantine in the

[1] Photius, i. 295.

year 330 had consecrated his new capital as Nova Roma, there began a continual exaltation, the work of the eastern emperors for their own purposes; after four centuries the bishops of Constantinople had in 733 reached the culmination of their hopes by receiving from the emperor Leo III. ten provinces out of the Roman jurisdiction, and twenty bishoprics of his own birth-land, Isauria, previously belonging to the patriarch of Antioch. They were in a Greek sense ecumenical, not because their authority extended over the world, but because by imperial gift it had become conterminous with that portion of the world which was considered by the Greek emperor the habitation of men,[1] that is, his subjects. The original and true patriarchates of Alexandria and Antioch had fallen under Mohammedan domination. So likewise had Jerusalem, which attained patriarchal rank only in the middle of the fifth century. The name of each as patriarch was carefully maintained, especially for appearance in the list of Greek councils, but in each case, and for hundreds of years, it was little more than "magni nominis umbra".[2] Of the fifty-eight bishops of the capital many have gained for themselves imperishable honour, many are venerated in the number of the saints by Greeks and Latins, and looked up to as intercessors and protectors, others have at least left behind them in one or other respect a distinguished memory. But more than a third, one and twenty, are branded as heretics or favourers of heresy. Almost as

---

[1] ἡ οἰκουμένη.
[2] Photius, i. p. 295.

many were for various reasons deposed, partly by heretical, partly by orthodox emperors. Several, also, of them received at the same time dishonouring treatment, such as Kallinikus, Anastasius, and Constantine. In three cases, those of St. Chrysostom, Eutychius, and Pyrrhus, deposed prelates, were restored, a case which much oftener recurs in later Byzantine history.

In the fourth century the names of Eusebius, Macedonius, Eudoxius, and Demophilus in the see of the capital are marked as supporters of the Arian heresy. In the fifth century the Nestorian heresy springs from its author in the very chair of Constantinople. Fifty years later the Acacian schism springs in like manner from the ambition of its author in the same chair, and the names of four successors, Fravitas, Euphemius, Macedonius II., and Timotheus are struck from the diptychs of their own church, when the schism was terminated under Pope Hormisdas. In less than twenty years after this, Anthimus, put into the see of the capital by the intrigues of the same empress Theodora who violently deposed Pope St. Silverius, was deposed by Pope Agapetus in his visit to Constantinople, as a Monophysite heretic. In the sixth century the Monothelite heresy was owing mainly to the political intrigues of Sergius, sitting for twenty-eight years in the see of Constantinople, also the prime minister and guide of the emperor Heraclius; he and his three successors, Pyrrhus, Paul, and Peter, were the main-stay of that most insidious and stubborn heresy, which for forty continuous years kept the Church in peril, and strove to overthrow the efforts of ten Popes to maintain the faith, and brought one of them to die a martyr under the rule of Constans II. But in the seventh and eighth centuries, the most terrible Iconoclast persecution found in six bishops of Constantinople its main support, in that they put to the service of the emperors Leo III. and Constantine Kopronymus, Leo V. and Theophilus, these immense ecclesiastical powers with which the emperors themselves had invested them over the eastern bishops. The single patriarch had himself become a despot in wielding the tyranny of the civil despot as his chief instrument. These six ecumenical patriarchs wielded their authority under Iconoclast emperors for a long time: Anastasius I. from 730 to 753; Constantine II. from 754 to 766; Nicetas I. from 766 to 780; then an orthodox sovereign brought with him an orthodox council. The patriarch Tarasius and union with the West might seem to have secured a deliverance from a renewed reign of the Iconoclast violence. On the contrary, three succeeding patriarchs, Theodotus from 815 to 821; Antonius I. from 821 to 832, and John VII. from 832 to 841, did what they could to carry out the wishes of their masters for that heresy.

Such was the conduct, as guardian of the faith, of the line of pseudo-popes set up by state policy at Constantinople, in virtue of the pretension that the bishop of Nova Roma should enjoy equal rights with the bishop of Old Rome.

It is to be noted that in this period the whole doctrine concerning the Person of our Lord Jesus Christ went through the most complete sifting and discussion in the Councils of the Church. During it, from St. Silvester to Gregory IV., seventy pontiffs sat in the chair of Peter. They lived in full five hundred years of perpetual struggle. One after another "apparent diræ facies inimicaque Troiæ numina"—Arius in the foreground heralding Mohammed in the rear; Nestorius and Eutyches tearing the unity of the Church on opposite sides; an able bishop of Constantinople seizing the moment of Rome's temporal captivity under Arian strangers to raise his see to parity: the East well nigh devoured by opposing sects. After this, an insidious Byzantine couple, Heraclius and Sergius, emperor and patriarch, covering up deep wounds with ambiguous words, and sacrificing the empire by their sacrifice of the faith; and lastly, emperors who disregard things human and divine, and mark their mastery over doctrine by the subversion of worship, a Leo III. and a Constantine Kopronymus. All secular power is in the hands of Nova Roma which Constantine has set up to be the Christian city from its cradle: the seven greater hills to take the place of the hills by the Tiber, and in these very hills of Constantine from age to age the evil vision nestles—his successor and his patriarch are the chief performers in this ever recruited drama of heresy. But through all these attacks the seventy successors on St. Peter's throne have kept the doctrine of the Church, that is the doctrine of the Incarnation itself, one and unchanged. The infidel has trampled upon Alexandria, Antioch, and Jerusalem; but while the old Christendom has sunk from debased nations into Saracen serfdom, a new Christendom has arisen among Teuton settlers, making their first steps in national life. Nova Roma has been false to the purpose for which Constantine founded it; and Old Rome has found among those whom the rival counts as barbarians, one more faithful as well as more powerful than she has been. Charlemagne stands at the end of the vista which Constantine begins. Of the two, does he not merit most in the Church of God?

But to estimate at its due value this long series of historic facts, it must be remembered that during at least three centuries of this period, the seventy Popes work as captives, the fifty-eight bishops of Constantinople work as the right hand of emperors. From the time indeed when St. Silvester passed from the catacombs to the Lateran palace, to the time when the Vandal robbers desolated Rome under the eyes of St. Leo, the Popes were not captives. They had severe persecution at times to undergo: especially under Constantius I., the whole fifty years of Arian trial were a special test of their fortitude, their clear undoubted maintenance of the Godhead of our Lord, their unfaltering trust in their apostolic right. But so long as there was a Christian western emperor he had a regard to the Apostolic See of the West: even a Valentinian III. could acknowledge St. Leo in an imperial edict in 447 as "Principem episcopalis coronæ"; words which present the very idea of St Peter's majesty, as the root, the bond, and the crown of the episcopate. But with the inroad of barbarians, as soldiers of fortune and civil masters of Rome, another time begins. And when to barbarous manners and brute force was added the Arian spirit, a period ensued which was calculated to test to the utmost the dowry of truth bestowed on the Apostolic See. Justinian as a civil ruler may be deemed worse than Odoacer, worse even than Theodorich. What the Popes did, they did often after being nominated without free election, often with the postponement of their confirmation after election (as when after the death of Pope Honorius, Pope Severinus had his three years diminished to two months, in the hope of Heraclius to bend him to the Monothelite heresy), sometimes with unjust depositions, as St. Silverius by Theodora, as St. Martin by Constans II., as St. Sergius attempted by Justinian II., as John VI. attempted by Apsimar, the emperor of a day : again by unlawful substitution for a living Pope, as Eugenius to St. Martin, when condemned but not yet martyred. Then again the eleven years preceding the great Pope Sergius from 676 to 687 witness the appointment of six Popes. At this time there is a series of Popes who show eastern lineage, as if the emperor's hand were busy in the choice of them. But no one of them fails, and St. Sergius and St. Gregory III., both easterns, are of the very greatest and most stedfast in the whole time of Popes.

Add to this that the civil condition of these Popes, from the entrance of the Lombards to the end of the exarchs, was often most perilous. It was plaintively alluded to by St. Agatho in addressing the Sixth Cou 1.

when forty years after the death of Honorius he set forth in most absolute language the unfaltering integrity of faith which had marked the Apostolic See to his own time, language which the Council accepted.

It is to be noted that a Pope, whose election had been long delayed by the mere arbitrary will of emperor or exarch, as soon as he was consecrated, entered into the full possession of his unrestricted rights. The exarch who had power to delay, who had power to plunder the Lateran treasury of the Church, as Isaac and John Platina did, had no power to lessen the dignity of St. Peter's succession when once acknowledged. Even Vigilius is admitted to have emancipated himself from the thraldom of Theodora; and Eugenius, forced upon the Romans by the tyranny of Constans II., was a blameless Pope, who did not yield to the heresy of Constans.

What manner of men were they who were loyal vassals to the most iniquitous rulers, and when solicited by their own faithful peoples to break an abhorred yoke yet held them back, and adhered to those who gave them neither protection nor justice? They did not rule as Satraps in a kingdom worn down to prostration by centuries of arbitrary power, but were acknowledged as sitting in the apostolic throne of Faith and Justice by rough lords from the North, to whom obedience in spiritual things was a Christian virtue learned with great difficulty by those who inherited a natural independence. Interminable intestine quarrels among the western potentates, who yet accept the voice of an unarmed Pope as the interpreter of faith, and the most upright arbiter of human justice, are a proof the more how deeply the rule of St. Peter had sunk into the western mind.

What guarantee of truth can be offered by the course of human things if this be not one? That is the testimony of the three centuries from Genseric the Vandal to Aistulf the Lombard. The testimony of Teuton conquerors, who burn what they once worshipped, and worship what they once burnt, who enter on their dominion as spoilers and develop into Christian monarchs. The testimony of Constantine's imperial successors, who own the papal succession to St. Peter, while they try to bend it to their will, and in the attempt subject half their empire to an anti-Christian tyranny. Lastly, the testimony of St. Leo the Great and fifty-one successors to the time when St. Leo III., invested with civil sovereignty, employed the acknowledged greatness of his spiritual power to restore the empire which the first Leo saw sinking in ruins.

CHAPTER VIII.

FROM SERVITUDE TO SOVEREIGNTY.

THE first land possession[1] of the Roman See appears to have been the Cæsarean palace of the Lateran, the gift to it of the emperor Constantine, in gratitude to God for having conquered the heathen empire at the Milvian Bridge. It noted the impression on the conqueror's soul of the divine sign, *in this prevail.* Therein St. Silvester took up his abode, and in it was built the Cathedral Church of Rome and of the world. For a thousand years it remained the abode of the Popes—the centre of the Church's visible life, whence her spiritual jurisdiction radiated, the proper residence of one hundred and sixty Popes, from St. Silvester to B. Pope Benedict XI.

It is not a little to be noted that the original root of the Pope's temporal power was his unique spiritual power, that the gift of Constantine foreshadowed the empire of Charlemagne ; that the first Christian emperor removed the Pope from the catacombs to a Cæsarean palace ; that the second emperor received back from the Pope that imperial title and power which so many successors seated in Constantine's Nova Roma had used

[1] I have in this chapter made continual use of Father Brunengo's two works, *I primi Papi-Re e l'Ultimo dei Re Longobardi*, and *Le Origini della Sovranità Temporale dei Papi.* They are quoted under the *Le Origini*, &c., and *I primi Papi-Re.*

so cruelly against the successor of St. Peter, whom yet they acknowledged. And still the Lateran Basilica bears on its front in barbarous Latin the title no less true than proved,

> "Dogmate Papali datur ac simul Imperiali,
> Quod sim cunctarum Mater Caput Ecclesiarum".

Nor is there any spot on the earth upon which the guiding hand of God in the fortunes of the world may be more profitably studied than before the entrance of that Church so well styled in her double character Mother and Head. If the Mother were not head her rule would be impotent; if the head were not mother it would be unbearable.

The munificence thus begun in his gratitude by Constantine was continued during centuries by great Roman families and by others also. The pastoral staff fixed itself in Roman earth, and became a great tree. In due time it flowered in a prince's sceptre. It is most interesting to mark in the gifts to the Roman See the heathen names of ancient patrician families commemorated. Under the properties administered by St. Gregory the Great we read of the Massa Papirianensis, the Massa Furiana, the Massa Varroniana, the Fundus Cornelii.

A fact[1] which enters deep into the world's history bears remarkable witness to the rapid increase of papal wealth and its inevitable accompaniment, the political independence of St. Peter's chair. From the time the unity of the Roman realm began to be dissolved into two empires,

[1] See Gfrörer, *Papst Gregorius VII.*, v. 10-11.

the eastern and the western, not a single western ruler fixed his seat abidingly in Rome, although almost all lived in Italy, and although many of them could have put to good use, amid the State's increasing weakness, the help which the charm of the Roman name offered. After the death of Constantine the Great in 337, of his three sons Constantius I. received the East, Constans I. received the West in union with his younger brother Constantine II., but after his murder, alone. This Constans usually dwelt in Gaul. When he visited Italy we find him prefer Milan and Aquileia to Rome. He yielded to the insurgent Maxentius, and then Constantius became sole master of the realm, and, when in the West, lived chiefly in Milan. In his whole reign once only did he enter Rome.[1]

The second division of the realm, which followed the emperor Jovian, gave Valentinian for ruler of the West, who selected at first Milan for residence, but was compelled by incursions of the German peoples to spend much time on the Rhine. We learn, partly from the history of St. Ambrose, partly from other documents, that the sons and successors of Valentinian I., Gratian, and Valentinian II., as well as the mother and guardian of the latter, the widowed empress Justina, when in Italy held their court chiefly at Milan and Aquileia.

The third and final partition, which severed the West for ever from the East, took place in 395 after the death of the Spaniard, Theodosius I., whom Gratian had taken for his partner. From that time not Rome, not

[1] See his visit described in chapter vi. vol. v. p. 243.

Milan, or Aquileia, but the seaport Ravenna appears the permanent residence of those phantom-emperors who ruled for nearly a century until the full dissolution of the western empire. The political significance of the last city even remarkably survived the name of the Roman empire.

We are expressly told that Odoacer, the first German king of Italy, who deposed Romulus Augustulus, the last West Roman, had his seat in Ravenna. The same was the case with Odoacer's conqueror, the great Ostrogoth, Theodorich. During his government Ravenna received the title of the royal city, though the Ostrogoth often lived in other great cities of upper Italy, such as Pavia and Verona. Finally Ravenna, after the extinction of the Ostrogothic state and people, remained for nearly two hundred years the seat of the exarchs, Byzantine viceroys of Italy.

Why of so many princes bearing the title of Roman emperors or kings of Italy did no single one make his seat in the former capital of the world? Why did the greater number pay it only a transitory visit, some perhaps not see it at all? I think only one sufficient answer can be given to this question. They shunned a longer stay at Rome because they felt that in a city which had assumed a priestly character they would no longer play the first part so much as kings desire and must desire it. That fact is, therefore, an incontestable proof not only of the papal power, but likewise of its wealth. Without property no co-active force, not even spiritual, can in the long run maintain itself.

The law of the year 321, allowing churches to receive landed[1] property from any testator, had results so astonishingly great, that in 50 years Valentinian I. thought it necessary to put a limit on it. We may pass at once to the time of St. Gregory the Great, the fourteen years 590 to 604. At that time the Bishop of Rome in his Lateran Palace, had become the greatest ground landlord in Italy, and even in all the West. He was the real protector of Rome. The eastern emperor bore the name, but in every need and trial it was not at Ravenna or at Constantinople that help was sought, but at the Lateran. Royal dignity waited already upon the Vicar of Christ; a dignity with which the spontaneous offerings of three hundred years had invested him. St. Gregory lived like a monk, and gave away as a king from the inexhaustible fountain of the apostolic charity.

His letters enable us to form a fair estimate of the domains of the Roman Church at that time. In his unresting activity to minister aright the material wealth of the Church, the son of St. Benedict ripened the recognition of his political independence. His death preceded by 150 years the legal acknowledgment of sovereignty attained by his successor, Stephen II., and that intervening period was, as we have seen, a time of exceedingly severe trial. A notice of the deacon John, biographer of St. Gregory, informs us that in his pontificate the Roman Church possessed at least twenty-three patrimonies. These were respectively, that of

[1] Hoensbroech, *P. Paul von.—Entstehung und Entwicklung des Kirchenstaates* in the *Stimmen aus Maria-Laach*, July 1, 1889.

Sicily, of Syracuse, of Palermo, of Calabria, of Apulia, the Samnite, the Neapolitan, the Campanian, the Tuscan, the Sabine, the Nursian, the Carseolan, that of Via Appia, of Ravenna, of Illyricum, the Istrian, Dalmatian, Sardinian, Corsican, Ligurian, that of the Cottian Alps, of Germanicia, and of Gaul.

The position of the Popes from the time of St. Gregory to the beginning of the State of the Church is thus described by a Jewish writer forty years ago.[1] "The Popes were usually the helpers out of every need. They supplied the money required for the payment of the troops, and for the requisite provisionment, to keep off the ever-impending threatenings of scarcity. They also frequently redeemed captives. Now as the Protector always exercised a decisive influence on the protected, and the distant emperors distinguished themselves as much by their neglect, as the Vicars of Christ by their activity in the interest of Italy, and especially of the seven-hilled city, nothing was more natural than that the estimation of those who were so often its preservers advanced more and more. Thus they soon came in fact to stand at the head of almost all secular matters in and about Rome, with almost sovereign power. That was especially the case since the pontificate of the great Gregory I., a Pope truly venerable both for his very distinguished mental gifts, and for his far-stretching, sound, practical discernment, and his inflexible will.

---

[1] Hoensbroech quoted from the Jew, Samuel Sugenheim, in his history of the rise and formation of the State of the Church, a prize essay crowned at Göttingen in 1854.

These were the reasons enabling him to assume a freer political position towards the Greek imperial court than his predecessors."

It has been computed[1] that the Popes were in all landlords of 1360 square miles, that is 870,400 acres, in the time of Leo the Isaurian, and that these lands produced to them 200,000 gold soldi in money, and 500,000 in kind. And if we add to this computation the very great secular powers which the policy of Justinian had placed throughout his empire in the hands of the bishops, we may form some notion of the secular authority wielded by the Popes before they obtained the technical rank of sovereigns, according to modern definition of that word. Constantine's gift of the Lateran palace may be considered the starting point which the continual generosity of so many succeeding generations extended, as has been recounted, until the unanimous voice of his people, delivered, as they hoped, from the Lombard burden, saluted Stephen II. on his return in 756, not only as Papa, but as Dominus Urbis.

Under the year 752, when Aistulf had attacked the exarchate and occupied the city of Ravenna, and was turning his arms against the Roman duchy and the cities depending on it, Muratori writes: "From what we have hitherto seen, although the Greek emperors had their ministers in Rome, yet the principal authority of government seems to have been seated in the Roman Pontiffs. They with the power and majesty of their rank and with the accompaniment of their virtues

[1] By Bianchini Giovini, quoted by Hoensbroech, p. 18, who gives 85 German square miles.

tranquilly governed that city and duchy, defending it moreover vigorously, when need arose, from the claws of the Lombards."[1]

Such was the position of the Pontiffs before that definitive rejection of the Byzantine sovereign made by Stephen II. when he was left naked to the assault of Aistulf by the cowardice or the impotence of Constantine Kopronymus. From his return in 756 he and his successors after him became kings as well as Popes of Rome. Scrupulous as the two Gregories, Zacharias and Stephen himself had been up to the time of the compact with Pipin, never after did any Pope acknowledge the Byzantine as his civil sovereign.

Never could an Italian of those ages have given to the Goth or the Lombard that heartfelt devotion which they felt for the perpetual defender of the Italian people, who was seated in the centre of Italy at once the champion of the Christian faith, and representative of Rome's old Commonwealth. The Byzantine slave-master revolted the Roman heart; the Arian politician revolted the Christian faith: but in the Roman see St. Sergius the Syrian emulated the courage of St. Martin the Roman, and St. Gregory III., also Syrian, was in no quality behind his predecessor St. Gregory II. the Roman. Is it any wonder that by the end of the seventh century when a Justinian II. tried to repeat on the person of St. Sergius the wickedness practised by his grandfather upon St. Martin, his own soldiers rose against the guardsman whom he had deputed to this atrocious work, and re-

[1] *Annali d'Italia*, anno 752.

cognised in the Pope the defender of all which they held dear, whether in the natural or the supernatural life.

And, again, had not the seven revolutions at Byzantium—ending in the exultation of a rough soldier who was able in the field, but ignorant in doctrine—given a sufficient lesson to the Italian peoples to cast off a force which disregarded all right in the natural order, and the whole tradition of faith in the supernatural realm of revealed truth?

That is the consummation which we have been following during a whole generation, from 726 to 756.

I will here insert the judgment of another historian, upon the gift of the exarchate, made by Pipin to St. Peter, in the person of the Popes:—[1] "To question the rightness of this donation is unreasonable and preposterous. Since the reconquest of Italy by Belisarius and Narses, Rome was regarded at Constantinople simply as a province, not as a member of the realm, or not as, what it had originally been, the seat of empire. On what could the right of Greek tyrants be founded constantly to receive back, even at second hand, conquests which they were able neither to govern nor to maintain? The assertions of some late historical writers seem to pre-suppose that all Europe, as far as the Rhine and the Danube, were placed by God for ever under the Byzantine yoke, and that the shaking off this yoke was an unpardonable injustice. Rome did under her

---

[1] Adolf Menzel, *Geschichte der Deutschen*, Book III. ch. xvi. 448, quoted by von Hoensbroech, p. 34.

bishops what peoples did under their kings. Rome took her opportunity to free herself from the yoke of foreign dominion and unnatural relations. No prince, no people of Europe has any other claim upon its soil to show than this and the centuries. Both tell for Rome. Before this testimony, the lesser but yet valid right disappears, that the Greek emperor had confiscated the Papal possessions situated in Lower Italy, and that nothing was more natural than that it should take the compensation which presented itself. The other question which has been also proposed, whether the office of a teacher and bishop of the Christian community can be united with a secular administration, had been long before answered. *Rome owed its actual existence solely to the protection of its bishops.* They had found their best right of sovereignty in the gratitude of the people, and long before the donation of Ravenna, they had been, if not in name, yet in fact, princes in Rome."

At the beginning of the year 756, Aistulf, the most aggressive of Lombard kings, had strictly invested Rome, ravaged its campagna, and destroyed the churches therein, while he devoutly exhumed the bodies of martyrs to transport them to new shrines in Pavia. In the spring of that year he surrendered his capital to the king of the Franks, and submitted to all the conditions imposed on him by Pipin. In the autumn, by a sudden stroke of God, he died out hunting. At the beginning of the year 757, Desiderius, by the help of the Pope, Stephen II. had succeeded to the Lombard throne, itself spared by Pipin, and these great changes are recorded in an extant letter of Pope Stephen, a hymn of gratitude and praise, to Pipin, who had placed the keys of the recovered cities, forming the new created State of the Church, on the tomb of St. Peter. Great is the contrast between the letters of 756, written to Pipin, in the height of Rome's distress and danger, and this letter from the first Pope-king to his benefactor.

"Words[1] cannot express, most excellent son, our delight at your work and your life. For we have seen miracles in our days wrought by the divine power. For the Roman Church, the holy mother and head of all the churches of God, the foundation of the Christian faith, which was groaning under the attacks of enemies, now through you, has been translated into the fulness of joy and security. Thus, by your work, and in our exultation, we rejoice to exclaim with the angels, 'Glory to God in the highest, and on earth peace to men of goodwill'. This time last year we were wounded and afflicted on all sides: now, in our deliverance through you, we cry out, 'This change is by the hand of the Most High,' and, again, 'In the evening, there shall be weeping, but in the morning joy'. What heart is there so stony that, knowing what your goodness has done, would not break into praise of God and affection to your excellency. This I am wont to say to those who come hither from all the nations of the earth: and I perpetually pray to God for your welfare, and that of the whole nation of the Franks. What can I call you but a new Moses and a glorious David, for, as they de-

---

[1] Mansi, xii. 546-9. Eleventh letter of the *Codex Carolinus*.

livered the people of God from the oppression of the heathen, so have you the Church of God. May the Lord, the beauty of justice, bless you and your children, Charles and Carloman, my spiritual sons, appointed by God kings of the Franks, and patricii of the Romans."

He then goes on to beg Pipin to execute fully all that he had promised to St. Peter by oath. He mentions specially Imola, Ferrara, Ancona, Bologna, with their complete territories; and begs him to favour the new king, Desiderius, if he restore, as he had promised, fully the *justitia*, which we may translate sovereignty, "to the Holy Church of God, or Commonwealth of the Romans, St. Peter, your protector". He also prays him that the Holy Catholic and Apostolic faith may be preserved by him from "the pestilent malice of the Greeks". He ends with the prayer:—"O victorious king, may God, in all your acts, extend His right hand over you, your queen, and mine and your dearest sons: and, as He has given you the royal power in this life, may you also hear the divine promise, 'Come, blessed of my Father, you have fought the good fight, you have finished your course, you have kept the faith, so take the crown laid up for you, and the kingdom prepared for you from the foundation of the world'".

A few days after this letter, that is, on the 24th April, 757, Stephen II. closed in peace his course on earth. He died in the Lateran patriarchal palace, acknowledged by all as king of Rome: and attended by his brother, Paul, who was to be his successor. He was buried with extraordinary honours in St. Peter's. In his short pontificate of five years he set the crown upon the work of his three great predecessors, Gregory II., Gregory III., and Zacharias, and is counted among the most illustrious of the Popes. He closed the seven centuries of Popes who were subjects: he opens the eleven centuries of Popes who have been kings. From the Pope who was crucified on the Roman hill to the Pope who died a king in the patriarchal Lateran palace, 93 in number, enemies have tried to deface the memory of two—but the voice of impartial history regards those rulers of the Church with unalloyed gratitude as men who, through trials and difficulties unsurpassed, kept the faith of the Church inviolate. That the city of Rome existed in their day, and exists now, is due to the pastoral staff of St. Peter, planted in its soil, which became, in the hand of Stephen II., the most gracious, the most prolific, the most honoured of sceptres.

Stephen II. was succeeded immediately by his brother Paul, who had been the chosen companion of his counsels and anxieties during the severe trials of his pontificate, ending so gloriously. It was the first instance of a brother to the Pope succeeding to his chair. He had been brought up, like his brother Stephen, in the Lateran patriarchal palace from the time of St. Gregory II., and was made a cardinal deacon by Pope Zacharias. "He was meek and very merciful, never rendering evil for evil to anyone."[1] He sat from 757 to 767, ten years and a month. During the whole time the

[1] Anastasius.

closest union was maintained between the Holy See and King Pipin. A series of letters from the Pope to the king is extant, testifying the affection and the confidence which existed between them. It was by the influence of Pope Stephen II. that the new king of the Lombards, Desiderius, was accepted by that people after the untimely death of King Aistulf. He bound himself strictly to carry out the compact at Pavia between the Franks, the Lombards, and the Romans, in virtue of which, at the subjection of King Aistulf to Pipin, the Lombard monarchy continued to exist. The reign of Desiderius from 757 until he was finally overthrown and deposed by Charles in 774 shows a repetition of attempts by fraud or by violence to evade the conditions which he had bound himself to accept. Already, in 757, Pope Paul I. wrote to King Pipin: "We[1] make known to your Excellence that we have hitherto received nothing of those things which by our legates we committed to your charge, for, according to their wont, those perfidious and malignant Lombards, persisting in great arrogance of heart, are by no means inclined to restore the justice of St. Peter". The possession of the cities and territories of Imola, Bologna, Osimo, Ancona, and Umana were in question. In the next year, 758, Desiderius ravaged with fire and sword the Pentapolis. Then he attacked the duchies of Spoleto and Benevento, which had put themselves under the protection of the Pope and the king of the Franks.

At another time the Greek emperor Kopronymus was

[1] *I primi Papi-Re*, p. 25.

bent upon recovering Ravenna and the Pentapolis, and upon attacking Rome itself. Desiderius met his agent and wrote to the emperor, exhorting him to send an army into Italy, and promising that he with all his Lombards would help him to recover Ravenna, and whatever else he desired.[1]

Through the whole ten years of Paul's pontificate, this king Pipin discharged with fidelity his office of Roman Patricius, that is, the sworn defender of the Holy See. It was this protection alone which enabled the Pope to maintain his newly founded State against the perpetual wiles of the Lombard, as well as against the Greek enmity. As to Kopronymus, the Iconoclastic heresy was the furious passion of his whole life. Pope Paul wrote to King Pipin:[2] " You know well how those most nefarious Greeks pursue us only to destroy and tread under foot the orthodox faith and the tradition of the fathers ".

When Pope Paul I. died, in 767, his pontificate of ten years had been throughout agitated by the perpetual oscillations of king Desiderius, alternating acts of devotion with acts of hostility, promises with violations of them, restitution of rights with fresh acts of plundering.[3] Scarcely had Paul I. closed his eyes when the duke Toto, a very powerful baron of the Roman Tuscany, conspired with his three brothers, Constantine, Passivus, and Paschalis, to get possession of Rome and the papacy.[4] Toto and his party, while preparation was being made

[1] *I primi Papi-Re*, p. 27.
[2] *Ib.*, p. 39.
[3] *Ib.*, p. 52.
[4] *Ib.*, 60-63.

for the solemn obsequies of Paul I. and the due election of his successor, broke into Rome, suddenly elected his brother Constantine, a layman, introduced him by violence into the Lateran palace. He seized upon George, bishop of Palestrina, and compelled him to confer minor orders upon Constantine. The next day he was made deacon by the same bishop, and on the following Sunday Toto, attended by a large body of armed men, carried the intruded Constantine to St. Peter's, where the three suburbican bishops, the said George of Palestrina, and the bishops of Albano and Porto, gave him episcopal consecration. In such fashion Constantine seated himself in the chair of Peter; he forced the people to make oath of fidelity to him. Thus the layman of a week before, thrust upon the clergy and people of Rome by the rudest violence, held possession of the Apostolic See for thirteen months. He wrote lying letters to King Pipin, who was not deceived by them. But Rome was filled with conspiracy and unrule.

A year after this event, in July, 768, the intruder Constantine was deposed, his brother Toto killed, while a second pretended Pope, named Philip, set up for the moment, was driven away. By the exertions of Christophorus, first of the seven Palatine judges, and his son Sergius, Stephen III., a Sicilian, and at the time cardinal priest of St. Cecilia, was duly elected Pope. He sat during three years and six months, in the course of which great events took place. His first act was to send Sergius to King Pipin and his sons, beseeching him to depute a number of Frankish bishops to Rome to hold a council there with him, and to make regulations which might prevent the recurrence of violence so deplorable.

Sergius found king Pipin dying. He expired at St. Denys on the 24th September, 768. There he was buried and afterwards his monument bore the inscription, "Pipin, the king, father of Charles the Great". He left his states, with the consent of the nobles and bishops, between his sons Charles and Carloman, who were crowned and anointed on the same day, 9th October, 768, Charles at Noyon, Carloman at Soissons. Pipin died aged fifty-five, having ruled France for twenty-seven years, ten as Mayor of the palace, seventeen as king of the Franks.

The legate Sergius proceeded at once to the kings, Charles and Carloman. They granted all which he desired. They gave him twelve Frankish bishops well instructed in the scriptures and the holy canons, the archbishop of Sens, the bishops of Mainz, Tours, Lyons, Bourges, Narbonne, Rheims, Langres, Noyon, Worms, and two others with sees of names unknown. These bishops came to Rome in April, 769, and Pope Stephen III. assembled bishops from Tuscany, Campania, and the rest of Italy, and held a council in the Lateran Basilica. Among other decrees they passed one under anathema: "that no laymen, nor any one save a cardinal, deacon or priest, ascending through the distinct degrees, be promoted to the honour of the sacred pontificate".[1] The Pope, all the priests, and the Roman people, prostrate on the pavement, deplored the sin they had

[1] *Anastasius*, Mansi, xii. p. 686.

committed in receiving Communion from the unhappy intruder, Constantine, who had been deprived of sight during the wild struggle which attended his deposition, and now in most abject guise confessed his crime before the council, and was condemned to penance.

In this terrible outburst of ambition and crime, which showed but too clearly to what sudden dangers Rome was exposed, the two great officers, Christophorus, the first of the seven Palatine judges, and his son Sergius, had done their utmost to prevent the usurpation, and in the end delivered the Holy See from the intruder Constantine. Desiderius had taken no part in the intrusion of the anti-pope. He even assisted Christophorus and Sergius in removing him. But in doing this a Lombard priest, Waldepert, sought to set up another anti-pope, and lost his life. After the due appointment of Stephen III., the master stroke of the Lombard king's policy was to sever, if he could, the two Frank kings from friendship with the Holy See, and so sooner or later to get possession of Rome. He proposed in 770 a double marriage; on one side the marriage of his daughter Desiderata or Ermengarde either with Charles or with Carloman; on the other that of their sister, the princess Gisela, with his son Adelchis. The queen mother, Bertrada, set her hand to accomplish the first. There is a most earnest letter from Pope Stephen III. to the kings Charles and Carloman, entreating them not to stain the noble Frank race, the most eminent of all, by a connection with the faithless and perfidious Lombard. "You have likewise," he said, "by the will of God, and the command of your father, contracted lawful marriages with excellent royal ladies out of your own people, conspicuous for their nobility and beauty. It is not lawful for you to repudiate them. To take other wives would be an impiety. Heathens only can so act. Forget not, most illustrious sons, that you received holy unction from St. Peter's successor, that your father of glorious memory listened to the injunctions of our predecessor Stephen, and forebore to separate from your mother, Bertrada, and be mindful of your repeated promise to St. Peter and his successor that you would ever be friends of our friends and enemies of our enemies. Would you now bind yourselves to our enemies? For the faithless people of the Lombards, which ceases not to attack the Church of God, and make incursions on our province of Rome, is our manifest enemy."[1]

Nevertheless the queen mother, Bertrada, carried out her design, and the king Desiderius seemed to attain the summit of security, so far at least as this, that though his son Adelchis did not obtain the princess Gisela, Charles took his daughter Ermengarde. He also sent her back to her father the next year, and his friend and secretary, Eginhard, has left unexplained the cause of this repudiation. No historian has thrown light upon this particular in the history of Charles, either how he came to brave the anathema of Pope Stephen III. by deserting a lawful wife, or how he came to send back in a year the unhappy princess whom he had unlawfully taken, or how we find Hildegarde acknowledged as his

[1] Mansi, xii. 695-8.

lawful wife from 771 to her death in 786. The blot remains unerased upon the memory of him who was otherwise the greatest of the Christian emperors.

With the marriage—if it is to be so called—of his daughter with Charles, Desiderius seemed to have reached well nigh the end of his ambition. Christophorus and his son Sergius had put an end to the usurpation of Constantine, were the heads of the national Roman party,[1] and the soul of Pope Stephen III.'s government. Desiderius in a visit to Rome managed to set the Pope against them. He had a Lombard party there, at the head of which was a certain Paul Afiarta, high in the Pope's service. Christophorus and his son Sergius both lost their lives. They had urged the king of the Lombards to restore to the Holy See the rights which he kept back. Desiderius was infuriated by their conduct[2] and strove to destroy them.[3] Desiderius was encamped outside of St. Peter's. A company of Lombard soldiers dragged the two victims, who had been taken out of St. Peter's, to the gate of the city, at the bridge: tore out their eyes, of which outrage Christophorus died in three days: Sergius survived in prison during two years, that is, to the death of Pope Stephen, when he was most atrociously murdered by order of Paul Afiarta.

But now the whole course of history was altered by a death which occurred on the 4th December. Carloman

---

[1] Kellner, p. 475.
Kellner, p. 475.
I primi Papi-Re, p. 109, 117.

died in the flower of his youth, leaving behind him two very young children by his wife Gilberga. Charles was called by the unanimous vote of the Frank magnates to rule the whole kingdom of the Franks increased greatly as it was by the late conquests of Charles in Aquitania and Gascony. Two months later, 1st February, 772, Stephen III. closed his pontificate of three years and a half. The Pope before his death had discovered how grievously he had been deceived by king Desiderius, to whom his two chief servants and ministers had been sacrificed. Desiderius kept none of the promises which he had made on the occasion of his coming to Rome: and when the Pope reminded him of them by a special embassy, mockingly replied:[1] "The Holy Father Stephen might have been contented that I delivered him from his two tyrants Christophorus and Sergius, and did not need to demand the rights of St. Peter. If I had not helped the Holy Father, great ruin would have fallen upon him, since Carloman, king of the Franks, the friend of both, was ready to bring an army to Rome to avenge their death, and carry away the Pope captive."

The repudiation of his daughter, Ermengarde, and the rupture of the desired alliance between Desiderius and Charles, terminated the good fortune of the Lombard king. From that time he seemed to lose his vigour of mind, and political insight. He continued to pursue, without check, the design of Aistulf, which he

---

[1] Kellner, p. 467, from *Anastasius*, who put these words into the mouth of Pope Adrian himself, addressing the ambassadors of Desiderius. Mansi, xii. 726.

had now fully made his own, to become master of Rome. But he had to deal with other adversaries. Eight days after the death of Pope Stephen III., he was succeeded by one of the greatest pontiffs who ever sat on the throne of St. Peter. Adrian, the son of Theodorus, was born in Rome of a very noble family, one of the most powerful in the city. Losing his parents early, he was brought up by a relation named Theodotus, Primicerius of the Roman See. He was distinguished from his youth by his purity of life, and his singular personal beauty. Pope Paul I. had placed him among the clergy, Pope Stephen III. created him a cardinal deacon, in which office his zeal, eloquence, learning, and management of affairs endeared him to the Roman people. On the very day of the Pope Stephen's death he was proclaimed unanimously his successor, and in eight days consecrated. He showed at once the vigour of mind and promptitude of execution which rendered his reign illustrious, and it continued nearly to twenty-four years, a period which no Pontiff reached in the seven hundred years from St. Peter before him, nor in the thousand years after him, until, at the end of the eighteenth century, it was slightly passed by that Pontiff who died a confessor, exiled, persecuted, and forlorn at Valence, in that land of the Franks, with whose greatest king Pope Adrian was bound in the closest personal friendship.

No sooner was Pope Adrian seated than he struck down that Lombard faction which the gold and intrigues of Desiderius had planted at Rome. Its head was Paul

Afiarta. In the very last days of Pope Stephen, he had caused the blinded Sergius to be assassinated, and banished from Rome certain judges, both of the clergy and the army, that he might have more weight in the forthcoming election. Adrian, the moment that he was elected, recalled the judges, and delivered from prison those who had been confined for the like reason. Desiderius, who desired to keep up appearances with him, sent him a solemn embassy of the three principal persons in his kingdom, Theodicius, duke of Spoleto, Tunno, duke of Ivrea, and the Lord Treasurer Praudulus. Their office was to profess friendship and alliance to the new Pope. Adrian replied :—[1]" It is my desire to have peace with all Christians, and even with your king, Desiderius, I will study to remain in that compact which was made between the Romans, the Franks, and the Lombards. But how can I trust your king in the matter in which my predecessor, Stephen, of holy memory, has spoken to me fully of his want of good faith : how he falsified everything which he promised on oath over the body of St. Peter, for the rights of holy Church, and only by his own hostile pleading, caused the eyes of Christophorus and Sergius to be put out, and worked out his own will upon those two chief men of the Church. Such is the faith of your king, Desiderius, and how can I trust in a treaty with him ?" In reply, the ambassadors made oath that Desiderius would fulfil what he had promised to Pope Stephen, and broken. The Pope thereupon despatched messengers to see that

[1] *Anastasius*, Mansi, xii. 726.

Desiderius fulfilled the promise. When these reached Perugia, they found that Desiderius had already taken the city of Faenza, and the duchy of Ferrara, and was pressing Ravenna with siege. It was only two months after the accession of Pope Adrian, and presently messengers from Ravenna came supplicating his help, just as thirty years before, when pressed by the arms of Liutprand, they had recourse to Pope Zacharias. But now the exarchate was fully subject to the Pope, and called upon him as part of his own State for defence.

When this conduct of Desiderius was reported to the Pope, he wrote in the gravest terms to the Lombard king, requiring him to restore the cities, and upbraiding him with the breach of those very promises which his own ambassadors had just made in his name. "The king," he said, "had taken cities which his predecessors, Stephen II., Paul I., and Stephen III., had possessed." Desiderius returned, for answer, "that he would not restore those cities, unless he first met the Pope". At the same time, he had received the widow and young children of the deceased Carloman, and wanted to induce the Pope to crown them, and so create division in the Frank empire, and alienate Charles, the Patricius of Rome, from the Pope, and thus subjugate the city of Rome and all Italy to the Lombard kingdom.[1] But Adrian stood firm as adamant. One of his two legates to the king, Paul Afiarta, was in league with the king, and promised to bring the Pope before him, even if it were with a rope round him. But, at this very moment,

---

[1] From *Anastasius*, textually. Mansi, xii. 727.

the body of the murdered Sergius was discovered at Rome. The Pope ordered an inquiry into the circumstances of his death. At the earnest entreaty of the Palatine judges, among whom Sergius had been second in rank, and of the whole Roman people, the Pope ordered the prefect of the city to try for homicide the parties inculpated. The crime was brought home to the legate, Paul Afiarta himself, at whose suggestion other highly placed officers had taken the blind Sergius out of prison, and pierced him with wounds. The Pope ordered the bodies of Christophorus and Sergius to be taken up and honourably buried in St. Peter's. He sent the Acts of the Court to the archbishop of Ravenna, instructing him to detain Paul Afiarta, when he returned from his embassy to the Lombard king. Archbishop Leo went beyond the Pope's instructions: handed over Paul Afiarta to the chief judge of Ravenna, before whom he acknowledged his guilt : and, instead of sending the criminal, as the Pope ordered, in exile to the East, had him executed by the judge.

Desiderius found himself bereft of his counsellor, Paul Afiarta : he refused to listen to the Pope's request to restore his cities. He committed further outrages and assaults. He rejected repeated letters and messengers of the Pope. His reply was that, instead of restoring cities, he would march with his whole army to Rome, and force it to surrender. The Pope had several of the gates of Rome built up and others carefully closed, and sent by sea messengers to Charles, begging him to help the Roman Church as his father had done, and force Desiderius to restore what he had taken from St. Peter.[1] Desiderius saw that his attempt to move the Pope to crown the sons of Carloman was vain; then, with the widowed Gilberga, these sons and the duke, Autchar, he advanced his troops from Pavia, on the way to Rome, and informed the Pope of it. Adrian replied, "If the king does not give up the cities, as he has promised, and fully satisfy us, it is useless for him to take the trouble to come to us. He shall not see my face."

Adrian, while awaiting the succour which he had asked from king Charles, had taken all measures necessary for the defence of Rome. He collected all the men of war whom he could from the Roman Tuscany, from Campania, from the duchy of Perugia, from such cities of the Pentapolis as the Lombards had not yet taken, who, with the Roman soldiers, might suffice to defend the vast circle of the walls and towers, and sustain a siege at least for a time. The two basilicas of St. Peter and St. Paul, being outside the walls, were defenceless. The Pope caused them to be stripped of all precious objects, which were brought for protection within the city. He had all the doors closed and barred up within: so that, if the Lombard king attempted an entrance, it would be as a burglar.

These were his acts as a sovereign prince—as pontiff, learning that the king was approaching the Roman frontiers, he sent to him the bishops of Albano, Palestrina, and Tibur, with an intimation in his own hand,

[1] Kellner, p. 479.

adjuring him by all the divine mysteries, and under threat of excommunication, that neither he, nor any Lombard, nor the Frank Autchar should set foot on the Roman territory without his leave.

Desiderius had reached Viterbo, the last city of the Lombard Tuscany. He was, at the head of his army, about to pass the frontier. On receiving the Pope's injunction he was struck with confusion and retired back with his army to his own city, Pavia. As the Hun had listened to St. Leo, the Lombard also listened to Adrian, and Rome was once more saved by her pontiff.

When Peter,[1] the legate of Adrian, reached France in the first months of 773, he found Charles wintering at Thionville, after his first expedition against the Saxons. He had destroyed the famous idol Irminoul. It was the beginning of his longest and fiercest war. Now, Pope Adrian called upon him, as Patricius of the Romans, to defend Rome and the State of St. Peter against Desiderius, from whom neither peace nor justice could any longer be hoped. At the same time a Lombard embassy reached him, professing that Desiderius had already restored every thing to the Pope. Charles sent three messengers of his own to Rome to ascertain the facts. They reached Rome just after its deliverance from the fear of a siege by the retreat of Desiderius from Viterbo. The Pope related to them in order all the late events : and sent with them other messengers of his own, conjuring Charles afresh to carry into effect

[1] Narrative chiefly drawn from *I primi Papi-Re*, p. 187, etc.

the promises which he had formerly made with his father to St. Peter, and to fulfil the redemption of the holy Church of God[1] by compelling the perfidious king of the Lombards to restore without contest to St. Peter, both the cities and the other rights which he had taken away. On their way to France the joint-messengers appeared at the court of Pavia, and, by instruction of Charles, urged Desiderius peacefully to restore the cities and rights. He gave an absolute refusal, which they carried to Charles.

Charles sent fresh messengers to Desiderius, and offered him 14,000 gold solidi, if he would make restitution. All was of no avail. When the messengers returned to Charles, he brought the whole matter before his dukes and chiefs, probably at the May diet, and an expedition into Italy was resolved upon for the autumn. The Frank army was summoned to meet at Geneva. One part of it Charles sent by the Mons Jovis, the St. Bernard; the other he conducted himself by the passes of Mont Cenis, the same route which Pipin had held in 754 and 756. When Charles reached the pass above Susa, he found it strongly fortified and valiantly defended by Desiderius in person, and his son, Adelchis. Here it is said the Franks were so long detained, being unable to break through the Lombard defence, that they were on the point of retiring, when a secret road was discovered to Charles, and their flank was turned. The result was a precipitate retreat of Desiderius to his fortified capital, Pavia, and of his son, Adelchis, to Verona.

---

[1] *Anastasius*, literally.

From that moment the chief struggle was concentred about these two cities. Other cities of Upper Italy, such as Turin, Ivrea, Vercelli, Novara, Piacenza, Milan, Parma, Tortona, and the maritime cities, with their castles, fell speedily into the hands of the Franks. Charles sat down before Pavia at the end of September or beginning of October, 773. That royal city of the Lombards, in the eighth century, was first among all the cities of Upper Italy, not only for its riches and magnificence, but for its military strength. Near the confluence of the Ticino and the Po, it was esteemed almost impregnable. It had resisted Odoacer, and Alboin required more than three years to take it, which he accomplished rather by famine than by force. Charles encamped with his army round it, and completely enclosed it with lines and trenches. He sent for the queen Hildegarde and her children. He made an attempt to take Verona, but found it too strong for anything short of a regular siege, defended, as it was, by the most valiant Adelchis. However, the widowed queen Gilberga, with her children, who were therein, surrendered themselves to him. They disappear henceforward from history, and are supposed to have been confined in Frank monasteries. Charles spent the feast of Christmas in the camp at Pavia. All we know of these months is the two words of Eginhard, that he spent them, "much employed".[1] We may conclude that not only the siege of Pavia, but the settlement of the

---

[1] Totum hiberni temporis spatium *multa moliendo* consumpsit.—*Annales*, ann., 773.

numerous cities in North Italy, which yielded to him, well occupied his time.

But Charles had hitherto never seen Rome, and the feast of Easter, which fell in that year, 774, on the 3rd April, drew him with a great attraction to visit the tombs of the apostles, and he resolved to be present for the Paschal rites. He left therefore his army under the command of his chief officers and with a great train of bishops, abbots, judges, dukes, and counts, and a large escort of warriors, took the road of Tuscany, which probably had been in a great part subdued, and advanced so quickly that he reached the gates of Rome on the morning of Holy Saturday.

Great was the joy of Pope Adrian to hear of this unexpected visit of Charles, and his rapid approach. He made the utmost preparation to receive so great a king, who had likewise the special dignity of Rome's Patricius, that is, her sworn defender. He sent out all the judges of Rome to a spot thirty miles away near the lake of Bracciano, where they awaited him with banners displayed. At a mile from Rome, near Monte Mario, by order of the Pope the soldiers under their respective leaders, and the children who were learning letters, were drawn up to meet him, and bearing in their hands branches of palm and olive sang welcome to him. The standards of crosses were carried, as in the reception of an exarch or a Patricius. When the king of the Franks, Patricius of the Romans, met these crosses, he descended from horseback with his officers, and walked the rest of the way on foot to St. Peter's. There, Pope Adrian, rising early with all the clergy and people of Rome waited, to receive the king of the Franks at the top of the steps leading into the court of the Basilica.

At that time there were thirty-five steps in five series of seven each. When Charles reached these steps, he threw himself on his knees, and so ascended,[1] kissing separately each one of the thirty-five in the fashion of a pilgrim. At the top he found Pope Adrian; they embraced each other, and the king holding the Pope's right hand they entered the church together, all the clergy and the monks singing, "Blessed is he who cometh in the name of the Lord". When the king with the bishops, abbots, judges, and all the Franks of his train, came to the Confession, they prostrated themselves to our almighty God, and rendered their vows to the Prince of the Apostles, glorifying the divine power in him, who had given them by his intercession such a victory.

After their prayer the king turned to the Pope and earnestly requested of him permission to enter Rome, in order to venerate the other churches of the city, and therein pay his vows. Whereupon the Pope and the king, together with Roman and Frank judges, descending to the body of St. Peter, bound themselves by oath to mutual protection. This permission to enter Rome was granted in after times by the Popes to Roman emperors themselves, as often as they approached the gates of Rome with armed force. After this permission received Charles and the Pope rode in solemn pomp

[1] *Anastasius*, Mansi xii. 736.

from St. Peter's to the Lateran, through the whole of Rome. And Charles, in the Lateran church, witnessed the Pope's celebration of the baptismal rite to the catechumens as usual on that day.

So the Romans on that day first beheld the flower of the greatest western nation passing in the pomp of armed men by their palaces, porticoes, Capitol, forum, and colosseum, with the greatest champion of Christendom then in the glory of his manhood at the age of thirty-two years. His secretary, Eginhard, attests his stature to have been seven of his own feet, and his whole aspect was full of majesty. When he ascended on his knees the thirty-five steps leading to St. Peter's, separately kissing each, he manifested in his own person the truth of the reply which nearly fifty years before Pope St. Gregory II. had made to the eastern emperor, Leo III. Leo threatened that he would tear down the statue of St. Peter. St. Gregory said that all the nations of the West regarded him as a God upon earth.

After this Charles returned to the meadows of Nero by St. Peter's wherein foreign armies usually encamped, At the following dawn of Easter day the Pope sent his chief officers and soldiers to conduct Charles in great pomp to Santa Maria Maggiore, where, with all his Franks, he heard the Pope sing Mass. After Mass the Pope received him to a banquet at the patriarchal palace of the Lateran. On the two following feasts the Pope, according to usage, celebrated Mass on the Monday at St. Peter's, on the Tuesday at St. Paul's, in presence of the king. At the Mass in St. Peter's, Anastasius mentions that the Pope caused the ceremony called Lauds to be inserted before the Epistle. It was sung before Popes and emperors at their accession. It consisted of the clergy dividing themselves in two bands before the altar, when the archdeacon on one side intoned with loud voice, "O Christ, hear us!" the other side responded, "Long life to our Lord decreed by God, Roman Pontiff and universal Pope!" This was repeated three times; a short litany followed, in which to each invocation made by the archdeacon, the other side replied, "Give him help": and it ended with a triple Kyrie Eleison. With this rite on that Easter Monday of 774 Charles was solemnly acclaimed as Patricius of the Romans. Eginhard in his "Life" says that Charlemagne would never put on a foreign dress, however splendid: and that he broke this rule twice only, both times at Rome, the first at the request of Pope Adrian: the second at the request of his successor, Pope Leo III., when he wore the long tunic and cloak, and was shod also in Roman fashion. Now twenty years before, that is, in 754, Pope Stephen II. had crowned Pipin and his two sons Charles and Carloman kings of the Franks, and created them also Patricii of the Romans. Charles would seem to have considered this ceremony a solemn inauguration of this dignity. It was from this time, 774, that in his public acts he styled himself king of the Franks and of the Lombards, and Patricius of the Romans.

In that same week before Charles left Rome he transacted affairs of the utmost importance with the Pope.

The ecclesiastical hierarchy in France, the rights of metropolitans, and the other churches had fallen in the last eighty years under great usurpations, which all the zeal of Pipin had not been able to remedy. Adrian prevailed on Charles to work a restoration of the ancient state. He also drew from the archives of the Roman See two authentic codes, one containing the old order of the ecclesiastical provinces and dioceses in France; the other, the councils and canons of the Greek and Latin church. These were of the greatest service to Charles in the synods and capitulars and wise regulations which he made for the restoration of the Church in France.

But further, the Pope addressed himself to obtain from Charles the renewal and confirmation of the promise made in April, 754, by king Pipin and Charles himself to Pope Stephen II. The king promised not only to reconquer for the Holy See the exarchate and Pentapolis, then occupied by Aistulf, but to add to them likewise all the provinces of nearly all Italy from the Po. That promise was grounded upon the design then entertained by the Pope and the king to put an end altogether to the Lombard rule. But at the siege of Pavia, in 754, the Pope and Pipin were so far moved by the supplications and promises of Aistulf, that they left him the Lombard kingdom. Giving up that first design, they made with him the treaty of Pavia, that compact between the Franks, the Lombards, and the Romans, which during eighteen years was appealed to as the basis of their political relations. But in this interval the incorrigible perfidy and ambition of Desiderius, and his obstinate refusal of all terms of agreement, had at last led Adrian and Charles to resume the original intention of Stephen and Pipin. Charles after forcing the pass above Susa resolved to pluck up by the roots the Lombard power. Thus the conditions of 754, having returned in 774, would bring back the first promise of Pipin, and the compact of Pavia in 756 having been trodden under foot by Desiderius, and torn at the sword's point, the compact of Quiersy was restored to force. It had not been annulled but suspended. Adrian therefore took the excellent opportunity of Charles's presence in Rome to complete the work so well begun by Stephen II. The fresh inauguration of Charles as Patricius helped to obtain from him a solemn confirmation of the former compact. His piety and devotion to St. Peter were not less marked than his father's, and he assented to the Pope's desire.

On Easter Wednesday, the 6th April, 774, the solemn act was completed which Anastasius has left carefully registered in the Liber Pontificalis.[1] The Pope with all the judges of the clergy and army, that is, all the ecclesiastical and lay dignitaries of Rome, went to St. Peter's, where he was met by Charles with all his train. Here Adrian in a public speech recorded the acts of kindness and attachment which for so long had joined together France and the Holy See. He reminded Charles of the promise which, in April, 754, his father Pipin of sacred memory and he himself with his brother Carloman and all the Frank judges had made and sworn

[1] *Anastasius*, Mansi xii. 737.

solemnly to St. Peter and Pope Stephen II. in the assembly of Quiersy. That was to assure to St. Peter and all his successors in perpetuity the possession of various cities and territories of Italy. He then earnestly exhorted and prayed the king to give entire accomplishment to that promise. Charles asked that the whole tenor of the promise of Quiersy should be read before him. Having heard it read, and greatly approved of it, with his judges, he most willingly accorded the request of the Pope. He immediately ordered his chaplain and notary Etherius to draw out another deed of promise and donation exactly similar to the first. In this he granted to St. Peter the same cities and lands and promised to give them over to Pope Adrian, marking out the limits. These are, says Anastasius, as we now read them in the text of donation, from Luni and the isle of Corsica, by Parma, Reggio, Mantua, and Monselice, embracing the whole exarchate of Ravenna as it was of old, the province of Venetia and Istria, the duchies of Spoleto and Benevento. This Charles subscribed with his own hand, and caused it to be subscribed by all his bishops, abbots, dukes, and counts. After this the king and his nobles, having placed the deed, first upon the altar of St. Peter, and then within the Confession, took a terrible oath to St. Peter and Pope Adrian, to maintain every syllable of its contents, and they placed the deed in the hands of the Pope. Further, Charles made Etherius write another copy of the same donation, placed it with his own hand on the inner altar of the Confession, under the gospels which were wont to be kissed there by the faithful, that it might remain in most secure guarantee and eternal memorial of the devotion of Charles and the Franks to the Prince of the Apostles. Other copies were afterwards made in authentic form by the proper officer of the Roman Church, which Charles carried with him into France.

Thus the original compact of Quiersy resumed its legal force, and became the foundation of political right in Italy. It is true that various reasons prevented the compact from ever receiving its entire effect, but it became, nevertheless, the standard which the Popes and the kings of the Franks kept before them, the archetype on which the public deeds and covenants renewed afterwards so often in the middle ages between the emperors and the Holy See were all framed. Adrian in thus claiming and securing the sovereign rights already acquired by the Roman Church may be called the second founder, after Stephen II., of the temporal monarchy of the Popes. Charles in crowning the work of Pipin showed himself not only worthy of the Roman Patriciate, but of that further dignity to which he was afterwards exalted by Leo III. In the twenty following years the union and cordial friendship which bound Adrian and Charles together, maintained and increased prosperity in the Church, and made closer still the old alliance of France with the Papacy. Adrian ordered a prayer for king Charles to be entered in the Roman liturgy, which thenceforward was made for the Roman emperors, who succeeded him in his office of Protector of the Church.

The Pope, in taking leave of Charles, predicted to

him, in the names of St. Peter and St. Paul, a quick and complete triumph over their common enemies, and the total conquest of the Lombard kingdom : "after which," he said, " you will render to St. Peter the gift which you have promised him, and will receive in reward greater and more signal victories ".

And Adrian ordered that in all the monasteries, and the twenty-eight titular churches, and the seven deaconries of Rome, every day perpetual prayers should be offered for victory to the Franks.

Thus Charles left Rome, and returned to his camp before Pavia. By the first days of June, Verona had fallen, notwithstanding all the valour of the prince Adelchis, and Pavia had yielded. With the submission of the capital, the few remaining cities, and Lombard lords, accepted Charles for their king. Thus, in the course of ten months, from September, 773, to June, 774, Charles effected, with great good fortune and little effusion of blood, the most brilliant of his conquests. He placed a strong Frank garrison in Pavia, he sent his counts to govern the various cities and provinces : in which, however, the chief Lombard dukes were comprised. Charles did not change the constitution of the kingdom : he did not make it a province of France. He left its integrity and autonomy. He became himself king of the Lombards, as before he had been king of the Franks.

One of his first deeds [1] was to restore to the Holy See all the cities and territories which, in his last years, De-

---

[1] Brunengo, *I primi Papi-Re*, 241-2.

siderius had invaded in the exarchate, the Pentapolis, or the duchy of Rome. He thus gave back to Pope Adrian full and pacific possession of the whole State of St. Peter, such as it was after the donation of Pipin. This was the chief, if not the sole, occasion of the war. It would be the first fruit of the victory. That he performed what he had promised is attested by his secretary, Eginhard: "Charles did not rest from the war which he had begun until he had restored to the Romans all which had been taken away from them. 'The end of this war was the subjection of Italy: and the restitution to Adrian, ruler of the Roman Church, of the things which had been seized by the Lombard kings.'"[1] Other contemporary annals of the year 774 say: "This year Pavia was surrendered to the Franks: and Desiderius was carried into France, and the lord king Charles sent his counts through all Italy: he joyfully restored to St. Peter the cities owed to him, and having arranged everything, came speedily into France". His return filled France with triumph.

"The Lombards[2] had been governed by their kings with good laws and exact justice, but they afterwards received better treatment under Charlemagne, a monarch who, in loftiness of mind, in power and rectitude of judgment, surpassed all Frank and Lombard kings." But this encomium on the good laws and exact justice of the Lombards belongs only to their treatment of

---

[1] *Vita Caroli*, M. n. 6. *Fasti Carolini*, found and quoted by Mai.

[2] Muratori, *Annali d'Italia*, a. 774, quoted by Brunengo, *I primi Papi-Re*, p. 260.

themselves, for the Romans[1] looked with horror upon the ignominious servitude with which Aistulf and Desiderius threatened them. These kings sought to crown that semi-barbarous occupation of North Italy during two centuries by throning themselves in Rome, and making the Pope their vassal. Aistulf sank before Pipin, and Desiderius before Charles. The oppressors of the Pope were swept away: his champion and protector, Charles, went on henceforth from victory to victory.

That the transition[2] of the lands secured to the Pope into the relation of vassals to a sovereign was a matter of time is explained by the insufficient material force at the command of the Pope, the love of independence in the population, their power to resist, and the general conditions of the time. Thus, from a letter of Adrian to Charles, in 787 or 788, we learn that he announced to the king how he had received the cities of Toscanella, Bagnorea, and Viterbo, and requested from him the tradition of Populania, and Rosella, near Piombino. Later, he shows him that he had not yet received them, though two messengers of Charles had been charged with their delivery. Thus it required fresh efforts on the part of the Franks, and fresh reminders on the part of the Pope, to obtain the complete execution of the gift. This does not show that Charles was unwilling to keep his word: but it does show the difficulty of the matter.

---

[1] For the felicity of *Italian* subjects of the Lombards, see Troya: *Della condizione dei Romani vinti dai Longobardi.* Brunengo, p. 260.

[2] Kellner, ii. 487-9.

It was a great undertaking to pacify the population in a number of cities, and to subject the great and the small proprietors in them to the papal lordship. Adrian had reason sometimes to express the wish to the king that it might be accomplished in their life-time. Sometimes Charles's own Commissioners were not trustworthy, were disinclined to the Pope, were liable to be corrupted or deceived, or made mistakes in executing their commission. In March, 781, Charles came again to Italy, celebrated Easter on the 15th of April at Rome, treated with the Pope, had his little son, Pipin, four years old, baptised, and made him, after the Pope had anointed him, king of the Lombards. The duchies of Spoleto and Benevento were to be vassal lands of the Pope. The distance of the latter from the Franks, the connection of the Duke Arichis with Desiderius, and the nearness to the Greeks, who occupied Gaieta, and other parts of Campania, caused special difficulties here. This gradual acquisition of the territories promised by Charles in 774 occupied a number of years; but in them Adrian had every reason to praise the good faith of Charles and the Franks.

From the time that all dependence on Constantinople was broken off, the sovereign authority of the Pope appears entire.[1] In all dealings with Pipin and the Franks, in the compact of alliance at Quiersy, in the two peaces of Pavia, in 754 and 756, between the Franks, the Romans, and the Lombards, the Pope appears as the sole actor and supreme arbiter of Rome's fortunes. He alone

[1] Origini, p. 317-319.

confers on Pipin and his sons the dignity of Patriciate of the Romans, thereby binding him to an armed defence of Rome and its State. To the Pope alone Fulrad consigns at St. Peter's the keys and the hostages of the cities of the exarchate. The Pope covenants with Desiderius the conditions for his elevation to the Lombard throne; demands of him the surrender of the cities not yet restored: guards against the schemes of the Lombards and the Greeks to take away the sovereignty of the Holy See; treats with the king of the Franks to frustrate them. He continually sends his ambassadors into France, usually prelates, sometimes dukes and Roman magnates. The kings of France send to him their messengers; treat with him of all public affairs of Italy. The people of Spoleto, Reate, and elsewhere, when at the fall of Desiderius they voluntarily became subjects of the Roman State, swear fealty to St. Peter and the Pope. In a word, in all political acts, in all concerning the government and defence of the State, the Pope alone speaks and acts in his own name with supreme and independent authority. No representative of the Senate or Roman people is seen at his side, clothed with proper and distinct authority. On the contrary, in the very gravest questions of State, no decree of the Senate, no plebiscite, no form of citizen suffrage is so much as hinted at. This is inexplicable had Rome been governed as a republic, or if its citizens had had any part of sovereign authority.

With this the language of the Pope himself exactly agrees. He speaks as a king of the cities and provinces of the Roman State. "The territories of our cities, and the patrimonies of St. Peter;" "our city of Sinigallia;" "our castle of Valens;" "this our city of Rome," "our city of Civita Vecchia;" "our city of Castle Felaty;" "our territories of the exarchate;" "this our province;" "they are attempting to withdraw from our dominion our cities of Campania, from the power and dominion of St. Peter and ours;" "we have resolved to send thither our main army;" "in all the parts which lie under the dominion of the holy Roman Church;" these and such like expressions occur everywhere in the letters of the Popes to the Frank kings. These also are no less frequent and significative. "The holy Church of God and its peculiar people;" "the Roman Church and all the people subject to it;" "our people;" "the people entrusted to us;" "all our people of the Romans of that province;" "our people of the commonwealth of the Romans". These expressions the Popes used without doubt or reserve in public letters to the Frank kings and nation. Adrian, in a letter to Charlemagne,[1] declares his will to maintain and exercise in the exarchate and Pentapolis exactly the same power which Stephen II. had received. "Our predecessor distributed all appointments in the exarchate, and all who ruled received their orders from this city of Rome. He sent judges to right all who suffered wrong, to reside in that city of Ravenna."

The interests of the Romans and the Franks, of the Papacy and the Frankish kingdom, of Adrian and Charles, became in this period blent together.[2] An indivisible

[1] *Codex Carolinus*, Ep. (Jaffe) 54. [2] Rohrbacher-Kellner, p. 489.

unity and sincere alliance existed between them. They were the result of that great visit of Charles to Rome in 774. When that visit took place, Charles was almost at the beginning of that wonderful career which has placed him at the head of modern history. By the death of his brother Carloman two years before, the whole Frank inheritance came into his hands. In the three years since 768, when Charles and Carloman had been crowned on the same day as kings of the Franks, but in different cities, there had been dissension between them, and had Carloman lived, it was to be feared that the young strength of the greatest western monarchy would have been turned against itself, instead of being gathered up together against the Saracen enemy who was bent on the conquest of the world. But now the single hand of Charles wrought it to a unity of power, moderation and wisdom, which first became conspicuous on this visit to Rome. By this act of spontaneous devotion he may be said to have inaugurated the unequalled success which afterwards attended on him. From that time, forty-two years of reign were appointed to him, in which he became greater and greater. The root may have been that first visit which he made to Rome, shortly after that Pontificate of Adrian began, in answer to his appeal. They became from this time fast personal friends. It is to be observed with what magnificent loyalty Charles took up, repeated, and ratified in his own person, the act of his father, Pipin, made twenty years before. That act of Pipin is almost unique in history. When Stephen II. came to him at Pontigny in 754, Pipin promised him *for the love of St. Peter* to defend the city and duchy of Rome from the intruding Lombard king, Aistulf, and so not to *give*, but to *preserve* its sovereignty to St. Peter, as throned in his successors, alike from Lombard robbery and Byzantine neglect and impotence. He promised also to recover the exarchate of Ravenna, and the province on the Adriatic called the Pentapolis, already taken by Aistulf from the Byzantine, and in his occupation, and to *give* them an inheritance to St. Peter. Also, he received the title of Patricius of the Romans, then bestowed upon him by Stephen II., with the engagement and the right of protection carried by it. His sons Charles and Carloman, then children, were associated with him in these promises, and in the dignity of Patricius. The nobles of the Franks assembled in diet gave their sanction to these things: Pipin accomplished them. He would not take to himself a palm of ground in that rich territory which he partly preserved for St. Peter alone, and partly bestowed upon him. Rome and its duchy he preserved; the exarchate and Pentapolis he bestowed. Stephen II. *reigned*, when he returned to Rome, in 756, and his brother, Paul I., after him. The Lombard kingdom, from the taking of Pavia in 756, continued by Pipin's permission. The last Lombard king, Desiderius, repaid all this by perpetual encroachment upon the cities given to St. Peter. The Lombard faithlessness is repeatedly dwelt upon in the contemporary writings of the Popes Stephen II., Paul I., Stephen III., and especially Adrian I. Charles had listened to the solemn appeal of Adrian to right him. He came to Rome, and the greatest warrior of the West ascended as a pilgrim on his knees the thirty-five steps which led to the tomb of the Prince of the Apostles. He was welcomed at St. Peter's Confession as Patricius, in the way that Popes and emperors alone, upon their accession, were welcomed. And before he left Rome, at the request of the Pope, he ordered his father's deed to be read before him ; in the midst of his princes, and with their consent, he re-affirmed it : and he guarded the throne of Adrian as Patricius during that pontificate, which, until seventeen hundred years from St. Peter had elapsed, had no equal in length. In all this Charles equalled and repeated the generosity of his father.

How greatly the Popes esteemed the deeds of Pipin and of Charlemagne is witnessed perpetually by the letters of the day contained in the Codex Carolinus.[1] In them the Frank king is constantly likened to Moses and to David, who delivered the people of Israel from Egyptian bondage and heathen oppression. He is called perpetually, " our helper and defender after God," " the guardian of holy Church," " the liberator of the Christian people," "the ransomer of the Roman Church, and all the people subject to it". To him is attributed the prosperity and security of Rome and the whole province of Roman Italy, which is said to be redeemed by him. No tongue can express or praise sufficiently his benefits. God alone can reward him. All nations must acknowledge his defence of the Church of God, and magnify him for it over all the kings of the earth.

[1] From Origini, etc., p. 297.

The effect of the Pipinian donation, confirmed in so splendid a manner by Charles, had two results at once of inestimable value : one to free the Popes and the inhabitants of Italy from the perpetual invasion, threats, and devastation of the Lombards. Thrice since the assault of the emperor Leo III., in 726, upon the faith and internal government of the Church, had Rome been in the utmost peril of subjugation, once by Liutprand, then by Aistulf, lastly by Desiderius. What would have been the condition of the Pope under such a king as Aistulf or Desiderius, seated at the Capitol? He could only expect a servitude far worse than had ever been suffered under the vice-cæsars of Ravenna, or the cæsars of Constantinople. The original Roman empire had been broken into a multitude of independent kingdoms. That changed condition of the Christian society of itself required that there should be lodged in its head a greater independence of the civil power. The hand of Charles, coming down upon the hand of Pipin, assured to Adrian the legal recognition of a sovereignty sufficiently large to secure him in the guardianship of the faith which was the chief work of St. Peter's See in every age. And so the misery which the rudest barbarian horde began in 568 was stayed at last in 774 : and if Gregory the Great, in his time, complained that he had been for thirty years keeping watch and ward against Lombard violence and intrigue, the four great pontiffs, Gregory II., Gregory III., Zacharias, and Stephen II., witnessed the last access of their attempt at domination, and the royal city of Ravenna acknowledged in

Pope Adrian, not only its spiritual head, but its temporal sovereign.

At the same time the second inestimable benefit of deliverance from the eastern despotism, fastened upon Italy since the time of Narses, took place. Some slight sketch of what the exarchate had been to Italy has been attempted. At last those two hundred years of misery were closed: the universal consent of the peoples of central Italy accepted with delight the Papal sovereignty. From the time of Justinian to Stephen II.—perhaps it should rather be said from the time of Leo the Great, the Popes alone had cared for Italy. They alone had possessed the power, the wisdom, and the charity to meet, in some degree at least, the calamities which rained down upon that land, reduced to the condition of a "servile province". Forty years after St. Gregory the Great, in the middle of the seventh century, a Pope had been torn from his sick bed, laid before the altar in the Lateran Basilica, carried to Byzantium, judged by the senate as a traitor for the exercise of his spiritual rights, and left to die of famine in the Crimea.[1] In the middle of the eighth century if we plant ourselves, and look through the events of two or three centuries, a certain fact comes out clearly. No one can assign the precise point of its completion, but it is seen attested by a multitude of indications. The Popes in gradually taking an acknowledged sovereignty, only yielded to the long and ardent desire of the peoples at whose head they stood, no less than to the stringent demand of public neces-

[1] Origini, p. 271 more or less followed in this page.

sity. The feeling of the subject here answered to the fact in the prince: that is, as the Popes were princes by actual necessity so long before they had the name and solemn right to it, so the Romans, and the Italians of the exarchate and the Pentapolis were spontaneous subjects of the Popes long before they bore the legal title. A mutual attraction joined the two together. The Popes through charity for the public good began to exercise in behalf of an ill-treated or a deserted population the part of provident civil governors; the people from gratitude and affection clung more and more to the Popes. The ever increasing calamities and the common trials which pressed on the Popes and the Italians in those miserable times, partly caused by the Byzantine emperors, partly by the barbarous Lombards, drew them more closely together, until the Popes found themselves sovereigns, and the people found themselves subjects, in a complete civil society. But the character of that society was indeed paternal: and as the civil bond sprung from a spiritual fathership, Pipin and Charlemagne named with the name of St. Peter himself the State which their love and reverence for him had partly preserved and partly created.

CHAPTER IX.

THE MAKING OF CHRISTENDOM.

AMONG the events of history, as the historic mind would ponder them, or the judgments of God, as the Christian mind would interpret them, there are none greater than the two which for some time past I have been attempting to narrate or to contemplate. One is the wandering of the nations on the north of the great inland sea: the other is, the wandering of the nations on its south. Having reached the last year of the eighth century, we may cast a glance back upon both, and unite, if it may be, in a single picture the action upon both of a power, which owed its institution only to the greatest fact of all facts concerning our race, the assumption of human nature, the soul and body of man, in His own Person, by the Creator of all things, the Son of God. That power existed only in virtue of certain words uttered and a certain will exercised, during His life upon earth. As the last of His thirty-three years was beginning, He had said to a man: Thou art the Rock, and upon this Rock I will build My Church, and the gates of hell shall not prevail against it. How far did the gates of hell advance upon the Church of God in the four hundred years which elapsed from the death of the great Theodosius?

When he closed his eyes in the year 395, the great empire of Augustus in the East and West was still intact. The fifth and the sixth centuries may be said to be filled by the fall of that empire in the West. I have required ten chapters to give even a slight account of the effects produced upon the Christian Church by the wandering of the northern nations to the time of St. Gregory the Great. But the seventh and eighth centuries are filled with the pouring out of the Mohammedan flood upon the Christian people, which had more or less remained after the wandering of the northern nations ended in their settlement. It is another convulsion equal in its range and perhaps still greater in its effects than that which made Teuton tribes the masters of Gaul and Spain and Britain, of Germany, of Italy, and Illyricum. The peoples of the north had struggled for hundreds of years to break the barriers of the Rhine and the Danube, and in their savage ferocity and tameless independence wrest the South, so long coveted, from the civilised but degenerate Roman. The prize, which they had almost reached in the third century, was saved from their grasp until the fifth by a succession of brave and able generals invested with imperial power. But the Teuton could both admire and receive the law and the religion of the empire which he overthrew. Far otherwise was it, when a savage tribe of Arabia, kindled to white heat by a fanatic and false belief, burst upon a despotic empire in which Christian faith and morality were deeply impaired. It needed but the third decade of one emperor's reign to abrogate the Roman sovereignty held during seven hundred years over Syria and Egypt, and to establish the sway of a false prophet, the bitterest enemy of the Christian faith, over the very city which contained the sepulchre of Christ. "The law had gone forth from Sion and the word of the Lord from Jerusalem," and thither all Christian nations sent a host of pilgrims to kindle anew their faith and love before the shrine which had held for a day the source of all that life, the Body of the God-man. Now that shrine, with all the memorial places of the Divine Life upon earth, fell into hands whose work it was to set up instead of the Christ, a man of turbulent passions and unmeasured ambition : instead of the Christian home, the denial of all Christian morality : instead of a Virgin Mother placed at the head of her sex, and unfolding from age to age the worth and dignity of woman, the dishonoured captives of a brigand warfare. All this took place within ten years after the death of Mohammed, and by the end of the reign of Heraclius, when the greatest triumph ever won by a Roman emperor over the rival Persian monarchy was followed by the most ignominious defeat from a troop of Arabian robbers, and the permanent abandonment of Roman territory. During the sixty following years, not only had Antioch and Alexandria, as well as Jerusalem, become Mohammedan, but the last fortress of Christian power in the East, the impregnable city of Constantine, trembled repeatedly at the approach of Saracen hosts, being rescued rather by its matchless position, its strong walls, and the invention of the Greek fire, than by the superior valour of its defenders. At the end of that seventh century, the whole northern coast of Africa had passed away from Roman to Saracenic rule : from the Christian faith to its Mohammedan antagonist. In ten years more, the Saracen banner crossed over. the straits of Gibraltar, and the Church of Spain fell under its domination. At this time the eastern empire, diminished as it had been, passed through severe revolutions. It seemed that from intestine dissension and the despotism of one crowned adventurer after another, the remnant of the eastern realm, which during seventy years could hardly maintain itself against Saracen aggression, was coming of itself to an end. In this uttermost extremity at Constantinople, a soldier had risen from the ranks to be a trusted general, and when the empire received him for its chief, a long prepared attack by the chalif on his capital was beaten back successfully by Leo III. In the time of the chalif Walid, who reigned from 705 to 715, the Arabian flag floated over the walls of Samarcand : its conquest had stretched to the foot of the Himalayas. His governor in Africa, Musa, had carried the bounds of his empire to the Atlantic ocean. The single city of Ceuta owned still the Byzantine sway. And the Christian count, Julian, for a private wrong, betrayed to the Saracen the city entrusted to his charge. Musa added almost all Spain to the Saracen domain. Constantinople had been besieged in 668, and saved under Constautine the Bearded ; it was saved again in 718, under Leo III.

These two deliverances, with the fact that it had not been taken in all the interval from the time of Heraclius, may be termed the only checks received from Christians by the Mohammedan conquest in the whole period from the death of Mohammed. Had it succeeded in gaining Constantinople when it gained Toledo, it is difficult to see how the universal enthralment of the Christian faith under the almost insufferable tyranny of the Arabian false prophet could have been prevented.

Thus when St. Gregory II. succeeded to the throne of Peter in 715, and Leo III. to the throne of Constantine in 717, the position of the Christian Faith before Islam seemed to stand in terrible danger.[1] The sons of Mohammed, lords of Asia, Egypt, Africa, and Spain, were besetting, with long prepared fleet and army, the last remains of the Greek power in Constantinople on the East, and on the West had only to look to the conquest of France. If they became masters of France, there was no strength left to resist them, neither Italy divided between Lombards, Greeks, and the old inhabitants, subjects of one or the other, nor Germany divided among various peoples. The whole world seemed to be reserved for the anti-Christian kingdom of Mohammed: all nations about to pass under the hard servitude of a conquering Arabian tribe, instinct with hatred to the Christian life; all women to become slaves of man's passion: all reason to endure subjection to a lie imposed by the scimitar. What we have since seen of Mohammedan rule in Asia and in Africa during

[1] Rohrbacher-Kellner, xi. p. 105.

twelve hundred years, seemed then on the point of becoming the general doom.

That was the time chosen by the eastern emperor, after a reign of ten years, to attempt the imposition of a fresh heresy upon Pope Gregory II. The man who was formally bound by his position as Roman emperor, and by the oath taken at his coronation to defend the Church as it had come down to him from the seven preceding centuries, was filled with a desire to remodel the practice of that Church in all its worship. He advanced claims which were not only an invasion of its independence by the civil power, but in themselves rested only upon the practice and the sentiments of the Church's two great enemies, the Jew and the Saracen. The Jew abhorred the relative worship paid to the images and pictures of our Lord, of His Mother, and of the saints, because he utterly denied the fact of the Incarnation, which these images and pictures were ever presenting in the daily worship of the faithful. The Mohammedan shared this abhorrence, because he denounced the Christian as an idolater for his belief in our Lord, as Son of God. Leo III. took up the mind of the Jew and the Saracen into his own rude and unformed nature, and bent the whole force of the imperial power to subdue the Pope to his will. Spain had just fallen into Mohammedan hands: and the lord at Damascus ruled from the Atlantic to Samarcand. Under his rule, which was the bitterest ignominy to every Christian, lay more than half the empire which Justinian had left. Then, in 726, a contest, the most unequal which can be conceived, began between Pope Gregory II. and the emperor Leo III. It continued fifty years under Leo and his son, Kopronymus, who died in 776. In the course of it, Leo sent a great fleet against the coast of Italy, whose commander was instructed to take and plunder Ravenna, to proceed to Rome, to put down all opposition to the imperial heresy, and to carry Pope Gregory captive to Constantinople, after the fashion used in the preceding century to Pope St. Martin. Pope Gregory II. endured to his death the joint heresy and tyranny of the eastern lord, and induced the irritated populations of Italy still to keep allegiance to him. His successor, Pope Gregory III., used the same forbearance. Pope Zacharias for ten years went on enduring, while the Frank nation accepted, on his judgment, a new dynasty. For twenty-eight years, from 726 to 754, no amount of wrong could induce four successive Popes to throw off the allegiance which had pressed upon Italy as a servile province since the conquest of Justinian. At length, the fourth Pope, Stephen II., was deserted in his utmost need by the emperor himself: was threatened with a Lombard poll tax laid upon Rome, and the position of vassal to an Aistulf in the city of St. Peter. Then the eastern servitude at last dropped, and the issue of the most unequal combat, begun in 726, was terminated by the compact ratified at Quiersy in 754, and carried out at Pavia in 756. This compact secured to Pope Stephen and his successors the position of sovereign princes in Rome, and the territory attached to it. In

756 Pope Stephen II. re-entered Rome as its acknowledged civil sovereign. Yet, in the eighteen years following this event, the last king of the Lombards renewed the ambition of Liutprand and Aistulf, to become the lord of Rome, and the renewal of Pipin's gift by Charlemagne, in 774, alone closed the momentous contest which, beginning in 726 with an attack on the unarmed Pope, ended in the deliverance of Italy from the most cruel of thraldoms, and made the Pope, who had long been Rome's only support and benefactor, its temporal as well as its spiritual head.

At the time of that event, more than four centuries had passed since Constantine, in 330, consecrated his city on the Bosphorus to be Nova Roma, pursuing his idea to found a capital which should be Christian from its birth, and the centre of a great Christian empire. Five years before the Church had met for the first time in General Council. The object of its meeting was to refute and censure an attack upon the Godhead of its Founder, and the place at which it met was a city immediately on the Asiatic side of the strait, on which what was then Byzantium stood. The position taken by Constantine was to guard with the imperial sword the chamber in which the Church's bishops sat, to accept their decrees as the utterance of Christ Himself, and to add the force of imperial law to the spiritual authority which he acknowledged them of themselves to possess.

From the baptism of Byzantium as Nova Roma in 330, fifty years succeed to 380, in which Constantinople becomes the chief seat of the very heresy condemned by the Church at the Council of 325. Its see is sought after immediately as the prize of worldly ecclesiastics in the East. Eusebius, the man who presently became its bishop, deceives Constantine into fostering the heresy which he abhorred: its bishop, Macedonius, was the docile servant of the emperor Constantius in his attempt to change the faith of the Church: its bishop, Eudoxius, nurtured the emperor Valens in the same heresy. But the succession of Popes in Julius, Liberius, and Damasus, frustrated these efforts of the bishops of Nova Roma in the first half century of its promotion: and when Theodosius sat on the throne of Constantine, with his colleagues, Gratian and Valentinian, their law of 380 called upon their peoples " to hold the religion which is proved to have been delivered to the Romans by the divine apostle, Peter, since it has been maintained there from his time to our own ".[1]

But the terrible effects wrought upon the eastern episcopate by the Arian assault had not been finally overcome. The next attack upon the Person of our Lord proceeded from the eloquent Syrian, Nestorius, who had been put in the see of Constantinople. It required all the energy of Pope Celestine and the patriarch Cyril of Alexandria, to overcome that heresy which still attacked the Incarnation, and was supported by court favour at the eastern capital, and the jealousy of its emperor for his bishop. It is remarkable that the First Council at Ephesus, in 431, should have been followed by

[1] See above, Vol. v. p. 254.

a Second Council at the same place in 447. This Second Council was, so far as its convocation and its constitution went, regularly entitled to be a General Council. Its decree was in favour of an opposite heresy to that of Nestorius, on the same subject of our Lord's Person, and its originator was the monk Eutyches, in high repute at the head of a monastery at Constantinople. The Council after its completion was rejected, and the heresy overthrown, by the single arm of St. Leo the Great. The whole Church at Chalcedon accepted his act and acknowledged his Primacy. But this Monophysite heresy had driven its roots deep into the Greek mind. During two hundred years, to the time of Mohammed himself, its effects may be traced, corrupting the unity of belief in the eastern patriarchates, encouraging perpetual party spirit, breaking constantly the succession of bishops in the hierarchy. In the time of St. Leo, the patriarch Proterius, who succeeded the deposed Dioscorus, was murdered by the Monophysite faction. A few years later the bishop of Constantinople used this heresy for the purpose of exalting his see against Rome, which had just been deprived of its emperor, and its government left in the hand of barbarians, who were also heretics. Thus supported by imperial power, Acacius brought about a schism which lasted for thirty-five years. The resistance of seven Popes, the last of whom, Hormisdas, obtained the full result which his predecessors had sought for, frustrated this second century of Byzantine aggression upon the faith and government of the Church.

Indeed, so striking and unquestionable was the submission of the Byzantine sovereign, and the recognition by the Byzantine bishop of the Papal authority, that from this time forth a somewhat new course was pursued by the eastern emperor and patriarch in regard to that authority. The purpose of Justinian in his subsequent reign was, while he acknowledged in very ample terms the papal primacy, to subject it in its practical execution to his own civil power. Thus when he had become by conquest immediate lord of Rome, he summoned Pope Vigilius to attend him at Constantinople. During eight years he subjected him to perpetual mortifications. He issued doctrinal decrees and required the Pope to accept them. His laws fully admitted the Pope's rank; he never denied his succession from St. Peter: but his pretension was to make the five patriarchs use their great authority in submission to himself; and he included the first of the patriarchs in this overweening claim, as his namesake Justinian II. signed his council in Trullo at the head of all, and left a line between himself and the patriarch of Constantinople for the signature of Pope Sergius, which was never given.

The result of Justinian's oppression of Pope Vigilius was to create temporary schisms in some parts of the West, through dread of the bishops that something had been conceded to the usurpation of the civil power. Not until the time of Gregory the Great could the Apostolic See recover the injury thus inflicted. But Justinian did much more than persecute a particular Pope. I think it may be said with truth, that from the conquest of Italy under his generals, Belisarius and Narses, it was the continual effort of the Byzantine emperors to subject the Papacy to the civil power in the exercise of its spiritual supremacy. From Justinian to Constantine Kopronymus—a period of more than two hundred years—that is the relation between the Two Powers which the eastern emperors carried in their minds and executed as far as they were able.

The fourth century of Nova Roma's exaltation opened with the strongest assertion of this claim which had yet been seen. The able and unscrupulous Sergius had become patriarch of Constantinople, and was prime minister of the emperor Heraclius. The whole East was teeming with Monophysite opinions, and every city, in proportion to its size and dignity, torn with party conflicts arising out of dissension respecting the Person of our Lord. Sergius thought he had devised a remedy by that Monothelite statement which, as he imagined, enabled him to present in a more conciliating form the old heresy put down by St. Leo and the Council of Chalcedon. He led the emperor Heraclius to publish this heresy in the imperial name. Then four successive patriarchs of Constantinople were found to put all their spiritual rank at the service of two emperors, Heraclius and Constans II., to formulate the heresy, and force it, if possible, on the Popes. Ten successive Popes resisted—one to martyrdom itself—and after a struggle of fifty years, Popes Agatho and Leo II. at the Sixth Council—when the eastern emperor for the moment became orthodox, and his patriarch and bishops followed him—condemned and expelled the heresy. But this fatal attempt of Sergius and Heraclius had been exactly coincident with the rise of Mohammed. The Greek contention respecting the Person of Christ had lasted three hundred years, from the Nicene Council, when the success of the false prophet led vast countries, once the most flourishing of Christian provinces, to yield to the human authority of a robber, and to put him in the place of the God-man whom by their works they had so often denied. And so the fourth century from the exaltation of Nova Roma had been completed.

Yet still it was reserved for the fifth century to Constantinople, at a time of its extreme humiliation, when for ninety years it had only just obtained from a new and undisclosed invention the power to keep the all-conquering Saracen outside its walls—to make its final and most absolute attack upon the elder sister whom it acknowledged as the leader of the Christian faith. Syria and Egypt and Africa and Spain were gone, and the Persian monarchy, for so many hundred years the rival of the Roman, equally was absorbed in the enormous Saracen dominion, and the cities of Asia Minor were in daily dread of the same foe prevailing over their religion and desecrating their homes. Such was the condition of things when the yet remaining Christian emperor assumed over the Christian Church the power of Mohammed's chalifs in the territory which they ruled in Mohammed's name. Another fifty years occur in which, when after the orthodox patriarch Germanus had been forced to lay the insignia of his rank on the altar of Sancta Sophia and depart, three Iconoclast patriarchs in succession, Anastasius from 730 to 753, Constantine from 753 to 766, and Nicetas I. from 766 to 780, placed themselves at the disposal of their emperors to corrupt the faith and subject the government of the Church, until at the Seventh Council once again an eastern emperor became orthodox: and an eastern orthodox patriarch followed again in Tarasius; and Adrian I. was received as Pope, being no longer a vassal of Constantinople, but a sovereign prince.

Upon these antecedents ensued the temporal sovereignty of the Pope. What is the witness of history to the spiritual action of the Popes during this long period of 426 years, from 330, when Byzantium became Constantinople, to 756, when the people of Rome welcomed with universal jubilee the return of their Pope, Stephen II., as sovereign?—when again in 774 Charles at the beginning of his great career approached St. Peter as a pilgrim, and renewed to him his father Pipin's act of munificent piety.

Let us follow the course of the heresies which, during four centuries and a half from the Nicene Council in 325, to the defeat of the Iconoclasts at the Seventh Council, attacked the faith of the Church. They turn upon the Person of our Lord: upon that mighty fact of the Incarnation which filled all men's minds. The Arian denied that He was God; the Nestorian and Monophysite sought in opposite methods to deal with His two natures. The Monothelite pursued the question to its inmost point as it touched the two natures in the operation of the Will; his error in its root was especially

Eutychean. When the question began the original eastern patriarchates of Alexandria and Antioch were in their primal state and glory. They held their descent from Peter, like the See of Rome. Like the Apostolic See their chairs were at the head of a great mass of bishops, Antioch in particular having a crowd of metropolitans governing important provinces, who looked up to the great see of the East, who, when the patriarchate was vacant, voted for the election, as they received from him the confirmation of their own election. Alexander in the mother see of Egypt had been the first to condemn his own insurgent priest, Arius, and at the Nicene Council he was attended by his deacon, Athanasius, who was soon to succeed to his place, and raise during his episcopate of forty-six years the See of St. Mark to its loftiest renown. Eustathius, at the same Council, the twenty-fourth bishop of Antioch, was a noted confessor, and with Alexander contributed to its decision; while Pope Silvester threw the whole weight of the West, which had no doubt as to the Godhead of Christ, in favour of the same result. As yet Constantinople was not; and the See of Jerusalem, though highly honoured, was in the hierarchy a simple bishopric suffragan to the metropolitan of Cesarea. There could be no controversy more reaching to the inmost heart of faith in the Church than that which concerned the Person of the Lord. Taking the four centuries and a half as a whole we find that the eastern patriarchates failed under the trial. The first of them, Alexandria, had for its two greatest teachers Athanasius and Cyril, both doctors of the Church, both renowned in their defence and illustration of the doctrine that God became man. But no sooner had Cyril died than his see became the centre of the Monophysite error. Almost the whole Christian people of Egypt followed its bad lead, and when the Saracen chief took Egypt and Alexandria in the name of Mohammed he found support rather than opposition in the mass of the Christians, who, in their bitter party hatred, called the remnant of Catholics still remaining Melchites or Royalists as the most opprobrious epithet they could devise. And in process of time, under Omar and his successors, the country of Athanasius has become the heart of Mohammedan learning and zeal.

Scarcely less melancholy is the history of Antioch and its twelve provinces of metropolitans, with their 163 bishops.[1] Eustathius was speedily deposed by the Arian faction, even before Athanasius, and during ninety years a perpetual schism preyed upon the dignity of the great eastern see. In the fifth century it was unable to prevent the advance of Constantinople. It fell a speedy prey to the Mohammed's chalif, and from that time the man who bore the name of its patriarch was often a dependent and pensioner at the eastern capital. Jerusalem had succeeded in obtaining the patriarchal dignity at the Council of Chalcedon. But in less than two hundred years Omar polluted its holy place by his presence, and the most stirring voice uttered by its patriarchs is that cry of its noble Sophronius, bidding his chief bishop go to the throne of Peter, "where the

---

[1] See Vol. v. p. 217.

foundations of holy doctrine are laid," and invite the sitter on that throne, who was Honorius, to rescue the faith imperilled by his brother patriarchs, Sergius at Constantinople, and Cyrus at Alexandria, leaders of the Monothelite heresy.

When therefore the emperor Constantine Kopronymus, in 754, took by the hand Constantine whom he had chosen to be ecumenical patriarch, and presented him as the elect of the emperor to the Council of more than three hundred bishops, whom he had convoked to sanction his own heresy, while twelve years afterwards, as the sequel of many torments, he executed him and had his body dissected ; we may say that the eastern patriarchs had utterly failed to defend either the faith or the hierarchy of the Church. Mohammed did not appear to complete the work of Arius, until the descendants of those who condemned Arius in 325 had obscured by interminable disputes during three hundred years what their spiritual ancestors had declared to be the faith of the Church. The causes of this failure had been internal. There had been great bishops in the East during this period. Chrysostom had sat in Constantinople, suffered, confessed, and been exiled before Nestorius, who sat there also, and was exiled for his heresy. Germanus, in the same see, did not yield to Leo III., and in that worst time confessed, and his place was forthwith taken by Anastasius, who subscribed all Leo's evil will. Kopronymus strove to exterminate the monks, who suffered every extremity for their maintenance of the faith. But as the main result the Byzantine despotism had overcome the eastern episcopate. I do not know how more telling proofs of that evil victory could be shown than that Philippicus Bardanes, in 711, during his ephemeral reign, should be able to assemble a council at Constantinople, which he required to restore the Monothelite heresy, condemned at the Sixth Council, and scarcely met with an episcopal opponent; and again that Kopronymus could assemble another large council in 754, to establish his Iconoclast aggression, which was received without dissent.

How then was the faith preserved during these four hundred and sixty years?

From Pope Sylvester to Pope Stephen II. we count sixty-one Popes. In that long period of time the doctrine of the Godhead and the Person of Christ with all its manifold consequences was fully drawn out. The variation which had been seen in the patriarchal and episcopal sees of the East was never found at Rome. All political and external help may be said to have failed the Popes. They lost their own western emperor, and the sole remaining eastern emperor turned against them. More also, he set up against them a new bishop who at the beginning of the time did not exist, the bishop of the eastern capital. The eastern lord added from generation to generation rank and influence to this bishop. He made him his own intermediate instrument of communication with all the bishops of his eastern realm, to whom it had been the continual policy of Justinian and his successors to grant great political privileges, making them in large degree partakers of civil authority.

They sought to rule the East throughout its manifold divided interests by the authority of the local bishops ; and they sought to rule the bishops themselves by their own patriarch. Rome, from being the head of the Roman monarchy at the beginning of the period, ceased to be the capital even of a "servile" Italy, the captive of Belisarius. The Popes passed through Odoacer, Theodorich, Theodatus, also Vitiges and Totila, also Liutprand, Aistulf, and Desiderius. Their elections, when made, were delayed in their recognition, or even controlled in their choice. They saw a crowd of northern raiders take possession of the whole West, and at one time the very heresy which at the beginning of the period had been condemned by the Church, was in possession of all the governments of the West but that of the Franks, and had for the chief ruler of its councils and the head of the regal league against the faith of Rome the greatest man whom the northern tribes can show during their time of immigration, and he had made Italy powerful and respected, and cultivated Rome with extreme solicitude. When St. Silvester sat in St. Peter's chair, Rome was the single capital of the whole empire ; when St. Leo sat there he witnessed the fall of the West, but stood imperturbable before Attila and Genseric ; when St. Gregory sat there, he divined from the temporal ruin and desolation of Rome, which he saw perishing piecemeal around him, that the world's last time was coming. When St. Martin sat there, he was torn from his sick bed by the eastern master to die in the Crimea; when St. Gregory II. sat there, the same eastern master threatened to break in pieces the statue of St. Peter in his Basilica. But in all the four hundred and sixty years from the first to the second Nicene Council, the witness of Rome to the Divine Person of her Lord was clear and distinct. Neither the greatest nor the worst of her opponents had subdued that witness, or rendered it faltering or indistinct. For this reason it was that the Pope, whose life the Iconoclast soldier, when clothed with the imperial purple, five times attempted, could reply to his threat, that all the West looked upon St. Peter as a God upon earth; that the one Teuton king before whose victorious reign that of Theodorich is pale and colourless, ascended on his knees the steps before St. Peter's tomb, laid upon the altar over his body the gift of temporal sovereignty, and went forth from that moment the predestined civil head of that new Christendom which St. Peter had made out of the northern adventurers.

Taking in all this time the simple witness of history, I ask if in it the words of our Lord to Peter were not palpably fulfilled: "Thou art the Rock, and upon this Rock I will build My Church". If the Rock had not been, each one in this long line of heresies would have destroyed the Church. The line of St. Athanasius was not infallible; the line of St. Ignatius of Antioch was annulled after frequent falls by the Mohammedan captivity; the line of Byzantium had some saints, but was prolific in heretics, and the last utterance of Jerusalem before it fell, when the Saracen ascetic voluptuary trod its courts, was uttered by its patriarch from Calvary itself, when he adjured his messenger: "Go swiftly from end to end of the earth, until thou reach the Apostolic See, in which the foundations of our holy doctrine rest".

The state of the eastern Church from the Council of Chalcedon to the final assault of the emperor Leo III. upon the whole fabric of Church government is one continual descent. It has certain recoveries, as the cessation of the Acacian schism, in 518; as the reversal of the Monothelite tyranny, under Constantine Pogonatus, in 680; as the repudiation of the still greater Iconoclast tyranny a century later, at the Seventh Council in 787, under Pope Adrian and the patriarch Tarasius. But even General Councils were attacked by eastern emperors in the last excesses of their overgrown domination. As Philippicus Bardanes got together a great Council in 711 to denounce the Sixth Council, so the Emperor Leo the Armenian had deposed an unbending patriarch, Nicephorus, in 815, supplied his place with the yielding Theodotus, and found another council in the same year to anathematise the work of the Seventh Council. Three more Iconoclast patriarchs—Theodotus from 815 to 821, Antonius I. from 821 to 832, John VII. from 831 to 841—close this evil list of heretical bishops. The feast of orthodoxy was established in 842. The incessant attempts of the Greek emperors to meddle with the faith took presently another development. They could no longer oppress as their subject a sovereign Pope. When they could not oppress him, they learnt to deny him. In less than another generation the schism of Photius began.

Such was the first century running from the time that Leo the Isaurian made, in 733, his creature Anastasius ecumenical in the sense that all the remaining Greek empire was put under his patriarchal jurisdiction. But it is plain that long before this, the Greek empire, so far as its own episcopate was concerned, had ceased to possess any inflexible rule of doctrine. The most venerable of its authorities, the original patriarchs of Alexandria and Antioch, had yielded before the Nestorian and Monothelite storms; had perpetual interruptions in their succession, sometimes had a double succession—one Catholic, another Monophysite—had submitted to the State-patriarch set over them at Constantinople; and being found in this condition by the Mohammedan flood, had seen their former dignity all but overwhelmed in its swelling waves. The western Church, which from the time of the northern wandering of the nations had been visited by unnumbered catastrophes, had, on the contrary, possessed in its bosom exactly that inflexible rule of doctrine which the East wanted: a rule of doctrine not imposed by civil despotism, but the very root as well as the bond of its episcopate. The Ostrogoth had made his kingdom in Italy, and the Visogoth his kingdom in Spain; the Frank, the Burgundian, and many more set up realms in France and Germany, whose limits were in perpetual fluctuation; seven or eight little Saxon kingdoms were dividing in Britain the old Roman unity. These Teuton tribes had two qualities in common—great personal valour and the most persisting spirit of division. Endless were the intestine quarrels and separations between those of the same northern race, who in political condition had hardly passed the tribal state. Every invading army whose commander became a king in the conquered territory had its own local interests, but none of that great political sense which had nurtured the empire of the Cæsars. The one Ostrogoth who had such a sense had grown up a hostage at Constantinople, and though it is said that he could not read, had certainly divined and carried off with him into the Italy which he captured the imperial secret of government: that is, the force of unity, justice, and subordination of the part to the whole; and Theodorich had come to the conclusion that he could not make Italian mind and Gothic manners coalesce in the structure of a kingdom. His device to rule them equally and separately scarcely lasted for his life. After ruling with equity, he died in remorse. No stronger instance of this great defeat can be found than the custom of the Merovingian race to the end. Their monarchy was in their eyes a family property. When their father died they took the throne as a part of the paternal inheritance. It was not delivered down in whole as a mighty trust of the nation itself. If there were several children, their swords cut the patrimony into slices, and each carried off his bit, like a wild beast. No political sense presided here. The sole solicitude of each was that his lot might not be of less value than his brother's.[1]

There exists no history giving in detail the most wonderful event of these troubled centuries—that is, the

[1] Kurth, vol. ii. 76.

process by which the Arian heresy, which, in the time of Theodorich, had possession of all these peoples—except the Franks, and the Saxons, who were pagans—finally became Catholic: a conquest of the northern warriors which one of the greatest enemies of the Christian faith seems to consider a more wonderful deed than the conquest of the former Roman world, so far as it was achieved at the time of Constantine's conversion.

At Rome the Pope sat through all these centuries, the visible representative of all that was good in the Roman empire, of law, justice, order, besides holding in himself the inflexible rule of faith. The Chair of Peter had no rival in the West, the eldest of its bishops looked up with reverence to his single and immemorial pre-eminence. Their local influence had in each of them its weight with their own people. For instance, St. Gregory of Tours was of an old senatorian Gallic family : all the interests of the population around him, whether Frank or Gallic, known to him as a native of the soil. In this double position much nearer and dearer to him was the Petrine descent, by consecration of which he maintained as bishop the Christian faith. Thus in the see of Tours he protected the temporal rights of his people, and resisted in particular the violent acts of king Chilperic. The faith itself was to him the strong exemplar of political sense : the one family of Christ bore in its very bosom the society of nations. He could not say the creed without feeling that the centre of faith was the natural centre of all humanising influence. The Saxon bishop in Northumberland would recognise the Saxon bishop in Kent in spite of intervening Mercia. The episcopate set up among the German tribes by St. Boniface in the name of the Popes, was the form of such unity as afterwards led these separate tribes to coalesce in an empire. And they coalesced with such difficulty as to show that without the spiritual bond they would have remained in their original antagonism.

In the last century of Merovingian rule the inapt government and private vices—if a king's vices can ever be called private—had inflicted a very great injury both on the civil and the ecclesiastical administration of the great Frank empire. The intercourse in writing between the Popes of the sixth century with the Frank rulers had been greatly interrupted in the seventh. While perpetual domestic murders and sensual crimes polluted the royal family, the nobility had become disordered; national councils were suspended, and in too many sees the bishops no longer answered in character to those who, in the time of Gregory the Great, had built up Gaul. At that moment there sprung from two great nobles of Austrasian Gaul, Arnulf, afterwards bishop of Metz, and Pipin of Landen, a family whose saintly virtues as well as their nobility raised it to great power. In 673 Pipin d'Herstal, who by his father descended in the second degree from Arnulf, and by his mother from Pipin of Landen, was mayor of the palace, and the degenerate blood of Chilperic and Fredegonde was put to shame by the chief minister of the kingdom. The race of Clovis was dying out in sensual cruelty: the family of Arnulf was raised up to take its place. In forty years, Pipin d'Herstal, as mayor of the palace, used the royal power with such effect as greatly to restore the unity of the kingdom. After his death and an interval of trouble his son Charles, in 707, united in his hands all the power of the Franks. It was just a hundred years from the death of Mohammed, when, in 732, the Saracen army having under his chalifs conquered all the East and the South, and over-run Spain, had only one more battle to fight with the bravest nation of the West, in order to trample the cross under their feet. The flood had passed the Pyrenees, and advanced over prostrate Aquitaine to Poitiers, which it had taken. As it issued from that city, the bastard son of Pipin d'Herstal, still mayor of the palace in name, but sovereign of the Franks in fact, met it with the rapidly collected warriors whom he had so often led to victory. Then, it is said, the Saracen and the Christian hosts for seven days watched each other; the Arabs on their light horses and in their white mantles, the Franks with their heavy iron-clad masses. On the eighth day, a Saturday at the end of October, the Arabs left their camp at the call of the Muezin to prayer, and drew out their order of battle. Their strength was in their horsemen, and twenty times they charged the Frankish squares, and were unable to break them. An Arab writer says: "Abd Errahman, trusting to his fortune, made a fierce attack. The Christians returned it with as much firmness. Then the fight became general and continued with great loss on both sides. Assault followed upon assault until four o'clock in the afternoon. The Frankish line stood like a wall of iron." Then a cry for succour was heard from the Arab camp. Duke Eudo with his Aquitains and Basques had surprised those left to guard it. Disorder and panic arose among the Saracens. Charles saw and ordered the whole line to advance. The wall of iron moved and all fell before it. Abd Errahman passed from rank to rank to check the flight, and did wonders. But when, struck by many lances, he fell from his horse, disorder and flight prevailed. They burst into the camp and expelled Eudo. Night came on, and Charles kept his army in its ranks on the plain, expecting a fresh battle on the morrow. On that morrow the Franks saw the white tents, but the Arabs had fled under cover of the night. The booty was great. The Franks report that there was no pursuit; the Arabs, that the Christians pursued their victory for many days, and compelled the fugitives to many battles, in which the loss was great, until the Moslem host threw itself into Narbonne.[1]

In that battle Charles merited his title of "the Hammer". Had he or his Franks blenched upon that day, Europe would have become Mohammedan, as three hundred years before in the battle of the nations by Macon it would have been the prey of the Mongol, had Attila prevailed. Carcassonne and Nimes and all southern France had yielded. But the hammer of Charles descended on the Saracen anvil. His son, king Pipin, carried on his work in southern France, and his grandson Charles, before his death, had become lord of an united realm from the Ebro to the Eyder. Islam never

[1] From Weiss, ii. 537-8.

advanced further in the West. As France in the fifteenth century owed its deliverance to the maiden of Arc, so in the eighth, not Gaul only, but all the West would seem to have owed its inheritance of the Christian name to the four great men whom Providence raised up in the family of Arnulf of Metz, and Pipin of Landen. Pipin, the mayor of the palace, Charles the Hammer, Pipin the king, and Charlemagne, are four continuous generations from grandfather to greatgrandson the like of which I know not that any other family can produce.

An old man so feeble that he had hardly strength to cross the Alps, and was almost killed by the exertion, laid his hand on the head of Pipin, and the mayor of the palace became king of the Franks. The hand was the hand of St. Peter. Forty-six years later the same hand will be laid upon the head of his son; and the king of the Franks will become emperor of the Romans; and the Saracens who felt the arm of one Charles in the battle by Tours, will feel another Charles rise up before them to meet the Moslem lord of the southern and eastern world on equal terms.

After Charles left Rome,[1] at Easter, 774, as above narrated, attempts were made against him by the Lombard dukes, and Adelchis, the son of Desiderius. In spite of the Saxon wars he was in upper Italy at the end of the winter of 776: he prevailed over his opponents, sent his counts to the various cities, and protected the State of the Church. At the end of 780 he was again at Pavia, and he celebrated the feast of Easter on April

[1] Reumont, ii. 128-9.

15, 781, at Rome. Here Pope Adrian crowned his son Pipin king of Lombardy, and the youngest, Louis, king of Aquitania. All seemed to go well. Greek messengers from the regent Irene, widow of Leo IV., brought proposals of agreement and treaty. During this longer sojourn the new arrangement of the Lombard kingdom would be completed. Frankish counts took the place of the old dukes, whose relation to the central power had been far looser than that of their successors was made.

The introduction of the royal missi and their action upon the administration of law likened subject Italy much more to the other states of Charles. The position of the native population was not essentially altered, but the improvement of the laws helped them. Charles all the while was carrying on war after war with the resisting Saxons, enlarging the Christian domain by founding bishoprics as far as the Weser and the Elbe, taking the Spanish marches from the Arab, and the eastern marches from the Avars, uniting the dukedom of Bavaria with his kingdom, and carrying out that mighty work of civilisation which has made his name immortal for its religious institutions, its legislation, and the encouragement which he gave to literature.

Early in the year 787 Charles was again with Pope Adrian at Rome. In a rapid campaign he reduced to his obedience Arichis, duke of Benevento, who was married to a daughter of Desiderius; and returning once more spent Easter with Adrian. It was the last meeting between those two fast friends. On Christmas day, 795, Adrian closed a pontificate of nearly twenty-four years. Three years before Rome had been desolated by one of its most fearful inundations, and the Pope had gone about in a boat succouring the needy. This pontificate was both in its spiritual and temporal consequences most brilliant.[1] Adrian possessed every quality which should adorn a great Pope, a tender and active piety, a zeal the ardour of which was tempered by wisdom; a union of goodness and resolution, so that in the exercise of his charge he combined the affection of a father with the authority of a teacher, and the vigilance of a Pope. Charles mourned for him both as a friend and father. He had an inscription of thirty-eight verses engraved in golden letters on the black marble stone which covered his tomb. He had Masses said for his soul in all churches; and dispensed great alms in distant lands, especially to England. In his letter to Offa, king of Mercia, he wrote :—" We have sent you these alms begging intercession for the Apostolic Lord Adrian, not that we doubt that that blessed soul is at peace, but to show our faith and affection for a most dear friend". It cannot be doubted that Adrian's influence upon the great king, since he first came to Rome in 774, had prepared him for the future exaltation which he was to receive in that same church of St. Peter, the steps of which he had ascended on his knees twenty-six years before. The day after Adrian's death, Leo III. was chosen his successor. He was by birth a Roman, and brought up in the patriarchal palace, and is described by contemporaries as learned, eloquent, and beneficent.

[1] Rohrbacher-Kellner, vol. xi. p. 553.

From the gift of king Pipin to Pope Stephen II., when the keys of the cities surrendered to him were laid upon the altar over the body of St. Peter, to the repetition of that gift by Charles in 774, and again from that most solemn action of Charles to the year 800, no difference in the relation of the Pope to the king of the Franks took place. In the first instance, in the year 754, Charles had been made Patricius of the Roman Church together with his father, and had as such taken on himself its protection and defence. Therefore the Popes took pains, in particular Leo III., that the Romans acknowledged under oath this relation, binding themselves to observe the rules which their Patricius should make for the security of the Church. No conclusion can be drawn from this, as to an overlordship of the king of the Franks in the territories assigned to the Pope. Pope Adrian and Leo III. sent to Charles a standard together with the keys of St. Peter's tomb.[1] The jurisdiction which the king of the Franks exercised in Rome as Patricius was not an overlordship; it was necessary for his office as Protector. But now an extraordinary event took place. In the year 799, three years after the accession of Leo III., a tumult broke out which in its savage violence surpassed that under Stephen III. On April 25, St. Mark's day, the Pope was conducting the solemn procession ordered by St. Gregory the Great, from the Lateran to St. Lorenzo in Lucina. A band of conspirators broke out of the Flaminian way, not far from the Church of St. Silvester. At their head were two

---

[1] Phillips, *Kirchenrecht*, vol. iii. 51.

nephews of the late Pope Adrian: Paschalis, the Primicerius, that is, the first of the seven Palatine judges, and Campulus, the treasurer, another of them, both in immediate attendance on the Pope. Leo III. was thrown to the ground, and an attempt made to tear out his eyes and his tongue. He was dragged into the Church of St. Silvester, and thence taken to the monastery of St. Erasmus on the Cælian.

The conspirators had not succeeded, as they hoped, in blinding the Pope. His wounds were wonderfully healed. His friends rescued him on a dark night from his confinement in the monastery, and brought him safely to St. Peter's. A large number of the people and clergy surrounded him. The Frank duke came from Spoleto with a hurriedly collected troop, took him from St. Peter's, and carried him to Spoleto, where again bishops, priests,. and laity surrounded him with congratulations.

When Charles heard of these events in Rome he caused the Pope to come into his kingdom. He was in the act of marching against the Saxons. At Paderborn he learnt of the Pope's approach. He sent to him[1] archbishop Hildebald, his chaplain ; the Count Anochar and his son Pipin, with many counts, and a considerable force to escort him, while he set in order the whole army for his reception. When the head of the Church appeared all fell on their knees to receive his blessing. Charles dismounted, tenderly embraced the oppressed fugitive before his army, and accompanied him to the cathedral.

---

[1] *Anastasius*, Mansi, xiii. 930.

Leo remained several days in the camp at Paderborn to consult with the king about the state of things at Rome, and what measures should be taken to meet them. No doubt it was felt that the powers of the Patricius at Rome must be increased, to give security in the future to the Pope.

The conspirators had acted with great violence at Rome, and sent to the king a list of accusations against the Pope.

The Pope returned to Rome accompanied by the archbishops of Cologne and Salzburg, and a large escort of Frank bishops and nobles. All the clergy, senate, people, soldiers, the schools of foreigners, Franks, Friesons, Saxons, and Lombards, also the chief matrons of Rome came out to Ponte Molle to meet him, with standards and crosses, attended him to St. Peter's, where he sang High Mass, and the next day he re-entered the city, and took again possession of the Lateran.

In the summer of the following year, 800, Charles left his capital, Aix-la-Chapelle. At Mainz he announced his intention to go to Rome, that he might punish those guilty of the ill-treatment of the Pope. It was his fifth campaign in Italy. He stayed seven days in Ravenna, which was now in the Pope's possession. At Mentana, twelve miles from Rome, the Pope went out to receive him. The next day, the 24th November, he came to St. Peter's, where the people waited for him in the usual order.

The king-protector declared that the chief object of his coming was to clear the Pope from the accusations brought against him, and for this purpose there was held on 1st December a great assembly at St. Peter's of archbishops and bishops, Frank and Roman nobility, before the king and the Pope. "Then all the archbishops, bishops, and abbots said with one voice :[1] 'We dare not judge the Apostolic See, which is the head of all the churches of God, for by it and by its successor we all are judged. But itself is judged by no man, as from of old has been the custom, but we will obey, as the canons require, according to the sentence of the supreme pontiff.' Then the Pope said : 'I follow the example of my predecessors, and am ready to clear myself of such false accusations'. And on another day, before the same presence, ascending the ambo, and holding the gospels in his hands, he said, under oath, with a loud voice : 'I have no knowledge of these false crimes which Romans, my unjust persecutors, have imputed to me, and I never committed them". Whereupon they gave thanks to God in a litany, and to our Lady the Mother of God and ever Virgin Mary, and to St. Peter, Prince of the Apostles, and to all the saints of God."

After these things, on the birthday of our Lord Jesus Christ, all were again assembled in the same church of St. Peter's.[2] Charles, at the request of the Pope, wore his Roman dress as Patricius of the Roman Church and Commonwealth. That majestic figure, seven of his own feet in stature, was vested in an inner robe of pure white, bearing over it the purple mantle which betokened his Frank monarchy. Pope Leo III.

[1] *Anastasius*, Mansi, xiii. 932.   [2] *Anastasius*.

celebrated High Mass in person; Charles knelt on the steps before the altar, his head bowed in prayer. Then the Pope took the crown which lay on the altar, and placed it on the head of the king of the Franks, and cried with a loud voice: "Life and victory to Charles Augustus, crowned of God, great and peace-bearing Emperor of the Romans!"

And from the Frank and the Roman nobles throughout the church the cry was echoed back: "To Charles Augustus, crowned of God, great and peace-bearing emperor of the Romans, life and victory!"

The title was thrice proclaimed before the Confession of St. Peter. And all the faithful of Rome seeing the great guardianship and affection which Charles bore to the Roman Church, and its ruler, assented with one accord. And the same day the Pope anointed with the holy oil Charles and the king his son.

Three hundred and twenty-four years had passed since at the bidding of Odoacer the Herule and Arian, the Roman senate had sent a message to the eastern emperor Zeno, declaring that no western emperor was needed. During the whole of that intervening period Rome had survived in virtue of St. Peter's primacy seated in her. She had subdued the Acacian schism. She had lived through the Gothic war and the five captures by friends and foes. During two centuries of Lombard invasion and of Byzantine oppression she had remained unbroken. Upon the judgment of Pope Zacharias, the most powerful nation of the West dethroned the unworthy race of Clovis, and placed a nobler and more religious house on the throne of the Franks. Another Pope, Stephen II., by his own authority had made the newly anointed monarch Patricius of the Romans, and he first, and then his son, during forty years, had in that character protected the sovereignty which he had partly recovered, so far as regarded Rome and its own territory, and partly bestowed, so far as regarded the exarchate as a gift to St. Peter. The external protection had proved to be inadequate to guard the papal succession in one case, the person of the Pope in another, from domestic treason. And now the word of the Pope alone summoned up from the past not only the title but the power of the emperor, and invested with it the greatest man of all those northern races, who since the time of Theodosius had subjugated the Roman western empire. Leo III. alone set the crown on the head of Charles; not the crown which belonged to him as king of the northern immigrants who had conquered Gaul, but the crown of Augustus, given by Christ. "To Charles Augustus, crowned of God," the word ran. This was the crown which Charles received, and which all the nations subject to his sway acknowledged, as the gift of St. Peter, seated in his see of Rome. The first and chief duty of the sovereign so created was to guard the Church of God. The four hundred years of Teuton immigration passed by that act into the definitive recognition of a new Christian people. Thereupon there became a family of nations, whose common life and law were the one Church of God, whose common territory was named from its master, Christendom. The eastern emperor in his ardour to impose heresy, had shown his impotence to protect what Justinian had once acquired, and Rome which created anew a western emperor was definitively free from any civil subjection to the eastern.

Three chief aspects of this great act are to be considered : how it regarded the West ; how it regarded the East ; how it regarded the enormous Mohammedan power which stretched from farthest West to farthest East, from the Tagus to the Indus.

First it is to be noted that the Pope alone, made the empire. As Stephen II. had conferred upon the newly made king of the Franks the office of Roman Patricius, and with it the jurisdiction in his own State requisite for the fulfilment of that office, so, where the jurisdiction of the Patricius had been proved to be insufficient, both by the intrusion of the anti-pope Constantine into the Papal See itself, and by the ferocious attack upon Leo III., a reigning pontiff, during a solemn procession in the streets of Rome, Leo III. created an emperor, who should have a jurisdiction in Rome over all persons. He did not make himself a vassal, but in making the emperor he gave judicial rights in the State of the Church for the carrying out the most important part of the emperor's charge, to be Protector of the Roman Church. That Protector was to be guardian of the whole Catholic Church : and so he bore the name and title, of all other civil titles the most respected, emperor of the Romans ; Rome alone, re-entering into the right lost in 476, and exercised now by the voice of her sovereign, gave the title, not drawn from the Franks or Germans, nor dependent on the

Byzantine, rather in itself a speaking sign that the Byzantine subjection had passed away. The Roman, and the Frank, and all the subjects of his vast domain accepted Charles as "crowned of God". That is, the Successor of St. Peter named him emperor of the Romans. As he had exalted a mayor of the palace to be king of the Franks, and Patricius of the Romans, so he had exalted the Patricius to be emperor; and because he was himself in spiritual things the head of the whole Church, he had made a particular king to be the advocate and defender of the whole Church. No one else could do what Leo III. did.

The annalists[2] of that age universally agree that it was Leo III. who devised and executed the exaltation of Charles to be emperor. The Pope in a deed granting certain privileges to a monastery, dated on the very day of his coronation, marks that his grant was made "in presence of our glorious and most excellent son Charles, whom by God's authority we have this day consecrated to be emperor for the defence and advancement of the universal Church". Charles himself everywhere said that he was "crowned by the divine will," "crowned by God". Most wise was the intention of Leo, that the supreme pontiff, the pastor and ruler of all the faithful, should institute this sacred empire by crowning and proclaiming Charles. It was thus that the Church and the supreme pontiff determined the peculiar and essential character, nature, and dignity of this empire. The purpose was that among the kings there should be one, already most

---

[2] Jungmann, 15th *Dissertation*, vol. iii. p. 176, translated.

powerful by the extent of his dominions, to whom besides a special charge and dignity should be given. This consisted in being the protector and defender of the Church and the Roman pontiff, and of the whole Christian society, to promote and spread abroad the Christian faith with all its blessings. The Church on her side, gave to this prince a pre-eminence over all other princes. That intimate union, which ought to subsist between the Two Powers, Spiritual and Temporal, preserving to each its own dignity and honour, found its practical and supreme expression in that mutual respect of Pontiff and emperor to each other. Five centuries of the Europe that was to be born came out of that act of Leo III. on Christmas Day, 800. Legitimate order and fixed possession were added to the innate courage and the love for self-government of the Teuton tribes, which thus grew into nations.

Divide into its chief parts the union thus consecrated before the eyes of all men, by an authority which all men admitted.

First of all we find the nature of civil government in general acknowledged by it. During five hundred years from the time of Constantine this had been upheld with unwavering steadfastness by the Popes. Never had they acknowledged a rule of despotism. One of the most marked characters of the Arian heresy was its disposition to exaggerate the civil sovereignty, admitting in it an absolute rule rather than a divine delegation, and extending that absolute rule into the spiritual order of things. So far already had Arius anticipated Mohammed. Against this confusion of the Two Powers, and their absorption into one, Athanasius, Hilary, and Basil, Popes Julius, Liberius, and Damasus had struggled. A hundred years later Pope Gelasius under Arian thraldom had maintained to the emperor Anastasius the essential independence of the spiritual power, and the defence in spiritual things due to it from emperors. When another emperor, Leo the Isaurian, had intruded, if possible, further into the fabric of the Church than Anastasius, he was met, as has been seen above, by St. Gregory II. Now, seventy years later, in the last days of the eighth century, the Iconoclast storm having broken in vain on the head of four successive Popes, Leo III. set his seal upon all these acts of his predecessors. He restored the empire, and in restoring set it forth once again in its character of the supreme earthly right consecrated to the defence of the divine right and Christian faith. The marvel was that he made the head of the Teutonic tribes the guardian of Christ's religion, and invested him with the privileges involved in that guardianship which a succession of degenerate Constantines on the eastern throne had abused. The chalifs had shaken to its centre the Christian structure in the East; had stripped the Christian empire of its fairest provinces; had set up against it a religion of internecine hatred to its faith, of perpetual pollution to its morals; and the Pope, when the loss of Italy was added to all its other losses, had established, in the person of Charles, Christian monarchy in the West. It was no longer an attempt to veneer with Christian name an empire, all whose bureaucratic despotism was founded in the heathen subjection of all power to the State, but the establishment in a great conqueror of an empire whose basis was essentially Christian. Charles was "Augustus crowned of God, great and peace-bearing emperor of the Romans," not an Augustus made by the senate and people of Rome, who had become in Diocletian the representative of armies, and in Byzantium continued a succession of dissolute adventurers.

Again, Charlemagne received from the Pope a complete code of Christian legislation, and as emperor he made it his own, and made it the centre of civil right. The act which constituted him emperor made Rome itself the point of a vast circumference of nations. It became for Christian contemplation what it had been for heathen: Christian voices united with the heathen. The imperial statute book spoke it out:[1] Rome is our common country. Already Charles, as Patricius, had received from Adrian I. a book of the councils and canons accepted by the Holy See. With it beside him he had restored order and law in the Frankish Church, which the last century of Merovingian misrule had so greatly impaired. He now added the imperial dignity and power to that peculiar combination of moderation and perseverance which marked his character. The harmonious equilibrium of qualities,[2] excelling equally in the arts of war and the arts of peace, and united with fidelity to the Church of God, made him the greatest of

[1] Reumont, ii. 133. [2] Kurth, ii. 242.

Christian sovereigns. Whatever he undertook he pursued with unfailing ardour. What he began, he finished; carrying on a multitude of things at once, he gave to each his full attention. In a reign of forty-seven years he made fifty-three military expeditions, most of which he led himself; eight years he fought the Avars; and thirty-three the Saxons. He enacted more laws than all his predecessors united, as well the Merovingians as the princes of his own family. Age, which brings fatigue and relaxation to other workers, saw his energies increase, for the fourteen years from 800 to his death showed his greatest legislative activity. The man in armour never laid aside his breastplate; his eye retained its penetration and his hand its vigour till he went down standing to his tomb, and there the great Christian emperor was found seated on his throne, with sackcloth under his imperial mantle, hundreds of years after his death.

To put the laws and customs of the Church in the hands of such a man as Augustus, crowned of God in St. Peter's Basilica, was of itself to change the wandering of the nations into an abode of settled peoples, capable of growing into the brotherhood of a Christian bond. So Leo III. completed the work of St. Gregory the Great. In Gregory's time the Visigothic kingdom of Spain had been already established on these same principles; now that it had been overthrown by the Moslem occupation, they were established on a vaster scale by the central empire of Charlemagne. So the Church carried her legislative wisdom, gained in the exercise of 800 years, into the civil counsels of princes.

Pipin le Bref,[1] great grandfather of Charles, had restored in France the great assembly of the Field of May. These assemblies were carefully held by Charles. Like his predecessors he took no measure and promulgated no law in opposition to the public wish. At Byzantium the practice which had triumphed was "the will of the prince has the force of law," but the emperor Louis II., in 862, expressed the practice of Charles: "Law is made by the consent of the people, and the sanction of the king". Every year at the Champs de Mai that principle became a reality. The king of the Franks appeared there the soul and centre of the assembly. He convoked it when and where he pleased. He proposed the subjects for its consideration, he gave his sanction to what it passed. He dissolved it at his pleasure. But it was consulted on all important acts of his government. It gave its advice with unlimited freedom; it had full right to amend the projects proposed. Often special commissions composed of the most competent persons considered what was brought before them; the bishops, ecclesiastical affairs; the lords, political. The government considered the interests of the Church with the most constant care. More than one Champ de Mai held by Charles bears the aspect at once of a council and a parliament. The king presided, listened, advised. The law which sprang from that familiar intercourse between king and nation perfectly expressed the harmony which reigned between an authority which was loved, and an obedience which was free. There was no written con-

Kurth, ii. 256-8, drawn from.

stitution, but it was one power exercised by sovereign and people. The Capitularies remain the monument of this immense activity.

The royal commissioners, Missi Dominici, an institution perfected by Charles, carried everywhere throughout his vast empire a knowledge of the laws thus passed, and reported to the sovereign how they were kept. By them the king touched each member of his political body. It was a class of removable functionaries, entirely under the order of the central power. It was composed chiefly, but not always, of bishops and counts. They went four times a year, usually two and two, an ecclesiastic and a layman, to inspect the district entrusted to them. All authorities were subject to this inspection. They reported to the sovereign upon all, and conveyed to him the popular feeling, as well as informed him as to the popular needs. This institution, together with the Champs de Mai, contributed to the empire's unity by maintaining its peace. It checked excesses of power in the great proprietors.

An account is extant how these commissioners acted in one of the remotest provinces, that of Istria. They consisted of two counts and a simple priest. At their arrival they held a public enquiry upon the conduct of the religious and civil authorities. The patriarch of Grado was obliged to appear in person, together with all the bishops and counts of the province. After that they considered the conduct of the duke John. The patriarch and the duke were alike compelled to give pledges to amend what had been wrongly done. All felt that

Charlemagne himself was behind his commissioners; and when they departed it was with the full assurance that their visit had not been in vain. It will be right to take this instance as representing the government of Charles everywhere, and at all times. For the first time since the origin of Frank society a power existed, each of whose acts indicated a resolution to maintain the general good and to impregnate the whole nation with the spirit of the sovereign.

In all this government the model of the Christian hierarchy was before the mind of Charles, and in the strength of union with it he worked. What is so singularly civilising in his power is the extinction in his personal character as ruler of anything local, bounded, and particular, together with the maintenance of every right in every place. The Pope was the head of the Church, and he looked upon himself as the head of the State; the Pope was surrounded in every province by bishops, his colleagues and coadjutors; they worked together in one mass. So Charles willed that his dukes and counts should work with him in one mass for one end, the pacific unity of his great empire. The act of the Pope[1] in making him Roman emperor helped him greatly to conceive of himself as the secular head of a Christian brotherhood of peoples, as the Pope was its spiritual head. But the act which made him emperor did not give him secular dominion over any people not already subject to him. For instance, it did not subject to him the Saxon kingdoms in Britain. He was not territorial, but

[1] Hergenröther, *Kirchengeschichte*, i. 507-8.

moral leader and president in the council of kings ; their chief in the defence of the Church. He did not take from the Greek empress or her successors any temporal lordship; though the Greek pride long refused to acknowledge him as an equal. The Pope remained what he had been from the time of Stephen II., an independent sovereign in the Papal State : he had not given himself a master in erecting a new empire. In fact we see Leo III. retain the exercise of his secular sovereignty, and the emperor appear only as defender of St. Peter's landed inheritance. Leo III. maintained the right of his own officers against the interference of some imperial commissioners, and distinguished accurately the limits of the State of the Church, from the imperial realm. He took measures against Arab inroads, to secure his State in full independence. What he needed was the emperor's support against the violent party spirit of the time; against such deeds as the intrusion of a Pope upon the Apostolic See by armed force ; against the assault upon a Pope by conspirators. This the authority of the emperor in Rome secured. For that he had a jurisdiction, as the Patricius had before. For this the Romans took an oath to the emperor as well as to the Pope; to the one as protector and advocate, to the other as temporal lord.

If in all this action Charlemagne had before him the model of the Christian hierarchy, not only his own vast kingdom, but all the nations of the West had spread out before them in the forty-six years of his reign, but especially in the last fourteen, when he had become, by the Pope's act, emperor of the Romans, the cordiality of union between the two great powers of human life, the spiritual and the temporal. The positive and intrinsic effect of the Holy See as the inflexible rule of doctrine and of justice on the Teuton features of the several northern tribes was seen when a man of immense natural capacity wielded so great a power in close conjunction and amity with it. What can be further than the action of Charles in the Champs de Mai, in the Missi Dominici, in a legislation which considered all the needs and desires of the subject, while it was supreme and final in its authority, from the condition of the northern tribes when they broke into the empire. The Vandals howled around the walls of Hippo when St. Augustine was repeating the penitential psalms on his death-bed; while Charles kept under his pillow St. Augustine's City of God, and strove to rule his empire for the maintenance of the Christian faith. He was accomplishing that union of many nations in one political bond as members of the same religion which Augustine himself, the most clear-sighted of saintly historians, was unable to contemplate. The mixture of earth with iron in the feet of the great heathen statue had wrought its dissolution; but the Teuton monarch, who mounted on his knees the steps of St. Peter's, kissing each separately, at the beginning of his career pledged his faith to the Pope over the tomb of the chief apostle, and before it ended he had given a final check to the intestine struggles of disunion. He had more than equalled the work of Constantine. The great Roman was indeed personally, though imperfectly, Christian. How much there was of policy, how much of faith in his conversion is a problem too hard to solve; but he was baptised on his death-bed, and the delay was probably of disastrous import to his inward life; and his empire was, in a great degree, still unconverted and heathen. His latter years were especially faulty in his practical execution of the relation between the Two Powers. From his time forward his own special foundation at Byzantium declined more and more, until the emperor who represented him became, in Leo, the Isaurian, and his son Kopronymus, the greatest enemy of the Church. But Charlemagne by his real union with St. Peter's successor, imparted Roman order, Christian civilisation, and civil constitution to that mass of seething peoples. If in the five hundred years succeeding Constantine his work deteriorated more and more, until the city which he wished to be the head of Christian empire yielded half of it to the Saracen, and then became the very seat of schism, the West, in the five hundred years which followed Charlemagne, saw a family of Christian and Catholic nations surround the throne of the chief apostle, nations which his Primacy had called into existence when he placed the imperial diadem on the head of "Charles Augustus, crowned of God".

If from the West we extend our view to Charlemagne's effect on the East, we find the new order of things which his empire introduced, present him as the temporal head of the Christian faith in union with its spiritual head over against the powerless Byzantine emperor. The Pope had ceased to be a subject, and his word had set a Teuton sovereign on full equality with the power which had so grievously maltreated Italy during two hundred years. Never could he have taken such a step had he been still a vassal of the Greek court, which had not only tyrannised itself, but left the Apostolic See defenceless to the Lombard aggression for many generations. The emperor Zeno had made Odoacer Roman Patricius for the subjugation of Italy and of Rome itself. Stephen II. had made Pipin Patricius for its delivery and defence of the Holy See. Leo III. had exalted the Patricius to be emperor for fuller defence. No Roman noble or bandit could resist the power thus created. The Greek influence in Italy was all but extinguished; the Roman Church was protected from that violation of its rights, that plundering of its property, which Cæsar and Exarch had so often inflicted. For the patrimonies which the Isaurian had confiscated, the Roman See was thus in another form compensated. The Pope had received a domain in central Italy, and was in the possession of full independence. Over against that free life and mounting sap of the West, the East presented but an image of decay and stagnation.

Harun al Raschid was reigning as chalif at Bagdad when Charles was made emperor at Rome. His troops advanced to Ephesus and compelled the empress Irene to pay tribute during a four years' suspension of hostilities. Again and again had Moslem armies polluted the Christian cities from Antioch to the Bosphorus with every iniquity. In 726, they took possession of St.

Basil's Cæsarea, in the year when the Isaurian was trying to force his Mohammedan hatred of images on Pope St. Gregory II., and seven years before he was stripping the Roman Church of its patrimony, and transferring ten provinces of the Papal patriarchate to the bishop of the eastern capital. From the death of Mohammed in 632 to the creation of Charles as emperor of the Romans in 800, was a time of scarcely interrupted disaster inflicted by the Saracen on the Christian through the East and the South. The outburst began as we have seen, by the betrayal of the faith on the part of Heraclius, the sole Roman emperor: Constans II., Leo III., and Kopronymus continued this betrayal. Mohammed waxed greater and greater through this whole period. The Christian successes consisted in *not* losing Constantinople, and in saving the south of France after the loss of Spain. In the reign of Harun al Raschid, that most terrible of destructions was at its greatest expansion and intensity. Then an emperor of the Romans was created by the Pope for the special defence of 'the Church. Exactly as Harun in his character of chalif was bound to lay waste and destroy the Christian Church and Faith, Charles was bound to watch over it. This was the tenure by which he held the empire, and his successors after him.[1] It was given, not for the glory and distinction of the wearer, but its true and proper significance lay in the fulfilment of the duties which the emperor was to discharge as protector of the Church.

---

[1] Phillips, sec. 127, vol. iii. p. 202, 205.

All imperial grandeur was an attribute of this duty. Exactly because the Greek emperor had not fulfilled this duty, the Pope undertook the renovation of the western Roman empire. It would be an entirely erroneous view of Leo's act to suppose that he could have done nothing else, that he must have made Charlemagne 'emperor, and by this single crowning bound himself and his successors to accept every succeeding emperor. Things in the East had come to that pass, but in the West the whole empire, in conception and in fact, was the Pope's work. The office thus created was a spiritual office, to which the spiritual head of Christendom should consecrate, anoint, and crown its temporal head. When there was a new king of the Franks, he was to come to Rome for consecration as emperor of the Romans: the Pope did not elect the new king, neither of the Franks then, nor of the Germans afterwards, but he, and he alone, invested the man chosen king with the title and power of the Roman emperor.

The chalifate, set up in the false pretension of succeeding a man whose whole claim to rule was founded on a falsehood, had become the most terrible despotism which human history had witnessed. It had taken possession of a very large part of what was Christian territory when it appeared in the world. Heraclius and his line trembled before it. At the time when a soldier of fortune closed seven revolutions at Byzantium Christian Spain was overwhelmed by it. And presently the Isaurian line helped its onward march by arrogating to itself that intrusion into spiritual government, which was the very basis of the chalifate. Then the action of Leo III., on Christmas Day, 800, created in the West a power adequate to resist the further advance of Mohammedan rule. As long continued dissension in the faith, decline in Christian morals, and an ever advancing despotism had given entrance to Saracen conquest, so from the very tomb of St. Peter, and at the voice of his Successor, arose that Christian king and Roman prince whom Pope Felix and his successors sought in vain from the heirs of Constantine. The vileness of oriental despotism was to meet in conflict Christian monarchy: the union of nations in the faith to give one spirit to the West: the flood which had almost overflowed the earth to stop before the Rock of Peter.

INDEX.

INDEX.

Abu Bekr, elected the first chalif, 118.

Adrian I., *Pope*, his accession and character, 441; replies to the embassy of king Desiderius, 442; his cities seized by Desiderius, 443; defends Rome against Desiderius, and stops him by interdict, 445; calls upon Charlemagne to rescue him, 446; whom he receives at St. Peter's as Patricius, at Easter, 474, 450; confers with Charles as to Pipin's donation, 453; receives the renewal of the donation from him, 455; visits of Charles to Rome during his pontificate, 497; dies in 795, mourned over by Charles, as a father, 498.

African Bishops repeat to Pope St. Martin the words of his predecessor, Innocent I., made in the time of St. Augustine, 72; acknowledge the special divine gift of maintaining the faith, dwelling in the Apostolic Chair, 73.

Agatho, *Pope*, holds councils preparatory to the Sixth Council, 239; describes the legates whom he sends to the Council, 239; restores St. Wilfrid to his see, 240; asserts before the Sixth Council the inerrancy of the Apostolic See, 245; his claims fully admitted by the Council, 247; and by the emperor, 249, who calls him "your most sacred Headship," 249; the Sixth Council beseeches him to confirm it, 247; dies before the Council ends in 681, 250.

Aistulf, king of the Lombards, takes Ravenna in 751, and names himself king of Italy, 350; attacks the duchy of Rome, and imposes a polltax on Rome, 353; will not listen to Pope Stephen II. at Pavia, 355; yields to Pipin, who besieges Pavia, 360; breaks his compact with Pipin, and begins a fresh siege of Rome, 361; yields Pavia to Pipin, and submits to his terms, 363; invests Rome at the beginning, and dies hunting at the end of 756, 365.

Alexandrine Patriarchate, its history from Dioscorus to Mohammed, 144-9.

Ali, fourth chalif, 656-661, assassinated in the mosque, 153.

Amalasunta, allowed to be murdered by her cousin, Theodatus, whom she had made king of the Goths, 380.

Anastasius made patriarch on the deposition of Germanus by Leo III. 336; made ecumenical by a tyrannical act of Leo III., 336; deposed by his son Kopronymus as a useless instrument, 337.

Anastasius, the Librarian, as authority for Roman history, 26; his account of Pope St. Martin, 52-5; of the visit of Constans II. to Rome, 230; his character of St. Gregory III., 332; describes his works, 343; his character of Pope Zacharias, 345, 352; describes the election and character of Pope Stephen III., 352; character and letter to Desiderius of Pope Adrian I., 441-3; describes Charlemagne ascending the steps to St. Peter's on his knees, 450; records the donation of Charlemagne in 774, 454; and the visit of Pope Leo III. to Charles at Paderborn, 500; his exculpation in St. Peter's and crowning of Charlemagne, 502; Justinian II., his captain of the guards sent to seize Pope Sergius, 272; entrance of Pope Constantine into Constantinople, 278; the election of Pelagius II. left free because of the Lombards, 382; his character of Pope Paul I., 432.

Antiochene Patriarchate, history from St. Chrysostom to Mohammed, 143.

Anastasius, formerly *Artemius*, and the first secretary, made emperor, 282; is deposed after a civil war of six months, and becomes a priest, 289; revolts against Leo III., and executed as a criminal by him, 289.

Athalarich, king of the Goths, perishes by his excesses in 534, 380; imposes a fine for confirming the Papal election, 380.

Augustine, St., his confession of the primacy of the Apostolic See praised by Pope St. Martin, 73.

Bardanes, Philippicus, reigns eighteen months, and tries to set up again the Monothelite heresy, 281; deposed and blinded, 282.

Baronius, his judgment as to the greatness of St. Gregory II. quoted, 332.

Bede, St., his account of archbishop Theodore, 236.

Boniface IV., Pope, consecrates Agrippa's Pantheon to be the Church of "the ever-virgin Mother of God and all martyrs," 28.

Brunengo, I primi Papi-Re and Le Origini della Sovranità Temporale dei Papi, quoted continually in the 8th chapter.

Byzantium, its despotism the Church's enemy from the time of St. Gregory, 5; its patriarch the special rival of the Pope, 6; tries for forty years to impose the Monothelite heresy on the Pope and the Church, 41; five acts of its theological despotism, 61; march of this despotism from Constantine to Constans II., 64; secular power declines, as spiritual usurpation advances, 65; development of its double despotism, civil and religious, from Constantine to Heraclius, 110-117; its fostering the heretical spirit destroys the empire, 117-118; two hundred years of eastern wickedness lead up to the Mohammedan conquest, 141, and the destruction of the eastern patriarchates, 143-6; triple despotism over the Popes, 1, controlling and confirming their election, 376-385; 2, the exarchal government, plundering and oppressing, 386-390; 3, interfering with doctrine, 393-400; eastern episcopate demoralised by it, 409; its advancement of its bishop from 381 to 733, 337.

Charlemagne, sent by his father Pipin to meet Pope Stephen II., 358; crowned with his father and brother by Pope Stephen at St. Denys in 754, 360; and made with them Patricius of the Romans, 360, 431; becomes with his brother Carloman, king of the Franks, 768, 436; marries Desiderata or Ermengarde, daughter of Desiderius, 437; sends her back repudiated after a year, 438; becomes king of the whole Frank empire, Dec. 4, 771, 440; marches into Italy against Desiderius, 446; invests Pavia, October, 773, 448; enters St. Peter's and welcomed by Pope Adrian as Patricius, at Easter, 774, 449; confers with Pope Adrian I., 450; renews and confirms the pact of Quieray, 454; lays the donation on the altar of the Confession, 455; captures Verona and Pavia and becomes king of the Lombards, 457; takes time to carry out the donation, but is never unfaithful, 459; his visit to Rome in 774 inaugurates his 40 years of triumphs, 463; his loyalty in repeating his father's acts, 465; visits to Rome in the pontificate of Adrian I., 497; receives Pope Leo III. at Paderborn, 501; comes from Aix-la-Chapelle to Rome, 502; the Pope acquitted on his personal word in St. Peter's before him, 503; crowned by Leo III. emperor of the Romans on Christmas Day, 800, 503; made emperor by the Pope alone, to be protector of the Church, 505; this making by the Pope acknowledged by all his subjects, 506; it recognises the proper nature of civil government, 508; it establishes Christian legislation in the person of Charles, 510; his action in the Champs de Mai, 511; his action by the Missi Dominici, 512; makes the Christian hierarchy the model of his civil government, 514; how his government civilises the West, 515; how his work surpasses that of Constantine, 516; how his empire bears on the Byzantine,

517; how it stands over against the chalifate, 518.

Charles Martell, saves Europe from Mohammed at the battle by Tours, 494; second of the four great Carlovingians, 496; called upon for aid by St. Gregory III., 339.

Church, the Catholic—the one kingdom of Christ in all ages, 2; unity of, as necessary as the unity of God, 2; want of the idea makes documents unintelligible, 4.

Constans II., emperor, charges the exarch Olympius to murder Pope St. Martin, 54; appoints another exarch, Kalliopas, to kidnap the Pope, 79; tortures and puts to death St. Maximus, the Confessor, 159-170; forces the election of Pope Eugenius in the life-time of St. Martin, 226; murders his brother, Theodosius, a deacon, 230; his visit to Rome described by Anastasius, 230; strips Rome of statues, and St. Mary of the Martyrs (the Pantheon) of its roof, 233; assassinated in his bath at Syracuse, 234.

Constantine and Charlemagne, their work on the Church compared, 516.

Constantine III., poisoned by the empress Martina, 159.

Constantine IV., Pogonatus, 236; solicits union with the Pope, 238; addresses the Pope at the Sixth Council as the living Peter, 249; his position as emperor, 261; reigns from 668 to 685, a great contrast to his father, Constans II., 262.

Constantine V., Kopronymus, emperor, leaves Pope Stephen II. undefended at the Lombard invasion, 354; Pope Stephen II. ceases to recognise his sovereignty over Rome, 357; asks Pipin to restore to him Rome and the exarchate, 364, 411; the last eastern emperor who exercises thraldom over Rome, 411.

Constantine, ecumenical patriarch of Constantinople, so presented to the bishops by the emperor in 754, 403; banished to Prince's Island in 766, 405; degraded in Sancta Sophia, 407; imprisoned, condemned, beheaded, and dissected, 768, 408.

Cyrus, made by Heraclius patriarch of Alexandria, 105; constructor with Sergius, of the Monothelite heresy, 105; supplies Heraclius with heresy drawn out scientifically, 253.

Desiderius, last king of the Lombards, 757-774, made by help of Pope Stephen II, 433; plots against Popes Paul I., Stephen III., and Adrian I., 433-438; marries his daughter to Charlemagne in 770, repudiated by him in 771, 437; gets rid of the Palatine judges Christophorus and Sergius, 439; encounters and is foiled by Pope Adrian I., 441-446; is invested in Pavia by Charlemagne in 773, 447; conquered and deposed by him in 774, 457.

De Vere, Aubrey, quoted, 373, the sin of Constantine cleaving his empire, note, 111.

Döllinger, quoted on the purpose of the Greek Council in Trullo, 264; analyses Mohammed's religion and estimates his work, 23, 208; sums up the effect of the Mohammedan attack, 224; makes absolute despotism the proper offspring of Mohammed, 220-224; what Mohammed was named by his companions, 217.

Eugenius, Pope, elected in the lifetime of St. Martin, 226, 229.

Gfrörer, Papst Gregorius, vii., vol. v. p. 10-11 quoted.

Gregorovius quoted, 25, 26, 28, 29, 37, 45, 257, 269, 270, 280, 290.

Gregory II., Pope, 19th May, 715, 290; extent of the Christian region at his accession, 290-293; his character and actions, 301; his letter to the emperor Leo III., 302-315; shows the bearing of a God Incarnate on the making of images, 306; compares the conduct of Leo III. with that of the Jewish king Ozias, 308; effects on the mind of portraying divine actions, 309; defines the bounds of Church and State, 311, 317; reproves the emperor's impiety in breaking up an image of Christ, 312; laughs to scorn his threats against St. Peter, 313; whom all the nations of the West look upon as a God upon earth, 314; contrasts Church discipline with State punishment, 318; the Pope and the patriarch bear God's commission to pardon the emperor, if penitent, 320; these letters, a picture of the time in which they were written, 321; especially as to the relation between the Two Powers, 322; and the unjealous unity of the Papal and the episcopal authority, 324; he rejects Leo's attack on the faith, but maintains allegiance, 328; causes king Liutprand to retire from before Rome, 329; Baronius esteems Pope Gregory II. as equal to St. Gregory the Great, 332; he dies in February, 731.

Gregory III., Pope, elected in 731, his character in Anastasius, 332, 343; holds a Council at Rome proscribing the Iconoclast heresy, 334; is deprived by Leo III. of the patrimonies in Leo's realm, and of his spiritual jurisdiction in ten provinces, 336; keeps king Liutprand at bay from Rome, 339; turns for aid to Charles Martell, 341; sends him the keys of St. Peter's Confession, 342; dies 27th November, 741, 344; having saved Rome from the Lombards, 344.

Heraclius, the emperor; mode of his accession, 9; his dynasty reigns for five generations, 10; tries to desert Constantinople, 14; his twelve years' inactivity, 14; his awakening, 15; conquers Persia in five campaigns, 17; brings back the Holy Cross to Jerusalem, 21; his success as a whole from 622 to 629, 21; subscribes and publishes the Ecthesis, 33; makes Pyrrhus patriarch of Constantinople, 36; triumphs when orthodox, and ruins the empire when heretical, 42; the revolution which follows his bringing back the Cross to Jerusalem, 102; he falls into the hands of Sergius, patriarch of Constantinople, and of Cyrus, patriarch of Alexandria, 103.

Hefele, quoted, 32, 37, 41, 51, 60, 68, 71, 103, 104, 107, 168, 169, 227, 264, 265.

Hergenröther, quoted, 7, 26, 48, 142, 169, 238, 240, 245, 264, 266, 268, 296, 325, 408, 411, 412, 513.

Honorius, Pope, his accession and acts, 30; his deception by the patriarch Sergius, 31; his death and burial at St. Peter's, 37; censured for neglect of his office by St. Leo II., in confirming the Sixth Council, 256; five Popes, who had been members of his clergy, condemn the Monothelite error, 56-7, 65; Muratori, Hergenröther, and Jungmann deny that he is chargeable with any error of faith, 252; he died before the Exposition of Sergius was presented for his acceptance, 253.

Hoensbroech, quoted, 424, 425, 426.

Isaac the model exarch, his tomb at Ravenna, 47.

Jerome, St., his account of the northern wandering of the nations, 138-141.

John IV., Pope, at his accession, censures the Monothelite heresy, 43; defends Honorius against having supported it, in a letter to the emperor, 44; calls upon the emperor Constantine III. to abolish the Ecthesis of his father, Heraclius, 155.

John, the Almsgiver, St., last great patriarch of Alexandria, 13.

John VI., patriarch of Constantinople, asks pardon of Pope Constantine, 282; describes his preeminence in the church as that of the head in the human body, 283.

John of Damascus, St., his record of Mohammed, 211; observes that Mohammed has no witness to his truth, 213; censures Iconoclasm as the invasion of a robber, 327.

Justinian I., embues all his successors with doctrinal despotism over the Church, 63; his conquest of Italy the source of woe, 113; confesses the Primacy of the Pope, while seeking to enthral it to himself, 115; his persecution of Pope Vigilius during eight years at Constantinople, 286, 393; as lord of Rome by right of conquest seizes on the confirmation and even nomination of Popes, 380; from his time the Byzantine emperors claimed the right of confirming Popes, 381; which they exercised down to Pope Gregory III. in 731, 385; the maker of the ecumenical patriarchate to hold under the emperor the portfolio of doctrine, 392; the chief of the theologising emperors, 393; moulder of the despotism which ate out the eastern episcopate, 410; which began by the deposition of Pope Silverius through his empress Theodora and continued to Constantine Kopronymus, 411; reduces Italy to be the "servile" province, deplored by Pope Agatho, 417; stands at the head of two centuries in which Byzantine oppression causes the Primacy to work in fetters, 503: as a civil ruler worse to the Church than Odoacer or Theodorich, 417.

Justinian II., succeeds in 685, 262; summons a Greek Council in Trullo, 263; strives to reduce the Pope to a patriarch, 265; claims to confirm the council in Trullo, 267; sends his guardsman Zacharias to carry Pope Sergius to Constantinople, 273; forces the patriarch Callinicus to demolish a church, 274; is deposed with his nose slit, 275; is restored in 705, his tyranny and savage cruelty, 276; his massacre at Ravenna, 277; summons Pope Constantine to Constantinople, 279; falls at the Pope's feet and acknowledges the privileges of the Roman See, 279; is deposed, murdered, and his head sent to Rome, 280.

Jungmann, quoted, 506—denies that Pope Honorius is chargeable with any error of faith, 252.

Kurth, quoted, 491, 509, 511.

Leo *II., Pope,* August, 682, to July, 683; confirms the Sixth Council, 250; modifies the condemnation of Honorius, 251-2; contrasts the negligence of Honorius with the four patriarchs, Sergius, Pyrrhus, Paul, and Peter, "who lurked as thieves in the See of Constantinople rather than acted as guides," 251.

Leo *III., Pope St.*, succeeds Adrian I. in 795, 498; attacked in a procession, 500; consultation with Charlemagne at Paderborn, 501; acquits himself upon his word, 502; crowns Charles, king of the Franks, as emperor of the Romans, 503.

Leo *III.,* the Isaurian, made emperor, 289, 298; begins in 726 the Iconoclast contest, 299; destroys the statue of Christ attached to his palace, 312; threatens the Pope to break in pieces the statue of St. Peter, 313; answers the Pope's letter by five attempts upon his life, 325; destroys the images and lays waste the churches, 326; censured by St. John Damascene, 327; deposes the patriarch Germanus, 326; sends a great fleet against Ravenna and Roric 335, confiscates the patrimonies of St Peter in his realm, 336; severs the Illyrian provinces from the Pope's patriarchal jurisdiction, 336; takes twenty Isaurian bishoprics from Antioch for Constantinople, dies in the year 741, the same year as Charles Martell and Pope Gregory III., 343.

Leo *XIII., Pope,* attests the witness borne by history to the Holy See, vii.

Liutprand, king of the Lombards, 712-744, 229; advances on Rome and retires at the Pope's intervention, 329; takes Spoleto, and takes four cities of the duchy of Rome, 338; yields to Pope Zacharias at Terni in 743, 346; receives the Pope at Pavia, and restores the province of Ravenna, 347-8; dies after 32 years' reign, the greatest of the Lombard kings, 348.

Martin, Pope St., his Council and his martyrdom, 51-100; condemns four patriarchs for heresy, 53; convokes a Lateran Council against the Monothelite heresy, 55; directs an encyclical to all bishops and peoples, 56; informs the emperor Constans II. that he has condemned his Typus, 56; his speech on opening the Lateran Council, 66; letter of the African bishops read at the Lateran Council, 72; answer of the Pope to it, 73; releases the people of Thessalonica from obedience to an heretical archbishop, his own vicar, 74; appoints a vicar in the eastern patriarchates of Antioch and Jerusalem, 75; describes his capture in the Lateran Church and deportation to Constantinople, 79-83; his sufferings described by an eye-witness, 85; arraigned for high treason before the Senate of Constantinople, 86; dragged through the city as a condemned criminal with the sword borne before him, 89; confined in the guard-house during 85 days, 95; starved to death at Cherson, 97; repeats in his death the Passion of Christ, and Constans II. the tyranny of Trajan, 100.

Mary, the Mother of God, declared by Sophronius, in his synodical letter, approved by the Sixth Council, "free from all spot in body, soul, and mind," 108; "whoever does not honour and worship her who is blessed above every creature —let him be anathema both in this world and the next". Pope St. Martin, the Martyr, 84; "the most chaste, immaculate, most excellent of all creatures, the fullest of grace, the maker and giver of joy," 100.

Maximus, the Confessor, his life, labours, and martyrdom, 157-170; the great opponent of the Monothelite heresy, 158; counsels Pope St. Martin to call the Lateran Council, 159; his testimonies to the Apostolic See, 160; carried to Byzantium, and tried before the Senate, 162; rejects the imperial offers of honour, 168; tortured and put to death by Constans II., 169; traces the danger of the empire to the misconduct of its rulers, 260.

Menzel, Adolph, quoted as to the right of Pipin and Charlemagne to make the donation, 428.

Mohammed, his work described by Döllinger, 23; his personal life and character, 172-189; change in his conduct after the death of his wife Chadidja, 173; proclaims force as the instrument of spreading his religion, 174; orders a marauding excursion in the holy months, 175; justifies it by verses of the Koran 176; his first battle at Bedr, 177; is defeated at Ohod, 179; defends Medina in a siege and loses reputation, 180; puts to death the men of a Jewish clan and enslaves their wives, 181; attempts a pilgrimage to Mecca and is forced to retire, 182; his polygamy after Chadidja's death, 183; rebukes by aid of the Koran a revolt of his wives, 184; takes the wife of his adopted son and justifies it as the command of God, 185; forbids by the Koran his wives to marry after his death, 186; obtains possession of Mecca, A.D. 630, 186; issues a new law of nations and war, and dies, 187; four principles of his life from the Hegira to his death, 190; employment of force to propagate Islam, 190; imposture in using the name of the angel Gabriel, 191; invents privileges as to the number and choice of his wives, 192; his disregard of human life, 193; his character as founder of a religion, 194; contrast between his character and that of Christ's, 195; how his life has infected the life of his followers, 196; degradation of woman in all Mohammedan countries, 197; his position at the time of his death, 199; his civil virtues, 200; effect of the invention of Gabriel on his title to belief, 201; at his death simply a successful robber, 203; the first twelve years of the Christian faith and the first twelve years of Islam, 206; holds in the Mohammedan system the place of Christ in the Christian, 208; radical antagonism of that system with the Christian faith, 202; his record by St. John Damascene, 211-214; character and formation of the Koran, 214; Christendom and Islam contemporaries in origin, 218; absolute despotism his proper offspring, 219; the locust people, 225.

Monothelite Heresy, pioneer of the Mohammedan conquest, 118.

Muratori on the Pope's position before the donation of Pipin, 426; absolves Pope Honorius from any error of doctrine, 252; justifies Pope Stephen II. in turning to Pipin for aid, 355; describes the government of the Lombard kings, 458; describes the tyranny of Constans II., 231; describes the massacre at Ravenna by order of Justinian II., 278; Leo III., the Isaurian, convulsed the Church with the Iconoclastic tragedy, 299.

Niehues, Kaiserthum und Papstthum, quoted, vol. i., 434, 436, 437, 446, 462.
Nova Roma, its ecclesiastical conduct, from A.D. 330 to 715, 476-481.

Odoacer, Patricius of Rome, by grant of the eastern emperor Zeno, 374; did not claim to confirm a Papal election, 377; five years of suffering to Italy before he is overthrown, 375; slain at a banquet by order of Theodorich, 378; results of his meddling with the Papal election, 379.

Olympius, the exarch, tries to murder St. Martin at Mass, 53.

Omar, the second chalif, 120; subdues Syria, 121; grants a capitulation to Jerusalem, 121-3; led into the holy places by the patriarch Sophronius, 123; takes Ctesiphon, Aleppo, Antioch, Alexandria, Egypt, and North Africa, as far as Tripolis, 124-127; character of his rule, 129; the churches he destroyed and the women he captured, 129; ascetic in outward bearing, a voluptuary in his life, 130; maker of the Mohammedan empire, 131; the empire ruled from Medina, 133; ruin which he brought on Constantine's empire and the Christian Church, 132; his union of the Two Powers, 134-135; his destruction of the Antiochene patriarchate, 137; mortally wounded in the mosque at Medina, A.D. 644, 152.

Osman, third chalif, 644 to 656, 152; slain by the son of the first chalif, Abu Bekr, 153.

Patrimonies of the Roman Church, the twenty-three in time of Gregory the Great, 424.

Paul I., Pope, 757-767; his new State maintained by Pipin against king Desiderius, 433; and against Greek as well as Lombard enmity, 434.

Persian Empire, strips the eastern empire of provinces from 610 to 622, 12, 14; is conquered by Heraclius from 622 to 627, 18; its emperor Chosroes destroyed by his son, 20; its ruin, nine emperors in four years, 24.

Phillips, Kirchenrecht, quoted, 499, 518.

Phocas, the emperor, his character, 7; puts to death his predecessor, the emperor Mauritius, and all his family, 9; his death, 9; his war with the Persian emperor Chosroes, 11; requires his patriarch to acknowledge the Roman Primacy, 25; presents the Pantheon to Pope Boniface IV., 28.

Pipin-le-bref; rise of the family of Arnulf and Pipin of Landen, 493; his forty years' work as mayor of the palace, 494; first of the four great Carlovingians, 496.

Pipin, the king, invites Pope Zacharias to sanction his assumption of the royal title, 351; elected king of the Franks at Soissons in 752, 351; meets Pope Stephen II. at Pontigny in 754, 357; promises to restore to the Pope the Lombard captures, 359; crowned by Pope Stephen II. in St. Denys', 360; forces king Aistulf to yield at Pavia, 360; called upon by Pope Stephen II. in the name of St. Peter, 362; relieves Rome by taking Pavia, 363; lays the keys of the surrendered cities on the tomb of the Prince of the Apostles, 364; refuses to be bribed by Constantine Kopronymus to give back these cities to him, 364; restores Rome to the Pope and gives him the exarchate and Pentapolis, 365, 400; letter of thanksgiving sent him by Pope Stephen II. in 757, 430; defends Pope Paul I. from king Desiderius, 433; dies in 768, his tomb inscribed: "Pipin the king, father of Charles the Great," 436; the Papal monarchy dates from the compact with him at Quiersy, 460; the greatness of his benefactions acknowledged in the Codex Carolinus, 465.

Popes, the succession of twenty-four, from 604 to 715, 26; the imperial confirmation of their election, 27, 30; then ten succeeding Honorius condemn the Monothelite heresy, 41, 56; are persecuted for forty years for condemning it, 57; the ten immediate successors of Honorius save the Church from heresy imposed by Byzantine emperors and patriarchs, 255-256; ground of their firmness, belief in the succession of St. Peter, 259; the five Popes who go to Constantinople, 284; the twenty-four Popes between the first and second Gregories, 295; their three hundred years of suffering and glory, A.D. 455-756, 369; mode of their election and confirmation under the exarchate, 383; their confirmation from 526 to 731, 385; their third oppression by the Byzantine lay power seeking to impose doctrine, 391; constancy of the successive Popes from Gelasius in 492, to St. Gregory II., in 726, 394; the Papal constancy makes martyrs; the patriarchal despotism corrupts the faith and destroys the empire, 395-396, 409-410; fifty-eight Byzantine bishops from Metrophanes, A.D. 325, to Methodius, 842, of whom twenty-one heretics, 411-414; seventy Popes in the same period, all of whom keep one faith, 415; the doctrine thus preserved is that of the Incarnation itself, 415; the line of subject succeeded by the line of sovereign Popes, 432; the Papal line the fountain head of political sense, 491-492; Christian Europe born from the alliance between Charlemagne and Popes Adrian I. and Leo III., 515.

Rachis, king of the Lombards, resigns his kingdom, 349; receives the cowl of St. Benedict from the hands of Pope Zacharias, 349.

Reumont, quoted, 301, 330, 332, 339, 359, 363, 365, 496, 509.

Severinus, Pope, his confirmation delayed for nineteen months and sixteen days, 37; is plundered by the exarch Isaac, 39; sat two months and sixteen days, during which he rejected the Ecthesis, 41.

Sergius, patriarch of Constantinople, deceives Pope Honorius, 106; draws up his Ecthesis against the doctrine of Sophronius, 33, 35, 109; supplies the emperor Heraclius with insidious heretical language, 254; condemned by the Sixth Council, 247; by St. Leo II., in confirming the Council, as one "who lurked as a thief rather than acted as a guide in the See of Constantinople," 251.

Stephen II., Pope, elected in 752, 352; resists Aistulf, attacking the duchy of Rome, and imposing a poll-tax, 353; appeals in vain to Constantine Kopronymus to defend Rome, 353; appeals to Pipin, king of the Franks, 354; leaves Rome for Pavia to persuade Aistulf to desist, 355; on his refusal, crosses the Alps to Pipin, 356; saves Europe from Mohammedan enthralment by union with Pipin, 357; meeting of Stephen and Pipin at Pontigny, described by Anastasius, 358; Pipin binds himself to protect the Roman Church and Commonwealth of which Stephen makes him Patricius, 359; anoints Pipin as king of the Franks in the Church of St. Denys, 360; is besieged in Rome by Aistulf, 361; writes to Pipin in the name of St. Peter, 362; is delivered by Pipin taking Pavia, 363; the keys of the cities laid by Pipin on the tomb of the Prince of the Apostles, 364; Pope Stephen II. recognised as head of the Roman State, 365; the State of the Church thus created, A.D. 756, 366; returns as king to Rome on the death of Aistulf, 756, 429; letter of the first Pope-king to Pipin, 430; dies in the Lateran palace, acknowledged by all as king of Rome, April 24, 757, 431; in him the line of Popes who are subjects closes; the line of Popes who are kings opens, 432.

Stephen III., Pope, his pontificate, 352, letter to the kings Charles and Carloman, 437.

Stephen, bishop of Dor, his memorial to the Lateran Council, 68.

Sophronius, patriarch of Jerusalem, appeals from Calvary to the Apostolic See under Honorius, as the chalif, Omar enters, 69; his synodical letter, a chief document against the Monothelite heresy, 107-109; calls the entrance of Omar "the abomination of desolation in the temple," 123.

Theodatus, King, tyrannises over the Romans, 380; allows the election of Pope Agapetus, 380; forces him to go as ambassador to Constantinople, 380; imposes the choice of Pope Silverius, 380.

INDEX. 531

Theodorich, the Ostrogoth, his domination Arian, 372; his political clemency ends in blood, 373; an emissary of the eastern emperor Zeno, 374; failed to assimilate the Roman and Gothic elements in stable union, 375; allows the election of Popes Hormisdas and John I., imposes that of Pope Felix IV., 378; did not claim to confirm the election of Pope Symmachus, 377; begins with slaying Odoacer: ends by slaying Boethius and Symmachus and Pope John I., 375, 378; ruled with equity and died in remorse, and with him died the Gothic kingdom, 491.

Theodorus, Pope, his accession, 46; receives the patriarch Pyrrhus, renouncing his heresy in St. Peter's, 48; condemns him when recalcitrant, 48; names an apostolic vicar in Palestine, 49; dies and is buried at St. Peter's, 50.

Theophanes, the Greek chronographist, marks the rise of the Arabian heresy as the scourge of Christian sins, 260; ascribes the conduct of the emperor Leo III. to a Mohammedan temper, 335-6; calls St. Gregory II. "the most holy apostolic man," 325; "the successor of Supreme Peter in his Chair," 325; describes the tyranny of Constans II., 234; the murders of Justinian II. and his son, 280; the persecution of the monks by Constantine Kopronymus, 403.

Toto, the duke, seizes the Papal Chair for his brother, a layman, 431.

Vitalian, Pope, elected in 657, 229; receives as sovereign of Rome the emperor Constans II., 230, 232; consecrates Theodore, archbishop of Canterbury, 235; cherishes the young English Church, 235; dies in 672, 237.

Wandering of the nations, the northern and the southern compared, 149-151.

Zacharias, Pope, elected and consecrated four days after the death of Gregory III. in 731, without the exarch's confirmation, 344; his character by Anastasius, 345; during ten years keeps at bay Liutprand, Rachis, and Aistulf, 345; in his first year prevails over Liutprand at Terni, 346; in his third year prevails over him at Pavia, 347; in 749 prevails over king Rachis at Perugia, 348; gives him on his abdication the Benedictine habit, 349; 'in 751 resists the seizure of the exarchate by king Aistulf, 350; is invited by Pipin, mayor of the palace, to sanction his becoming king, 351; declares that it is lawful for him to depose the Merovingian and become king in his stead, 351; dies the 14th March, 752, having thrice saved Rome, 352.

SELECTION

FROM

BURNS & OATES'

Catalogue

OF

PUBLICATIONS.

LONDON: BURNS AND OATES, Ld.
28 ORCHARD ST., W., & 63 PATERNOSTER ROW, E.C.
NEW YORK, CINCINNATI, CHICAGO: BENZIGER BROTHERS.

1893.

Messrs. BURNS & OATES have recently acquired the Stock and Copyrights of:—

Ceremonial according to the Roman Rite. Translated from the Italian of JOSEPH BALDESCHI, Master of Ceremonies of the Basilica of St. Peter at Rome; with the Pontifical Offices of a Bishop in his own diocese, compiled from the "Cæremoniale Episcoporum"; to which are added various other Functions and copious explanatory Notes; the whole harmonized with the latest Decrees of the Sacred Congregation of Rites. By the Rev. J. D. HILARIUS DALE. New Edition. Handsomely bound in cloth, 6s. 6d.

The Sacristan's Manual; or, Handbook of Church Furniture, Ornament, &c. Harmonized with the most approved commentaries on the Roman Ceremonial and latest Decrees of the Sacred Congregation of Rites. By the Rev. J. D. HILARIUS DALE. New Edition, with numerous Additions. Cloth, 2s. 6d.

Perry's Practical Sermons for all the Sundays of the Year. FIRST AND SECOND SERIES. Sixth Edition. In Two Volumes. Cloth. Price 3s. 6d. per Volume.

Controversial Catechism; or, Protestantism refuted and Catholicism established by an appeal to the Holy Scriptures, the testimony of the Holy Fathers, and the Dictates of Reason; in which such portions of Scheffmacher's Catechism as suit modern Controversy are embodied. By the Rev. STEPHEN KEENAN. New Edition, Revised and Enlarged. Cloth, 2s.

Latest Publications.

Jesus, the All-Beautiful. A devotional Treatise on the character and actions of Our Lord. By the Author of "The Voice of the Sacred Heart," &c. Edited by the Rev. J. G. MACLEOD, S.J. Quarterly Series. 6s. 6d.

Analysis of the Gospels of the Sundays of the Year. From the Italian of ANGELO CAGNOLA. By the Rev. D. A. LAMBERT, LL.D., Author of "Answers to Atheists," &c. 8vo. Cloth, net, 5s.

The Manna of the Soul. By Father PAUL SEGNERI. Second Edition. In Two Volumes. Cloth, 12s.

Socialism, Exposed and Refuted. By Rev. VICTOR CATHREIN, S.J. Translated from the German by Rev. JAMES CONWAY, S.J. Crown 8vo. Cloth 4s.

Sermons for all Sundays and Festivals of the Year. By J. N. SWEENEY, D.D., Priest of the English Benedictine Congregation. A New Edition is in the Press and will be issued early in 1893. Price 10s. 6d.

The Blessed Virgin Mary in the Fathers of the First Six Centuries. By the Rev. THOMAS LIVIUS, C.SS.R., M.A., Author of "Mary in the Epistles," &c., &c. [*In the Press.*

No. 1.   1893.

SELECTION
FROM
BURNS AND OATES' CATALOGUE OF PUBLICATIONS.

ALLIES, T. W. (K.C.S.G.)

    Formation of Christendom. Vols. I., II., and III., (all out of print.) . . . .

    Church and State as seen in the Formation of Christendom, 8vo, pp. 472, cloth . (out of print.)

    The Throne of the Fisherman, built by the Carpenter's Son, the Root, the Bond, and the Crown of Christendom. Demy 8vo £0 10 6

    The Holy See and the Wandering of the Nations. Demy 8vo. 0 10 6

    Peter's Rock in Mohammed's Flood. Demy 8vo. . 0 10 6

"It would be quite superfluous at this hour of the day to recommend Mr. Allies' writings to English Catholics. Those of our readers who remember the article on his writings in the *Katholik*, know that he is esteemed in Germany as one of our foremost writers."—*Dublin Review.*

ALLIES, MARY.

    Leaves from St. John Chrysostom, With introduction by T. W. Allies, K.C.S.G. Crown 8vo, cloth . 0 6 0

"Miss Allies' 'Leaves' are delightful reading; the English is remarkably pure and graceful; page after page reads as if it were original. No commentator, Catholic or Protestant, has ever surpassed St. John Chrysostom in the knowledge of Holy Scripture, and his learning was of a kind which is of service now as it was at the time when the inhabitants of a great city hung on his words."—*Tablet.*

    History of the Church in England, from the beginning of the Christian Era to the accession of Henry VIII. Crown 8vo, cloth . . . 0 6 0

"Miss Allies has in this volume admirably compressed the substance, or such as was necessary to her purpose, of a number of authorities, judiciously selected. . . . Considering how scanty was the material available for the due performance of much of her task, she has secured a proportion and continuity which is surprising. . . . As a narrative the volume is capitally written, as a summary it is skilful, and not its least excellence is its value as an index of the best available sources which deal with the period it covers."—*Birmingham Daily Gazette.*

ANNUS SANCTUS:

    Hymns of the Church for the Ecclesiastical Year. Translated from the Sacred Offices by various Authors, with Modern, Original, and other Hymns, and an Appendix of Earlier Versions. Selected and Arranged by ORBY SHIPLEY, M.A.

    Plain Cloth, lettered 0 5 0

    Edition de luxe 0 10 6

ANSWERS TO ATHEISTS: OR NOTES ON

Ingersoll. By the Rev. A. Lambert, (over 100,000 copies sold in America). Tenth edition. Paper. . . . £0 0 6
Cloth 0 1 0

B. N.

The Jesuits: their Foundation and History. 2 vols. crown 8vo, cloth, red edges 0 15 0

"The book is just what it professes to be—*a popular history*, drawn from well-known sources," &c.—*Month.*

BAKER, VEN. FATHER AUGUSTIN.

Holy Wisdom; or, Directions for the Prayer of Contemplation, &c. Extracted from Treatises written by the Ven. Father F. Augustin Baker, O.S.B., and edited by Abbot Sweeney, D.D. Beautifully bound in half leather 0 6 0

"We earnestly recommend this most beautiful work to all our readers. We are sure that every community will use it as a constant manual. If any persons have friends in convents, we cannot conceive a better present they can make them, or a better claim they can have on their prayers, than by providing them with a copy."—*Weekly Register.*

BOWDEN, REV. H. S. (of the Oratory) Edited by.

Dante's Divina Commedia: Its scope and value. From the German of FRANCIS HETTINGER, D.D. With an engraving of Dante. Crown 8vo . . 0 10 6

"All that Venturi attempted to do has been now approached with far greater power and learning by Dr. Hettinger, who, as the author of the 'Apologie des Christenthums,' and as a great Catholic theologian, is eminently well qualified for the task he has undertaken."—*The Saturday Review.*

Natural Religion. Being Vol. I. of Dr. Hettinger's Evidences of Christianity. With an Introduction on Certainty. Second edition. Crown 8vo, cloth 0 7 6

"As an able statement of the Catholic Doctrine of Certitude, and a defence, from the Romanist point of view, of the truth of Christianity, it was well worth while translating Dr. Franz Hettinger's 'Apologie des Christenthums,' of which the first part is now published."—*Scotsman.*

BRIDGETT, REV. T. E. (C.SS.R.).

Discipline of Drink 0 3 6

"The historical information with which the book abounds gives evidence of deep research and patient study, and imparts a permanent interest to the volume, which will elevate it to a position of authority and importance enjoyed by few of its compeers."—*The Arrow.*

Our Lady's Dowry; how England Won that Title. New and Enlarged Edition. 0 5 0

"This book is the ablest vindication of Catholic devotion to Our Lady, drawn from tradition, that we know of in the English language."—*Tablet.*

BRIDGETT, REV. T. E. (C.SS.R.)—*continued.*

Ritual of the New Testament. An essay on the principles and origin of Catholic Ritual in reference to the New Testament. Third edition . . . £0 5 0

The Life of the Blessed John Fisher. With a reproduction of the famous portrait of Blessed JOHN FISHER by HOLBEIN, and other Illustrations. 2nd Ed. 0 7 6

"The Life of Blessed John Fisher could hardly fail to be interesting and instructive. Sketched by Father Bridgett's practised pen, the portrait of this holy martyr is no less vividly displayed in the printed pages of the book than in the wonderful picture of Holbein, which forms the frontispiece."—*Tablet.*

The True Story of the Catholic Hierarchy deposed by Queen Elizabeth, with fuller Memoirs of its Last Two Survivors. By the Rev. T. E. BRIDGETT, C.SS.R., and the late Rev. T. F. KNOX, D.D., of the London Oratory. Crown 8vo, cloth, 0 7 6

"We gladly acknowledge the value of this work on a subject which has been obscured by prejudice and carelessness."—*Saturday Review.*

The Life and Writings of Blessed Thomas More, Lord Chancellor of England and Martyr under Henry VIII. With Portrait of the Martyr taken from the Crayon Sketch made by Holbein in 1527. 2nd Ed. 0 7 5

"Father Bridgett has followed up his valuable Life of Bishop Fisher with a still more valuable Life of Thomas More. It is, as the title declares, a study not only of the life, but also of the writings of Sir Thomas. Father Bridgett has considered him from every point of view, and the result is, it seems to us, a more complete and finished portrait of the man, mentally and physically, than has been hitherto presented."—*Athenæum.*

The Wisdom and Wit of Blessed Thomas More . . 0 6 0

"It would be hard to find another such collection of true wisdom and keen, pungent, yet gentle wit and humour, as this volume contains."—*American Catholic Quarterly.*

BRIDGETT, REV. T. E. (C.SS.R.), Edited by.

Souls Departed. By CARDINAL ALLEN. First published in 1565, now edited in modern spelling by the Rev. T. E. Bridgett 0 6 0

BROWNLOW, VERY REV. CANON

A Memoir of the late Sir James Marshall, C.M.G., K.C.S.G., taken chiefly from his own letters. With Portrait. Crown 8vo, cloth . . . 0 3 6

Lectures on Slavery and Serfdom in Europe. Cloth 0 3 6

"The general impression left by the perusal of this interesting book is one of great fairness and thorough grasp of the subject."—*Month.*

BUCKLER, REV. H. REGINALD (O.P.)

The Perfection of Man by Charity: a Spiritual Treatise. Crown 8vo, cloth. . . . 0 5 0

"We have read this unpretending, but solid and edifying work, with much pleasure, and heartily commend it to our readers. . . Its scope is sufficiently explained by the title."—*The Month.*

CASWALL, FATHER.

Catholic Latin Instructor in the Principal Church Offices and Devotions, for the Use of Choirs, Convents, and Mission Schools, and for Self-Teaching. 1 vol., complete £0 3 6
Or Part I., containing Benediction, Mass, Serving at Mass, and various Latin Prayers in ordinary use . 0 1 6
May Pageant: A Tale of Tintern. (A Poem) Second edition 0 2 0
Poems 0 5 0
Lyra Catholica, containing all the Breviary and Missal Hymns, with others from various sources. 32mo, cloth, red edges 0 2 6

CATHOLIC BELIEF: OR, A SHORT AND

Simple Exposition of Catholic Doctrine. By the Very Rev. Joseph Faà di Bruno, D.D. Tenth edition . . . . . Price 6d.; post free, 0 0 8½
Cloth, lettered, ... 0 0 10
Also an edition on better paper and bound in cloth, with gilt lettering and steel frontispiece 0 2 0

CHALLONER, BISHOP.

Meditations for every day in the year. New edition. Revised and edited by the Right Rev. John Virtue, D.D., Bishop of Portsmouth. 8vo. 6th edition . 0 3 0
And in other bindings.

COLERIDGE, REV. H. J. (S.J.) *(See Quarterly Series.)*

DEVAS, C. S.

Studies of Family Life: a contribution to Social Science. Crown 8vo 0 5 0
"We recommend these pages and the remarkable evidence brought together in them to the careful attention of all who are interested in the well-being of our common humanity."—*Guardian.*
"Both thoughtful and stimulating."—*Saturday Review.*

DRANE, AUGUSTA THEODOSIA, Edited by.

The Autobiography of Archbishop Ullathorne. Demy 8vo., cloth. Second edition 0 7 6
"Admirably edited and excellently produced."—*Weekly Register.*
The Letters of Archbishop Ullathorne. (Sequel to the *Autobiography.*) Demy 8vo, cloth . . 0 9 0
"Compiled with admirable judgment for the purpose of displaying in a thousand various ways the real man who was Archbishop Ullathorne."—*Tablet.*

EYRE MOST REV. CHARLES, (Abp. of Glasgow).

The History of St. Cuthbert: or, An Account of his Life, Decease, and Miracles. Third edition, Illustrated with maps, charts, &c., and handsomely bound in cloth. Royal 8vo 0 14 0
"A handsome, well appointed volume, in every way worthy of its illustrious subject. . . . The chief impression of the whole is the picture of a great and good man drawn by a sympathetic hand."—*Spectator.*

FABER, REV. FREDERICK WILLIAM, (D.D.)

	£	s	d
All for Jesus	0	5	0
Bethlehem	0	7	0
Blessed Sacrament	0	7	6
Creator and Creature	0	6	0
Ethel's Book of the Angels	0	5	0
Foot of the Cross	0	6	0
Growth in Holiness	0	6	0
Hymns	0	6	0
Notes on Doctrinal and Spiritual Subjects, 2 vols. each	0	5	0
Poems	0	5	0
Precious Blood	0	5	0
Sir Lancelot	0	5	0
Spiritual Conferences	0	6	0
Life and Letters of Frederick William Faber, D.D., Priest of the Oratory of St. Philip Neri. By John Edward Bowden of the same Congregation	0	6	0

FOLEY, REV. HENRY, (S.J.)

Records of the English Province of the Society of Jesus.

	£	s	d
Vol. I., Series I. . . . . net	1	6	0
Vol. II., Series II., III., IV. . . net	1	6	0
Vol. III., Series V., VI., VII., VIII. . . net	1	10	0
Vol. IV. Series IX., X., XI. . . . net	1	6	0
Vol. V., Series XII. with nine Photographs of Martyrs	1	10	0
Vol. VI., Diary and Pilgrim-Book of the English College, Rome. The Diary from 1579 to 1773, with Biographical and Historical Notes. The Pilgrim-Book of the Ancient English Hospice attached to the College from 1580 to 1656, with Historical Notes . . . . net	1	6	0
Vol. VII. Part the First: General Statistics of the Province; and Collectanea, giving Biographical Notices of its Members and of many Irish and Scotch Jesuits. With 20 Photographs . . . . . net	1	6	0
Vol. VII. Part the Second: Collectanea, Completed; With Appendices. Catalogues of Assumed and Real Names; Annual Letters; Biographies and Miscellanea. . . . . net	1	6	0

"As a biographical dictionary of English Jesuits, it deserves a place in every well-selected library, and, as a collection of marvellous occurrences, persecutions, martyrdoms, and evidences of the results of faith, amongst the books of all who belong to the Catholic Church."—*Genealogist.*

FORMBY, REV. HENRY.

Monotheism: in the main derived from the Hebrew nation and the Law of Moses. The Primitive Religion of the City of Rome: An historical Investigation. Demy 8vo. 0 5 0

FRANCIS DE SALES, ST.: THE WORKS OF.
Translated into the English Language by the Very Rev. Canon Mackey, O.S.B., under the direction of the Right Rev. Bishop Hedley, O.S.B.
Vol. I. Letters to Persons in the World. Cloth . £0 6 0
"The letters must be read in order to comprehend the charm and sweetness of their style."—*Tablet.*
Vol. II.—The Treatise on the Love of God. Father Carr's translation of 1630 has been taken as a basis, but it has been modernized and thoroughly revised and corrected. 0 9 0
"To those who are seeking perfection by the path of contemplation this volume will be an armoury of help."—*Saturday Review.*
Vol. III. The Catholic Controversy. . . . 0 6 0
"No one who has not read it can conceive how clear, how convincing, and how well adapted to our present needs are these controversial 'leaves.'"—*Tablet.*
Vol. IV. Letters to Persons in Religion, with introduction by Bishop Hedley on "St. Francis de Sales and the Religious State." 0 6 0
"The sincere piety and goodness, the grave wisdom, the knowledge of human nature, the tenderness for its weakness, and the desire for its perfection that pervade the letters, make them pregnant of instruction for all serious persons. The translation and editing have been admirably done."—*Scotsman.*
*** Other vols. in preparation.

GALLWEY, REV. PETER, (S.J.)
Precious Pearl of Hope in the Mercy of God, The. Translated from the Italian. With Preface by the Rev. Father Gallwey. Cloth. 0 4 6
Lectures on Ritualism and on the Anglican Orders. 2 vols. (Or may be had separately.) 0 8 0
Salvage from the Wreck. A few Memories of the Dead, preserved in Funeral Discourses. With Portraits. Crown 8vo. 0 7 6

GIBSON, REV. H.
Catechism Made Easy. Being an Explanation of the Christian Doctrine. Eighth edition. 2 vols., cloth. 0 7 6
"This work must be of priceless worth to any who are engaged in any form of catechetical instruction. It is the best book of the kind that we have seen in English."—*Irish Monthly.*

GILLOW, JOSEPH.
Literary and Biographical History, or, Bibliographical Dictionary of the English Catholics. From the Breach with Rome, in 1534, to the Present Time. Vols. *I., II. and III. cloth, demy 8vo* . . each. 0 15 0
*** Other vols. in preparation.
"The patient research of Mr. Gillow, his conscientious record of minute particulars, and especially his exhaustive bibliographical information in connection with each name, are beyond praise."—*British Quarterly Review.*
The Haydock Papers. Illustrated. Demy 8vo. . 0 7 6
"We commend this collection to the attention of every one that is interested in the records of the sufferings and struggles of our ancestors to hand down the faith to their children. It is in the perusal of such details that we bring home to ourselves the truly heroic sacrifices that our forefathers endured in those dark and dismal times."—*Tablet.*

GRADWELL, MONSIGNOR.

Succat, The Story of Sixty Years of the Life of St. Patrick. Crown 8vo, cloth £0 5 0
"A work at once bright, picturesque, and truthful."—*Tablet.*

GROWTH IN THE KNOWLEDGE OF OUR LORD.

Meditations for every Day in the Year, exclusive of those for Festivals, Days of Retreat, &c. Adapted from the original of Abbé de Brandt, by Sister Mary Fidelis. A new and Improved Edition, in 3 Vols. Sold only in sets. Price per set, ... 1 2 6
"The praise, though high, bestowed on these excellent meditations by the Bishop of Salford is well deserved. The language, like good spectacles, spreads treasures before our vision without attracting attention to itself."—*Dublin Review.*

HEDLEY, BISHOP.

Our Divine Saviour, and other Discourses. Crown 8vo. 0 6 0
"A distinct and noteworthy feature of these sermons is, we certainly think, their freshness—freshness of thought, treatment, and style; nowhere do we meet pulpit commonplace or hackneyed phrase —everywhere, on the contrary, it is the heart of the preacher pouring out to his flock his own deep convictions, enforcing them from the 'Treasures, old and new,' of a cultivated mind."—*Dublin Review.*

HUMPHREY, REV. W. (S.J.)

Suarez on the Religious State: A Digest of the Doctrine contained in his Treatise, "De Statû Religionis." 3 vols., pp. 1200. Cloth, roy. 8vo. . . . 1 10 0
"This laborious and skilfully executed work is a distinct addition to English theological literature. Father Humphrey's style is quiet, methodical, precise, and as clear as the subject admits. Every one will be struck with the air of legal exposition which pervades the book. He takes a grip of his author, under which the text yields up every atom of its meaning and force."—*Dublin Review.*

The One Mediator; or, Sacrifice and Sacraments. Crown 8vo, cloth 0 5 0
"An exceedingly accurate theological exposition of doctrines which are the life of Christianity and which make up the soul of the Christian religion. . . . A profound work, but so far from being dark, obscure, and of metaphysical difficulty, the meaning of each paragraph shines with a crystalline clearness."—*Tablet.*

KING, FRANCIS.

The Church of my Baptism, and why I returned to it. Crown 8vo, cloth 0 2 6
"Altogether a book of an excellent spirit, written with freshness and distinction."—*Weekly Register.*

LEDOUX, REV. S. M.

History of the Seven Holy Founders of the Order of the Servants of Mary. Crown 8vo, cloth . . 0 4 6
"Throws a full light upon the Seven Saints recently canonized, whom we see as they really were. All that was marvellous in their call, their works, and their death is given with the charm of a picturesque and speaking style."—*Messenger of the Sacred Heart.*

LEE, REV. F. G., D.D. (of All Saints, Lambeth.)
  Edward the Sixth: Supreme Head. Second edition.
  Crown 8vo £0 6 0
  "In vivid interest and in literary power, no less than in solid historical value, Dr. Lee's present work comes fully up to the standard of its predecessors; and to say that is to bestow high praise. The book evinces Dr. Lee's customary diligence of research in amassing facts, and his rare artistic power in welding them into a harmonious and effective whole."—*John Bull.*

LIGUORI, ST. ALPHONSUS.
  New and Improved Translation of the Complete Works of St. Alphonsus, edited by the late Bishop Coffin:—
  Vol. I. The Christian Virtues, and the Means for Obtaining them. Cloth 0 3 0
  Or separately:—
    1. The Love of our Lord Jesus Christ . . . 0 1 0
    2. Treatise on Prayer. (*In the ordinary editions a great part of this work is omitted*) . . . 0 1 0
    3. A Christian's rule of Life 0 1 0
  Vol. II. The Mysteries of the Faith—The Incarnation; containing Meditations and Devotions on the Birth and Infancy of Jesus Christ, &c., suited for Advent and Christmas. 0 2 6
  Vol. III. The Mysteries of the Faith—The Blessed Sacrament 0 2 6
  Vol. IV. Eternal Truths—Preparation for Death . 0 2 6
  Vol. V. The Redemption—Meditations on the Passion. 0 2 6
  Vol. VI. Glories of Mary. New edition . . . 0 3 6
  Reflections on Spiritual Subjects 0 2 6

LIVIUS, REV. T. (M.A., C.SS.R.)
  St. Peter, Bishop of Rome; or, the Roman Episcopate of the Prince of the Apostles, proved from the Fathers, History and Chronology, and illustrated by arguments from other sources. Dedicated to his Eminence Cardinal Newman. Demy 8vo, cloth . 0 12 0
  "A book which deserves careful attention. In respect of literary qualities, such as effective arrangement, and correct and lucid diction, this essay, by an English Catholic scholar, is not unworthy of Cardinal Newman, to whom it is dedicated."—*The Sun.*
  Explanation of the Psalms and Canticles in the Divine Office. By ST. ALPHONSUS LIGUORI. Translated from the Italian by THOMAS LIVIUS, C.SS.R. With a Preface by his Eminence Cardinal MANNING. Crown 8vo, cloth 0 7 6
  "To nuns and others who know little or no Latin, the book will be of immense importance."—*Dublin Review.*
  "Father Livius has in our opinion even improved on the original, so far as the arrangement of the book goes. New priests will find it especially useful."—*Month.*
  Mary in the Epistles; or, The Implicit Teaching of the Apostles concerning the Blessed Virgin, set forth in devout comments on their writings. Illustrated from Fathers and other Authors, and prefaced by introductory Chapters. Crown 8vo. Cloth 0 5 0

MANNING, CARDINAL. Popular Edition of the Works of

	£	s	d
Four Great Evils of the Day. 6th edition.	0	2	6
Fourfold Sovereignty of God. 3rd edition.	0	2	6
Glories of the Sacred Heart. 5th edition	0	4	0
Grounds of Faith. 10th edition.	0	1	6
Independence of the Holy See. 2nd edition	0	2	6
Internal Mission of the Holy Ghost. 5th edition	0	5	0
Miscellanies. 3 vols. . . . the set	0	18	0
Religio Viatoris. 4th edition,	0	1	6
Sermons on Ecclesiastical Subjects. Vol. I..	0	6	0
(Vols. II. and III. out of Print.)			
Sin and its Consequences. 7th edition	0	4	0
Temporal Mission of the Holy Ghost. 3rd edition	0	5	0
True Story of the Vatican Council. 2nd edition	0	2	6
The Eternal Priesthood. 10th edition	0	2	6
The Office of the Church in the Higher Catholic Education. A Pastoral Letter	0	0	6
Workings of the Holy Spirit in the Church of England. Reprint of a letter addressed to Dr. Pusey in 1864	0	1	6
Lost Sheep Found. A Sermon	0	0	6
Rights and Dignity of Labour	0	0	1

The Westminster Series

In handy pocket size. All bound in cloth.

The Blessed Sacrament, the Centre of Immutable Truth .	0	1	0
Confidence in God.	0	1	0
Holy Gospel of Our Lord Jesus Christ according to St. John.	0	1	0
Love of Jesus to Penitents.	0	1	0
Office of the Holy Ghost under the Gospel	0	1	0
Holy Ghost the Sanctifier	0	2	0

MANNING, CARDINAL, Edited by.

Life of the Curé of Ars. Popular edition	0	2	6

MEDAILLE, REV. P.

Meditations on the Gospels for Every Day in the Year. Translated into English from the new Edition, enlarged by the Besançon Missionaries, under the direction of the Rev. W. H. Eyre, S.J. Cloth . . 0 6 0
(This work has already been translated into Latin, Italian, Spanish, German, and Dutch.)

"We have carefully examined these Meditations, and are fain to confess that we admire them very much. They are short, succinct, pithy, always to the point, and wonderfully suggestive."—*Tablet.*

MIVART, PROF. ST. GEORGE (M.D., F.R.S.)

Nature and Thought. Second edition	0	4	0

"The complete command of the subject, the wide grasp, the subtlety, the readiness of illustration, the grace of style, contrive to render this one of the most admirable books of its class."—*British Quarterly Review.*

A Philosophical Catechism. Fifth edition	0	1	0

"It should become the *vade mecum* of Catholic students."—*Tablet.*

MONTGOMERY, HON. MRS.

Approved by the Most Rev. G. Porter, Achbp. of Bombay.
The Eternal Years. With an Introduction by the
Most Rev. G. Porter, Achbp. of Bombay. Cloth. £0 3 6
The Divine Ideal. Cloth 0 3 6

"A work of original thought carefully developed and expressed in lucid and richly imaged style."—*Tablet.*
"The writing of a pious, thoughtful, earnest woman."—*Church Review.*
"Full of truth, and sound reason, and confidence."—*American Catholic Book News.*

MORRIS, REV. JOHN (S.J.)

Letter Books of Sir Amias Poulet, keeper of Mary
Queen of Scots. Demy 8vo 0 10 6
Two Missionaries under Elizabeth 0 14 0
The Catholics under Elizabeth 0 14 0
The Life of Father John Gerard, S.J. Third edition,
rewritten and enlarged 0 14 0
The Life and Martyrdom of St. Thomas Becket. Second
and enlarged edition. In one volume, large post 8vo,
cloth, pp. xxxvi., 632, ... 0 12 6
or bound in two parts, cloth 0 13 0

MORRIS, REV. W. B. (of the Oratory.)

The Life of St. Patrick, Apostle of Ireland. Fourth
edition. Crown 8vo. cloth 0 5 0

"Promises to become the standard biography of Ireland's Apostle. For clear statement of facts, and calm judicious discussion of controverted points, it surpasses any work we know of in the literature of the subject."—*American Catholic Quarterly.*

Ireland and St. Patrick. A study of the Saint's
character and of the results of his apostolate.
Second edition. Crown 8vo. Cloth. . . . 0 5 0

"We read with pleasure this volume of essays, which, though the Saint's name is taken by no means in vain, really contains a sort of discussion of current events and current English views of Irish character."—*Saturday Review.*

NEWMAN, CARDINAL.

Church of the Fathers 0 4 0
Prices of other works by Cardinal Newman on
application.

PAGANI, VERY REV. JOHN BAPTIST,

The Science of the Saints in Practice. By John Baptist Pagani, Second General of the Institute of
Charity. Complete in three volumes. Vol. 1,
January to April (out of print). Vol. 2, May to
August. Vol. 3, September to December . each 0 5 0

"'The Science of the Saints' is a practical treatise on the principal Christian virtues, abundantly illustrated with interesting examples from Holy Scripture as well as from the Lives of the Saints. Written chiefly for devout souls, such as are trying to live an interior and supernatural life by following in the footsteps of our Lord and His saints, this work is eminently adapted for the use of ecclesiastics and of religious communities."—*Irish Ecclesiastical Record.*

PAYNE, JOHN ORLEBAR, (M.A.)

Records of the English Catholics of 1715. Demy 8vo. Half-bound, gilt top £0 15 0

"A book of the kind Mr. Payne has given us would have astonished Bishop Milner or Dr. Lingard. They would have treasured it, for both of them knew the value of minute fragments of historical information. The Editor has derived nearly the whole of the information which he has given, from unprinted sources, and we must congratulate him on having found a few incidents here and there which may bring the old times back before us in a most touching manner."—*Tablet.*

English Catholic Non-Jurors of 1715. Being a Summary of the Register of their Estates, with Genealogical and other Notes, and an Appendix of Unpublished Documents in the Public Record Office. In one Volume. Demy 8vo. . . 1 1 0

"Most carefully and creditably brought out . . . From first to last, full of social interest and biographical details, for which we may search in vain elsewhere."—*Antiquarian Magazine.*

Old English Catholic Missions. Demy 8vo, half-bound. 0 7 6

"A book to hunt about in for curious odds and ends."—*Saturday Review.*

"These registers tell us in their too brief records, teeming with interest for all their scantiness, many a tale of patient heroism."—*Tablet.*

PORTER, ARCHBISHOP.

The Letters of the late Father George Porter, S.J., Archbishop of Bombay. Demy 8vo. Cloth. . 0 7 6

"Brimful of good things . . . . . In them the priest will find a storehouse of hints on matters spiritual; from them the layman will reap crisp and clear information on many ecclesiastical points; the critic can listen to frank opinions of literature of every shade; and the general reader can enjoy the choice bits of description and morcels of humour scattered lavishly brough the book."—*Tablet.*

QUARTERLY SERIES Edited by the Rev. John Morris, S.J. 83 volumes published to date.

Selection.

The Life and Letters of St. Francis Xavier. By the Rev. H. J. Coleridge, S.J. 2 vols. . . . 0 10 6
The History of the Sacred Passion. By Father Luis de la Palma, of the Society of Jesus. Translated from the Spanish. 0 5 0
The Life of Dona Louisa de Carvajal. By Lady Georgiana Fullerton. Small edition . . . 0 3 6
The Life and Letters of St. Teresa. 3 vols. By Rev. H. J. Coleridge, S.J. . . . . . . each 0 7 6
The Life of Mary Ward. By Mary Catherine Elizabeth Chalmers, of the Institute of the Blessed Virgin. Edited by the Rev. H. J. Coleridge, S.J. 2 vols. 0 15 0
The Return of the King. Discourses on the Latter Days. By the Rev. H. J. Coleridge, S.J. . . 0 7 6

QUARTERLY SERIES—*(selection) continued.*

Pious Affections towards God and the Saints. Meditations for every Day in the Year, and for the Principal Festivals. From the Latin of the Ven. Nicolas Lancicius, S.J.	£0	7	6
The Life and Teaching of Jesus Christ in Meditations for Every Day in the Year. By Fr. Nicolas Avancino, S.J. Two vols.	0	10	6
The Baptism of the King: Considerations on the Sacred Passion. By the Rev. H. J. Coleridge, S.J.	0	7	6
The Mother of the King. Mary during the Life of Our Lord.	0	7	6
The Hours of the Passion. Taken from the *Life of Christ* by Ludolph the Saxon	0	7	6
The Mother of the Church. Mary during the first Apostolic Age	0	6	0
The Life of St. Bridget of Sweden. By the late F. J. M. A. Partridge	0	6	0
The Teachings and Counsels of St. Francis Xavier. From his Letters	0	5	0
Garcia Moreno, President of Ecuador. 1821—1875. From the French of the Rev. P. A. Berthe, C.SS.R. By Lady Herbert	0	7	6
The Life of St. Alonso Rodriguez. By Francis Goldie, of the Society of Jesus	0	7	6
Letters of St. Augustine. Selected and arranged by Mary H. Allies	0	6	6
A Martyr from the Quarter-Deck—Alexis Clerc, S.J. By Lady Herbert	0	5	0
Acts of the English Martyrs, hitherto unpublished. By the Rev. John H. Pollen, S.J., with a Preface by the Rev. John Morris, S.J.	0	7	6
Life of St. Francis di Geronimo, S.J. By A. M. Clarke.	0	7	6
Aquinas Ethicus; or the Moral Teaching of St. Thomas By the Rev. Joseph Rickaby, S.J. 2 vols.	0	12	0
The Spirit of St. Ignatius, Founder of the Society of Jesus From the French of the Rev. Fr. Xavier de Franciosi, S.J.	0	6	0
Jesus, the All-Beautiful. A devotional Treatise on the character and actions of Our Lord. Edited by Rev. J. G. MacLeod, S.J.	0	6	6
The Manna of the Soul. By Fr. Paul Segneri. New edition. In two volumes.	0	12	0

VOLUMES ON THE LIFE OF OUR LORD.
The Holy Infancy.

The Preparation of the Incarnation	0	7	6
The Nine Months. The Life of our Lord in the Womb.	0	7	6
The Thirty Years. Our Lord's Infancy and Early Life.	0	7	6

The Public Life of Our Lord.

The Ministry of St. John Baptist	0	6	6
The Preaching of the Beatitudes	0	6	6
The Sermon on the Mount. Continued. 2 Parts, each	0	6	6

QUARTERLY SERIES—*(selection) continued.*

	£ s. d.
The Training of the Apostles. Parts I., II., III., IV. each	£0 6 6
The Preaching of the Cross. Part I.	0 6 6
The Preaching of the Cross. Parts II., III. each	0 6 0
Passiontide. Parts I. II. and III., each	0 6 6
Chapters on the Parables of Our Lord	0 7 6

Introductory Volumes.

The Life of our Life. Harmony of the Life of Our Lord, with Introductory Chapters and Indices. Second edition. Two vols.	0 15 0
The Passage of our Lord to the Father. Conclusion of The Life of our Life.	0 7 6
The Works and Words of our Saviour, gathered from the Four Gospels	0 7 6
The Story of the Gospels. Harmonised for Meditation	0 7 6

ROSE, STEWART.
St. Ignatius Loyola and The Early Jesuits, with more than 100 Illustrations by H. W. and H. C. Brewer and L. Wain. The whole produced under the immediate superintendence of the Rev. W. H. Eyre, S.J. Super Royal 8vo. Handsomely bound in Cloth, extra gilt. . . . . . net. 0 15 0

"This magnificent volume is one of which Catholics have justly reason to be proud. Its historical as well as its literary value is very great, and the illustrations from the pencils of Mr. Louis Wain and Messrs. H. W. and H. C. Brewer are models of what the illustrations of such a book should be. We hope that this book will be found in every Catholic drawing-room, as a proof that 'we Catholics' are in no way behind those around us in the beauty of the illustrated books that issue from our hands, or in the interest which is added to the subject by a skilful pen and finished style."—*Month.*

RYDER, REV. H. I. D. (of the Oratory.)
Catholic Controversy: A Reply to Dr. Littledale's "Plain Reasons." Seventh edition . . . 0 2 6

"Father Ryder of the Birmingham Oratory, has now furnished in a small volume a masterly reply to this assailant from without. The lighter charms of a brilliant and graceful style are added to the solid merits of this handbook of contemporary controversy."—*Irish Monthly.*

SOULIER, REV. P.
Life of St. Philip Benizi, of the Order of the Servants of Mary. Crown 8vo 0 8 0

"A clear and interesting account of the life and labours of this eminent Servant of Mary."—*American Catholic Quarterly.*
"Very scholar-like, devout and complete."—*Dublin Review.*

STANTON, REV. R. (of the Oratory.)
A Menology of England and Wales; or, Brief Memorials of the British and English Saints, arranged according to the Calendar. Together with the Martyrs of the 16th and 17th centuries. Compiled by order of the Cardinal Archbishop and the Bishops of the Province of Westminster. With Supplement, containing Notes and other additions, together with enlarged Appendices, and a new Index. Demy 8vo, cloth 0 16 0
The Supplement, separately 0 2 0

THOMPSON, EDWARD HEALY, (M.A.)

The Life of Jean-Jacques Olier, Founder of the Seminary of St. Sulpice. New and Enlarged Edition. Post 8vo, cloth, pp. xxxvi. 628 . . . . £0 15 0

"It provides us with just what we most need, a model to look up to and imitate; one whose circumstances and surroundings were sufficiently like our own to admit of an easy and direct application to our own personal duties and daily occupations."—*Dublin Review.*

The Life and Glories of St. Joseph, Husband of Mary, Foster-Father of Jesus, and Patron of the Universal Church. Grounded on the Dissertations of Canon Antonio Vitalis, Father José Moreno, and other writers. Second Edition. Crown 8vo, cloth . 0 6 0

ULLATHORNE ARCHBISHOP.

Autobiography of, (*see* Drane, A. T.)	.	0	7 6
Letters of, do. ,,	.	0	9 0
Endowments of Man, &c. Popular edition.	.	0	7 0
Groundwork of the Christian Virtues: do.	.	0	7 0
Christian Patience, . . do. do.	.	0	7 0
Memoir of Bishop Willson.	.	0	2 6

VAUGHAN, ARCHBISHOP, (O.S.B.)

The Life and Labours of St. Thomas of Aquin. Abridged and edited by Dom Jerome Vaughan, O.S.B. Second Edition. (Vol. I., Benedictine Library.) Crown 8vo. Attractively bound . . 0 6 6

"Popularly written, in the best sense of the word, skilfully avoids all wearisome detail, whilst omitting nothing that is of importance in the incidents of the Saint's existence, or for a clear understanding of the nature and the purpose of those sublime theological works on which so many Pontiffs, and notably Leo XIII., have pronounced such remarkable and repeated commendations."—*Freeman's Journal.*

WARD, WILFRID.

The Clothes of Religion. A reply to popular Positivism. 0 3 6

"Very witty and interesting."—*Spectator.*
"Really models of what such essays should be."—*Ch.Quart.Review.*

WATERWORTH, REV. J.

The Canons and Decrees of the Sacred and Œcumenical Council of Trent, celebrated under the Sovereign Pontiffs, Paul III., Julius III., and Pius IV., translated by the Rev. J. WATERWORTH. To which are prefixed Essays on the External and Internal History of the Council. A new edition. Demy 8vo, cloth 0 10 6

WESTMINSTER DECREES.

Decreta Quatuor Conciliorum Provincialum Westmonast.: 1853-1873. Adjectis Pluribus Decretis Rescriptis aliisque Documentis . . . net 0 6 0

WISEMAN, CARDINAL.

Fabiola. A Tale of the Catacombs. . . 3s. 6d. and 0 4 0
Also a new and splendid edition printed on large quarto paper, embellished with thirty-one full-page illustrations, and a coloured portrait of St. Agnes. Handsomely bound. 1 1 0

www.ingramcontent.com/pod-product-compliance
Lightning Source LLC
Chambersburg PA
CBHW031935290426
44108CB00011B/560